A Climber's Guide to Glacier National Park

A guidebook is not a substitute for mountaineering skill,
nor can it make climbing safe for those who do not practice the
principles of safety. Inexperienced climbers are urged to avail
themselves of the instruction given by the various
mountain clubs before trying difficult ascents.

REMEMBER TO REGISTER WITH THE PARK RANGERS

FALCON™

COVER PHOTO BY BRIAN KENNEDY
Tim Hooley atop Mt. Wilbur

Strolling up Mt. Altyn in early June. Mt. Wilbur in background.

A
CLIMBER'S
GUIDE
TO

Glacier
National Park

J. Gordon Edwards

Robert Megard

©1995 by Glacier Natural History Association. Published in cooperation with Falcon Press Publishing Co., Inc., Helena, Montana.
First edition published in 1961.

Library of Congress Catalog Card Number 90-83821
ISBN 0-87842-177-7

Publishing Consultant: SkyHouse Publishers, an imprint of Falcon Press Publishing Co., Inc., Helena, Montana.

Distributed by Falcon Press Publishing Co., Inc.

Contents

Two thousand vertical feet of class 3 terrain — Brian Kennedy

Foreword

J. Gordon Edwards is the patron saint of climbing in Glacier National Park. He is the focal point around which experience about climbing in this special place has collected. By profession, J. Gordon Edwards is a scientist. By style, he is a naturalist and a teacher. *A Climber's Guide to Glacier National Park* is a treasury of material opening up not only the high, secret passageways to Glacier's hidden valleys and cathedral peaks, but shares the wealth of myth and history that have been attached to this special place by the people whose lives have been touched by these high summits.

When I reflect on the significance of Gordon Edwards, both principal author and editor of this guide, two strong images come to mind:

The first image is of Gordon on a mountain slope, always looking up, attentively studying the rock above for routes, unseen delights, and dangers.

The second image is of Gordon, often joined by his wife Alice and daughter Jane in the Swiftcurrent Motor Inn Coffee Shop, surrounded by Glacier enthusiasts. I like to think of it as the Swiftcurrent "cracker barrel" where Glacier news is being discussed. Sometimes Gordon tells stories or offers route information, but more often, he is listening to another's story about a hike or climb, collecting information about a climb that is new to him, or speculating about a new route. What is important is not who is there, or what is said, but the celebration of the special place—Glacier National Park!

J. Gordon Edwards' love affair with Glacier National Park began in the late 1940s when he took a job as a park ranger-naturalist. Initially, he climbed to collect exotic insects at the mountaintops, but soon it became evident that his enjoyment of climbing was an end in itself.

Both his wife Alice and daughter Jane have been lifelong climbing companions. Alice began climbing because she worried less when she came along. But she quickly developed a pleasure for climbing that over the years has included climbing all of the 10,000-foot peaks in the park. Jane began following in the "family footsteps" at about the age of eight.

Impressed by the enthusiasm and accomplishments of the Edwards family, many of his park service colleagues encouraged Gordon to compile route descriptions. Descriptions first became available as mimeographed sheets at ranger stations. Year by year, descriptions grew in number until the climber's guide that was published by the Sierra Club.

With passing time, Gordon has become more editor than writer as other climbers, inspired by his enthusiasm and example, have submitted routes for consideration. The guide that exists at this time offers a wide variety of detailed routes, sharing with us the experience of many different types of climbers with varying skill levels and physical abilities.

The aim of this guide is to present routes that are interesting to a broad range of climbers. Some of the routes included here are extremely challenging. But there are also a variety of detailed route descriptions that are less hazardous, but do not just send people up scree slopes. One of the key elements of this guide is that the choice of routes is motivated as much by such factors as hidden cirques, high ridges, hidden animal trails, and fantastic views, as by challenging rock.

What is most important to me is the overriding perception that Gordon has brought to the sport of climbing in Glacier National Park. He enjoys the entire mountain environment and attempts to share that broader enthusiasm with all of us who seek guidance from this climbing guide. He guides our hearts as well as our hands and feet. My own personal understanding and appreciation of Glacier has been profoundly molded by J. Gordon Edwards' perception of Glacier.

In this edition, there are many who deserve to be recognized for their efforts in the completion of the guide. But most important to Gordon, has been the considerable assistance he has received from his daughter, Jane.

Glacier National Park is a very special place. The Glacier Park horizon fuels the imagination, inviting the adventuresome spirit to explore beyond the roads and trails, allowing the curious to better know what lies on the horizon.

These "shining mountains" have been a sacred place for as long as there has been a human presence along this section of the Continental Divide. *A Climber's Guide to Glacier National Park* is a chronicle of this very special place. Throughout its pages, it gives us the benefit of insights that Gordon Edwards has collected during a good portion of his life.

You will enjoy this new edition of *A Climber's Guide to Glacier National Park*. Whether you are reading it to plan out a route for a specific climb, or as a way of passing a dreamy winter evening in an easy chair, let its words caress your imagination like a cool, suggestive breeze. Permit the images to inspire you to explore with Gordon's guidance. Allow yourself to be drawn into the magic of Glacier National Park. It will touch your life in special ways.

ROLF LARSON

GLACIER NATIONAL PARK

A Mecca For Mountaineers

The mountains of Glacier National Park offer supreme experiences for all hikers and mountaineers. There are wonderful ascents for those whose main objective is simply to revel in the majesty of tremendous surroundings, as well as sheer walls for the most experienced technical climbers. The rock is very old, and the huge sweeping mountainsides are usually composed of hundreds of fractured little cliffs, interspersed with scree-covered shelves. Other extensive slopes are entirely made up of talus or scree, but mountaineers can gain elevation rapidly by ascending dry watercourses or by traversing to firm-walled couloirs or giant staircases up rocky ribs and ridges. Above the ledges and scree slopes there are usually steep cliffs rising almost to the summits. Those soaring rock faces present an abundance of challenges to qualified climbers equipped with ropes, pitons, chocks, and carabiners. They are very similar in structure and difficulty to the rock faces of the European Alps and Dolomites. High up on the massive mountainsides, usually nestled in ancient glacial cirques, are more than sixty small glaciers, and the north and eastern faces of many of the peaks are liberally sprinkled with sparkling snowbanks and snowfields even in late summer. Snowstorms may occur at any time during the short summer season, and during most of July and the first half of August the cool clear air offers refreshing relief from the hot lowlands from which most park visitors have recently escaped.

The broad valleys where prehistoric glaciers once ground deep are now filled with lush forests and punctuated by chains of lovely clear lakes. Many valleys are accessible by human trails, about 700 miles of which are maintained by the National Park Service. Equally enjoyable are the extensive meadows extending into the eastern valleys (Cut Bank, St. Mary, Swiftcurrent, and Belly River) and stretching unbroken for hundreds of miles across the rolling prairies east of the park.

These unspoiled surroundings are enjoyed by humans and wildlife alike; quantities of large mammals make their home within the park. Several hundred Rocky Mountain goats and bands of bighorn sheep roam the high rocky slopes and ledges. About 3,000 wapiti, or American elk, inhabit the more remote valleys and hillsides, maintaining the well-worn trails that often provide mountain climbers with easy approaches which would otherwise require many hours of tiresome bushwhacking. There are more black bears in Glacier than in Yellowstone, but most of them are exceedingly shy during the daytime and remain by choice in areas far from noises and fumes. Grizzlies are also numerous and can be found in all areas of the park. Black bears seldom attack people unless teased or in fear of danger to their cubs, but grizzlies are surly animals with little fear of man, and should be avoided whenever possible. All animals should be treated with respect and none should be approached. Walking about in the dark poses the danger of stumbling into porcupines, which are common at night near back-country campgrounds.

A constant companion of those who explore above timberline is the inquisitive marmot. As you travel through the alpine meadows, a relay of long, shrill whistles precedes you as each marmot within earshot repeats the warning that a non-marmot is approaching. Smaller mammals that also abound in the park are chipmunks, ground squirrels, pikas, wood rats, snowshoe hares, beavers, and tree squirrels. Less abundant are the weasels, martens, otters, fishers, skunks, foxes, coyotes, lynxes, mountain lions, and wolverines. In recent years the wolves have increased in numbers and are the object of much interest and scientific study. Wherever you travel, from the deepest valleys to the highest summits, you will never be alone. Countless eyes will be upon you and dozens of noses will test the air as you approach. Some of the wild creatures can scarcely resist the delicious odors emanating from human lunches and may appear almost fearless as they edge closer and closer. Articles of clothing should never be left unguarded along the trail, for marmots and porcupines enjoy gnawing on anything that has been flavored by the salts of perspiration.

At least 250 different kinds of birds have been recorded in the park, and in a single outing a competent ornithologist is likely to observe as many as thirty or forty of them. Most of these birds depend upon insects for a large part of their diet, as do also the fish which abound in most lakes and streams within the great valleys. Reptiles and amphibians are rare, and there are no poisonous snakes at all, probably because of the shortage of suitable food (since they do live in some nearby areas that must be just as cold and snowy as any place in Glacier National Park). To keep the ecological relationships balanced there must naturally be tremendous numbers of insects present, and certainly more than 4,000 species are represented in the local fauna. Occasionally hordes of horse flies, deer flies, black flies, or snipe flies will swarm over hikers along the trails or on the mountainsides and make life temporarily miserable. Fortunately, none of those bloodsuckers feed after dark, so one may still get a good night's sleep in the area. Mosquitoes are even more abundant at times, and sometimes will hum musically about your face at night or at first light of dawn. A bottle of good insect repellent should always be included with the equipment carried by mountaineers, and liquids or creams are recommended over sticks and sprays.

Only about eighteen different kinds of trees are known in Glacier, but there are more than thirty additional species of shrubs and bushes. Many of the latter bear edible berries, and in late summer when the whortleberries are ripe it is difficult to hurry any hiking party through those thickets (they usually emerge from the back country with purple mouths and fingers). Over a hundred different kinds of wildflowers may be seen during any visit to Glacier National Park, many of them in such profusion that they impart their colors to vast areas of the landscape. The most abundant and showy of these at medium to high elevations are the yellow glacier lilies, white globe-flowers, red paintbrush, bright blue phacelia, and (in late summer) brilliant purple asters. In the eastern meadows, huge yellow-orange Gaillardia heads and masses of blue lupines predominate. The great three-foot-high heads of white lilies known as "beargrass" (Xerophyllum tenax) bloom around Lake McDonald in June and follow the season altitudinally, so the high meadows above timberline become a waving white blanket of them by late July.

Books concerning the natural history and geology of the park are on sale at hotels, stores, and ranger stations throughout the area. Publications of value to hikers and climbers are also listed below, including many that have long been out of print but may be enjoyed by "Glacierites" in libraries across the nation while they are making preparations for expeditions in that great national park.

Leave No Trace
Steve Frye, Chief Ranger

With the 1995 revision and reprinting of *A Climber's Guide to Glacier National Park,* it is important to stress the need for all climbers to recognize their responsibilities regarding the protection of the magnificent resource that is Glacier National Park. Climbing and scrambling in the park continue to grow in popularity. The challenge is how to allow these activities to continue, yet preserve the naturalness and integrity of the plant and animal communities.

The ideas of minimum or low impact use are collected in a national program called **Leave No Trace** that calls on all users of backcountry and wilderness areas to limit the impacts of their visit. Human waste, litter, disturbance of wildlife, destruction of plant communities, and the subsequent development of informal trails and soil loss are all cause for concern. Increasing numbers of people have created crowding problems in some areas, destroying the solitude many have come to seek. Route marking as with paint and cairns have compromised the wild character of many areas.

Alpine areas are especially vulnerable to human use. Impacts associated with human use are cumulative and landscapes may take decades to recover. Without the cooperation and understanding of all off-trail users, the success of protective measures will be limited. Leaving no trace requires a positive, respectful attitude toward the wild country you are entering.

Once you leave the maintained trail to travel cross-country or to begin a climb, carefully choose your route. Try to avoid fragile areas such as wet meadows or streamsides and travel on durable surfaces such as rock, snow, or unvegetated areas. Small groups of four to six people create fewer impacts to vegetation, wildlife, and other users than larger groups, and they are safer. Spread out when walking over vegetation; repeated trampling can damage or kill plants. Scree sliding may be fun but it is extremely destructive to fragile vegetation and can accelerate erosion.

The park staff prepared the following list of plant community sensitivity to assist you in evaluating the suitability of routes. To minimize damage, select a route that travels over snow and durable surfaces and avoids vulnerable plant communities.

Most Durable

Stable talus: level or stable talus and boulder fields with high lichen cover and few plants.

Dry ledges: areas with thin soil, either bedrock outcrops or relatively level alpine cobble (flat stable rocks with soil between).

Durable

Krummholtz: dwarf or windswept conifer islands.

Meadow: moist to dry meadows, dominated by relatively robust herbaceous species: asters, fleabane, paintbrush, glacier lily, and grasses and sedges. These areas may be more susceptible when they are just emerging from snowpack.

Cushion plant: low-growing, mat-like plants, often on windswept ridges or steep slopes: moss campion, draba, and phlox.

Vulnerable

Heath: low shrubs of heath and heather.

Tundra: turf (dense plant cover) less than 6" high, moist until late into the year; dominated by grasses, sedges, and dwarf willow.

Unstable talus: scree slopes with sparse vegetation—very susceptible to damage or uprooting.

Wet ledges: seeping water running over rock; mosses, saxifrage and plants in crevasses.

Most Vulnerable

Saturated soil: mossy streambanks, boggy sites, wet meadows; characterized by monkey flowers, sedges, saxifrages, and moss.

A backcountry permit is required for all overnight trips. Although most climbing is done as a day trip or from one of the designated backcountry campgrounds, a limited number of undesignated site permits are given. These permits are a special privilege with specific rules and considerations. When you are issued a permit for an undesignated site, you will also receive additional information on campsite selection and bear safety. Every effort will be made to disperse users.

Climbers need to be particularly cautious regarding bear encounters as climbing routes frequently involve brushy areas or isolated locations where you may surprise unwary animals. Make plenty of noise and always give bears and all other wildlife plenty of room. Never approach any wild animals; keep food and garbage away from them. Bear resistant food containers are available for camps in areas where no trees are available for hanging food.

Please pack out all garbage and litter. Bury human waste at least 200 feet from water when soil is present; when soil is absent, waste will degrade faster when spread out in the open air on rocks. Burn toilet paper or pack it out. Try to urinate on rock or snow, so animals will not dig or paw to get the salt, thus destroying vegetation and causing soil erosion.

Wear the lightest boot you can safely climb with, as studies have shown heavy boots with lug soles more readily damage moist soils. Bring flat-soled shoes or sandals for around camp. Try to leave as little evidence of your visit as possible. Ribbons, paint, and tree blazes should never be used as trail or route markers. Temporary cairns or ducks may be helpful, but should never be left behind after the climb. Never pull embedded rocks to construct markers, as this may destroy adjacent plants and accelerate soil erosion.

A major modification in this edition of *A Climbers's Guide* resulted from the closure of an area around the east approach to Chief Mountain by the Blackfeet Tribe to minimize disturbance to religious activities. This has resulted in the closure of the Chevron or Humble oil road as a short route to the base. Please respect this closure. No portion of the mountain or any of the climbing routes are closed. The road closure just means a little longer and more arduous approach.

Heavy usage of the Logan Pass area and special concern for rare or threatened species of plants has led to the publication, by the park, of approach routes to Mt. Clements, Mt. Reynolds, and Mt. Oberlin that avoid sensitive habitats. Please use these approaches for all the routes, except when the area is snow covered. Seasonal closures may also affect available routes.

Read the bear and other safety warnings in the park newspaper, *Waterton Glacier Guide*, for the most recent information. Remember that if an accident should occur, a rescue effort may be many hours or even several days away. Come prepared for such emergencies. We hope you have a safe and enjoyable visit to the park whether you are climbing or not. It is important for all of us to "leave no trace" during our visit to Glacier so that the beauty and wildness may be enjoyed by present and future generations.

The inspiring west face of Kinnerly Peak looms above Upper Kintla Lake—Glacier National Park photo

Climbers nearing a pristine summit—Glacier National Park photo

Preface

Americans continue to display an increasing interest in the sport of mountaineering. The climbs of Mount Everest, K2, Annapurna, Nanda Devi, Nanga Parbat, Kanchenjunga, Makalu, Dhualagiri, Aconcagua, Yerupaja, Salcantay, St. Elias, Logan, McKinley, and (most recently) Mt. Tyree in the Antarctic have engaged the attention of the entire civilized world. Such high adventures as these lead climber's too far afield and are too costly and gruelling for any but the most highly trained and well-financed mountaineers. Fortunately, one need not travel to the Himalayas, Cordillera Blanca, Antarctic, or Alaska to experience climbing challenges. Many of the men who have participated in major mountaineering campaigns attest that there is much more pleasure to be derived from their climbs of smaller peaks in milder areas, where weather is less severe and where highly organized caravans of porters are not required. Many Europeans travel to our continent to test their skills in the rugged Tetons of Wyoming, the great volcanoes of our Pacific Northwest, the massive Canadian Rockies, and the remote ranges of Alaska and the Yukon Territory. The stupendous walls of Yosemite Valley are perhaps the ultimate arena in the world for technical rock-climbing, but in every mountainous region of North America climbers will find walls of rock suitable for mountaineering adventures involving ropes, pitons, chocks, carabiners, and an occasional expansion bolt. Other mountaineers find equally challenging the densely vegetated slopes capped by steep ridges and couloirs of less-solid rock that may require more stamina and perseverence than the ascents in some of the regions mentioned above. It is this type of mountaineering that characterizes most of the climbs in Glacier National Park, although an abundance of class 5 and 6 climbs are available for capable climbers who relish nights spent hanging from cliff faces thousands of vertical feet above the verdant valleys.

What does the climber gain from his activities in the spectacular heights he seeks to gain? What satisfaction from the "conquest" of a challenging summit? Perhaps the reader would not have picked up this book unless some of the answers were known already. No person who has yet to discover the pleasures of climbing can possibly be aware of the intangibles associated with a day on the mountain. In addition to the exhilaration from outdoor exercise and the pleasure of coping successfully with obstacles, there is usually a spiritual exultation also. If the challenging hours culminate in the attainment of a cherished goal they become especially significant. George Leigh-Mallory (of Everest fame), seeking to express feelings shared by most climbers, asked: "Have we vanquished an enemy?". . . then quickly answered: "None but ourselves!" Whatever the reasons for climbing, there has been a steady increase in the numbers of men and women who search out the pleasures known only to those who explore the wild lonely summits and wonder at the vastness of their surroundings.

It is important that these people learn correct climbing procedures, thereby increasing their pleasure while almost eliminating the dangers which laymen generally associate with mountaineering. Instruction and supervision is offered by a great many outdoor organizations, such as: Adirondack Mountain Club (Albany), Alpine Club of Canada (Toronto), American Alpine Club (New York), Appalachian Mountain Club (Boston), Chemeketans (Salem, Oregon), Chicago Mountaineering Club, Chinook Outdoor Club (Canada), Colorado Mountain Club (Denver), Dartmouth Mountaineering Club, Glacier Mountaineering Society (Whitefish, Montana), Harvard Mountaineering Club, Iowa Mountaineers (Iowa City), Maryland Mountain Club, Mazamas (Portland), Seattle Mountaineers, Sierra Club, Spokane Mountaineers, Stanford Alpine Club, Washington Alpine Club, and the Yale Mountaineering Club. Climbers are sociable people who are always ready to welcome new converts and share knowledge about how to most safely enjoy their spectacular sport. Attending their meetings or sharing some of their outdoor activities will always be entertaining and valuable to participants, and subscribing to their publications will help support those groups as well as bring pleasure to the readers.

Hopefully this little book will further encourage appreciative men and women to ascend the wild steep slopes and walk the long high ridges of Glacier National Park. Surely an abundance of pleasant memories will then haunt them all the rest of their lives! The architecture of the mountains in Glacier Park is so unique as to require a distinctive approach and attitude on the part of the mountaineers who wish to enjoy the climbs there. Two key adjectives that apply again and again in this park are "massive" and "great." The entire park is built of massive layers of stone, and those who relish long exposed leads on homogeneous igneous rock may not feel at home on the cliffs here. The great sheer faces are quite similar to those of the Austrian Alps and comparable in some cases even to the famous European Eigerwand. Many climbers do not desire such supreme challenges, however, and will traverse on shelves and ledges

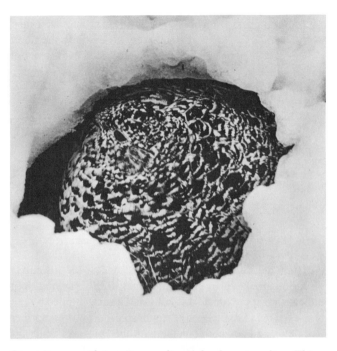

Ptarmigan, or Alpine Grouse, live only above tree line. This female remained on her nest of eggs while covered by eleven inches of fresh snow — J. G. Edwards

while seeking the best route up through the next cliff. Unless the climber deliberately chooses routes demanding tight belays or direct aid, or involving hazardous snow and ice work, superb alpine techniques are seldom essential here. Most mountaineers in Glacier National Park are likely to enjoy just "getting up high" more than facing horrendous challenges or piling stupendosity upon spectacularity.

Climbing here is pleasant, although strenuous, and elevation is usually gained rapidly (often 2,000 vertical feet per hour). The culmination of the climb comes as you stroll up the final ridge to the summit, breathing in the fresh air while exclaiming over the beauty of the deep green valleys, the surrounding peaks and spires in all directions. The mountaineering experiences are great fun and the summit views are almost always more impressive than anticipated.

The routes suggested in this guide are certainly not the only ways of reaching the summits, but if they are followed carefully and cautiously the ascents should prove to be interesting and often spectacular, without exposing climbers to unnecessary risks. These routes were mostly climbed by the author in person, but in every case where the description was provided by someone else, that source has been indicated. For those who would rather pioneer their own routes there remain hundreds of outstanding climbs in the park that are not described here.

The pleasures of roaming the valleys and peaks are legion, but a lapse of attention or judgment at the wrong time may transform the sunniest and most enjoyable moment of your life into your last one on earth. Please, try to keep that always in mind while among the peaks!

Classification of Climbs

Throughout this guide references are made to the difficulty and hazards of various routes or portions of routes. The following definitions will indicate the approximate difficulty and hazard implied by each of the six classes. This classification is applicable only to the northern Montana Rockies, and does not coincide with the "classes" devised for areas in which the rock is more solid and the hazards are of a different sort. David Brower, in his forward in the original edition of this guide, explained the reasons for using this different system in Glacier National Park. So did Bill March of the National Mountaineering School of North Wales in *Off Belay* (February 1976).

CLASS 1. Very easy. May be followed by any hiker with average stamina and wearing serviceable footgear. No rock climbing involved.

CLASS 2. Easy. May be climbed by any strong hiker with proper footgear. A few low rock ledges may be present but no dangerous pitches (in good weather).

CLASS 3. Moderate. Small cliffs on the route may be difficult, and steep scree may require great exertion, but there is little danger of physical injury if reasonable caution is exercised.

CLASS 4. Difficult. The route ascends pitches where a fall might be serious or may lead to a long tumble down steep pitches and narrow ledges. The actual climbing may not be very difficult but the potential hazard is great. Rock-climbing experience and proper techniques of belaying are essential to minimize the risk and great care must be taken to avoid any slips.

CLASS 5. Severe. High rock work where pitons may be used and climbers should be roped for safety. Each member of the party should have had previous rock-climbing experience and should be capable of employing correct belaying techniques.

CLASS 6. Very severe. High rock work where pitons must be used for direct support for the climbers during part of the ascent. Much greater climbing skill is required in these mountains than on corresponding cliffs of granite in Yosemite or the Tetons because climbers must be able to evaluate each pitch and hold according to the quality of the rock, rather than simply grabbing any knob or crack for support. Greater knowledge and ability is also required for the placement of pitons and chocks in these sedimentary formations.

Registration of Climbers

Regardless of your level of experience and the difficulty or ease of the planned climb or cross-country trip, always be sure to register at the nearest ranger station or visitor center. Searches will not be initiated unless positive evidence is received regarding overdue climbers, but the registration information is valuable. If the station is unoccupied when you go to register, leave an explanatory note that outlines your plans and indicates when you expect to return. (You can also indicate that you will check out at another ranger station or even make a telephone call to inform the rangers that you are out.) Cooperation between the park and the mountaineers will help assure that enjoyable alpine experiences can continue in Glacier National Park!

If the ranger station is closed when you return there will usually be a box in which you should place a note that you are out and safe. Be SURE you do not forget to sign out in some manner, to avoid having worried search parties out there looking for you after you have left the area. The rangers are very deeply concerned for the safety of each mountaineer. Many of those rangers are mountaineers also and they have personal concern for fellow climbers in their part of the park.

Obviously if you are not climbing alone, there is a great chance that someone in your party will survive accidents and go for help. Solo climbing is discouraged for many other reasons, also, but this alone should be sufficient incentive for climbers to go up the slopes with companions. If there is no way in which you can register for a climb that you impulsively decided to try while far from the ranger station, then you should either get someone else to deliver a note to the rangers stating your intentions very clearly and indicating where you will report upon completion of your climb. It is also wise to notify a close friend or relative and tell them exactly what you intend to do and when you will return.

No matter where or how you register your intentions, it is very important that you do not change plans during the day and go elsewhere. It is also very important that you remember to notify the proper persons upon your return, so the rangers will not be out searching for you in the darkness and the storm.

Routes Among the Peaks

It is hoped that most mountaineers in Glacier National Park enjoy high altitude experiences other than just those that culminate on the very tops of the mountains. Routes such as those discussed near the beginning of each chapter are included for those persons to consider. Many are useful shortcuts to places that require far more time and energy to reach via the lowland trails or humanized passes, but others are simply hikes to interesting places that we think most climbers would enjoy visiting.

The shortcuts between Stoney Indian Pass and Fifty Mountain Camp will surely be well-traveled by climbers in the future, because they save a long half-day of trail hiking between those two locations while at the same time providing the mountaineer with fantastic views and lovely alpine terrain en route. Routes such as the Norris Traverse and the Ipasha Connection provide much longer and even more unique experiences. High altitude game trails such as those from Ptarmigan Tunnel are interesting because they are so scenic, but have added interest when we realize how many centuries the animals have been following those same remarkable routes. The Iceberg Notch serves mountaineers especially well, for they can go directly from Iceberg Lake to Ahern Pass via that notch and thus gain access to Iceberg Peak, Ahern Peak, and Ipasha Peak, or can drop into the head of the Belly River Valley, or can follow the Ipasha Connection to Chaney Glacier, Sue Lake, and Stoney Indian Pass (or Fifty Mountain), or can hike the human trail from Ahern Pass to Canada, or can simply complete a marvelous circular route to the Many Glacier area via Granite Park and Swiftcurrent Pass.

Before attempting any of those routes, be sure to register at the nearest ranger facility. Even though they are not actually climbs to the summits, those routes can be dangerous or deadly, and climbers should always take advantage of the protection gained by registering. Any injury that immobilizes a person while far from traveled trails may prove fatal unless somebody knows where you are and takes action if you do not return in a reasonable length of time. Another incentive to register may be the advantage of learning more information concerning the routes!

The Rocks of Glacier Park

The rocks of Glacier Park are mainly of sedimentary origin and are mostly more than a billion years old. For this reason they are often extremely unsound and fracture unpredictably. There are usually gullies and easy chimneys affording routes through even the most impressive cliffs. Interspersed between the cliffs are ledges covered with small fragments of loose rock (scree). With few exceptions, such ledges, gullies, and chimneys provide relatively safe routes up the peaks. Below the great cliffs there are tremendous accumulations of fallen rock fragments of larger sizes (talus). Throughout Glacier National Park climbers will encounter great talus slopes extending from the forests or alpine meadows up to the cliffs. These slopes are resting at a comfortable pitch and can be safely ascended, descended, or traversed without danger of causing major rock slides. The differentiation between talus and scree is one of size. In this book talus is used only for the great slopes at the mountain base, and scree is for all other accumulations of small rock, sand, and gravel lying loose on the mountainside. When approaching solid rock outcroppings beware of scree, because on a firm surface it functions almost like ball-bearings.

The following rock formations are easily recognized within Glacier National Park:

Cretaceous limestone—A pale, compact formation lying immediately below the Altyn limestone in most parts of the park, hence not usually exposed. Along the eastern edge of the Lewis Range this formation may be examined in many places, the most obvious being the bases of Chief Mountain and Wynn Mountain. In these places a very distinct horizontal line of contact between this rock and the Altyn limestone can be seen even from a distance of more than a mile.

Altyn limestone—A pale buff-colored formation, hard and brittle, exposed only near the eastern edge of the park. It forms the prominent ridge between Many Glacier Hotel and the parking area, the sheer cliffs near the campgrounds at Rising Sun, and the pale rock over which Trick Falls descends. Most of Chief Mountain and Divide Mountain are also composed of this rock. Although it is not encountered on other summit climbs, the Altyn limestone cliffs near Rising Sun and Many Glacier afford excellent places for rock-climbing practice.

Argillites—Red or green shales which approach the hardness of slate. This rock usually splits or fractures easily. The cliffs have deteriorated into tremendous scree slopes on some mountains, down which you can run with amazing speed.

The argillite in the park is of two major types: Appekunny (green) and Grinnell (red). Appekunny argillite lies immediately above the Altyn limestone, the greenish-gray rock strata being at least 2,000 feet in thickness. This sort of rock is prominent in the cliffs of Appekunny Mountain and also occurs just below the bright red Grinnell argillite in most of the peaks near the eastern side of the park. Grinnell argillite is a great formation, nearly 2,000 feet thick, composed of brilliant red strata with occasional thin layers of quartzite interspersed. This rock predominates in most peaks of the Two Medicine area around St. Mary Lake and around Swiftcurrent Lake. It contributes greatly to the sculptural qualities of many mountains in Glacier National Park.

Siyeh limestone—Light gray to dark gray rocks; constitute the major portion of all of the higher peaks in the park. Frequently as much as 4,000 vertical feet of a sheer mountainside may be composed of Siyeh limestone, but faces composed of this material are usually broken into cliffs five to twenty-five feet high, separated by narrow, steep slopes or small scree-covered ledges. The stratified rocks in these cliffs tend to break suddenly under pressure, and all holds should be thoroughly tested before being trusted. Angle pitons or long horizontals may sometimes be used if carefully placed. Despite the broken condition of the Siyeh limestone exposures, the slope is usually still very steep, and a slip from one of the small ledges might result in a bounding fall of several thousand feet. The structure of these ledges usually prevents good belays, so the best method of climbing here is simply to recognize the danger and climb slowly and with great individual care.

Diorite sill—Dark greenish-black crystalline rock of an igneous origin (formerly molten because of subterranean heat). This intrusion between sedimentary strata occurs within the Siyeh formation, forming a dark band across the face of Mt. Gould, Mt. Wilbur, Mt. Cleveland, Mt. Stimson, and many other major peaks. The band is about 100 feet thick wherever it appears, and may form sheer cliffs. It is easy to climb, however, because of its hardness, excellent handholds, and ability to hold pitons firmly. Immediately above and below the diorite sill there is always about fifteen feet of very pale, easily fractured rock that is poor for climbing. This was originally Siyeh limestone, but has been partly metamorphosed because of its close contact with the molten magma that forced apart the layers of limestone, then intruded between them and cooled to form the present diorite sill. The more or less vertical fissures up through which the molten magma was extruded were also composed of that dark igneous rock after it cooled. Many of the deep, narrow notches in ridge tops in the park are places where the vertical "dikes" of diorite have weathered more rapidly than the strata of limestone on either side.

Reef of fossil algae (stromatolites) — A pale gray formation up to sixty feet thick, running throughout the Siyeh limestone formation, sometimes above and sometimes below the diorite sill. This is actually an extensive fossilized reef of Proterozoic algae, which thrived in the shallow sea here more than a billion years before the uplift occurred. The rock is easily recognized because it is composed of concentric circles, each rosette being the remains of a separate colony of algae of the genus Collenia. These colonies may be a yard or more in diameter, and they superficially resemble large heads of lettuce but are composed of extremely hard stone with a very sharp, rough, abrasive surface. Fortunately, the reef is not as difficult to climb as might be expected at first sight, and it will accept pitons well.

Purcell lava—A dark brown or black consolidation of lava that flowed through surface vents before this area was uplifted from the sea. This magma reached the surface in several regions, and is now visible at Granite Park, Boulder Pass, near Fifty Mountain Camp, and on Thunderbird Mountain. On Thunderbird it creates a formidable cliff more than 200 feet high, running the entire length of the mountain, below the long summit ridge. (The lava atop Rainbow Peak is believed to represent a separate flow, millions of years later.)

Other formations—There are a few other types of rock exposed, including the Shepard formation of quartzite-bearing material above the Purcell lava in some places, such as the Logan Pass meadows, and the red Kintla formation above the Siyeh formation in some of the high peaks in the northwestern part of the park. None of these other formations need be discussed here, for they closely resemble in color, hardness, and texture, formations already described, and they never interfere with the ascent of any of these mountains.

Consider These Other Factors

Weather Conditions—Glacier's mountains are big enough to make their own weather as well as to conceal the approach of weather fronts until they are almost upon you. Very severe storms can come up very quickly. Be prepared for such disagreeable developments by carrying extra food, warm clothing, and emergency bivouac equipment, especially on overnight trips into the back country. Summer snowstorms are interesting, and they enhance the scenery, but they sometimes last for two or three days, even in July and August, and make off-trail travel exceedingly hazardous if not impossible. Plan for the worst and hope for the best!

Lightning—Because the weather can change so unexpectedly in these mountains, climbers often find themselves high above the valley when thunderheads suddenly appear over the western ridge. They must be aware of the hazards and select the lesser of many evils. Stay out of gullies and couloirs, because precipitation will bring down much rock fall. Stay away from ridges and summits, because that is where most lightning strikes. Resist the temptation to get into caves or semicaves, for it has been demonstrated that the electrical charge from the ceiling of a cavern or an overhang often passes to the floor through the body of any person crouching there. (It is better to be soaked than stroked.) The charge of a strike of lightning disperses over the surface of the mountain, rapidly diminishing the further it goes from the point of impact. If a person crouches low on the surface carrying the charge, and has only his feet on the ground, he may not feel it at all. If, however, several parts of the body are in contact with the surface then it may serve as an alternate route for part of the charge. If lightning is imminent (as indicated by the approach of thunderheads, by whining or buzzing sounds around the summit, by the hair standing on end, by St. Elmo's fire around the nearby boulders, or by the obvious proximity of lightning strikes in the area), then the climber should get away from the ridges and peaks as rapidly as possible, should lower his profile by crouching while running down the slopes, and should not carry erect metallic objects that may attract electricity. Of course it would be even better to be able to predict such adverse weather far enough in advance to avoid getting into such situations at all.

Loose rock—As a result of the structure of the mountains here, climbing parties can often be fairly large and the members unroped, or roped only rarely. This creates a special danger from falling rock, the most common danger to the rock climber. We recommend the following advice, taken from the *Manual of Ski Mountaineering*. Weather is a frequent cause of rock fall; rocks are brought down by change of temperature and resultant splitting action of intermittent freezing and thawing, as well as by heavy rain. Rock falls occur on all peaks, particularly in gullies and chutes. Areas of frequent rock fall may be indicated by abundant fresh scars on the rock walls, fine dust on the talus piles, or lines, grooves, and rock-strewn areas on snow beneath cliffs. A more immediate cause of rock fall is carelessness in climbing by both man and beast.

Warning of a rock fall, if detected, should be a vigorous cry, *Rock!* Other warnings are whistling sounds, a grating, a thunderous crashing, or sparks where the rocks strike at night. The immediate action is to seek cover — if one can move and if cover is available. If not, the climber should watch the falling rock, present his narrowest profile, and not commit himself until he knows he is in direct peril. Otherwise he may move into the path of a falling rock by blindly or prematurely trying to avoid it.

Rock fall danger is minimized by judgment and choice of routes. Clean and careful climbing will reduce it further. Holds should be tested before use by striking with the heel or hand or foot, but not with such vigor or indirection as to launch loose rock on the party below. Careful appraisal will prevent many insecure rocks being stepped on or grasped. Many insecure rocks should deliberately be moved into safe position so as to avoid accidental falls due to action of the rope or careless movement. The body will not brush rock loose if it is properly balanced—away from the rock. The rear foot is a bad offender, and the climber should be sure, as he brings it forward, that it does not kick rocks.

When a large party is climbing, slopes with loose rock on them may be negotiated safely in several ways. Disperse the party so that no individual ever climbs while directly above another. The uppermost climbers should always stop moving when one of the following persons is beneath him, and wait until the lower climber moves out of the line of potential rockfall. The lower climbers should, however, protect themselves by being constantly aware of the location of those higher on the mountain and by reducing the hazard by being prepared to quickly take shelter or evasive action. Too often the warning calls from above are not heard because of wind or the sound of nearby rock movement. (Even when climbing alone a climber should keep looking up and listening intently at all times . . . and should never stop to rest in places that might be raked by spontaneous rockfall.)

Fortunately, most of the large rocks in Glacier National Park are rather flat and do not travel far down the slope. As they bounce, they usually fracture into even smaller flat slabs that soon come to rest. A flat slab will sometimes get on edge, however, and roll like a wheel, even changing direction and rolling laterally across the slope for unexpected distances, so it is essential to be aware of such hazards. Compared with other mountain ranges, the distance covered by falling or rolling rocks is very much shorter here than elsewhere. On the other hand there is more loose rock hanging from the slopes here than anywhere else!

When the party must all ascend the same narrow couloir, bounding rocks cannot be avoided by those lower in the gully. The safest procedure is to ascend (or descend) such couloirs one person at a time, while everyone else waits off to one side. Those above should not be above the gully, obviously, and those below should be under protective walls out of harm's way. This does slow progress, but often it is welcomed because it permits time for a drink or a snack, or for picture-taking and a leisurely look around. If parallel gullies are available, both can be climbed simultaneously. If there are only two or three people in the party another possible procedure is for them to climb side by side in the couloir, or at least so close to each other that any dislodged rock will not gain momentum before reaching someone else. There are many times when the leader warns followers of a hazard and they can reach a safe position to the side while he takes the risky move. Remember, of course, that a goat or sheep above, or a gust of wind, may trigger rockfall that sweeps down the gully. In such an event the persons who can most quickly reach safety beneath a ledge or far out of the center of the gully will be those most likely to avoid injury. Try to anticipate such events at all times, even though they may only occur once a year!

On the great mountainsides which make up a large part of nearly every climb here there are hundreds or thousands of small cliffs and ledges. Parties should never climb straight up such slopes. The recommended technique is to ascend via a long zig-zag route so that there is seldom a time when one climber is directly below another. The leader usually pauses at each directional change to see where the followers are and waits until they are nearly beside him before heading up in the opposite direction. As the leader passes briefly above them the followers (who must protect themselves at all times) halt in safe places. If the followers are not near any safe places they should ask the climbers above to stop moving for a minute until they can reach a safe place. This procedure quickly becomes understood by everyone in the party, so there is no need for such requests. Each person protects those below, and each person below takes the proper precautions. The party ascends the slopes and the walls of broken cliffs almost as rapidly as it would be climbed by only two or three in a group . . . and they do it without risking injury to anyone.

When climbing on class 4 cliffs, follow the customary procedures for cliff-climbing elsewhere. It is even more important here, however, that you never climb directly below another climber, for rocks are very frequently dislodged, even by careful climbers. Class 4 pitches often deserve secure rope belays, but in these mountains the belayer often cannot find a place secure enough to enable him to stop a falling companion. Rather than risking a "bolo fall," with both the belayer and the belayee bounding down the slope on opposite ends of the same rope, it seems preferable for the climbers to remain unroped! Usually the pitches are actually very safe IF adequate care is taken to test all holds before trusting them and IF the climber only moves one hand or one foot at a time while keeping the other three points firm. Of course, when an obviously risky pitch must be belayed the leader (or belayer) can use an anchor piton or can find a solid belay point above the top of the cliff. (Of course, on class 5 and 6 cliffs, climbers must take the same precautions as on cliffs of that difficulty elsewhere, and in Glacier National Park the really great sheer cliffs are composed of relatively solid rock.)

Pitons—Pitons are not often needed in Glacier National Park except on class 5 and 6 pitches. Driving a piton: Study the rock to see if a piton will be likely to weaken the formation. Select a crack that is wide enough to take one-third to one-half of the piton shaft before hammering begins. Select the type and size of piton that the rock will support best, and one that the carabiner can be snapped into after the piton has been driven. While driving, watch the piton to see that it goes in smoothly and to notice if the point hits a dead end. Listen to the sound at each blow; good verticals and horizontals usually go in with a rising pitch (wafers and angles will have no noticeable pitch so long as the ring is swinging free). Drive the piton hard, until the head begins to change shape. The greater the resistance overcome in driving the piton, the firmer it will be. A well-driven piton will withstand a direct outward pull of 1,000 to 2,000 pounds.

On some difficult routes in the park, pitons may have been driven and then left on the cliffs. They may sometimes be useful to later climbers there, but such pitons should always be viewed with great suspicion. Weathering will loosen them in time and only the person who drove it really knows how reliable it was in the first place. Before trusting your life to a piton found embedded in a Montana cliff, be sure it is solid. To test it, strike it with a hammer (or a hard rock) while listening for a rising pitch like a musical saw, rather than a dull "clunk." (Angle pitons will not provide that reassuring sound, so try to determine how solid they are by striking them in two or three directions to see if they move, by carefully examining the rock into which they were driven, and by testing them with a sling rope. Snap the rope into the carabiner or thread it through the eye of the piton, and grasp the doubled rope at least two feet from the piton. Jerk it vigorously outward, downward, and to each side, while observing the piton.) Generally speaking, a poorly anchored piton is worse than no piton at all. Do not trust them unless you are really certain that they are capable of stopping a fall that may end your life!

Rappelling —The novice rappeller is usually more concerned with where he is going than with where he lays the rope against the cliff as he descends. Actually, he should be very much aware of rocks which may cut the rope, jam it, or be dislodged by it. Rappel slings are an even worse potential hazard, for they weaken rapidly when left exposed to the elements. NEVER use a sling that was left on the mountain by someone else. Rappelling should never be done just "for fun," because climbing history is filled with stories of deaths resulting from this practice. People fall out of rappels for a number of reasons, all of which can be avoided if the rappeller is well-trained and very careful at all times during the rappel. Due to the relatively high mortality rate, most climbing organizations urge members to rappel ONLY when necessary, and to be extremely careful. Pitons may pull out, sling ropes may fail, bowlines may reverse and pull loose, the rappel rope may be too short, the rope may dislodge a rock that strikes the climber and causes a fall, the rope may be wrenched out of a jammed carabiner, or any of a number of other difficulties may occur, any of which may be fatal.

Snow and ice —Progressive training is just as essential for snow climbing as it is for rock climbing. An improperly handled ice ax can be a great liability. Steep snowbanks have been responsible for a large number of accidents and deaths in Glacier National Park. Once a person starts sliding, it is often impossible to stop unless an ice ax is used for "self-arrest." Glissading down steep snow may be fun, but should be never be done on slopes that the mountaineer is not familiar with. A good general rule is not to glissade down any slope that you did not walk up recently. Snow ices over badly in late afternoon, often thus becoming deadly, and in early mornings most snow surfaces are as hard as rock but extremely slippery.

Snow fields, snowbanks, and snow chutes abound in Glacier Park all summer, and are often extremely dangerous to cross. Everyone should get a personal introduction to steep snow on Logan Pass, so they will realize how impossible it is to stop themselves when they are sliding without ice axes. When a party not thus equipped is forced to traverse steep snow by kicking steps in it, a good belay should always be used. Otherwise serious injury or death may result when a kick-hole breaks out or a climber loses his or her balance. Mountaineers with ice axes can safely cross, ascend, or descend almost any snow surface in Glacier National Park IF

Ice axes and nylon rope are essential for much climbing in early summer — Robert Megard

they know how to use the ax for support, for belays, and especially for self-arrest. For those who have not had previous training or experience with them, and who have not read detailed instructions in other books, the following condensed instructions may be useful. Practice these moves on a safe slope (with a gentle "run-out" at the bottom) before facing serious challenges on the mountain. Another hazard which should be emphasized is that of a person being struck by rocks that slide down the snow silently and strike climbers on the snow OR JUST BELOW THE SNOW! When someone is getting water at the bottom of a snowfield it is wise for someone else to keep looking up, so the water gatherer can be warned if a rock is sliding down the snow.

When traversing gentle snow slopes, always hold the ax in your uphill hand and lean on it to prevent yourself from slipping. The thong should be around your wrist while on steep snow so that it will not be lost down the slope for any reason. If you fall and begin sliding it is often possible to stop yourself by simply digging the end of the shaft in and dragging it, but if any momentum has been gained, that will not work. The *self-arrest* may then be accomplished as follows: kick around until you are sliding feet first down the snow while lying on your back, with the left arm extending across the chest and that left hand gripping the ice ax head where the handle is attached (with the palm of the hand on top of the head and the thumb and fingers extending downward around the head at that point). The long point of the head should be extending out beyond the little finger (i.e. forward), and the right hand should hold the shaft at the middle. Then you slowly roll over toward your left, with the hand holding the ax head just a little above your right shoulder. As you roll onto your stomach, the long point of the head begins to scrape the surface of the snow. Your right shoulder and right side press down on the wooden shaft while your left hand directs the point into the snow (with your thumb UP). Take it easy, because if you dig the point in too abruptly the ax may be jerked out of your hands! (It should be noted that you may reverse the instructions given here, if you prefer to hold the head with the right hand across your chest and roll over toward your right side.) Practice this technique on a steep slope with a safe "run-out" at the bottom before you are forced to use it on dangerous ice and snow.

To traverse steep snow safely, hold the ice ax in the same grip as for self-arrest. Keep the thong around your wrist so that if you fall you can quickly assume the self-arrest position. If you are traversing toward your left, hold the head in your left hand and the shaft in your right hand. Take two "kick-steps," digging the uphill sides of the feet into the snow crust, then keep the feet firmly in position while leaning slightly forward and placing the bottom of the ice ax shaft into the snow above and in front of the left foot. While keeping slight pressure down on the ice ax shaft with both hands, move the right foot and then the left foot forward again, kicking their uphill edges into the snow crust again. If a foot slips, lean harder on the nearly-vertical ax handle and it will usually stop you on the spot. If you slip so far that the handle slants and pulls out, you still have the perfect self-arrest grip on the ax with both hands and can quickly halt your slide using the technique described above.

When traversing to your right across a steep slope, hold the ax in the same manner as above, but move the ax after your right foot has been kicked into place. When moving in this direction, your right arm extends across the front of your body and grips the middle of the ice ax shaft (the left hand still grips the head in the self-arrest grip). Lean slightly on the ax while taking another step with your left foot and one with your right foot, then move the ax forward again while keeping both feet motionless. As with left traverses, if the ax handle pulls out it will be easy to use the basic self-arrest technique before you have fallen very far.

Ascending steep snow is very similar to traversing. Hold the ax in exactly the same manner with both hands. Stretch your arms uphill and jam the point of the ice ax handle into the snow there, while keeping the handle nearly vertical and using it as support to prevent you from falling backwards if a foot slips. While leaning lightly on the ax, kick the edges of your boots into the snow crust for two steps. Either use the "herring-bone" technique or angle steeply up in one direction or the other. Keep the feet in position while reaching uphill with the ax shaft again. If you have a sudden small slip it will occur while the ice ax handle is stuck into the snow (or is being quickly moved to a higher position and can be quickly jabbed into the snow again). If there is a major fall (as might occur if you are roped to someone else who suddenly slips and yanks you violently into a back-flip down the steep slope) you are still in good shape because you already have the self-arrest grip on the ax and can soon stop yourself *and* the other person!

Descending steep snow can be accomplished by walking downhill or by glissading (sliding on your feet). Other methods are not highly recommended because they may result in torn clothing. Grip the ice ax head in the same grip as for all the above techniques. As the slope steepens it becomes increasingly difficult to walk down it without slipping. Keep the self-arrest grip on the ax and you will be able to stop if you have a fall. Many mountaineers enjoy glissading by keeping their weight on their heels, with their toes very slightly raised, while gliding down the steep snow. If the slope is so steep or so rough that you cannot stay on your feet, use the handle of the ax as a rudder and a brake. Hold the handle at a forty-five degree angle alongside your thigh and lean back on the hand that is gripping the shaft about halfway down. Keep the other hand on the head in the usual self-arrest grip. The harder you lean on the handle, the slower will be your slide. It is customary to zig-zag down the long slopes but a straight swoop down a smooth steep snowfield is graceful, rapid, and exhilarating. As usual, a fall can be terminated quickly by dropping into the self-arrest position. When the slope ends abruptly above cliffs or boulder fields, the first people to the bottom should wait eight or ten feet above the edge of the snow so they can halt or slow the progress of other sliders who may be out of control at that point.

WARNING: *The self-arrest technique that is so useful on steep snow will not work on bare ice or extremely hard-surfaced snow.* This is why climbers are told not to glissade down slopes they have not recently walked up. Do NOT descend any unknown snow slopes that may be icy near the bottom. Alternative routes are almost always available. If the ice MUST be descended, the leader should be belayed from above while he or she chops large steps in the ice with the ax (make each step angle down and inward, so feet will slip deeper into the step rather than slipping out of it). Climbers who anticipate such pitches should carry reliable ice screws along for use as belay points.

Glacier travel —The glaciers in this park are small in comparison with those in the Pacific Northwest and the Canadian Rockies but they can still be quite hazardous. When those masses of moving ice are forced over a hump in the bed of the glacier and the top must go further than the bottom, the top splits open, forming crevasses. In the winter those great cracks fill with soft snow, and in early summer it is difficult to see any crevasses on the surface of the glaciers in this park. As the season warms the snow melts from the surface and the snow plugging the crevasses melts from below until only a thin layer covers the top of the crevasse. That layer quickly gives way when a person walks onto it, dropping the victim into the crevasse. The victim slips rapidly down the hard, slick walls of the crevasse and is deeply wedged between the converging walls twenty to forty feet below the surface of the glacier. Breathing immediately becomes difficult or impossible, and freezing of the victim proceeds rapidly even if capable of breathing. Climbers should never walk on glaciers unroped unless it is possible to take every step on solid ice that has been exposed when all the snow cover melted away. Only then can the crevasses be seen and avoided, and even then there is the risk of slipping over the lip and falling into one of the crevasses. Travel across glaciers, either snowcovered or bare, is strongly discouraged unless the mountaineer is equipped with an ice ax and knows how to use it correctly. If the ice is snow-covered it is also essential that climbers be roped together and trained in the use of ice ax belays and in the use of prusik cinches to help the fallen climber work his or her way up out of the crevasse while being held firmly on belay by anchored climbers on the glacier's surface.

Because so few users of this Guide will be climbing on glaciers and because so much space would be required to discuss glacier travel, ice ax belays, tying the knots needed for roping up, tying prusik cinches for self-rescue techniques that might permit a climber to get out of a crevasse, and other crevasse rescue techniques, details will not be covered here. Persons who anticipate glacier traveling must have ice axes and climbing ropes, so presumably they have already had access to instruction or literature dealing with the above topics. When they register for their climb, they can also ask the rangers for details and suggestions. As a general safety precaution, in view of the fact that most glacier crossings in this park will probably be brief, the party can be relatively safe if they advance very slowly across the ice, cross crevassed areas at right angles (so not more than one will fall into the same hidden crevasse), and probe every step of the way with ice axes to detect soft places where the point of the ax handle fails to strike rock-solid ice beneath the snow cover. When hidden crevasses are thus detected, the party can safely detour around them.

Crossing steep slippery slopes — Although the only damage suffered by mountaineers who fall repeatedly while crossing beargrass-covered hillsides or steep slopes of "ball-bearing scree" will usually be injury to the ego or minor scratches, it is nice to avoid such falls if possible. Climbers carrying ice axes have a great advantage. Many carry ice axes specifically for protection on slick slopes of that sort. This is especially valuable for backpackers carrying heavy loads. In addition to avoiding painful slips, those backpackers actually make the load lighter by partially supporting their upper body as they lean on the ice ax with every step. While using the ax for support such as this, do NOT keep the thong around your wrist. (If you fall, it is best to shove the ax aside rather than falling on it!) The support gained is great. Always carry the ax in your uphill hand to minimize the chance of falling downhill on it, and place the point of the handle into solid places above your body, rather than below you where there is a greater possibility of it slipping off and causing you to plunge headfirst down the slope. It is especially important that the thong not be used while climbers are running down scree or steep slopes of mixed vegetation and rock, since there are a great number of slips under those conditions and falling on the ax head must be avoided if possible. The ice ax can also be used while climbing broken cliffy hillsides where steep grassy lodges are encountered between the vertical pitches. The ax must be suspended from the wrist during the actual steep rocky pitches, but it is possible to lay it on a ledge above you frequently (or leave it below and let following climbers pass all the ice axes up at one time). When a grassy slope is at the top of a small cliff there are often no handholds available there. The long point of the ice ax head is very useful there, since it can be pushed into the soil or between rocks and then the handle adjacent to the head is pulled on while the handle itself is held horizontal to the surface of the ledge. Other uses of the ice ax touted by some include stirring hot coffee, opening cans, smoothing the ground while preparing a campsite, substituting for a tent pole, and being wielded as a weapon.

Grizzly bears—Glacier is grizzly country. Use good techniques of watchful awareness of your surroundings and of making your presence known to wildlife around you while far above tree line, just as when in densely forested areas. Climbers should heed the warnings provided in the literature given to all persons entering the park, including the information about behavior recommended in grizzly bear country.

Some of the higher mountains of the park have grizzly bears (often with cubs) roaming about above the 8,000-foot level in July and August (Kintla, Kinnerly, Cleveland, Stimson, and Rising Wolf are notorious examples). They are turning over rocks and eating the larvae of cutworm moths or the spicy adult ladybug beetles that migrate upward by the thousands in late summer. Although bears have not been very hostile under such conditions, climbers should be aware of this behavior and remain alert as they approach ridgetops even though thousands of feet above tree line.

Great Photographers

Almost every mountain climber carries at least one camera and most are quite adept at the art of photography. They often respond to the hushed exclamations evoked by their pictures when projected on the large screen by modestly saying "you couldn't miss—just point the camera in any direction and shoot." Well, it MAY be easy to get spectacular kodachromes on mountain summits, but most mountain climbers have surely taken a few that were never shown in public! All admire the TRULY outstanding pictures that occasionally show up at gatherings of climber-photographers and appreciate the skill of those who took them. There are many great photographers who seldom even get to the summits, yet they take thrilling photographs of mountain scenery. Those pictures appear in books, magazines, and newspapers, impressing mountaineers and non-climbers alike, and the names of the photographers become well-known to all mountain-lovers.

A few of the photographers who have been especially effective in portraying the beauty of Glacier National Park deserve special mention in this book. The early artists whose pictures have illustrated numerous publications and brochures are usually cited only as Hileman and Kabel. Later, there were marvelous photographs by Marion Lacy, Walt Dyke, and Ira Spring. Outstanding pictures taken by Ansel Adams, Cedric Wright, and Philip Hyde were included in the first edition of this guide. During the last thirty years the greatest contributions in local newspapers have been those by Mel Ruder, Hal Kanzler, Brian Kennedy, Bob Kennedy, Scott Crandell, and George Ostrom. The ranks of excellent Glacier National Park photographers include Kathleen Ahlenslager, Bill Blunk, Larry Burton, Diane Ensign, Jeff Gnass, Rick Graetz, Wade Laird, Rolf Larson, John Mauff, Bruce Selyem, Ralph Thornton, Larry Ulrich, and also a great many others. In a different category are those who photograph plants, birds, and mammals. Nobody could surpass Alan Nelson's flower portraits, or the marvelous photographs of birds and mammals by Danny On and Stewart Cassidy. Cassidy's huge color prints are fortunately still readily available in state and national parks and in hundreds of museums and zoos throughout the United States at very reasonable prices, and Stewart continues to travel and take additional pictures that are becoming available to the public.

T. J. Hileman, a portrait photographer from Kalispell, took hundreds of 5 x 7 photographs in the park between 1910 and 1942. He was commissioned by the Great Northern Railroad in 1925 to photograph mountain landscapes and tourist activities throughout the park. Although much of Hileman's time was spent traveling throughout the park on horseback, he also became a very capable mountaineer. He is probably the only person who has ever recorded the views from the summit of Mt. Wilbur with a professional view camera. Hileman's photographs have been used extensively by both the Great Northern Railroad and the National Park Service in their promotions of tourism in Glacier National Park. A great many of Hileman's outstanding mountain pictures were used by Dr. George Ruhle in his *Guide to Glacier National Park* .

Ira Spring has been the greatest photographer and writer of outdoor books in the Pacific Northwest, in my opinion. He was employed by the Great Northern Railroad to take hundreds of 5 x 7 color transparencies in the park in the early l950s. The results were magnificent. When Alice and I hiked to Boulder Peak with him his pack must have weighed seventy pounds, but he stopped only to set up for dramatic photographs or to reload the film holders for his huge cameras. His great color prints have appeared in countless books and journals, as well as Glacier National Park brochures, and I have never seen any photos of this area that were better than Ira's.

A Chronological History of Climbing

The following brief chronology includes many of the major events in the history of mountaineering in Glacier National Park. It is unfortunate that so many worthy explorers must be omitted because of space limitations. The author must also apologize to numerous men and women who have climbed throughout the park during the last twenty years without his having been aware of them and their exploits! It would be great if every climb in the various areas could have been accurately recorded for the information of succeeding generations, but our record is unfortunately very sketchy. With anticipation of future revisions of this guide it is hoped that readers will inform the publisher or the author of significant omissions (and corrections) so that later editions can be more complete in this respect.

1883. James Willard Schultz, with friends including Jim Rutherford, Charlie Phemmister, and Oliver Sandoval, traveled to Lower St. Mary by way of Duck Lake. They then climbed and named Flattop Mountain.

1884. Schultz made a second trip with Rutherford and others and met a trapper called Medicine Beaver. They climbed and named Goat Mountain. Schultz sent a manuscript describing that trip to *Field and Stream* magazine, where it attracted the attention of publisher George Bird Grinnell. He wrote to Schultz and made arrangements to visit the country the following year.

1885. James Willard Schultz, with George Bird Grinnell and an Indian named Yellowfish (Charles Rose) climbed and named Singleshot Mtn. and Divide Mtn. This was Grinnell's first visit to the Rockies.

1887. Schultz, Grinnell, George H. Gould (Santa Barbara, California), and Lt. J. H. Beacon camped in the park. They hired a second guide, Jack Monroe. Some of the party climbed Mt. Allen, Mt. Gould, Mt. Henkel, and other peaks, and discovered Grinnell Glacier. It was named by Lt. Beacon, who also named a mountain Apikuni, which was Schultz's Indian name. They also named Mt. Wilbur (for E. R. Wilbur, who was an editor at *Field and Stream*).

1891. George Grinnell, with William H. Seward III (grandson of Lincoln's Secretary of State), Henry L. Stimson (later the Secretary of War and Secretary of State), and Billy Jackson (Indian grandson of Hugh Monroe, he was Reno's scout with General Custer at the Little Bighorn). They explored Blackfoot Glacier and named Mt. Jackson, Blackfoot Mtn., Mt. Reynolds, Citadel Mtn., and Mt. Stimson. Stimson was admired for his bravery and courage. (He often sat beside a grizzly bear bait in the dark, with a single-load rifle!) Mt. Stimson was later renamed Mt. Logan, and the name (Stimson) was then transferred to the massive peak above the Nyack Valley.

1892. Stimson, accompanied by Dr. Walter B. James (NY) and William Fox (a Blackfoot Indian) climbed the east face of Chief Mountain and authenticated the legend that a famous Flathead Indian had earlier fasted on that summit until experiencing the vision that guided him to a future as one of the greatest chiefs. He had left on the summit the bison skull which had served as his pillow, and Stimson's party indeed found a weathered old bison skull there after their frightening ascent! Stimson also made the first ascent of Blackfoot Mountain in 1892 and Little Chief in 1894.

1895-1906. Dr. Lyman Sperry (Oberlin College) explored the region around the glacier that now bears his name and supervised (at his own expense) the construction of the foot trail from Lake McDonald to the headwall near the glacier. He climbed Gunsight Mountain, and Longfellow and Vaught later climbed it and signed his register there in 1905. The Park naturalists requested this author to bring the register down in 1955, for the Park's historical museum, where it will be preserved for posterity.

1896. A register was placed in a small bottle and buried a foot deep on the summit of Chief Mountain by the original survey party. There were two engineers and three army officers in the party. In 1976 Eric Schwab, of Santa Ana, California, while on Chief Mountain with his family, discovered that historical document. Digging a foot deeper, the Schwabs found two very old bison teeth and a few deteriorated bone fragments! They reburied all of those objects in safe places nearby.

1900-1901. Francois E. Matthes climbed many peaks throughout the park while surveying it for the first topographic maps, including Chief, Little Chief, Red Eagle, Pinchot, and Blackfoot.

1910. Glacier National Park was established by an act of Congress and President Taft signed the bill creating the Park on May 11th.

1914. The Seattle Mountaineers held their annual summer outing in the new national park. For two weeks 115 members hiked and climbed, following an amazing pathway from Two Medicine Lake to Red Eagle Pass, cross-country from there to Gunsight Lake, then over Piegan Pass and Swiftcurrent Pass and north to Waterton Lake. They then hiked back to Lake McDonald by trail. Snow prevented the party from reaching the top of Blackfoot Mountain on August 4th, and another blizzard on August 11th turned back thirty members after they had reached a high camp on Mt. Cleveland.

1915. The Many Glacier Hotel opened for the first time, on July 4th. This was the summer that Howard Eaton led the first of his horseback parties through the park, from East Glacier Park to Many Glacier and then to Lake McDonald. His parties of more than fifty riders were comprised mainly of guests from his dude ranch at Wolf, Wyoming. With him on that 1915 tour were Mary Roberts Rinehart and Charlie Russell. Also during that summer James Willard Schultz led a camping expedition of thirty-three of his old Blackfeet friends through the eastern side of the Park, and one result of that trip was the writing of *Blackfeet Tales of Glacier National Park,* by Schultz.

1917. Robert H. Chapman climbed extensively with his survey crew. They erected the small wooden platform that is still atop Mt. Carter, and left the batch of heavy batteries wrapped in an old tarp there. They also ascended Rainbow, Vulture, and Kintla Peaks.

1918. Warren L. Hanna, while a law student at the University of Minnesota, worked at Many Glacier Hotel in the summer. He was so impressed by the park that during the next few years he wrote a manuscript for a general book on the subject. After a lapse of nearly fifty years his wife, Frances, ran across the old manuscript and encouraged Warren to work on it again. Despite many other responsibilities (such as heading a law firm with dozens of attorneys and writing huge legal volumes every year) Mr. Hanna did complete his book. It became the classic entitled *Many Splendored Glacierland*, which was published in 1975 and is treasured by all who share the love of Glacier Park with Frances and Warren Hanna.

1918. The High Trail from Granite Park to what is now called Logan Pass was completed. Late in August, even though the trail was not quite finished, the party including William Gibbs McAdoo, Secretary of the Interior, was permitted to travel over the route.

1919-1922. Members of the Nature Study Club of Indiana climbed many peaks and left registers in flat metal boxes on Edwards Mountain, Going-to-the-Sun Mountain, Mt. Gould, Mt. Jackson, Mt. Reynolds, Chief Mountain, and Grinnell Mountain. On each summit they built a small fire with twigs carried up from the valleys, then "as the smoke ascended heavenward" Dr. Frank B. Wynn read a "dedication." Many may find it overly effusive today, but it is pleasant to picture those enthusiastic gentlemen sitting on the summit with rapt attention as the following dedication was read: "To the God of the open air we dedicate this mountain summit. To us has been given the rare privilege of its attainment. Splendid and inspiring is the reward of the toilsome ascent! Its rugged course most trying was, but now triumphant visions greet us everywhere, symbolizing the blessings to the steadfast traveler along life's trail. The flame we here do kindle typifies the awakening of the inert dead into flaming life, effulgent and eternal. Its smoke, rising far beyond our reach and ken, wafts upward the spirit of our aspiration toward the beneficent and Infinite One, whose presence and power we acknowledge with grateful hearts."

As a member of the Nature Study Club, the author had heard of a mountain-climbing president of prior years, but never knew where he had climbed. Twenty years later, on my first climb of Mt. Jackson, I opened the metal box on the summit and was startled to see the register book headed "Guest Register of the Nature Study Club of Indiana." The mystery was solved! I later found identical registers on all of the mountains mentioned above, and left them all in place. Gradually they have all disappeared, but a few are preserved in the historic archives at Park headquarters.

Dr. Wynn, the Nature Study Club president, died near the top of Mt. Siyeh on July 27, 1922, after which Point Mountain was renamed Wynn Mountain in his honor.

1921. The trail over Red Gap Pass to the Belly River country was opened to travel. Dr. George C. Ruhle came to Glacier to serve as the first Park Naturalist and liked it so well that he stayed for twelve years. In addition to hiking almost every trail in the park, he also climbed dozens of mountains. Later he wrote two excellent Guides to the roads and trails of Glacier National Park (mentioned later) and he returned again in 1978 and 1990, still in great physical condition. (He has been helping other countries around the world establish national parks!)

1923. Norman Clyde, already a famous mountaineer and the most active climber in the Sierra Nevada of California, visited Glacier National Park. He climbed thirty-eight peaks, at least ten of them first ascents. The most notable first ascents were of Mt. Rockwell, Norris Mountain, Mt. Logan, Clements Mountain, Mt. Cannon, and Mt. Wilbur. Most of those climbs were solo, a practice which has more recently been strongly discouraged because of the potentially serious consequences that could result from even a minor accident.

1924. The Sierra Club held its summer outing in Glacier National Park. For three weeks 210 club members (with fifty employees and 135 horses) traveled through the northern section of the park. The trip was marred by bad weather but several mountains were climbed, including Pyramid Peak, Sentinel Peak, The Guardhouse, Appekunny Mountain, Goat Mountain, Heavens Peak, and Mt. Cleveland. Norman Clyde accompanied the Club on that outing and climbed twenty-one more peaks, including Vaught, Allen, Red Eagle, Gould, Siyeh, Guardhouse, Sentinel, Going-to-the-Sun, Cleveland, and Merritt. With Lee L. Stopple and Fred O. Herz he made a first ascent of Heavens Peak, and they later also descended Mt. Cleveland via a high traverse around Stoney Indian Peaks to Stoney Indian Lake.

1924-1938. DeWight Wanser, while employed by George Noffsinger (saddle horse concessionaire) established tent house camps around the great "North Circle" in the park, then led saddle parties from camp to camp, supplied the camps, collected receipts, etc. He rode nearly 30,000 miles over park trails, but his main base was the Crossley (Cosley) Lake camp which his wife, Berith, operated from 1924 to 1938. Their son, William, grew up there, spending each summer around the camp until he was eighteen years old. In 1930 he and his father made the first ascent of

Kaina Mountain, and they also roamed over all the surrounding ridges and peaks. Bill then spent seventeen years on ice breakers, serving Eskimo communities all along the Alaska coast. He and his versatile wife, Ethel, spent a part of each summer in Glacier National Park and have been mainstays in the Glacier Mountaineering Society. DeWight Wanser was still visiting the park in the late 1970s, and it was marvelous to hear first-hand accounts by the man who knew the park best! The tent camps were closed prior to the war and never reopened. Crossley Lake camp had eighteen tent houses with large double beds and accommodated about fifty "dudes" each night. Great meals were served in the dining tent, and the guests slept between clean sheets.

1926. Reverend Conrad Wellen, of Havre, made the first ascent of Mt. St. Nicholas. That rocky spire had been considered unclimbable after several experienced mountaineers had attempted it and failed. It is more frequently climbed now, but is seldom considered easy!

1927. G. M. Kilbourn went to work for the saddle horse company at Many Glacier Hotel. He had previously hiked most of the trails in the park and climbed a great number of mountains, so he often guided parties up to the high places he knew so well. He made several ascents of Mt. Wilbur, as well as climbing all the peaks overlooking the valleys radiating from the Swiftcurrent Lake region. Kilbourn's letters to the author were very helpful in researching the early days of the eastern part of Glacier National Park.

1928. Leo Seethaler served as Grinnell Glacier guide and contributed to the alpine atmosphere at Many Glacier by climbing the huge rock chimney in the dining room of the Hotel as part of the advertising for guided trips to the glacier.

1930. Dr. Morton J. Elrod published a revised edition of his 1924 *Guide to Glacier National Park.* Every hiker in the park carried a copy of that well-written booklet.

1931. The trail through the new Ptarmigan Tunnel was completed, thereby rendering the Red Gap Pass route to Belly River largely obsolete.

1934. The Seattle Mountaineers held another summer outing in the park, and their members climbed Reynolds, Siyeh, Wilbur, Cleveland, Goathaunt, and Rising Wolf.

1935. James L. Dyson, an outstanding geologist who worked as a Ranger-Naturalist for eight summers until 1948, devoted his lieu days to climbing mountains and studying glaciation and other geological features in the park. His climbs included the first ascent of Citadel Mountain. (In 1962, Dr. Dyson's new book, *World of Ice,* won the Phi Beta Kappa award as the outstanding non-fiction book in the United States that year.) Dyson returned to Glacier Park in 1962 and made a speedy climb of Mt. Gould with Dr. Herbert Alberding (another geologist of note, in the naturalist service), Gordon Tjernlund, and J. Gordon Edwards.

1937. Norman Clyde again visited Glacier National Park with a Sierra Club outing led by Richard M. Leonard, who had made notable contributions to the technique of rope management in rock climbing (and later was to lead in the development of nylon climbing rope by the Quartermaster Corps). The peaks climbed included Mt. Logan, Mt. Wilbur, Mt. Cleveland, Grinnell Mountain, Going-to-the-Sun, and a first ascent of Kinnerly Peak.

1937. Three climbers from Whitefish, Montana, climbed Mt. St. Nicholas. They were Robert F. Haines, James Caughren, and Lloyd A. Muldown. These men had already climbed many other peaks, together with Roger W. Haines, including Going-to-the-Sun, Heavens Peak, and Mt. Cleveland.

1940-1950. The postwar years brought an increase in park travel and a corresponding influx of climbers. Unfortunately, many trails that had been neglected during the war years were never reopened, and the backcountry "camps" remained closed forever (i.e. permanent facilities with board and room for riders and hikers who formerly could go from camp to camp, traveling light while enjoying the entire north circle route). The marvelous old chalets at Cutbank, Two Medicine, and Going-to-the-Sun Point were boarded up and, in a few years, destroyed by the Park Service. There was relatively little climbing being done, however a few of the ranger-naturalists enjoyed hiking the high trails on their lieu days and inevitably they began scrambling to higher points to take pictures with which to illustrate their evening talks. They were joined occasionally by other park employees and by adventuresome park visitors. The record of who did that sporadic climbing is extremely incomplete, however the following persons are known to have been active: Gerald Baden, ranger-naturalist from southern California, was an avid climber-photographer for many summers, but later began spending more time in the mountains of Canada. Gordon Edwards, ranger-naturalist from Ohio State University, came out with his wife, Alice, in 1947 and has been in the park each summer since that time. He was a seasonal ranger until 1956. His first interest was in high altitude entomology and ecology, but the pleasure of climbing and the views from the summits became every bit as interesting as the insects. John Mauff, of Chicago, visited the park in 1946 and immediately began climbing numerous peaks and seeking to hike every trail in the park. He returned almost every summer, made hundreds of ascents, and is still active here. He shared the first ascent of Split Mountain with Edwards in 1956. Joe Steffen, of Portland, took a night job at the Many Glacier Hotel about 1950, then discovered the mountaintops. He began climbing every day, after working all night! In later years he returned to devote full time to hiking and climbing, and to share the pleasures with his wife, Sharron, and daughter, Coowee. He is still going strong: in 1983 he led three parties up Mt. Wilbur during one two-week period and by 1989 he had been atop that great peak more than forty times!

1949. Dr. George C. Ruhle's *Guide to Glacier National Park* was published. It was a great aid to all hikers and mountaineers in the area. After slight revision in the 1950s it continued to fulfill everyone's needs until going out of print in the 1960s. On every hike, even after that, someone in the party would always have *Ruhle's Guide* in their pack, but a great void existed for most younger visitors until 1972, when Dr. Ruhle wrote a big, new, updated Guide.

1950-60. The popularity of climbing increased every year, but it was still an unusual occasion when someone met another person above the trails and only once every two or three years would parties meet on a summit. Edwards had been asked by Chief Naturalist Ed Beatty to write a description of each new route he climbed, and he and Don Robinson (the Assistant Chief Naturalist for the park) mimeographed those descriptions for distribution to interested persons at each ranger station. An incomplete listing of the persons who were most notorious for their climbing during that decade is presented below (in alphabetical order).

Larry Burton, after serving as a park ranger, returned almost every year to hike, climb, and photograph. He took the most impressive kodachromes of the great Garden Wall fire (August 1967) as it exploded up the west side of Mt. Gould. In recent years he and Sylvia Geshell have been in the park every summer completing a series of environmental lesson plans, tapes, and pictures for the Montana Department of Education dealing with biology and ecology. They are deeply involved in national park management procedures and participate actively in conferences dealing with those matters. They are at the University in Missoula during the winters.

Stewart Cassidy, from Arizona, worked for many summers as a ranger. He did a lot of serious hiking and climbing in the park, but gradually photography overtook climbing in his life, and by the 1970s he was so busy mailing thousands of his great wildlife pictures out each week that he seldom had a chance to get out onto the trails. In every national park and museum in the United States you now see his large clear color portraits of wild animals and birds in interesting poses. Every naturalist should have a complete set of Cassidy's pictures! Stewart has added many exotic pictures to his stock and visited very remote regions, such as Antarctica, with his versatile camera. He still intends to have more time in the future to get back up to his favorite peaks in Glacier National Park.

Jack Donnan and his wife, Marcia, from San Jose, climbed Reynolds, Gould, Siyeh, Divide, Rising Wolf, and Wilbur during the years he was a ranger. A picture of Jack looking down at Cracker Lake from Mt. Siyeh was a spectacular part of the American Heritage *Book of Natural Wonders* in 1963 (full page, in great color).

Martin Faulkner made the ninth ascent of Mt. St. Nicholas with John Merriam in 1954. During his years in the Park Service he also reached the summits of many other peaks in the park.

Robert Jasperson climbed Kinnerly Peak and Mt. Cleveland, among many others. A grizzly bear chased him up a sheer cliff (to escape her) above Agassiz Glacier while he was climbing Kintla Peak. He is an ardent conservationist, and after earning a law degree he became the attorney for prestigious California environmental groups.

Hal Kanzler was a well-known Columbia Falls business leader with a tremendous love of the outdoors. His enthusiasm led large numbers of friends and neighbors to follow wherever he went. For example, in 1964 he led a group of twenty-five mountaineers high up into the Mission Mountains for a three-day outing, including Dr. David Downey and Janet (his wife), Charles Fisher of Columbia Falls, David Line (well-known local artist and photographer), Dr. Loren Kreck (Kalispell), and Hal's sons, Jerry and Jim Kanzler. Hal's great photographs have appeared on magazine covers and in countless books and magazine articles. He truly excelled at everything he attempted! After the tragic deaths of Hal (1967) and Jerry (1969), Jim Kanzler continues to accomplish remarkable feats of mountaineering—including the only ascents ever made of the north face of Mt. Cleveland and the north face of Mt. Siyeh (both with ranger Terry Kennedy). Rangvold Kvelstad, of Poulsbo, Washington, was in charge of food supplies at Many Glacier Hotel for many years. He went climbing on every free day, and always took along groups of bellhops and waitresses. They, in turn, took other interested employees (and guests) on climbs they made later as a result of Kvelstad's introduction to the sport.

Marion Lacy, professional photographer from Whitefish, did a great amount of hiking and climbing in Glacier National Park. This remarkable man produced tremendous wall-sized photographic murals of great clarity, as well as photographs reproduced in almost every book or pamphlet or magazine article dealing with the park. His huge murals cover the walls of the largest restaurant in West Glacier, and hopefully will always remain there. In search of spectacular viewpoints, he even climbed Kintla Peak in 1952 and Mt. St. Nicholas in 1958!

Clyde Lockwood began his national park career in Glacier, and did considerable climbing in the early l950s. Later he was assigned to several other parks, including Mt. Rainier (where he was on the mountain rescue teams) and Yosemite. Eventually he returned to Glacier as Chief Park Naturalist, until retiring in 1989. He became the General Manager of the Glacier Natural History Association, and was largely responsible for the publication of the 1991 edition of the *Climber's Guide.*

George McFarland, who grew up at the family ranch on the west edge of Glacier National Park, has surely climbed every peak and hump in the entire Livingston Range. In the early days he climbed alone much of the time, but as the park rangers became more interested in such activities he enjoyed their company on many strenuous hikes and climbs. If anyone has questions about the peaks, ridges, valleys, lakes, and streams in that great mountain range, George McFarland is the person most likely to know the answer. After thirty years of mountaineering in that area, he is still in good condition and still exploring the wilderness.

Robert Megard joined Rangvold Kvelstad on many climbs, including Chief Mountain's east face, Mt. Merritt, and Mt. Jackson. He later completed his Ph.D. and is now Professor of Biology at the University of Minnesota, doing critical research in aquatic biology. He is also an outstanding photographer, as evidenced by his spectacular mountain pictures in several editions of the *Climber's Guide.*

Alan G. Nelson served as a ranger-naturalist during the 1960s and was constantly hiking and climbing. He suffered grave injury on one occasion when he dropped out of a safe tree to rush at a grizzly sow as she was in the process of killing a young boy. He saved that boy's life but could not get back up the tree when the grizzly turned her attention to him, and he suffered severe injury to his leg as a result. As Alan's photographic prowess developed, he began spending more time taking pictures than breathing rarified air. His 1972 book on the wildflowers of the park contains eighty marvelous color photographs that he took himself, close-up. He has also photographed many exotic areas, such as Prudhoe Bay, Alaska, and the Galapagos Islands. He teaches school in the winter but he and his wife, Kaydell, spend much of each summer in and near Glacier National Park.

G. George Ostrom, a Kalispell resident, was a close friend of Hal Kanzler and a frequent companion on camping, hunting, and climbing trips. George wrote columns for the *Hungry Horse News,* which were marvelous for their wit and insight. Perhaps that is why, in a moment of weakness, he bought the *Kalispell Weekly News* in 1974 and became the publisher. The circulation of that four-page newspaper was less than

1,000, but it grew to thirty pages with a circulation of over 20,000 before he sold it in 1982 after 820 wonderful issues. The photographs rivalled those published by Mel Ruder in the *Hungry Horse News,* which have received many national awards, and the writing was always interesting. Ostrom included great photographic coverage of climbs made by him and his staff, and also liked to take photographic flights over the mountains.

Kenneth Proctor, a ranger from southern California, was quite at home on any mountain. He shared with Edwards such things as Wilbur, Rockwell, Gould, Reynolds, and the traverse from Rainbow Peak to Mt. Carter. Ken later became a ranger in Grand Teton National Park, where he shared a first ascent of The Grand, via the Otter Body Snowfield, on the south side of that tremendous mountain.

Dick Rieman of Whitefish made the first ascent of South Vulture Peak with Don Eberlie in 1958. That same year he climbed Mt. St. Nicholas with Eddie Gilliland. They liked it so well that they returned the following year, accompanied by Marion Lacy, and stood on that elusive summit for the second time.

Edward Risse, while working on trail crews and fire suppression in 1955-1959, climbed a dozen major peaks. In 1957 he and Clyde Lockwood participated in a famous rescue high on the east face of Chief Mountain with Don Alford, Don Dayton, and Lou Wendt. Ed returned to the park for more climbing in 1986 with his son, Michael.

Garth Uibel of Calgary did much climbing in Waterton and Glacier national parks, as well as in the Canadian Rockies. He has improved the coverage in this guide by writing descriptions of his routes on Mt. Chapman, Kinnerly Peak, and other mountains in Glacier National Park.

Klindt Vielbig from Portland visited the park and went climbing with Richard Parker from Oberlin, Ohio. Their climbs included the seventh ascent of Mt. St. Nicholas. Klindt described it in an article in the *Mazama Annual* . . . not omitting the discussion of a jar of honey that drained inside his pack. They ascended the south side of St. Nick until they ran out of pitons, then descended and traversed to the great notch and ascended the traditional route . . . a long day even for excellent climbers!

A great many other good mountaineers were active during this decade and I must apologize to those I have unintentionally neglected to mention.

1952. The Seattle Mountaineers again came to Glacier for their summer outing with eighty campers. They climbed fifteen peaks, including Chief, Jackson, Going-to-the-Sun, Reynolds, Siyeh, and the east face of Clements. They placed 185 signatures in the various summit registers and left aluminum register tubes on four of these peaks.

1954. The Sierra Club arrived for a high trip co-led by Dr. H. Stewart

Kimball and David Brower, Executive Director of the Club. The party contained 144 people, plus commissary crew and packers. They entered the park at Many Glacier and hiked over Stoney Indian Pass and onward to Hole-in-the-Wall Cirque. The weather was so bad it inhibited most activities on mountains.

1955 and 1957. A small contingent of Sierra Clubbers returned each year and enjoyed excellent weather. They entered the park at Two Medicine and hiked to St. Mary Lake. Dave Brower and Philip Berry led parties up the east face of Triple Divide Peak in 1955. A highlight of the 1957 trip was the second ascent of Split Mountain accomplished by Philip Berry and Richard Miller.

1958. The Colorado Mountain Club held a summer outing in the park. Some of the group hiked the highline trail for thirty miles to Waterton Lake. Others climbed Mt Jackson, Mt. Siyeh, and Mt. Wilbur.

1960-1970. Many new climbers became extremely active during this period and it was not uncommon to meet other parties on or near the summits. There were days when climbers were simultaneously atop Gould, Reynolds, Oberlin, Going-to-the-Sun, Allen, and Mt. Wilbur . . . with no previous coordination planned! In 1960 the first edition of Edwards' book, *A Climber's Guide to Glacier National Park,* was published by the Sierra Club; however, the great impetus in mountaineering had already been provided by the press coverage of serious climbing around the world, and by the strong movement toward physical fitness among Americans of all ages. By 1966, when the next edition appeared (with a fifteen-page supplement), it seemed as though the majority of employees in the Park Service as well as those in the hotels and restaurants around the park were spending a great many of their lieu days enjoying thrilling views from the mountaintops. It would be impossible to mention every climber of note who ascended mountains during this decade, and space obviously is not available to discuss the individual exploits of many of them here. Just for the record, however, it seems appropriate to list those who attracted the most attention.

The first section includes employees of the Park Service who were enthusiastic climbers. These were mostly rangers; however many fire guards and trail crew members are included also. Typically, the climbing parties included a mixture of all these categories. Arranged alphabetically, the outstanding climbers were: Gerald Baden; Oakley Blair; Marc Boyd; Asa Brooks; Dave Bush; Dave Casteel (and wife, Marilyn); Stewart Cassidy; William Colony; Jerry DeSanto; Doug Erskine; Greg Evans (and wife, Sue); Bob Frauson; Bob Fullerton; Marshall Gingery; Fred Goodsell; Bill (and son, Keith) Hollister; Steve Jorgenson; Dick Mattson; Lloyd

Parrat (and sons, Mark and Monte); Bob Pfister; Fred Reese; Lewis Sabo; Bob Schuster; Charles Scribner; Dave Shea; Roger Shewmake; Stu Swanberg; Chris Tesar; Tom Tschohl; Bob Wood (and wife, Stephanie); and Wyatt Woodsmall. Most of these park employees are still actively hiking in the 1980s, wherever they may be, and a great many still enjoy the wild country and lofty peaks of Glacier National Park.

Large numbers of park visitors were also known to be climbing mountains here during the 1960s. The following came quickly to mind when the author sought to list those with whom he was associated at that time (or heard about through the grapevine or the newspapers). Alphabetically listed, they are: Jim Anderson; Gil Averill; Tom Best; Reverend Hugh Black; Mona Brown; Larry Burton; Richard Buys; Michele Casteel; Tom Choate; Bruce Cook; Dave and Janet Downey; Bob Emerson; Brock Evans (now a U.S. senator); Erling Evenson; Martin Faulkner; Renn Fenton; Charles Fisher; Keith Hollister; Richard E. Johnson; Cal Jorgensen; Hal Kanzler; Jerry Kanzler; Jim Kanzler; Randy Kay; Fred Koesling; Rolf Larson; Russ Landt; Mark Levitan; H. M. Louderback; John Mauff; Ray Martin; Helmuth Matdies; William Matthews; George McFarland; Bruce Murphy; Donald Nellis; Alan Nelson; Arthur Noskowiak; George Ostrom; Mark Parratt; Monte Parratt; Clare Pogreba; Leo Renfrow; Kathleen Sabo; Steve Sabo; Carl Sanders; Philip Shinn; Dave Shoup; Dick Wallner; Kris Wallner; and Reverend John Ward.

1968. The Sierra Club had another outing in the park from the 16th to 25th of July. With fifty-five hikers and twelve horses, plus the work crew, they hiked from Logan Pass to Hole-in-the-Wall Cirque. From Fifty Mountain Camp they took a great detour over Chaney Notch to Chaney Glacier, thence to Stoney Indian Pass and Kootenai Lake. The leader of the group was H. Stewart Kimball, assisted by Gordon Edwards.

Since 1970. The numbers of tourists enjoying Glacier National Park continued to increase every year, and many of them were eager to leave the highway and admire the majestic scenery "close-up." The appearance of appropriate books to help us all appreciate experiences in the park deserves special mention.

In 1972, Dr. George C. Ruhle published a new book, *The Roads and Trails of Waterton-Glacier National Parks.* In some ways it was even better than his original guide. That book and many others were available through the Glacier Natural History Association at the Belton Depot in West Glacier 59936.

In 1976 another great reference source for persons interested in the park appeared in print. It is *Montana's Many-Splendored Glacierland,* by

Warren L. Hanna. In its 215 pages there are details of the past history of the area, the people who have developed it into the great park as it is today, and the nature of its mountains and valleys. Chapters deal with the flowers, the animals, the glaciers, the bears, the trails, the passes, the mountain climbing, the environmental problems, and every other topic that should be of interest to mountaineers. Hanna's research has been extremely thorough and reflects his long experience as an attorney accustomed to getting every detail exactly right. The book is illustrated with marvelous photographs, many of them in color.

In 1979 Denis and Shirley Twohig began the publication of *Going-to-the-Sun,* a beautiful magazine devoted to Glacier National Park in all its aspects (trails, history, flora and fauna, climbing, etc.). In 1981 a group of mountaineering enthusiasts formed the Glacier Mountaineering Society under the leadership of Denis and Shirley. Initially the GMS News was printed inside the *Going-to-the-Sun* magazine and was edited by Brian Kennedy (the publisher of the *Hungry Horse News*). In 1982 the magazine ceased publication, but the name and the logo were adopted by the Glacier Mountaineering Society. That publication now keeps members abreast of the climbing activities of the membership, publishes descriptions of new routes, and discusses various other activities of Society members. The Glacier Mountaineering Society's schedule of activities includes weekly climbs during the summer, and the third week of July each year is designated as GMS Week by the Society. Members from throughout the U. S. and Canada gather in the park at that time to renew friendships and share in numerous climbs, clinics, and evening programs. The activities culminate with the annual "grand luncheon" and social program, during which the prestigious GMS Alpine Awards are presented. The address of the Society is P.O. Box 291, Whitefish, Montana 59937, and new members are always welcome.

There have been several notable winter climbs in Glacier National Park. On 29 November 1969 six outstanding mountaineers reached the summit of Mt. Wilbur, then spent the night near the summit. The climbers were Jim Kanzler, Jim Anderson, Mark Leviton, Clare Pogreba, Pat Callis, and Jung Hofer. Mt. Cleveland was climbed in February 1977 by Glen H. Milner, Robert L. Talbot, and Richard Olmsted, of Jackson Hole, Wyoming. The first winter ascent of Mt. Siyeh was made in February 1982 by Ed Sondeno, of Bozeman, and in winter of 1984 Ted Steiner and Kenny Kasselder ascended the north face of the Little Matterhorn. In December 1985 Trenton Cladouhos and his son Tom miraculously gained the summit of Mt. St. Nicholas. In 1986 Dan McComb and Tom Otto stood atop Kintla Peak amid frigid winter conditions. February 1987 found Roger Semler and Bruce Weide skiing and camping for three days as they ascended Rainbow Peak. Mt. Jackson was finally climbed in winter by Don Scharfe, Scott Thomas, and Orrin Webber of Kalispell on February 25, 1988. In 1989 Lane Johnson of Whitefish climbed Mt. Stimson in February with John Head and Marty Loefflad, of Moscow, Idaho. Steve Niday, of Missoula, skied and climbed to the top of Mt. Merritt on 23 February 1991, the first known winter ascent. In a blizzard, he slept 1,000 feet below the summit until the weather cleared. On 2 January 1992 Ted Steiner, a climbing instructor from Whitefish, climbed the northwest ridge of Mt. Jackson. The wind was so ferocious that he had to *crawl* the last hundred feet to the summit (in a total whiteout). These are all major peaks to conquer, even under pleasant summer conditions, and the hardiness and perseverance of mountaineers who reach the frigid summits in winter are truly amazing!

The marvelous newspaper called the *Hungry Horse News* was published and edited by Mel Ruder in Columbia Falls for thirty-two years. Ruder specialized in writing human interest stories and Glacier National Park was his major "beat." He is an excellent photographer and enjoyed carrying his big camera into every corner of the park. His scenic specials were superb. Every issue included pictures that mountain-lovers cut out and saved. He reported on every notable climb and provided accurate information on mountaineering and hiking activities in the park.

National Park Service employees who are known to have made note-worthy climbs in recent years include the following: Bob Adams; Kathy Ahlenslager; Rich Altemus; Reginald Altop; Jim Bellamy; Curt Buchholtz; Chuck Cameron; Dave Casteel (and wife, Marilyn); Randy Coffman; Robin Cox (and wife, Sarah); Jerry DeSanto; Dennis Divoky; Ed Dunleavy; Greg Evans (and wife, Sue); Robert Frauson; Steve Frye; Al Hoffs; Robert Isdahl; Steve Jackson; Kyle Johnson; Terry Kennedy; Dallas Koehn; John Kramer; Wade Laird; Rolf Larson; Doug Mason; Dick Mattson (and wife, Ursula); Dan Maturen (and wife, Katryn); Russ Miller; Rick Millsap; Greg Nelson; Greg Notess; Michael Ober; Bill Pierce; Jack Polzin; Jack Potter (and wife, Rachel); Fred Reese; Joe Reis; Ed Rosette; Tim Savee; Carol Savage; Mary Schneider; Robert Schuster; Roger Semler; Dave Shea; Roger Shewmake; Chuck Sigler (former Chief Ranger); Greg Smith; Tom Sweeney; Lisa Tuvecek; Gary Vodehnal; Tom Walsh; Becky Williams; Cindy White; Allie Wood; Gary Yates (and wife, Karla); and Rick Yates.

There were impressive numbers of friendly mountaineers on the high goat trails and soaring summits of Glacier National Park during the 1970s.

Many were residents of the surrounding area, but even more came from great distances. Those who did most of their climbing in the Many Glacier area or elsewhere on the east side of the Park became known to this author, either personally or via mutual friends. Many of those climbers are mentioned below, but there are certainly a great many other worthy persons whose accomplishments were not adequately heralded. Throughout the book specific references have been made to the activities of many of these men and women, whose contributions will be recognized and appreciated by future mountaineers who follow in their footsteps.

The following are the mountaineers who have attracted the most attention since 1970: Kathleen Ahlenslager; Grant Bernard; James Best; Joe Biby; Roscoe and Rocky Black; Dan Block; Bill Blunk ; Tom Bulleit; Scott Burch; Lavonne Burgard; Larry Burton; Edwin and Steve Cady; Pat Caffrey who authored the book, *Climber's Guide to Montana*; Mike Cheek; Trenton and Tom Cladouhos; Becky Cousins; Sarah Cox; Scott Crandell; Dwight Crosier; Chester Davis; Vic Davis; Jerry DeSanto; Dave and Janet Downey, and sons Dan and Mark Downey; Carl Fiedler; Ken Fielder; Jack Fisher; Marty Fulsaas; Sylvia Geshell; Bruce Gillis; Bobbie Gilmore; Dave and Mark Going; Carl Hansen; Greg Harrah; Monte and Lee Hartman; Joe Haugestuen; Bill Hedglin; George Hollerbach; Jim and Tom Hooley; Robert Horodyski; Rick Hull; Mark Jefferson; Rolf Larson; Jerry Lundgren; Paul Jensen; Jaime and Lisa Johnson; Lane Johnson; Jim Kanzler; Kenny Kasselder; Randy Kay; Brian Kennedy; Terry Kennedy; Ron Knaus; Wade Laird; Rolf Larson; Dale Lee; Dave Leppert; Mavis Lorenz; Wayne Lugenbuehl; Doug Mason; Dan and Katryn Maturen; John Mauff; Dan McComb; George McFarland; Paul Meierding; Glen Milner; Worth Moffet; Alan and Kaydell Nelson; Greg Nelson; Meg Nelson; Arthur Noskowiack; Greg Notess; Richard Olmsted; George Ostrom; Tom Otto; Wayne and Kelly Phillips; William Rideg; Steve Sabo; Larry and Arnie Sandefur; Carl Sanders; Dean Sayles; Mike Scarano; Don Scharfe; Dick Schwab, with Mark and Heidi Schwab; Eric Schwab; Phil and Jo Schwab, with Sarah and Anne Schwab; Bruce Selyem; Roger Semler; Dave Shea; Laura Shearin; Dave Shoup; Tom Shreve; Allen Smith; Anthony and Carol Somkin; Dan Spencer; Tim Speyer; Joe Steffen (and daughter Coowee Mennen and granddaughter Valah); Shari Stahl; Ted Steiner; Al Streitmatter; Robert Talbot; Ralph Thornton; Denis and Shirley Twohig; Ken Wade; Lou Wendt; Ann Williamson; Matt and Charles Wilson; Dave Wing; Dan Wirth; Don Wolfe; Gary and Karla Yates; Chip Youlden; Maggy Young; and Mike Young.

Another group of local climbers deserve special mention. George Ostrom recently informed me that "The Thursday Mountain Club members are still peak-bagging, with a membership that averages 65 years of age." Still active are Doc "Hi" Gibson, Ivan O'Neil, Spencer Ryder, George Ostrom, and Ambrose Measure (who was eighty in December 1988). Recent additions have been Pat Gyrion, Elmer Searles, Hank Good, and Bob Dundas (but Dundas, "being a kid in his late fifties," has lowered our average age level). The gang has had more and more "guest" hikers the last few years, "including a few young fellas, and two ladies." Seventy-year-old Elmer Searles keeps a record which shows they have made a total of ninety hikes or climbs in the past three years, most of them being reruns or new routes on fun peaks they had done before, such as Painted Tepee, Altyn, Sinopah, Grinnell, Rising Wolf, Clements, and Siyeh. As anyone who has climbed here is aware, several of those peaks are NOT easily ascended!

Ostrom sadly reports "We lost Harry Isch, on July 21,1988. He died of heart failure while climbing Mt. Cannon. He made a joke just seconds before dropping: a peaceful death, with good friends, in a beautiful place."

To these senior citizens who are continuing to attain such lofty heights in Glacier National Park every younger climber must render deep respect. They give us all great hope for continuing outdoor activities in our own future!

Acknowledgments

This book could not have materialized without the aid of many persons to whom I wish to express my appreciation.

Alice Edwards, my wife, seems to enjoy hiking and climbing as much as I, and has climbed all of the 10,000-foot peaks in the park with me, as well as dozens of lesser summits during the past thirty-seven years. Without her companionship, and that of our daughter, Jane, many of these ascents would not have been made. Without their interest and assistance the descriptions presented here would probably never have been written.

When the Glacier Natural History Association decided to publish this new edition of the guide, I volunteered to duplicate the older edition by "scanning" it and revising it on the word processor at San Jose State

ACKNOWLEDGMENTS

University. I had no previous experience with word processing, but the staff of the Electronic Learning Laboratory on the campus provided me with all of the necessary equipment and facilities and explained how to use them. Dr. Donald Perrin and Ken Watson are in charge of the Laboratory, and Jeff Engell and Victoria Whisner were assigned to assist the professors seeking to learn in that laboratory. We are extremely grateful to these experts and to San Jose State University for making it possible to produce the revised manuscript in its final form, ready for use by the publishers in Helena, Montana.

Dr. Jane A. Edwards, my daughter, is doing research at the University of California in Berkeley and has had years of experience with various kinds of word processors. I sometimes went to her laboratory to work on the manuscript at nights and on weekends, and am extremely grateful for her advice and assistance in the laboratory as well as on many of the mountains that are discussed in this guide.

Chief Park Naturalist M. E. Beatty and Assistant Naturalist Donald H. Robinson encouraged me to climb as many mountains as possible during the nine years I worked there as Ranger-Naturalist, and to write descriptions of the routes I discovered. They then gave copies to each ranger station for distribution to interested climbers.

After I had compiled several dozen descriptions I was approached by the Sierra Club's Executive Director, David Brower, who asked if I would consider having the guide published by the Club. I was delighted, and Brower personally edited the manuscript and rushed it into print in 1961. He had been climbing in Glacier National Park and found it to be pleasant, challenging, and spectacular. He soon had the guide in print, with sixteen large glossy photographs by Ansel Adams and many others by Cedric Wright and Philip Hyde. The Club later reprinted it, with a fifteen-page supplement describing more recently discovered routes.

When the Sierra Club became more active in politics than in mountaineering they ceased publication of guides to the Grand Tetons, Glacier National Park, etc. The Mountain Press, in Missoula, then was permitted to make exact copies of the Sierra Club book, except for the photographs, and published two revised editions.

During the compilation of this information I have enjoyed climbing with an abundance of good climbers and pleasant companions. Each of them has contributed to my knowledge of this great wild area. I owe a debt to every one of those men and women. Many are mentioned specifically under the section on the "Chronological History of Climbing" in the park, but there were a great many others whose names I have failed to recall.

In the 1940s very few of the park's permanent rangers ever thought of going climbing. Indeed it was hard to remember a single one who had ever really gotten to the top of a trailless peak in the park. The temporary summer employees, on the other hand, devoted most of their lieu days to exploring the remote back country and roaming about on the summits. A great change began during the late 1950s. By the 1960s there were many permanent as well as seasonal rangers who devoted their lieu days to climbing the ridges and peaks and taking beautiful photographs from the highest places they could reach. Meanwhile the park was taking action to safeguard the lives of the novice climbers who had been scrambling up the peaks. They purchased two "deer carriers" for rescue work and employed some excellent climbers as permanent rangers. Those men, led by Robert Frauson, soon had developed rescue teams that handled every conceivable sort of emergency in and near the park. A great many climbers certainly owe their lives to Frauson and his cohorts! Not only did they save many lives, but they also permitted the sport of climbing to flourish in Glacier National Park rather than being inhibited because of the possibility of accidents on the peaks. The cooperation between the rangers and the climbers who now come from throughout the nation has been remarkable. Hopefully that fine relationship will continue.

In addition to Bob Frauson's constant aid, we have received valuable help and encouragement in the preparation of this new edition from former Chief Ranger Charles B. Sigler and Rangers Jerry DeSanto, Dick Mattson, Dan Maturen, and Terry Kennedy. Their information has been particularly useful in the preparation of route descriptions for several peaks in the northern Livingston Range and the North Central Area.

We are also indebted to some very unusual park visitors for supplying details regarding parts of the park that are difficult or very time-consuming to reach. William Blunk and Ralph Thornton took strenuous trips through the wild Red Eagle Pass area and the entire Norris Traverse. They also explored the remote alpine regions around Kintla Peak and Parke Peak, and prepared reliable descriptions for others who may follow their routes in the future. Dan Spencer has climbed with Dan Maturen and Katryn Maturen throughout the park and they have contributed espe- cially valuable information concerning the "Continental Divide Route" from Brown Pass to Jefferson Pass and southward to Trapper Peak and the Fifty Mountain meadows. (See "Jefferson Pass Approaches.") Several "techni- cal climbers" who are widely recognized as leaders in that field have also climbed in Glacier National Park. The exploits of Jim Kanzler and Terry Kennedy on the monstrous faces of Glacier's highest peaks are legendary (see details under Mt. Siyeh, Mt. Cleveland, and Mt. St. Nicholas, for examples).

ACKNOWLEDGMENTS

The photographs selected for inclusion in these guides have been obtained from a great variety of sources. The generosity of the following donors is greatly appreciated: The Glacier National Park film library; The Glacier Park Company; the Great Northern Railroad and Burlington Northern Railroad; *Hungry Horse News* publishers Mel Ruder and Brian Kennedy; *Going-to-the-Sun* magazine editor Denis Twohig; and the following individuals: Tony Blueman, Bill Blunk, James Dyson, Diane Ensign, Bill Hedglin, Hal Kanzler, Bob Kennedy, Rolf Larson, John Mauff, Robert Megard, George Ostrom, Carl Sanders, Dan Spencer, Ira Spring, Ralph Thornton, and many others.

In 1979 Mel Ruder decided to retire, so he sold his famous *Hungry Horse News* to Brian Kennedy. Fortunately, Brian is an enthusiastic mountaineer himself, so the *News* continues to carry spectacular mountain photographs, including many taken from the summits by the editor and his brother, Bob. Everyone interested in hiking or mountaineering in Glacier National Park should enjoy a year-round subscription to this spectacular newspaper (Columbia Falls, MT 59912).

Lake McDonald in May (left to right: Mt. Vaught, Mt. Cannon, and Mt. Brown) — NPS Photo

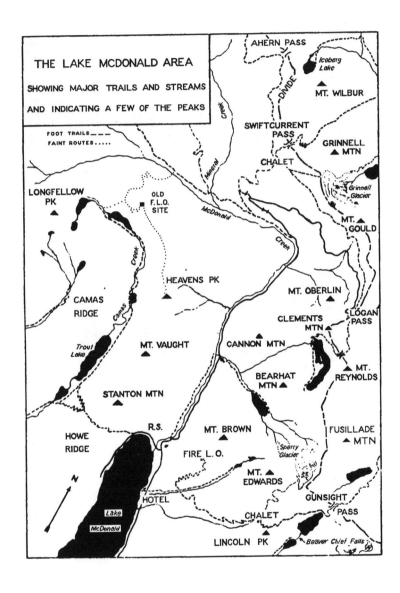

THE LAKE McDONALD AREA

SHOWING MAJOR TRAILS AND STREAMS
AND INDICATING A FEW OF THE PEAKS

FOOT TRAILS ___
FAINT ROUTES .....

THE LAKE McDONALD AREA

Routes Among the Peaks

Ten-mile-long Lake McDonald is only 3,153 feet above sea level, so it is the lowest valley in the entire park. For great views of the rugged area surrounding this great lake, hike up Apgar Mountain (5,236 ft.) on the old fire lookout trail that begins one-half mile west of the lower McDonald Creek bridge. The ridges along each side of the lake are 2,000 feet high. Snyder Ridge is on the east and Howe Ridge parallels the west shore of Lake McDonald. The only trail that crosses Howe Ridge is the one from the head of the lake. It provides access to a string of attractive lakes in the next valley (Rogers, Trout, Arrow, Camas, Evangeline, and Ruger Lakes).

The mountains rising immediately above the north end of the lake are Stanton Mountain (7,750) and Mt. Vaught (8,850) on the west and Mt. Brown (8,565) and Mt. Cannon (8,952) on the east side of the valley.

Six miles up a good trail from Lake McDonald Hotel are the Sperry Chalets. From there, the climb up Lincoln Peak (7,440) is popular for climbers going over Lincoln Pass en route to the St. Mary Valley, a twenty-two mile hike that also crosses Gunsight Pass.

It is about three miles from the chalets up to Sperry Glacier Basin, from which there are easy climbs of Mt. Edwards and Gunsight Peak and hundreds of acres of snow and ice to explore. For details of the cross-country routes between Logan Pass and Sperry Glacier, see the Logan Pass chapter of this guide.

A challenging four-mile side trip from the Sperry trail is the steep trail up to the Mt. Brown fire lookout, 4,300 vertical feet above Lake McDonald. (The summit is 1,100 vertical feet higher than the lookout.)

The pleasant drive up the McDonald Valley soon takes you to Avalanche Gorge, from which a fascinating trail leads quickly to Avalanche Lake. Persistent climbers can fight their way directly up into the Sperry Glacier basin from there. The great mountain face that rises immediately north of Avalanche Creek is 5,700 vertical feet in height. It is Cannon Mountain, which is *much* more easily climbed from Logan Pass. Across the valley from Cannon, snowy Heavens Peak presents some formidable obstacles to mountaineers even though its elevation is only 8,987 feet.

About 6.2 miles from Avalanche Camp (twenty-two miles from the entrance station) a small dirt lane descends 0.7 miles from the highway, to "Packers Roost." Pack strings supplying Granite Park Chalets are loaded here, and private saddle trips to the North Central Area of the park frequently begin here also. From Packer's Roost it is twelve miles to Fifty Mountain Camp via the Flattop Mountain trail, and seventeen miles via the circuitous McDonald Creek trail. (The latter is the quickest route to Trapper Peak and the extensive meadows that straddle the Continental Divide from West Flattop Mountain to Jefferson Pass.)

Continuing up the highway for a couple of miles will bring you to the "Heavens Peak Tunnel," where most visitors will want to stop (parking south of the tunnel) and take pictures looking at Heavens Peak through the photogenic rock window in the side of the tunnel. A short distance further up the road is the "Loop" where the highway abruptly turns toward Logan Pass. A large parking area is above the loop, for the convenience of those who wish to leave their vehicles for a few days and take to the trails. It is four miles up the trail to Granite Park Chalets, and from there hikers may go over the pass to Swiftcurrent Valley or take the Garden Wall trail (7.6 miles) to Logan Pass. For persons with greater ambitions than that, the Highline Trail heading north from Granite Park leads to Waterton Lake, by way of Fifty Mountain Camp. Many mountaineering attractions are available in that great area, discussed under the chapter on "The North Central Area" in this guide.

Routes to the Summits

Mt. Brown (8,565)

The Southwest Ridge Route. Distance to summit about six miles, 4.7 of it on human trail. Elevation gained is about 5,300 feet. Class 2, except the wall near the summit ridge, which is class 4 or 5.

Views from the top are extremely rewarding. St. Mary Lake, Going-to-the-Sun Mountain, Mt. Siyeh, the entire Lewis and Livingston Ranges, and many southern peaks are very prominent from this lofty prominence, and most of the McDonald Valley is visible. Avalanche Creek and the lake at its head lie 4,600 feet below the summit. Sperry Glacier and its guardian peaks are close at hand to the southeast with a plethora of snowfields and glacial features. Further south, in the middle distance, are the thumb-like spire of St. Nicholas and the broad, snow-covered pyramid of graceful Great Northern Mountain. The huge peak near Mt. St. Nicholas is 10,000-foot Mt. Stimson, deep in the rugged and remote area of upper Nyack Creek.

Leave Lake McDonald Hotel and hike to Mt. Brown Fire Lookout by trail, a distance of 4.7 miles, with more than thirty switchbacks in the last two miles. From the fire lookout it is a little more than a mile to the summit, with a climb of about 1,500 feet in vertical elevation.

Follow the goat trails from the lookout to the top of the large, gentle slope northeast of the fire lookout. From there you must climb around seven or eight rugged, rocky humps arranged as a jagged wall (class 4 and 5 in places). Two of these (including the first) may be most easily traversed on the east side, but the others are best passed by climbing around the wall on their western faces. Beyond this wall it is an easy walk up the ridge to the summit. NOTICE: Persons not equipped for rock climbing should not attempt this wall, but may instead traverse below it along the west side (on goat trails) then climb straight up to the summit ridge by means of class 3 pitches.

A much more strenuous climb, which will offer good experience for people intending to make more serious climbs in the future, is the ascent of Mt. Brown (to the fire lookout) from Going-to-the-Sun Highway near McDonald Falls via the largest gully on its west face. It includes a few class 3 and 4 pitches and plenty of bushwacking en route.

Edwards Mountain (9,055)

The East Face Route. Distance to summit about 8.5 miles, eight miles of it on human trail. Elevation gained is about 5,800 feet. Class 2 and 3 all the way, if correct routes taken.

The summit views are very attractive, although not quite so rewarding as those from Gunsight Mountain. This is probably the very best vantage point for observing Sperry Glacier, however, and is well worth the climb just for that reason. It is interesting to watch Sperry Chalets and any people moving near it, and to trace much of the trail toward Lake McDonald, itself a handsome spectacle. Beyond Mt. Brown, toward the north, may be seen the snowy giants of the Livingston Range. Massive Cannon Mountain conceals many of the peaks in the northeast sector of the park, while Mt. Jackson blocks out much of the southern horizon. Beyond the cirque of Sperry Glacier is the Logan Pass area and its surrounding peaks, while farther to the east brilliant blue St. Mary Lake extends far out toward the prairies, impressively flanked by many tremendous peaks — most notably Citadel, Little Chief, Red Eagle, and Going-to-the-Sun Mountain.

From Lake McDonald Hotel follow the Sperry Glacier trail eight miles to the headwall just west of the Sperry Glacier basin, where steps have been blasted out of solid rock to give hikers access to the glacier. Leave the trail just above the stairway and proceed northward along the east side of Edwards Mountain. When an easy-appearing route is seen, walk up the talus slopes and scramble up small cliffs (class 3) to the east end of the summit ridge. If you take care in route-finding you need climb no dangerous pitches, although some can be found if desired. Once atop the ridge, it is a short, easy, remarkable walk to the true summit and its cairn. A register in a thin metal box was placed in the cairn by the Nature Study Club of Indiana in 1921. After reading it and signing it, please replace it with care where wind and rain won't damage it and where it can be seen from a side view by the next climbers who seek it. The trip from the hotel to the summit should not take more than eight hours. If some members of the party are not in excellent condition, it may be wise to spend the night in or near Sperry Chalets and make a leisurely climb the next morning. Usually the views are more attractive early in the day, frequently becoming hazy in the afternoon, especially late in the season.

The West Ridge Route. For experienced rock climbers (many class 4 and 5 cliffs along this high, narrow ridge). Distance to summit from hotel about 8.5 miles, 6.5 of it by trail.

This is a more interesting route than the East Face Route but requires greater skill and is fraught with more danger to the climbers. A rope should be carried on this route because there are many interesting cliffs of fairly good rock which may challenge the party. (Most can be avoided, if desired, if you work back and forth over the ridge when necessary.)

Head directly up the slope north of Sperry Chalets, staying just west of the cliffs, until you reach the top of that prominent ridge (class 2 or 3 up to that point). Once atop the ridge, you will enjoy one of the most pleasant hours imaginable as you work along this knife-edge, alternately following it and paralleling it, and choosing pitches as difficult as desired or walking through gaps and scrambling along ledges near the top. As you climb this ridge you will often be looking down 3,000 feet to tiny Snyder Lakes and beyond them to the Mt. Brown fire lookout. In the other direction lies Sperry Glacier, surrounded by jagged walls and extensive snowfields. After traveling along the ridge for a considerable distance your party will find two cairns on small humps near the east end of the ridge. The register should be found in the higher of these two prominent cairns.

Time required to reach the summit by this route should not exceed eight hours from the hotel, but a more enjoyable climb may be one including a high camp near Sperry Chalets.

Gunsight Mountain (9,258)

Distance to summit about 9.5 miles, eight miles of it on human trail. Elevation gained is about 6,050 feet. Class 2 to 5, depending upon routes taken. First known ascent was by Dr. Lyman Sperry and party in 1905 (register book is now in the Park Museum).

The views from the true summit are similar to those from the lower western peak, but much more spectacular. Directly south, below almost sheer cliffs, lies deep blue Lake Ellen Wilson with the stupendous bulk of 10,000-foot Mt. Jackson rising far above the shore. This peak blots out most of the view toward the south, but it is still possible to see the horizontal summit ridge of 10,000-foot Mt. Stimson and the impressive thumb-like spire of Mt. St. Nicholas toward the southeast. To the right, beyond Mt. Jackson, rises a graceful extremely snowy massif with many broad white glaciers. This is Great Northern Mountain, just south of the park boundary in Flathead National Forest. The most prominent peaks visible in the foreground toward the north include Mt. Edwards (with greatly folded strata), Cannon Mountain, and Clements Mountain. These peaks partly conceal the mountains of the Lewis and Livingston ranges farther north, and their snowfields and glaciers. Going-to-the-Sun Mountain and Mt. Siyeh loom beyond Logan Pass, and far beyond them the pastel prairies extend endlessly. Sperry Glacier (one of the three largest

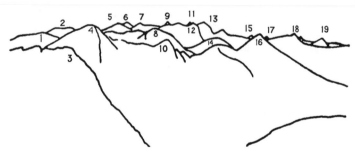

Looking Northwest From Gunsight Mountain. (1) Rogers Pk.; (2) Wolf Gun Mtn.; (3) Edwards Mtn.; (4) Mt. Vaught; (5) Logging Mtn.; (6) Parke Pk.; (7) West Ridge of Kintla Pk.; (8) Longfellow Pk.; (9) Rainbow Pk.; (10) McPartland Mtn.; (11) Kinnerly Pk.; (12) Vulture Pk.; (13) Mt. Carter; (14) East Ridge of Longfellow Pk.; (15) Boulder Pk. (?); (16) Heavens Pk.; (17) Thunderbird Mtn.; (18) Mt. Chapman; (19) Mt. Alderson.

in the park) covers half the basin between Gunsight and Bearhat mountains but is not so easily observed from this vantage point as it is from the top of Mt. Brown or Edwards Mountain, or from the slightly lower eastern peak of Gunsight Mountain.

This delightful climb may be completed in a single day from the hotel, but is more enjoyable if the first night is spent in comfort at or near Sperry Chalets. Time required from the headwall to the summit should not exceed four hours, regardless of the route followed.

Hike about eight miles from Lake McDonald Hotel to the headwall of Sperry Glacier, above the stairway that has been blasted through the cliff there. Several routes are possible from that point, three of which should be included here. There are two distinct summits on Gunsight, the rocky, bare, west summit being a few feet higher than the snowy eastern crag. A rather large cairn adorns the bare summit dome, but the register of the Nature Study Club of Indiana was placed in the cairn atop the *eastern* summit, possibly because Dr. Sperry and his friends left their names in a can there in 1905. The register was also signed by Vaught and Longfellow prior to 1920.

The Northeast Slope Route. WARNING: Stay off the steep snowfields unless you are equipped with ice axes and familiar with techniques of self-arrest.

This route is very obvious when Gunsight is viewed from the top of the Sperry Headwall stairway. Stay on the scree east of the steep snowfields, on easy class 2 or 3 cliffs that extend to the lowest part of the summit ridge. It is an easy walk from that ridge to either of the summits.

The Northwest Ridge Route. For expert climbers only. From the top of the stairway, climb up the rocky north ridge of this mountain toward the west summit. Routes exist around the dangerous cliffs for some distance, but eventually a very sheer and difficult cliff is reached. Climb the class 5 east side of the ridge, above steep snow slopes (stay roped). Above that cliff it is an easy scramble to the summit.

The West Face Route. For mountaineers who prefer to avoid the extremely unsafe cliffs and enjoy more diverse terrain en route.

At the bottom of the very difficult cliff mentioned above, look down the scree slope toward the west and locate a ledge that leads around the west face of the mountain. (Several prominent stone ducks marked this traverse in 1955.) Walk around that narrow ledge, dropping shortly to a wider and safer ledge, then continue to traverse until at least halfway to the sharp southwest ridge of the mountain. When you see an easy couloir leading upward, mark the traverse ledge prominently so it can be found on the descent, and scramble upward. From the ledge to the summit is easy.

Aptly named Heavens Peak, from Granite Park Chalets—Hal Kanzler

Heavens Peak (8,987)

Views in every direction are amazing. To the north the entire Lewis and Livingston Ranges and the valley between them lie at your feet. Southward is nearby Mt. Vaught, with beautifully folded strata in its west face. Beyond Cannon Mountain rises the great dome of 10,000-foot Mt. Jackson. Far south, beyond the McDonald Lake basin, are the graceful glacier-covered slopes of Great Northern Mountain. The peaks around Logan Pass are evident at the upper end of Going-to-the-Sun Highway, which is visible all the way from the pass, along the jagged Garden Wall and down into the deep green McDonald Valley. The many small mountain ranges of western Montana extend as far as the eye can see, while directly below you, to the west, is a string of beautiful blue lakes 5,000 feet lower, and not the mere stone's-throw away they seem to be. First known ascent: Norman Clyde, Fred Herz and Lee Stopple, July 15, 1924 (via Camas Lake).

When my wife, Ray Ozman, and I climbed this peak in 1950 we saw and photographed a remarkable spectacle. It was afternoon and the sun was low. McDonald Valley was so filled with clouds that we could see nothing below the Garden Wall and Haystack Butte. As the clouds rose out of the valley a strong west wind leveled them off even with our summit, over which the wind was whipping rather violently. Each of us saw his shadow cast upon this sea of clouds and around each shadow was a complete circle rainbow—the "Specter of the Brocken," which is often seen from the air but seldom by climbers on the ground. (See page 134.)

The North Ridge Route. Distance to summit about 12 miles, 8 miles of it by human trail. Elevation gained is about 4,700 feet, mostly class 2 and 3, but at least one class 4 pitch along the ridge. For beginning climbers who are strong hikers.

Leave auto at the big switchback on Going-to-the-Sun Highway about 9 miles west of Logan Pass. The trail northward soon hits a trail coming from Granite Park, which leads into the McDonald Valley (dropping 500 ft. in elevation). Follow the trail northward in the valley to the trail junction beside Mineral Creek. Go westward until beneath the north end of the great north ridge of Heavens Peak, then leave the trail. Wade McDonald Creek and climb 2,000 vertical feet through alders, to the divide between McDonald and Camas Creek valleys. Above this divide the old trail climbs steeply for a thousand feet to the fire lookout at the end of the long north ridge of Heavens Peak. Follow good goat trails south along the ridgetop for over a mile, to the small notch just north of the summit pyramid. The remaining 2,000 feet of elevation are ascended easily except for a place where a steep snow slope leads to a class 4 cliff, above which is another steep snow slope. The last thousand feet to the peak is easy class 1 or 2 walking up the scree just west of the snowy north ridge.

Climbers should leave the road by 6:30 A.M. and be equipped for night hiking on the descent.

The South Ridge Route. This route is shorter and more exciting than the North Ridge Route but it is also more dangerous. Distance to summit about 4 miles, none of it by trail.

The route goes up beside the large stream that drains the great basin southeast of the mountain. Wade across McDonald Creek about 6.5 miles north of the McDonald Hotel. Bushwhack up beside the stream, to the top of the waterfall, then follow the top edge of the cliff upward toward the south for several hundred feet. Eventually a stream is reached which drops down to McDonald Creek. Follow the north shore of that stream for about

40 feet, to a rock outcrop, then follow the outcrop up into the great basin southeast of the mountain. After getting above the alders and brush in the lower part of that basin, cross the big basin and climb to the crest of the prominent ridge which ascends toward the summit. Climb up that ridge, angling slightly to the left after passing the highest patches of vegetation. Stay near a stream that drains the huge snowfield high on the south face of the mountain. When that snowfield has been reached (about 800 feet from the summit) traverse below it to the southwest ridge of the mountain. Early in the summer this traverse might be difficult, but by mid-July there is a bare ledge of rock below the big snowfield. That ledge climbs very steeply up to the southwest ridge. Climb up that ridge until it becomes too steep, then traverse along the west face, losing elevation, until almost beneath the summit. Scramble up easy scree slopes from there to the top.

The East Face Route. Distance to the summit about 3 miles, none of it by trail. Elevation gained is about 5,000 vertical feet from McDonald Creek. Class 3 all the way, if the correct route is followed, but dangerous on the steep upper snowfields. First known ascent of the route: Rolf Larson, Jere Johnson, and Drew Paslawski, August 29, 1982.

Drive to a parking area on the east side of the highway south of Logan Creek, about 10 miles north of Lake McDonald Hotel. Observe two prominent gullies directly across McDonald Creek, on the steep Glacier Wall. Both gullies extend up through the brush on that wall, but the one on the east is best. Ford the creek, proceed to the east gully, and climb to the base of the cliffs near the top of the Glacier Wall (class 3). A hundred feet below the ridgetop traverse to the west, to an easily-climbed break in the cliffs (bearing small alpine firs).

Cross over the ridgetop and hike up the north side of the ridge toward the snowfield that is on the northeast face just below the summit. Traverse beneath the terminal and lateral moraines then climb to the top of the north ridge (class 3). That ridge leads to the summit (see details under the *North Ridge* route).

The Northeast Ridge Route. This very steep ridge, complicated by snow and ice, was climbed for the first time, in 1979, by Glacier National Park Rangers Steve Frye and Michael Ober.

Little Matterhorn (7,886)

The Southeast Face Route. Distance to summit about 9 miles, 8 miles of it by human trail. Elevation gained is about 4,800 feet. Mostly class 3, but some class 4 near the summit.

This peak seems not difficult up the southeast face, directly above the ridge separating the Sperry Glacier basin from the Snyder Lake basin. Possibly near the summit it will be necessary to work onto the east face for a short distance. Hike the Sperry trail to the top of the stairway up the Sperry Headwall. From the small pond above the headwall, traverse snow slopes toward the north, losing a little elevation as you approach the long ridge of snow that extends from the cliffs down toward the east. Climb that snow ridge and walk carefully down it toward the east to a place where the red rock outcroppings most closely approach the snow ridge. Walk down the steep snow to the rocks (don't glissade or take a chance of sliding unless you have an ice ax or ice ax belay and are experienced with both). From the red rock outcroppings, walk to the base of the Little Matterhorn. The routes upward seem numerous; with care, you will encounter nothing more difficult than class 3 or class 4 cliffs. Play it safe, and carry a climbing rope and at least one ice ax if climbing before August. The base of this sharp spire may also be reached from the Snyder Lake basin, by scrambling up class 3 slopes.

The North Face Route. Ted Steiner and Kenny Kasselder climbed from Avalanche Lake directly to the summit of the Little Matterhorn. They described their first ascent as a grueling technical ascent involving seven very intense pitches. They had difficulty finding safe rappel routes on the descent, and reached Avalanche Lake after sixteen hours on the face.

Longfellow Peak (8,904)

The Northeast Ridge Route. Distance to summit about eleven miles, 5.5 miles of it by human trail. Elevation gained is about 4,600 feet. Class 2 and 3, except in the chimney leading to the summit snowfield, which may be class 4 or 5. Ropes should be carried for belays, and at least one ice ax in each party is essential in June and early July.

The views from the summit are quite remarkable. Westward are only small wooded ridges, but north toward Vulture Peak and beyond it are many rugged peaks massed close together, with notable amounts of snow and ice. A little more to the east Waterton Lake is visible for its entire length (Longfellow is the beautiful snowy peak that is rather prominent from the launch *International* as it cruises on Waterton Lake). South of the lake is massive Mt. Cleveland (highest in the park), flanked by the Stoney Indian peaks to its south; then Mt. Merritt (with three high humps on its summit); and (even farther to the right) Mt. Wilbur. South of Wilbur is low, sharp, pointed Swiftcurrent Peak with its crowning hut for the fire lookout. Granite Park Chalets are just below this peak, on the alpine benches below Swiftcurrent Pass. Nearer at hand the Heavens Peak fire lookout stands atop the ridge that leads north from Heavens Peak. Across the McDonald Valley the Garden Wall dominates the scene, with Mt. Gould in the center of it. Going-to-the-Sun Highway is clearly visible for much of its upper length, but the big switchback and lower areas are concealed by Heavens Peak ridge. Southeast, beyond Heavens Peak and Mt. Vaught, arise a host of impressive peaks, particularly Gunsight Mountain (with Sperry Glacier on its northern slopes), Mt. Jackson (a broad, round dome beyond Gunsight), and Mt. St. Nicholas (the sharp, thumblike spire far to the southeast). A few small lakes are visible east and north of Longfellow, but the upper two lakes along Camas Creek are so close that they are not easily seen from the summit.

Do not attempt this climb unless the northeast ridge is bare of snow up to the elevation of the bottom of the huge broad snowfields that extend downward nearly a thousand feet below the summit. If this ridge is snow-covered, then certainly the broken chimneys leading from it up to the upper reaches of the peak will be filled with ice and snow, preventing access to the broad snow slopes above them. (The northeast ridge above these cliffs, beside the tremendous snowfields which cover the entire upper east slopes, is bare of snow by mid-July, even though it appears to be snowy when the mountain is viewed from the road.)

Park at the big switchback on Going-to-the-Sun Highway about nine miles west of Logan Pass. A trail heads north from this point and soon meets a trail leading down into the McDonald Valley (half a mile). After reaching the valley floor, follow the lane northward until it ends at the northern edge of the 1936 burn area. Take the Waterton Valley trail to the old junction just past the suspension bridge, then follow the west fork (along McDonald Creek) for 2.5 miles more. The old bridge across the creek below the trail to the Heavens Peak fire lookout has disappeared; the fire lookout was abandoned in the 1940s. Ford McDonald Creek and follow elk trails up the alder-covered hillside to the broad saddle (5,900) between the McDonald Valley and the Camas Creek Valley. (This was a popular pass with the Indians in the early days, for easy travel between the Flathead Valley and the Waterton Valley.) There is no water at the saddle, but a stream is crossed about a hundred yards north of the saddle. A high camp here is recommended.

Leave camp before 9 A.M. if you intend to climb the peak and reach the highway again before midnight. Hike westward through small green meadows following a very distinct game trail which is south of the high-

*Male and female ptarmigans are very visible on the
snow, in summer. —J. G. Edwards*

est part of the ridge. This trail soon begins to descend toward Lake
Evangeline and may be lost below the lush alpine meadows (delightful
views of Longfellow Peak). The traverse around the south side of the two
high forested humps east of Longfellow may require as long as two hours.
The 1938 topographic map fails to show either of these humps in their true
size, and also fails to reveal the true depth of the valley which separates
these humps from the main mass of Longfellow Peak. The eastern hump
rises several hundred feet above the pass where the campground is and ter-
minates in high, forbidding cliffs along the western end. A deep notch lies
between this hump and the lower one west of it and a broad pass inter-
venes between this western hump and the ridge leading up Longfellow.
This broad pass has an intermittent stream in it and is about midway in
elevation between the top of the western hump and the shore of Lake
Evangeline. Owing to the presence of this low pass, it is necessary to lose
elevation during the traverse around the south side of the two high humps,
dropping from 5,900 feet at the campsite to an estimated 5,400 feet elevation in the low pass. (Don't be tempted into climbing upward during the
traverse.) We found no good route across the traverse. It is a walk across
steep sidehills of hard earth mixed with small cliffs, brush and saplings,
and while game trails may exist lower down, there are none at the elevation of the meadows near the campsite.

From the deep valley, follow good game trails up the right side of the ridge that extends from Lake Evangeline straight toward the prominent rocky spire just northeast of the main summit mass of Longfellow (high on the ridge, near the summit). NOTICE: This ridge leading to the spire can also be reached from the head of Camas Creek Valley, via an easy walk up the slopes above Evangeline Lake. The approach to that valley can be made either from old Rogers Ranch (two miles below Trout Lake) or from Lake McDonald (via the Howe Ridge trail). Continue around the south base of the prominent rocky spire, across scree slopes and gentle ravines, then climb upward to the ridge west of the spire. Scramble higher along this northeast ridge to the elevation of the ominous-looking over-hanging cliff that extends entirely across the east face beneath the broad summit snow-fields. This cliff is at least fifteen feet high and the top extends outward possibly ten feet farther than the base. It cannot be climbed by conventional methods.

A glance around the other side of the ridge reveals the sheer nature of the north face of the mountain, with tremendous cliffs extending from high above you to the snowfields a thousand feet below. This face appears to be devoid of sensible climbing routes. Fortunately, just at the base of the overhang it is easy to work around and slightly upward, onto the north face (actually the northeast corner). The route is not visible from lower on the ridge. A narrow, deep ravine extends down from the top of the cliffs above the overhang. Only one possible cleft leads upward through that ravine. The climbing is easy unless the cleft is snow-clogged (in which case it may be impossible), but exercise great care in climbing over the rocks that are thickly covered with moss. If possible, veer toward the left at first, so as to avoid the extreme exposures for awhile, then work upward and almost into the center of the ravine near its top. If inexperienced rock-climbers are in the party, it would be wise to use the rope here for greater safety, only one person climbing at a time. When you emerge above this ravine, carefully note or mark the location of the top of it, so that you can find it easily on the descent (there is a similar ravine slightly farther west that eventually ends in sheer cliffs below). Above this fortuitous ravine lies a broad prominent snowfield extending across the upper middle por-tion of the east face and upward clear to the summit. If equipped with an ice ax, the leading climber may safely lead the others (roped together, of course) up the snow all the way to the summit. Otherwise, it is safer to follow the bare north ridge around the north edge of the snowfield to the steep, slender snow slope which connects with the smaller but steeper upper part that extends to the top of the mountain. Where this ridge abuts against another cliff, three alternative routes are possible. In order of their safety, these are: (1) While belayed from the rocky ridge, go out onto the steep snow, climb up it for several yards, then return to the bare ridge above the troublesome cliff; (2) Climb the cliff immediately beside the steep snowbank to reach the upper ridge; or (3) Drop down slightly toward the west and follow a broad, ascending, scree-covered ledge across the north face and up the summit ridge (this latter route was climbed by us). Above these routes no obstacles exist and a few minutes' easy walk up the bare ridge leads to the summit. Two low peaks of almost equal height are connected by a long ridge of scree.

The Western Approach Route. Distance to summit about seventeen miles, thirteen miles of it by human trail. Elevation gained is 5,200 vertical feet. Nothing more severe than class 3, if the correct route is followed.

Hike the trail from the old North Fork Road up to Dutch Lake (elevation 5,600 ft.), then follow a fisherman's trail around the south shore of the lake. Climb up toward the northwest, to the pass between Longfellow and the smaller peak south of it. According to Richard Johnson (1963) there is no brush encountered on this route. From the pass it is an easy class 3 walk to the summit, with no snowy obstacles. For climbers with time and energy to spare, it is also possible to climb Paul Bunyan's Cabin on the way (that name has been locally applied to the huge rectangular prominence on the south ridge of Longfellow Peak).

The views from the summit are just as remarkable from the top as they are when approached via the much more difficult *Northeast Ridge Route.* The feeling of being on an extremely remote peak surrounded by incredible wilderness adds to the satisfaction gained by climbers who reach this spectacular summit.

Mt. McPartland (8,413)

Distance to the summit about seven miles, four miles of it by human trail. Elevation gained is about 5,200 vertical feet, class 3 except for a possible class 4 pitch near the summit ridge. (Based on the description by Rolf Larson and Gary Vodehnal, September 14, 1983.)

Cross the horse bridge half a mile upstream from Lake McDonald, then follow the west bank of McDonald Creek for about four miles. (It is possible to ford the creek further upstream; however it is very cold and may be thigh-deep even late in the season.) Leave the trail when beneath the cirque between Mt. Vaught and Mt. McPartland, and bushwhack straight uphill. This part of the climb, although discouraging, should not last more than two hours.

Above the worst bushwhacking there is a troublesome band of cliffs.

They are deceptively difficult (possibly class 4), with bad angles for foot and handholds (and an abundance of moss). Above those cliffs, head for the saddle south of McPartland's summit. That saddle is reached via an impressive spine of violently-folded argillite. Although challenging to follow, it is an effective route to the saddle between McPartland and Vaught. Pick a route up the final 500 vertical feet of cliffs, staying slightly to the east of the ridge.

The summit is a small, rounded dome about fifty by twenty feet, with sheer cliffs below the east and west sides, a difficult class 4 ridge descending toward the north, and the class 3 or 4 pitches toward the south and southeast. There are spectacular views almost directly down onto Arrow and Trout Lake, and a marvelous panorama of the region around Sperry Glacier and the Avalanche Lake basin toward the east and southeast.

Mt. Stanton (7,750)

The Southeast Slope Route. Distance to summit about 2.5 miles, none of it by trail. Elevation gained is about 4,550 feet. Class 2 and 3 except for one class 4 cliff near the false summit.

This is a good climb for hikers with a bit more than the average amount of perseverance. It affords remarkable scenic opportunities, especially views of Lake McDonald, the Livingston range (along the western border of the park), and the area near Sperry Chalets and Sperry Glacier. Beyond Lake McDonald the biggest peak is the round dome of Mt. Jackson (exceeding 10,000 ft. in elevation), while south of the lake is a graceful peak with several large snowfields and glaciers on its north slopes. It is Great Northern Mountain, which is south of Glacier National Park.

It is advisable to carry along some insect repellent, since black flies are often abundant on the very top of Mt. Stanton; mosquitoes, too.

Drive westward past the Lake McDonald Ranger Station at the north end of Lake McDonald to the top of the first small hill on that road (about one-quarter mile).

Bushwhack up the stream course above this road, through an old avalanche area. After fighting through underbrush and timber for ten or fifteen minutes you will emerge in rather open terrain a little farther north (a different drainage system). Cross to the north bank of the large stream there and follow it uphill at varying distances from the creek, wherever the walking is easiest. About halfway up the mountain is a fork in the gully. Bear to your right there and continue upstream to the low cliff beneath the false summit of the mountain. This may be surmounted easily (class 3 or

4) at several places, so don't make risky rock climbs. Always search for the easier, safer routes and use them.

Above the false summit, walk up the ridge to the actual summit pyramid. This is easily climbed on its south side, where it is just a slope of scree and small rock outcroppings. Time to the summit from the road should not exceed three or four hours, if the scenery isn't contemplated too often on the way.

This sharp little peak can also be reached from the highest point (5,200 ft. elevation) on the trail over Howe Ridge, 2.3 miles from the head of Lake McDonald.

Mt. Vaught (8,850)

The Southwest Ridge Route. Distance to summit about 6.5 miles, none of it by human trail. Elevation gained is about 5,650 feet. Mostly class 2 or 3, but with at least two class 4 pitches between Mt. Stanton and the summit of Mt. Vaught.

This is a very beautiful and appealing climb with summit views of the Livingston Range, the Lewis Range, and much of the region south of Logan Pass. The steep west face of Heavens Peak and the snowy grandeur of Longfellow and Vulture peaks are terrific to behold. Lake McDonald shimmers at your feet to the south, with graceful Great Northern Mountain rising beyond it. Eastward the vista includes Avalanche Lake, Hidden Lake, Cannon Mountain, part of the Logan Pass area, Going-to-the-Sun Mountain, just beyond Cannon), Little Chief Mountain, Red Eagle Mountain, and the vast open expanses of the prairies far east of St. Mary Lake. A vertical mile below is a chain of bright blue lakes dotting the narrow, steep-walled valley west of Vaught and Heavens peaks. Large numbers of insects which normally frequent the vegetation along the shores of these lakes may usually be found embedded in the snowfield atop Mt. Vaught, carried there by strong convection currents.

Climb to the top of Mt. Stanton, then walk north along the ridge toward Mt. Vaught to the lowest part of the shoulder between Stanton and Vaught (about 500 ft. lower than the summit of Stanton). There is only one really dangerous cliff on the descent of this ridge and it may be climbed via an exposed chimney on the east side of the ridge (a place to use a rope), the most dangerous part of the entire climb. North of the low point in this saddle, stay on the talus slopes east of the pinnacles and cliffs along the ridge, until you reach the head of the stream valley near the bottom of the southwest ridge of Mt. Vaught. It is easy to climb out of the head of this valley and follow a goat trail up the ridge until you are above the scattered trees there. Then follow up the east side of the southwest ridge for a considerable distance (still on the goat trail) through breaks in the cliffs, which are class 3 or 4 in places.

For the last thousand feet of elevation this trail veers onto the western side of the ridge, affording constant views of the beautiful Livingston Range to the north and the attractive series of lakes far below. No climbing difficulties exist and the rock is pleasant to work on. The summit itself is a bare scree ridge above the huge eastern snowfield so prominent from Lake McDonald. A register, from the 1930s, is in the cairn at the summit and should be carefully replaced after it is read and signed.

This climb is a hard day's work for most people, so plan to leave the road not later than 7:00 A.M. and be sure to carry flashlights (which may be left on Stanton and picked up on the way back). WARNING: Be sure you do not go down into the tempting valley between Stanton and Vaught, because it is almost impossible to follow that stream down to the McDonald Valley — it is extremely tough going there, with numerous steep creek banks to negotiate, and almost every step must be forced through one of the thickest tangles of windfalls and shrubs in the park.

In 1924, while returning from his first ascent of Heavens Peak, Norman Clyde traversed to Mt. Vaught and then, after watching sunset from the peak, he descended to the Camas Creek trail in the gathering darkness. The steep descending ridge led to a cliff that "threatened to block my course," he wrote, then "there followed a long descent through thickets and forest in the dark."

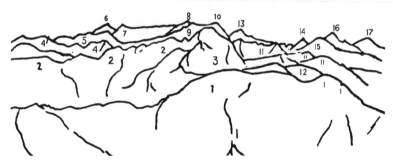

Looking Northwest From Mt. Vaught: (1) Camas Ridge (curves to join South Ridge of Longfellow Pk.); (2) Dutch Ridge; (3) Longfellow Pk.; (4) Wolf Gun Mtn. (Adair Ridge); (5) Logging Ridge; (6) Parke Pk.; (7) West Ridge of Kintla Pk.; (8) Rainbow Pk.; (9) West Summit of Vulture Pk.; (10) East Summit of Vulture Pk.; (11) Mt. Geduhn (many summits); (12) East Ridge of Longfellow Pk.; (13) East Ridge of Mt. Carter; (14) Thunderbird Mtn.; (15) The Guardhouse; (16) Mt. Chapman; (17) Mt. Alderson.

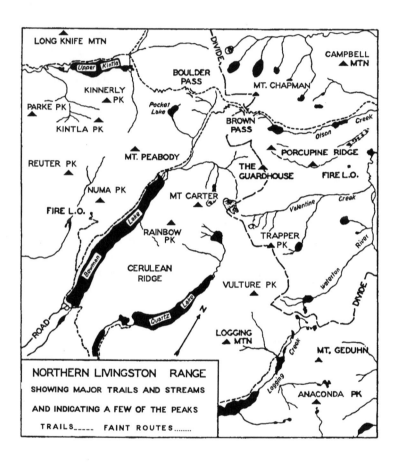

NORTHERN LIVINGSTON RANGE

SHOWING MAJOR TRAILS AND STREAMS

AND INDICATING A FEW OF THE PEAKS

TRAILS_____ FAINT ROUTES........

THE LIVINGSTON RANGE

Routes Among the Peaks

This magnificent area embraces the most rugged terrain in the park, extending north from Heavens Peak to Kintla Lake and culminating in the vicinity of Boulder Pass (7,600 ft). The region is relatively inaccessible except for persons who are willing to pack in enough supplies and equipment to enable them to spend at least one or two nights in the high country. Most climbs in the northwestern part of the park are approached by trail or boat after a long, long drive up the valley of the North Fork of the Flathead River. Vulture Peak (9,638) can be reached by hiking fourteen miles up the faint trail to the head of Logging Valley then climbing 5,000 vertical feet through dense brush, rocky slopes and ridges, and steep snow and ice. Wild, remote Quartz Valley has been used by very hardy fishermen for many years, but climbers have very seldom reached the head of the valley and ascended the headwall or reached the distant summit of Vulture Peak via the north face. Rainbow Peak (9,891) and Mt. Carter (9,843) are best climbed from Bowman Lake, while Long Knife (9,784), Kintla (10,101), and Kinnerly (9,944) are approached by way of the long, wild Kintla Valley. The peaks around Brown Pass and Boulder Pass may also be reached from the east, where the commercial launch service to the foot of Waterton Lake can be used to reduce the hiking distance to less than fourteen miles up an excellent trail to those passes. Attractive peaks just south of Brown Pass include Thunderbird Mountain (8,800), The Guardhouse (9,336), and The Sentinel (8,840), while Chapman Peak (9,406), Mt. Custer (8,883), and Boulder Peak (8,300) surround Hole-in-the-Wall Cirque. East of Brown Pass is more great mountain scenery, dominated by Mt. Cleveland (10,466), the highest peak in Glacier National Park. Extending in that direction from the pass is the great ridgetop of Porcupine Ridge, with a series of remarkable spires (the Citadel Peaks) capping its far eastern extremity.

In addition to the exciting summit climbs in this spectacular region there are many exploratory trips not involving actual summits that will nevertheless interest most mountaineers. From the head of Bowman Lake it is possible, but difficult, to scramble up to Weasel Collar Glacier on the northeast face of Mt. Carter, and see the great icefall near the snout of the glacier. Fifty years ago a faint trail continued up Jefferson Creek to Jefferson Pass; however, in recent decades not one person a year has been able to force a passage through all that brush and downed trees. Perhaps some intrepid explorer can find a good game trail leading from the Weasel Collar Glacier basin around the ridge and up to Jefferson Pass!

From Brown Pass, bushwhack up to the small glacier beneath the north face of Thunderbird Mountain then follow the goat trail around the west and south sides of that mountain and on to the notch between The Sentinel and The Guardhouse. The route from there to Fifty Mountain meadows is described later, under "Jefferson Pass Approaches."

From Boulder Pass, mountaineers can go north through the flat glacier-scoured area with an extensive alpine larch forest, descend twenty feet beside the waterfall that drains the basin, and traverse game trails below the great cliffs to the head of Kintla Creek. A short climb to Forum Peak from there yields unique views and it is an easy descent to the road at Cameron Lake. In the opposite direction from Boulder Pass there is a ridge-walk to Mt. Peabody, with a possible descent to the shores of Pocket Lake. Also, the approaches to Aggasiz Glacier basin from Boulder Pass are described later, under the climbing route to Kintla Peak.

To reach the viewpoint for photographs of Hole-in-the-Wall Falls, go west on a grassy bench from Hole-in-the-Wall basin. Descend a small streambed (overgrown with grass) for fifty feet, to a big tree. Go further west below a six-foot cliff for about 100 yards, then straight down through prostrate trees, to the cliff edge. This is the only place for good views of the fall emerging from the famous hole!

Before making any climbs or cross-country trips in this region, register at one of the ranger stations . . . and be SURE to check in upon your return. Any minor injury in such wild surroundings can be fatal if rescuers do not know exactly where to look for you!

Routes to the Summits

East and West 9430 Peaks

The ridge between Kintla Peak and Parke Peak bears two prominent unnamed peaks that are designated as "9430" on the Kintla Peak Quadrangle topo map. Bill Blunk and Ralph Thornton have proposed that they be designated as "East 9430 Peak" and "West 9430 Peak," and since those two mountaineers have spent more time exploring and climbing in that area than anyone else, it seems appropriate to honor their suggestion in this guide. The approaches used by Thornton and Blunk in 1985 and 1987 are described briefly in the following pages.

From Bowman Lake, follow the old West Lakes Trail northward. Beyond the junction with the Akokola Lake Trail the West Lakes Trail is overgrown, unmaintained, and often obscure. From the trail crossing at Long Bow Creek, ascend the ridge west of that creek. The ridge, covered by brush, with open stands of lodgepole, parallels Long Bow Creek but rises so abruptly that water is inaccessible. It is necessary to cross several steep brushy gullies that dissect the ridgetop. Above 6,400 feet the forest becomes more open. Traverse the west (left) side of the ridge from this point and climb into a cirque at the 6,900-foot elevation. A good campsite is in this cirque, which contains two small intermittent ponds and is just west across the ridge from Long Bow Lake. With full packs, it usually takes all day to reach this campsite.

WARNING: Ranger Jerry DeSanto, who has spent many years exploring in the northwest section of the park, warns that while it is comparatively easy to find the route going UP the ridge from Long Bow Creek to the high cirque with the two ponds, it is very difficult to keep on the proper ridge while descending. It is too easy, in the thick brush, to accidentally follow one of the many spur ridges that lead off to the west into increasingly difficult terrain. Refer to the map, compass, and altimeter constantly. Fortunately, if you realize you are off the route, it is fairly simple to follow a course due east until again within sound of Long Bow Creek.

Bill Blunk and Ralph Thornton contacted Jerry DeSanto and Russell Miller for more details about this remote area. Those rangers had been near the ridge earlier, and Russ pioneered an approach route to Long Bow Basin several years ago.

West 9430 Peak provides outstanding views. The entire width of Kintla Glacier is spread out far below. Kinnerly Peak appears as a very striking matterhorn from this angle. Far to the south the familiar peaks of Mt. Merritt, Mt. Siyeh, Mt. Gould, and many others are visible. The climb is all class 3 except for one short class 4 pitch. The known routes are described below:

The Southwest Ridge Route to West 9430 Peak. Climb the western wall of the cirque to gain the top of the ridge that extends southwest from West 9430 Peak. The route along the top of that ridge is surprisingly interesting, because the sedimentary rock there has been so badly folded that the strata are nearly vertical and form an impressive serrated wall. Scramble over the top of most of the gendarmes there, or bypass them via small ledges west of the ridgetop. A short class 4 pitch with considerable exposure must be climbed where the ridge abuts the main mass of the peak. Above this it is an easy scree slog to the summit. The first known ascent was by Blunk and Thornton, in August 1985. They found no evidence of previous visitors, so they built a cairn and left a register there. From the summit, they also traversed easy goat trail ledges to the westernmost knob on the ridge which was also apparently unclimbed.

The South Face Route to West 9430 Peak. From the Long Bow Lake cirque, ascend the direct south face of the peak. This route is very steep, but is easier than the ridge route. Class 3 all the way, if care is taken in route-finding.

East 9430 Peak is a most enjoyable climb for anyone willing to endure the difficulties of getting into upper Long Bow Basin. Views from the summit are spectacular in all directions. Below, to the north, is the multi-colored cirque of Kintla Glacier. To the west is the West 9430 Peak, with its summit snowfield and the great ridge beyond it continuing to Parke Peak. Longknife Mountain is superb from this viewpoint. To the south is the spectacular North Fork Valley, and the foot of beautiful azure Bowman Lake. Further southward the view encompasses a sea of magnificent peaks all the way to Mt. Stimson and Mt. St. Nicholas.

The West Ridge Route. Ascend the south face route on the West 9430 Peak to an elevation of 8,650 feet. An improbable-looking ledge leads eastward, with several detours to higher or lower ledges (including one scramble up a narrow gully and a descent behind a detached block) all the way to the saddle between West and East 9430 Peaks. This "Happy Ledge" (as it was called by Thornton and Blunk) descends gradually but remains high enough to allow passage above the head of the great vertical couloir that blocks access to the saddle from all approaches on the lower scree fields. Beyond this major couloir, the "Happy Ledge" opens onto a scree slope and route-finding becomes simple.

As the saddle is approached, notice three diagonal gullies ascending to the south ridge of that peak. The middle gully is very interesting and enjoyable (mostly class 3), with danger only from falling rocks. At the top of the gully, at about 9,000 feet on the south ridge of East 9430 Peak, the whole south face of the peak can be seen . . . and it is *all* a sheer-sided vertical wall! The ridge continues upward, however, with great exposure but remarkably good handholds, and is much easier than it looks from below. (Thornton and Blunk carried a rope, but did not use it there.) Near the top, they describe an especially interesting section. "The route reaches the top of a buttress and then, to continue the climb, you must walk (or crawl) along an exposed horizontal knife edge of rock to get back to the main face of the mountain."

There was no evidence of previous climbers on the summit, so Blunk and Thornton built a small cairn and left a register there.

The ridge extending east from the top of East 9430 Peak does not appear to be passable (up to Peak 9826). As for descending to Kintla Glacier from the saddle, these climbers concluded that there were simply too many difficulties and dangers discouraging a backpackable route, but believed that perhaps "a tough, lightly-loaded party could descend to the upper snow slopes of Kintla Glacier and (properly roped) cross to the easy scree slopes southwest of Kintla Peak."

ADDITIONAL NOTES: Blunk and Thornton were also interested in possible routes between West 9430 Peak and Parke Peak. They explored ledges from the far western knob that might lead to the southeast ridge of Parke Peak. They could find no passable route there, so traversed back east a short distance to a notch in the ridge, overlooking a vertical gully full of loose rock. It appeared impossible, but a little further west on the ridge "we found a narrow ledge that descended steeply eastward and safely reached the bottom of that vertical gully. The beginning of that narrow ledge descent is about 130 feet east of the small cairn we left on a high point of the ridge. The bottom of the steep gully is directly above a sheer 500-foot cliff. Fortunately there is an easy horizontal goat trail there that leads back to the west, crosses a rib of rock and reaches the top of the lower ridge that descends easily to the côl between West 9430 Peak and Parke Peak. The route up to the 9430 Ridge would be obvious to anyone coming from Parke Peak, but is difficult to find when going the other direction." This exploration results in the knowledge that climbers can traverse from the deep saddle southeast of Parke Peak to the West 9430 Peak. Attempting to traverse this route with full packs to Longbow Lake is strongly discouraged.

Mt. Carter (9,843)

The Northwest Couloir Route. Distance to summit about fourteen miles, ten miles of it by human trail. Elevation gained is about 5,800 feet. Class 2 and 3, with severe bushwhacking on the lower slopes and one or two small class 3 pitches near timberline.

Views are almost the same as those seen from Rainbow Peak, but the acres of ice in Rainbow Glacier are more easily seen from here and Cerulean Lake is also fully visible. Logan Pass is evident, with Mt. Stimson rising beyond it, and far beyond Stimson's long flat summit is the sharp thumb-like spire of Mt. St. Nicholas. As explained under Rainbow Peak, it is possible to traverse the ridge between Rainbow and Carter, but it is likely to be dangerous if there are snowbanks along the south slope of the ridge where the best traversing may otherwise be done.

Drive to the campground at the foot of Bowman Lake and hike seven miles to the head of the lake. Continue on the new trail toward Brown Pass for about a mile. At the top of the hill, study the route up Carter for the last time, then go straight downhill toward the mountain. The old Jefferson Creek Cabin is less than one-half mile away, but horrible brush makes it seem further. Near Bowman Creek are remains of the old trail and the trail branching south across the creek to the old cabin. The bridge is gone, but the ruins of the cabin are only a few hundred feet away . . . IF you can find it. Shortly after crossing Bowman Creek, leave the faint trail and plunge through dense brush toward Mt. Carter, seeking the lowest part of the valley that extends northwest from the descending east ridge of that massive mountain.

High on the mountain a pleasant stream flows down the rocky basin, plunges over a waterfall far above tree line, then suddenly disappears. Down in the forest the water emerges again in a large red pothole, only to vanish again within a few hundred yards. Still farther down the streambed is again filled with water, but in late summer it seems to come only from a nearby spring. Finally, near the valley floor, this water again sinks into the gravel, and the streambed becomes smaller and smaller until it eventually disappears completely. On the ascent, after gaining a slight elevation south of the valley floor, begin to search for that stream. Once it is found, the route upward becomes easy. Stay in the woods west of the streambed but always near it. After a few hundred feet of climbing, the down timber ceases to be a problem and it is easy to hike up the steep, forested hillside by the streambed. Continue upward beside the stream (or in the bed, if there is no water) and enter the large hanging valley above the timberline. In this broad valley the stream draining the snowfields near the summit plunges over a large cliff as a lovely waterfall. The cliff extends far to the right and left of the waterfall, but fortunately there is a break at the extreme left (northeast) end of the cliffs. Follow a game trail up a steep, grassy ravine far over on that side of the basin until almost even with the top of the waterfall, then a rather narrow, grassy ledge angles back toward the waterfall and reaches the broad valley above it. The route upward is now obvious, going up scree slopes and easy little cliffs. In the upper part of the basin, stay far northeast of the snowbanks and reach the ridgetop by going up an easy scree couloir toward the east. Mark the head of that couloir with a pile of rock to aid on the descent, then walk up the ridge to the summit. The active, narrow glacier southeast of that ridge is

Kinnerly Peak (right) and Kintla Peak, seen from Boulder Pass—Bob and Ira Spring

Weasel-Collar Glacier, famous because of the icefall that is so spectacular. On the summit of the mountain is a wooden platform that was probably built by the U.S. Geological Survey crew before 1936, and two U.S.G.S. benchmarks are cemented into the rocks there. Remnants of a tent, the tent poles, and numerous batteries wrapped in the tent canvas were still there in the 1960s.

Mt. Geduhn (8,375)

The route is described under the "North Central Area" chapter. The approach is made from Jefferson Pass or from Fifty Mountain Camp or from the McDonald Creek trail near West Flattop Mountain, as discussed there.

The Guardhouse (9,336)

The route is described under the "North Central Area" chapter. The approach is made from Brown Pass or from Frances Lake, as discussed there.

Kinnerly Peak (9,944)

The summit views are splendid, and include most of the scenes observed from the top of Kintla Peak. Some of the sights from this peak are better than anything seen from Kintla, however. Upper Kintla lake is a vertical 4,800 feet below, and just beyond it looms the 5,000-foot south face of Long Knife Mountain in British Columbia. The deep blue color of the lake has developed relatively recently. Dr. Ruhle, in his *Guide to Glacier National Park,* describes it as being turquoise in the early 1950s. Norman Clyde in 1937 wrote: "Lying inset in the dark green forest 5,000 feet below, the jade green Kintla Lakes shimmered and scintillated in the sunshine of late afternoon." (There was evidently much more "glacial milk" entering the valley lakes at that time.) Looking over at the rugged northwest face of Kintla Peak, some climbers will find its steep glaciers and great cliffs to have a chilling effect (but see the description of the west face route up that great mountain). Southward, beyond the soaring peaks of the Livingston and Lewis Ranges, is the tenuous thread of Going-to-the-Sun Highway winding up to Logan Pass. The pass itself, flanked by Clements Mountain and Mt. Reynolds, is clearly visible.

The Northwest Face Route. Distance to summit about fourteen miles, 10.5 miles of it by human trail. Elevation gained is about 5,100 feet.

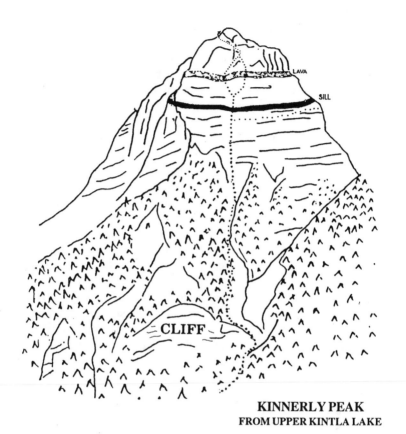

KINNERLY PEAK
FROM UPPER KINTLA LAKE

Mostly class 3, but at least two class 4 or 5 pitches.

Drive to Kintla Lake, then hike about 10.5 miles up the valley to Upper Kintla Lake. Ford the cold, swift stream below the lake, and proceed around the southwest shore on good game trails for about a mile. When the stream is reached which drains the entire northwest basin of Kinnerly Peak, ascend the steep hillside near the west bank. Several hundred feet above the lake the stream rushes over a cliff (A), which must next be reached. Below the cliff the main streambed becomes a rocky gorge that would be difficult to climb, but it can be avoided by climbing up a steep, narrow ravine just west of the main gully. The ravine is filled with dense vegetation, but it is easily trampled down and there is good footing beneath it. The ravine ends at the base of the twenty-to-thirty- foot cliff (the same cliff that the waterfall goes over). Climb the cliff west of the water-

85

fall via a class 4 pitch that is steep and difficult but has no "exposure" beneath it. (Further to the west it becomes much easier to climb, and it is easy to traverse back to the stream above the cliff.) A short distance upstream from the fall a distinct game trail crosses the creek and then skirts the eastern edge of a broad valley choked with alder thickets. One particularly good trail climbs the steep, sparsely-wooded hillside (B) above the alders, soon reaching a point higher than the big fork in the drainage system. Traverse southward across ledges and easy cliffs and enter the deep gully of the northeast fork of the drainage system. It is a class 3 climb up the boulders, ledges, and cliffs in that streambed, and elevation is gained very rapidly. When the broad, scree-covered slope is reached (C), scramble straight up toward the prominent breaks in the upper cliffs far, far above. (This entire slope is a rapid scree-run on the descent!)

The left-hand (north) couloir through the upper cliffs has at least one class 5 cliff, with a slight overhang near the top and a fair amount of exposure. Blunk and Thornton traversed to the right and found a gully with good holds that was much easier to climb (class 4). There is a large block at the top of that "openbook" gully around which a nylon sling can be placed for protection on the descent. (They had already traversed further to the right but found difficult cliffs on each possible route.) Above the cliffs, skirt the northeast edge of the large snowfield that was so easily visible from Upper Kintla Lake, then climb easy chimneys and scree ledges until just below the steep, rotten end of the summit ridge. (Good class 3 routes exist above the snowfield but it takes patience to locate them.)

Stay below and north of the long, narrow west ridge of crumbly pinnacles and blocks and traverse eastward for several hundred feet along goat trails below the sheer summit ridge. When nearly under the highest hump on that ridge, leave the goat trails and climb easy pitches (class 3) to the summit.

The Southwest Face, from the Notch. The first known ascent was by Dave Leppert, Eric Schwab, Tim Lewis, and Marty Shimko, on July 31, 1984. The following description is based upon their excellent article in *Going-to-the-Sun* magazine. From the Great Notch between Kinnerly and Kintla Peaks, traverse across the southwest face of Kinnerly (class 2 and 3), staying about 200 feet above the saddle and 6,500 feet below the dark igneous diorite sill. (Leave numerous distinctive "ducks" of rock to help find the route back.) When the largest gully on that mountainside is reached, scramble up beside it, and climb easily through the diorite formation. The red cliffs above become increasingly difficult, and more ducks were constructed above each chute that was used. The gully widens into a Y-shaped basin above the red rock. It is a class 3 or 4 climb up the east side of the "Y" to a prominent ten-foot-wide shelf that extends across the entire face. Above that shelf there are thick formations of basalt (igneous rocks of the Purcell formation). Traverse eastward beneath the sheer faces until seeing a large gully above, which angles back toward the left (west).The route upward there was steep, but the rock is very solid and climbing was fairly easy. They climbed the lower portion of the basalt, then traversed westward around a spur and found a good route up through an obvious break in the cliffs. From the top of that spur, a short climb to the west leads to the summit ridge, and it is a narrow ridge walk from there to the top. It only required two hours for the party to go from the Notch to the summit.

NOTE: These mountaineers reached the Notch by struggling directly up from Kintla Lake, and found it to be a very exhausting climb with full packs. Approaching from Boulder Pass via the Agassiz Glacier Basin would be much easier and probably much faster. For more details, refer to *Going-to-the-Sun*, Spring/Summer 1985, pp. 6-11 (with map and photos).

The Southwest Ridge Route, from Kintla-Kinnerly Notch . First ascent by Glacier National Park Ranger Dick Mattson, August 28, 1981.

From the flood-plain below Agassiz Glacier climb 2,400 vertical feet to the notch between Kintla and Kinnerly Peaks. The steep snowfield leading up to this notch requires an ice ax, and crampons would be an asset. From the notch, climb up broken cliffs, angling to the left (west) until reaching a climbable gully. Go up this gully until reaching the diorite sill, then traverse to the left just below the sill of dark igneous rock. A break through this formation of hard black rock is soon found. Climb up through cliffs, angling to the left when necessary, and then up another gully which extends to a band of scree. Traverse further to the left on this scree, below vertical cliffs, until passing around the steep west ridge of Kinnerly. From that corner there is suddenly a view of Kintla Lake, and a snowfield is directly below. Ascend more ledges and easy cliffs, angling to the northeast, then traverse eastward north of the very unstable blocks of igneous rock along the summit ridge. Near the far east end of that ridge it is an easy scramble to the very summit.

This route is only class 3 and 4 if the proper route is followed, but great care must be taken to mark and memorize the route for the descent, because straying from the route could lead to tremendous exposures and unclimbable pitches.

The Southeast Face Routes. There are two very different approaches to this face: (l) Take the launch from Waterton to Goathaunt (or walk eight miles along the west shore of Waterton Lake), then hike fifteen miles to Boulder Pass; or (2) Drive up the gravel road to Kintla Lake and then hike nineteen miles, almost to Boulder Pass. Either way, leave the trail at the 6,000-foot contour level (below the many sharp switchbacks) and descend to the nearby streambed, then follow the suggestions given in the guide to the approach to the East Ridge Route up Kintla Peak. After ascending 800 vertical feet while crossing the basin, you reach the moraine region below Agassiz Glacier, still 2,300 feet from the summit.

At least three parties have climbed up this great horn via the Agassiz Glacier approach. Norman Clyde and his friends made the first ascent of the Peak in 1937, Garth Uibel of Calgary, with Canadian friends, climbed it in 1956, and Hugh Black (with John Ward and James Hazelton) succeeded in their assault in 1963. Drawing upon their letters and notes, the author presents the varying details of each of these ascents.

The approach to Agassiz Glacier from Boulder Pass is strenuous but not hazardous. All three parties traversed the talus and scrub forests below Mt. Peabody for several hours, then crossed the outlet of the glacier and continued to the steep rocky slope with many rivulets (described in route to Kintla Peak elsewhere in this guide). They then climbed up a series of cliffs to a small meadow and headed toward the southeast end of Kinnerly Peak by walking along a small moraine that ends at the base of the actual mountain. They all ascended easy cliffs on the south face above that moraine, then up a short class 4 chimney. Above that, they scrambled up about 500 feet of scree to reach the great southeast shoulder or ridge and climbed on that shoulder (or just south of it) until about two-thirds the way to the top of the peak. A huge sheer cliff halted upward progress above that point along the ridge, and the three parties found three different routes from there as follows:

From the great cliff on the southeast shoulder, Clyde's group angled upward toward the northeast, "with several thousand feet of space below waiting in case you should lose your footing." Having crossed the entire east face, they climbed easily up the sharp northeast ridge on good diorite and argillite, to the summit.

From the great cliff on the southeast shoulder, Uibel's group climbed to a small snowfield on the east face, then straight up over small ledges "and around to the south ridge on the skyline," up which they went easily to the summit.

From the great cliff on the southeast shoulder, Black's group went forty feet to the left (south) of the ridgetop and upward about 100 feet to a difficult class 4 chimney. Above that chimney they climbed further to the left, "to the hard gray igneous rock that is almost at the edge of a couloir on the left." They climbed a class 5 chimney up the middle of that gray cliff, above which it was a class 3 scramble to the summit, "keeping to the left (south) of the gendarme."

Hopefully, everyone seeking to climb up this impressive side of Kinnerly Peak will benefit by reading these discussions, and will find a good route to the summit based upon the experiences of these three groups of talented mountaineers.

Kintla Peak (10,101)

This is the most arduous climb in the northwest section of the park and must never be attempted without adequate leadership. At all times after leaving the trail keep constantly in mind the amount of time and danger which any rescue operation would entail. Don't take any chances, for if injured here you cannot possibly be carried to a doctor in less than two days! Helicopter availability can cut one day off that time — maybe!!

There are remarkable views into British Columbia, Alberta, western Montana, the Flathead Valley, and the broad expanses of prairies far east of Glacier National Park. Nearly every peak in the park is visible from this high point, as well as those in the national parks of southern Canada. On a clear day the Purcell and Selkirk ranges of British Columbia are visible, and it is believed that one peak seen from nearby Kinnerly Peak is actually Mt. Assiniboine, the Matterhorn of the Canadian Rockies. Kintla Glacier is quite impressive (in 1950); far below is the deep basin of Upper Kintla Lake.

There are two reasonable ways to get into the Agassiz Basin, from which the most popular routes begin: (1) Take the launch from Waterton to Goathaunt (or walk eight miles along the west shore of Waterton Lake), then hike fifteen miles up to Boulder Pass; or (2) Drive up the unpaved road to Kintla Lake and then hike nearly twenty miles toward Boulder Pass. Elevation gained, either way, is about 2,000 vertical feet from the road to Boulder Pass. Leave the trail west of Boulder Pass, and head into the great Aggasiz Basin.

The best approach route to Agassiz Glacier was pioneered by rangers DeSanto and Mattson, and described in detail by Thornton and Blunk (below). Leave the foot trail west of Boulder Pass, at the lower of the two sharp switchbacks (7,100 ft. elevation). Drop fifty to 100 feet below the trail level while crossing a flower-covered basin, then traverse low around a small ridge on your left. The next basin has small trees, but is easily crossed. Traverse a little lower around the next ridge (on a faint game trail below the cliffs). The next cirque is compound and after traversing some

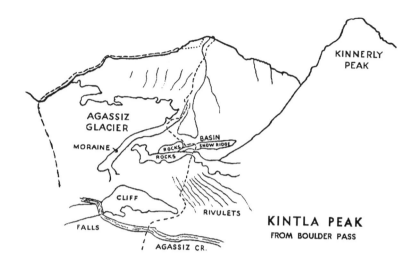

easy tree-studded meadows the route drops down into a rocky talus bowl. Traverse the bowl and reach its southwestern rim at the level of some small cliffs. A short easy descent then leads to the long, wide, slanting ledges (with a big snowdrift) that are visible from the foot trail far below Boulder Pass. Those ledges lead to the obvious saddle on the ridge, and a gully extends down from there to the meadows below Agassiz Glacier. Looking down the correct gully, one can see that it points directly toward a large waterfall further down in the basin. Descend to the meadows, then proceed to the route selected for the ascent of Kintla.

Dave Leppert and Eric Schwab briefly described the *return* to Boulder Pass from Aggasiz Glacier via this route, as follows: After climbing up the gully from the great meadows (mentioned above) "traverse around the south wall of the great basin at about 7,200 ft. elevation, staying just about at tree line, to reach the human trail a short distance below Boulder Pass." They had climbed both Kintla and Kinnerly Peaks from base camp in the great gap between the mountains. (See *Going-to-the-Sun* magazine, Spring 1985.)

There are at least two good routes up the mountain from the meadows below glacier–scoured Agassiz Basin, described below:

The Southeast Ridge Route. Follow the approach to the Agassiz Glacier basin that was described above. From the great meadows, traverse southward, crossing a large lateral moraine at its lowest point, then take the easiest route toward the côl between Mt. Peabody and the great south ridge of Kintla Peak. (Probe with ice axes while crossing the snow and ice there, for it may be undercut by stream action.) From the côl it is an easy ascent up the ridge toward the west. High above Agassiz Glacier the ridge angles north, and there are fantastic views both to the east and the west. When the upper ridge becomes cliffy, easy ledges on the west face lead to a class 4 gully providing access to the summit.

The first ascent of this route was by Jerry DeSanto and Steve Bracken in 1984, but it has been repeated by others, including Thornton and Blunk. This is probably the *best* route, because of pleasant climbing conditions and tremendous scenery all the way to the summit.

The East Ridge Route. After crossing Agassiz creek, veer to the right (west) and pass around the northeast end of the large cliff which parallels Agassiz Creek. Climb up the gentler slope (class 2) at that end of the cliff and walk uphill across the large, sloping region which is crossed by many small, closely-spaced rivulets. Traverse this watery area for about an eighth of a mile, bearing uphill and toward the north, almost directly toward the gap between Kintla and Kinnerly peaks. Above this watery region rises another cliff, which is easy to climb in only one place — where a small stream has worn a steep class 3 gully through it. (This is the only place along the entire cliff where snow does not normally extend up to the base of the cliff in mid-summer.) Climb up this easy break through the cliff. At the top of this cleft leave a cairn to aid you in finding the route on the descent. Above the cliff thus surmounted there is a high steep snowbank lying on the east slope of a large moraine. Take care in climbing this snow slope (it is recommended that an ice ax be carried to arrest a fall on the snow) especially if there is still a hard glaze on it from the preceding night. After surmounting this snowbank and continuing over the top of the moraine pause to scout the route above you.

Toward the northwest you will now be able to see the sharp gap between Kintla and Kinnerly peaks. Straight ahead of you is the cliffy east ridge of Kintla with a snow-choked gully coming down it (this is a dangerous avalanche area so stay away from beneath it!). Drop down into the snowy valley before you and work around to the left (south) of Kintla's east ridge. Now angle southward as you climb up steep snow and small rocky slopes (class 2) to the very large prominent moraine extending southeast from the cliffs along the east base of the massive mountain. Two climbers in 1950 met a grizzly sow and a cub atop this moraine as she climbed it from the upper part of the glacier and they from the lower side. Fortunately they were closer to the upper cliffs than she was, and won a foot race to the safety of the rocks. The grizzly chased them all the way to the cliffs, reared up as high as she could reach and woofed at them, then she and the cub ran down the moraine and down the lower part of the glacier at full speed and disappeared. It required about fifteen minutes for the men to climb down the cliff they had darted up in a matter of seconds.

Walk up this moraine (run, if pursued by grizzlies) to the point where it abuts against the cliffs. Three prominent chimneys are now dead ahead leading through the steep lower cliffs of this side of the east range. Two of these are dangerous and difficult climbs but the large one farther to the right (usually with a snow tongue extending far up it) is not unduly difficult. This couloir may be entered by climbing toward it up a small cliff then traversing thirty feet of sloping scree ledge (class 3 and 4). It is easy to climb upward in this snowy chimney on rocks and talus (class 3) for about sixty feet (avoiding the snow if possible). At this juncture climb out of the couloir, cross the ridge west of it and continue upward in the next couloir. It is most important to mark the exact place where you cross over this small ridge with a distinctive cairn of rocks else it may be impossible for you to find this safe route down later (the wrong couloirs all end in sheer cliffs near the base). After climbing upward to the left leave another cairn to aid in finding your way back. Orient yourself carefully with respect to the moraine far below you so that you won't traverse too far (or not far enough) on your descent.

Now climb the talus slopes and easy class 3 ledges to the top of the east ridge. (This is easier if you angle upward to the left while climbing and attain the ridge near its junction with the ridge that extends north toward Kinnerly Peak.) Mark the route very carefully here so that you do not get off onto the wrong ridge during the descent (which may be made during darkness or in inclement weather).

Follow up that east ridge of Kintla to the summit pyramid. This pyramid consists of very thin layers of dark-colored rock, upon which are more massive blocks near the actual summit of the mountain. If climbing difficulties are encountered here, veer to the right and climb up a diagonal crack in the cliffs (merely a walk up a loose scree passageway). Above this diagonal, traverse below the upper north wall of the summit pyramid and go up easy little cliffs to the ridgetop west of the summit. It is a pleasant walk along that ridge to the summit.

If you are approaching from the west side, plan to backpack in to the head of Upper Kintla Lake for the first night. If approaching from Waterton Lake, it is best to camp at Hole-in-the-Wall Basin (*or* near the top of Boulder Pass). Either way, it is wise to be on the trail by 6:30 A.M. the next day, in order to make the climb and return to camp by dusk. Keep in mind that the time-consuming part of the climb does not begin until you leave the foot trail below Boulder Pass, and that after leaving Agassiz Glacier it may take three more hours to reach the summit. When you return to camp that evening you may not feel like backpacking fifteen miles more, so perhaps you should plan on a second night in camp.

The West Face Route. Distance to summit about fourteen miles, about 8.5 miles of it by trail. Elevation gained is about 6,100 feet. First ascent was by Rangers Jerry DeSanto and Jim Reilly, July 23, 1977. This description of the route was condensed from their written report. They say of the climb: "this is a long and tiring trip and should not be attempted in less than two full days from the head of Kintla Lake . . . . Climbers should be mentally as well as physically prepared for the difficult approach — and the equally difficult return, which is by far the worst part of the trip."

Backpack eight strenuous miles on the undulating trail along the north side of Kintla Lake and camp near the head of that lake or near the outlet of Upper Kintla Lake. Ford the outlet of Upper Kintla Lake and head due south into the great valley between Kintla and Kinnerly Peaks. Stay high along the east edge of the valley, near the cliff base, seeking to avoid the jumble of downed timber and brush. Many streams encountered are not shown on the newest topographic maps (not even the major stream draining Kintla Glacier). Eventually the long scree slope near the southeastern corner of the valley is approached. Plan on four or five hours to cover that first difficult 2.5 miles!

Scramble up the long, hard scree-slope for the next two hours. (The scree is "cemented" in many places, like hard moraine surfaces, making it very difficult to climb without slipping, and even more hazardous to *descend* with heavy packs. Ice axes will be of great help on that slope.) There are suitable campsites above the scree slope, at about 7,000 feet in elevation.

The remaining 3,000 vertical feet of the climb will be relatively easy, straightforward and enjoyable the next day. From the campsite, head directly east toward a horizontally-banded cliff about eighty feet high. Climb up a snow chute at the south end of the cliff, directly beneath a vertical face of glacier ice. (The snow is coated with hard ice in the mornings.) Above the snow chute, head directly toward Kintla Peak, crossing several lobes of the glacier, then ascending a series of small cliffs and scree slopes. Reach the ridge just south of the peak, then work upward through a maze of balanced rock formations, crumbling ledges, and chimneys, to the majestic, aloof summit.

Return carefully to the high camp and, if possible, spend another night there and pack out to the road on the third day. DeSanto and Reilly summarized the route as follows: "a genuine wilderness experience through wild and remote country. . .The many high waterfalls and the vertical ice faces of Kintla Glacier are great sights but the brush and blowdowns are always on your mind. Consequently, we recommend this trip only to the hardy and persevering."

The Upper North Face Route. This not a reasonable route unless the party is already in or near the great notch between Kintla and Kinnerly Peaks. That would probably only be recommended if ascents of both peaks have been planned, as it was by Schwab, Leppert, Lewis, and Shimko (see details under *The Southwest Face Route* up Kinnerly Peak). From the Notch it is a very easy class 3 scramble up to the summit ridge of Kintla Peak.

Long Knife Peak (9,784)

The views into Canada and those toward Kintla and Kinnerly Peaks are unique. Much of the newly-designated wilderness area in southeast British Columbia is visible, and the only sign of civilization is the evidence of logging in the Kishinena Valley of B.C. and along the north fork of the Flathead River. This area is seldom visited, and climbers will sense a remoteness not found on most Glacier Park climbs. It is recommended that the climb be made only in late summer, so that steep snow will be avoided. Even then, ice axes will be handy, and half a length of climbing rope should also be carried along.

This forbidding peak was evidently first climbed by the Boundary Survey team about 1901, but has been very seldom ascended during recent decades. Chief Ranger Chuck Sigler, with Park Ranger Dick Mattson and Jerry DeSanto, climbed the mountain on August 7, 1981, and provided a written account for the benefit of other climbers. The following description of the route was gleaned from that account.

The East Ridge Route. Distance to the summit about sixteen miles, twelve miles of it by human trail. Elevation gained, from Upper Kintla Lake, is about 5,400 vertical feet. Class 3 all the way; however, there is danger on steep snowfields early in the summer. From afar there appear to be three summits on this mountain, but the climber will find that there are actually four. The two middle knobs are the highest, and the western one of these is the true summit. Because of the difficulty of the approach to the peak, this ascent will usually require a round trip time of three days.

Leave the Boulder Pass trail just west of the stream crossing west of the upper end of Upper Kintla Lake, and head northwest toward the great basin above. The next three or four hours are the worst part of the trip — this is a grueling climb through brush, downed trees, and slippery beargrass slopes while gaining 2,900 vertical feet. Leave the main stream at about the 5,600 feet contour, cross the stream, and head north toward the easternmost notch where there is a watercourse (usually dry by midsummer). From above that watercourse bear to the northwest through large jumbled boulderfields and subalpine larch trees to the UTM coordinates 5430.9 x 705.7 (where there is a good campsite in the broad saddle between Long Knife Peak and the unnamed peak just east of it).

From the campsite, head toward the northwest, where five knobs are silhouetted on the skyline, then angle back to the southwest to reach the boundary monument number 269 (see map). That monument was backpacked to this location in 1904! After reaching the monument look for the goat trail about fifty feet below the monument, which leads to the saddle between the first two peaks. From that saddle, climb straight up to the western peak over cliffs and through one or two chimneys. That is the second summit, and it is marked with a small cairn and a register placed on August 1,1977. The peak can be reached in two or three hours from the high camp. There is considerable exposure below the top, especially to the west and south.

The next peak to the northwest is the actual summit. It is reached by traversing around the secondary summit on the north. The traverse is made about half-way up the peak, via a scree shelf that becomes quite narrow and sloping in places. From the saddle between there and the true summit a little route-finding is necessary. There is a route up the left (south) side, above the saddle. A few cliffs require some maneuvering, but the rope was used only once while going up and not at all during the descent.

There was a small cairn on the summit but no register. The rangers placed a register there after building up the cairn. The summit has plenty of exposure and overhangs, but there is room enough to move around.

Numa Peak (9,003)

The views from the summit are spectacular toward the east and southeast, and the great jagged walls in the north and northeast are tremendously impressive. Bowman Lake is beautiful in its deep basin, and the seemingly endless slopes of heavily-forested wilderness west of the Livingston Range are nowhere observed any better than from here.

The South Face Route. Distance to the summit about eight miles, six miles of it by human trail. Elevation gained is about 4,900 vertical feet. Class 3 and 4 pitches are in the long steep couloir in the upper south face. This route was discovered by Robin Cox and Russ Miller on July 31, 1983.

From the Bowman Lake auto campground, travel by trail or boat about two-thirds the way up Bowman Lake, to the stream that drains the basin just below the south face of Numa Peak. (This stream lies almost directly across the lake from the stream that drains the area between Rainbow and Square Peaks.) Bushwhack up the east side of the creek for two or three hours, until reaching the upper basin (in late summer it is easy to go right up the dry creek bed).

From the basin, observe a ramp of vegetation just east of the center of the southeast face, that extends up the peak for 600 to 900 feet. Go up that ramp almost to the cliff above it, until finding a distinctive couloir on your left (recognizable because there is a huge two-ton chock-stone bridging the upper part of it). The ascent of that couloir is the easiest known route up the south face. The most difficult part of the entire climb is within the first several hundred yards up this couloir, where there are occasional class 4 pitches mixed with class 3 ledges. (Early in the summer lingering snow will make that couloir extremely hazardous!)

The couloir continues upward for several hundred yards, then a natural ramp continues out onto the south face. Move into the middle of the south face there, and pick a route up through the broken cliffs to the summit.

Other Routes. For those interested in a more challenging rock climb, George McFarland reports that at least one of the couloirs on the northeast side of the mountain can be climbed (class 4). It can be approached from the south basin, via a traverse around the upper east shoulder above Baby Glacier. Numa Peak has also been climbed by McFarland via the ridge from the Numa Fire Lookout, but most climbers who have studied that ridge believe that it looks like a terrible way to reach the summit.

Parke Peak (9,038)

This peak is interesting because of its use as an early triangulation point (perhaps as early as 1902 or 1903). The remains of a wooden platform still mark the station. Three brass caps from 1924 (one triangulation station and two reference markers) are also on the summit. It was named after Lt. Parke, astronomer of the U.S. Northwest Boundary Survey in 1859-1861.

Views are mostly toward the west and north, since larger peaks block out views into the rest of the park. Most interesting, perhaps, will be the inspection of the lake at the head of Red Medicine Bow Creek and of the region around Harris Glacier. Kintla Lake is beautiful, of course, and Long Knife Peak is very impressive.

The Northwest Route. Distance to the summit about eleven miles, seven miles of it by human trail. (OR approach by boat and travel only about two miles up the slopes and ridges to the summit.) Elevation gained from Kintla Lake is about 5,000 vertical feet. Class 2 or 3 all the way.

Unless approaching by boat, hike the trail along the north shore of Kintla Lake, ford the inlet stream, and bushwhack westward along the south shore to the stream that enters the lake by the "a" in "Lake" on the 1968 topographic map. Follow up that stream drainage, staying east of the 1964 timber blowdown. Above the first steep hillside, angle upward to avoid the down timber in the valley floor and approach the small lake just west of the peak (concealed by the "K" of "Kintla" on the 7.5-minute Kintla Lake Quadrangle map, and at coordinates UTM 5425.0 x 701.4).

Proceed through the west bowl and up onto the ridgetop north of Parke Peak. It is an easy walk up that ridge to the summit. From the small lake to the top should not take more than two hours.

The 7,718-foot peak labelled "Parke" is the location of a reference point by that name used by the old mappers, and the "Kintla" label on Parke Peak is the name of the triangulation station used by the Boundary Commission in 1903.

If a boat is used for this trip, it should take no more than ten hours, round trip, but if the approach is made via the trail, climbers should plan on two full days for the climb. The first known ascent by this route was made by Rangers Jerry DeSanto and Russell Miller.

The Gully Route.   Distance and approach similar to the other route. From the head of Kintla Lake, cross the inlet stream (Kintla Cr.) and wade to the major gully just south of the lakehead. Scramble up the (hopefully) dry streambed shown on the map there until reaching the waterfall just above the dense forest. About 30 feet west of the waterfall there is a deep narrow crack in the wall (beyond a gnarled tree). Climb westward over the rock outcrop below and west of this crack and traverse further west to the base of a steep mossy wall. Carefully ascend this wall (possible even with full packs), then traverse east, into the gully above the waterfall. Now walk up the west (right) fork of the stream gully. At the 6,600-foot level, cross the boulder field and approach the west wall of the huge basin. An obvious vegetated ledge angles up to your right, to the ridgetop. Follow the ridge to the top of "Peak 7718" and continue up the ridge toward the main summit. A flat, but dry, campsite is atop the ridge.

From the campsite, ascend and traverse around the west side of the next peak on the ridge. The first view of Parke Peak is seen from there! Traverse onto the northwest face of Parke Peak on a good ledge just above the saddle. (Mark the end of the ledge so it can be located on the descent.) The remainder of the climb is straight forward. Just below the top it is easier to traverse west and go up an obvious gully to the summit ridge.

The first ascent of this route was made by Ralph Thornton and Bill Blunk, in August 1984. It took three days, but with lighter packs it would be much faster. (The summit is 5,000 vertical ft. above Kintla Lake!!)

Mt. Peabody (9,216)

The views from this rugged peak are dominated by Kintla, Kinnerly, Long Knife, Rainbow, and Carter Mountains. Canadian views are wide-ranging, as are the vistas toward the east. The greatest views of all, however, are those of the lakes, meadows and snowfields around Bowman Lake and the impressive glacier scenes in the opposite direction around Agassiz Glacier.

First ascent, August 1978, by Chief Ranger Chuck Sigler with Park Rangers Jerry DeSanto and Jeff Ellington. DeSanto provided a copy of the account of the climb, upon which this description is based. Along the summit ridge toward the south are three more peaks that are only slightly lower than the true summit of Peabody. Two of them are very sharp and have great exposure, and are almost certainly unclimbed as of 1983.

The Pocket Lake Route. Distance to the summit about seventeen miles, 11.5 miles of it by human trail. Class 3 all the way IF care is taken in route-finding along the summit ridgetop.

This tall, sheer-sided peak is only visible from a few places, because it is hidden from view behind and between nearby mountains on all sides (except from the head of Bowman Lake). It is a long way from roads and trailheads, so it is rarely climbed. Jerry DeSanto provided a copy of the account, in response to a letter from the author.

Hike up Bowman Valley for about 4.5 miles above the head of the Lake, to the junction of Bowman Creek and Pocket Creek. Follow Pocket Creek uphill, staying well to the west of the waterfalls until it is possible to traverse above them to Pocket Lake. Most climbers may want to make a high camp there, nearly 3,000 vertical feet above the great valley.

From Pocket Lake, scramble up to the saddle southwest of the "knob" overlooking Pocket Lake. (The coordinates for the saddle are UTM 5425 x 710.) (This saddle is easily reached from Boulder Pass, since it is just above the rocky talus bowl described on page 90, on the high approach to Kintla Peak via Agassiz Glacier.)

Follow the ridge south from the saddle to an 8-foot cliff that requires use of hands. Continue up the prow of the ridge to a very wide portion of ridge that ascends for a long distance. The peak above is a false summit. Rather than climb it and then descend tricky pitches, traverse around the west (right) side of the false summit until just below the northwest ridge of the false summit. From here it is best to descend 60 feet, to another obvious ledge that leads southward to the deep notch between the false summit and the true summit of Mt. Peabody. The climb to the true summit from the notch follows the ridgetop and ledges along the east side of the ridge. The time required to travel from the saddle to the summit should be about three hours.

Rainbow Peak (9,891)

The West Face Route. Distance to summit about nine miles, including five miles by boat (none by trail). Elevation gained is about 5,800 feet. Class 2 and 3 except for possible class 4 pitches just above upper limit of tree growth.

Views from the summit are enthralling. To the north, Peabody Mountain, Kintla and Kinnerly peaks, and Long Knife Peak are striking because of the extreme stratification, with all strata sloping uniformly down east. The small snowy lakes of the near side of Mt. Peabody are Numa and Pocket lakes, which may be entirely concealed by snow and ice. Hole-in-the-Wall cirque and the tremendous waterfall below it are easily seen, as well as glimpses of the trail from Boulder Pass to Brown Pass. In the near foreground looms the gigantic pyramid of Mt. Carter, connected by a rocky ridge. In the basin between Rainbow and Carter lies Rainbow Glacier, with acres of active ice moving downward toward Cerulean Lake. Farther to the right of Carter may be seen Mt. Cleveland with its long flat top, then Mt. Merritt, with three humps at the summit. Chief Mountain is visible beyond these peaks, at the edge of the vast prairies. Toward the southeast may be seen Going-to-the-Sun Highway winding up to Logan Pass and far beyond those familiar landmarks the sharp spire of Mt. St. Nicholas pokes at the sky. To the right of St. Nicholas is Great Northern Mountain, beyond the south boundary of the park. Just beyond the deep valley southeast of Rainbow, Vulture Peak (a tiring climb) effectively blocks the view of any other peaks in the Livingston Range. In the south and west there are vast stretches of densely wooded wilderness, the home of most of the big game in Glacier National Park, and the large lakes glistening in that dark green setting are Lower Quartz Lake and Bowman Lake, almost 6,000 vertical feet below you. Quartz Lake itself is concealed by Square Peak, and Logging Ridge blocks the view of Logging Lake.

This route makes it almost imperative to use a boat to carry you from the campground at the foot of Bowman Lake to the correct place on the south shore for beginning the climb. No trails lead along the south shore

Great fields of beargrass along the trail near Brown Pass —John Mauff

and a full day of bushwhacking would be needed to that point. Someone in the camp should be willing to transport the climbing party down the lake for a reasonable fee. Be sure to make arrangements to have a boat pick you up at the same place later!

About five miles up the lake a stream empties into it, draining the large basin between Rainbow Peak and Square Peak. Study the southwest face of Rainbow as you approach it. Two large, nonforested streambeds extend upward along the forested western portion of this face. The left-hand bed ends below cliffs near the west ridge just above timberline, but the one farther to your right extends upward into a small cirque or amphitheater. This cirque is about halfway to the summit and usually contains a few small snow patches. The quickest known route leads up the first of these streambeds until cliffs become annoying, then traverses to the right into the other drainage and climbs upward into the cirque. From that cirque either climb directly upward through broken cliffs (danger of finding class 4 cliffs if great care is not take in route-choosing there) or traverse far to your right from the cirque to class 2 scree slopes which lead all the way to the summit.

It may prove difficult to get from the lakeshore up to the open streambeds, but the following directions should help. Land on the shore at east bank of the drainage stream (which is only four or five feet wide) and walk up the east bank, staying a few yards from the water for easier footing. All rocks in this stream are extremely slippery. Soon a low ridge begins to form a little to your left. When that ridge approaches the stream climb it and walk up its crest. That ridge leads into a much larger one, the side of which is crisscrossed with game trails. Ascend those trails, angling back toward the stream and always staying within easy hearing distance of it. Eventually a good elk trail parallels the stream less than a hundred yards from it. Whenever the trail branches, follow the more deeply worn branch and you will gain elevation at a steady rapid rate. Eventually the hill levels off and the trail leads through an almost flat forested area. Keep watching for an extensive nonforested area at your left. When that is reached, proceed up the grassy slopes and enter the rocky streambed there. Follow the stream uphill through heavy forest until the trees on the north bank give way to an open hillside. Traverse from there toward your right until reaching another stream drainage, which is much larger than the one just discussed. This is the large denuded passageway that was so prominent from the lake, and it leads directly upward to the cirque.

Above the cirque, the farther east you traverse before climbing, the easier the route becomes. The scree slopes above the cirque offer no difficulties after the first 200 feet of cliffs are climbed or outflanked. The upper part of the climb is easiest if the southwest ridge is topped and followed upward along a faint game trail. Plan to leave the lakeshore no later than 8:30 A.M. if you intend to be back to meet the boat there at dusk.

On and near the summit there are abundant deposits of a very dark formation of lava, which originated as a flow of molten rock long before this mountain range was uplifted.

It is possible to traverse the ridge from Rainbow to Mt. Carter, but it is a long traverse and if much snow is left it can also be dangerous. Once on the flanks of Carter, traverse far to your right before scrambling up the scree slopes to its summit. (The cliffs on the north, as well as those on the western ridge, are dangerous and time-consuming.) The views from Carter almost duplicate those from Rainbow; on its summit are the remnants of the tent and batteries left there by the Geologic Survey team many years ago, as well as the weathered platform of wood they built.

Square Peak (8,700)

Distance to summit a little over a mile, after leaving the boat. Elevation gained is more than 4,500 vertical feet above the lakeshore.

Proceed along the south shore of Bowman Lake, to the inlet of the stream draining the valley between Rainbow and Square Peaks. A game trail goes up the hillside east of the stream, but close to it. It can be followed most of the way from the lake to the major fork in the stream. This is the same approach as that to Rainbow Peak, and it takes about forty-five minutes to reach the fork. A boulder field has accumulated between the forks of that stream and the northwest face of Square Peak. Skirt the north edge of the boulder field to avoid the brush, and head for the main drainage channel on the face of the mountain. In an average year there will be snowbanks at the base of the peak throughout the summer, but they pose no difficulty.

Follow up the main drainage (a couloir) all the way to the ridgetop west of the summit. It will occasionally be necessary to climb class 4 cliffs and traverse on ledges, but most of the climb is right up the couloir. After reaching the ridge several different routes to the summit are obvious, and not difficult.

Time from the lakeshore to the summit should not exceed four hours, according to ranger Jerry DeSanto (but he has always been a "tiger" on these mountains). It was he who provided the details regarding this route and many others in the northwest part of the park.

Views are very good to the north, south, and east, but the tremendous bulk of Rainbow Peak blocks out most of the northeastern peaks. Cerulean Lake is especially spectacular, nestled 4,000 feet below in the green pocket at the base of Vulture Peak, and of course the majesty of Bowman Lake and its surrounding peaks is always thrilling to contemplate.

Thunderbird Mountain rises above Brown Pass —John Mauff

Vulture Peak (9,638)

The summit views are very distinctive, quite unlike those from any other peak. The only nearby peaks of comparable size are Rainbow and Carter, with Rainbow Glacier between them. The stream from this glacier drops into colorful Cerulean Lake, which is aptly named. Farther down the valley Quartz Creek widens into long, slender Quartz Lake, then passes through Middle and Lower Quartz Lakes. All these lakes lie 5,500 vertical feet below you. Beyond and between Rainbow and Mt. Carter may be seen the broad pyramid of Kintla Peak and the matterhorn of Kinnerly Peak. Farther to the right is the Boulder Pass area with a view of Hole-in-the-Wall Cirque, Mt. Chapman, Thunderbird Peak, and The Guardhouse. Porcupine Ridge is east of The Guardhouse, but it curves northward so soon that the Citadel Peaks are not visible, nor is Waterton Lake. Across the Waterton Valley, Mt. Cleveland and the Stoney Indian Peaks dominate the northeastern horizon, with great three-humped Mt. Merritt a little more to the south. Chief Mountain appears between Merritt and Stoney Indian peaks, but much farther to the east, with just a glimpse of the prairies visible beyond it. Southeast of Vulture, beyond Trapper Peak and Flattop Mountain, is the small sharp cone of Swiftcurrent Peak and its fire lookout. The high hump north of that lookout is Mt. Wilbur, while the bulky mountain south of it (with three transverse snow bands on its north face) is Mt. Gould. Going-to-the-Sun Mountain rises above the Garden Wall south of Mt. Gould, and Little Chief Mountain is seen straight through Logan Pass. The highway is visible from Logan Pass almost to the big switchback below Granite Park Chalet. Farther south the broad round dome of 10,000-foot Mt. Jackson conceals Mt. Stimson, but the spire of Mt. St. Nicholas looms up west of Jackson, and Great Northern Mountain (covered with snowfields) is even farther west and far beyond the southern boundaries of the park. Between Vulture and Jackson is the snowy summit of Heavens Peak.

The Logging Lake Route. Distance to summit about nineteen miles, fourteen miles of it by human trail. Elevation gained is about 6,150 feet. Class 2 and 3 all the way, if correct route is followed.

Leave the North Fork Road at Logging Creek Ranger Station. Hike 4.5 miles to Logging Lake, then six miles along the north shore to the lakehead. Another 3.5 miles up the valley takes you beyond Grace Lake to two small unnamed lakes, but the trail becomes worse and worse, and is difficult to follow beyond Grace Lake. When the second small lake is approached, leave the valley floor and head uphill, angling toward the northwest. Game trails go up the steep forested ridge west of the streams that plunge down from Vulture Glacier into that small lake. About 1,000 vertical feet above the valley is a cliff over which two widely separated waterfalls leap. Walk across grassy areas below the cliff and cross the western stream near the falls. Descend slightly while continuing toward the east (stay below the brush as much as possible). Follow the easterly stream uphill almost to the foot of the waterfall. A fairly good elk trail goes up the brush-covered bank west of this waterfall. Take the time to find where it leaves the grassy, open area near the stream, or you will encounter tiresome bushwhacking there. This trail leads upward steeply for a short distance, then makes an abrupt turn to the west. Just short of a small streambed, it abruptly turns uphill again (stay away from that streambed) and soon emerges above the heavy brush angling up toward the west and following grassy slopes through some small cliffs there.

No further obstacles will be encountered for a least a thousand vertical feet. Scramble up anywhere between the two streams, pass a beautiful waterfall made by the easterly stream, and continue until the steep hillside levels off into a gentle region of alpine meadows, snow slopes and rivulets of ice water. (The westerly stream comes from the snow above this gentler area.)

Climb up the steep snowfields directly above the alpine meadows, or up the scree along the east edge of the snowfields, and pass west of the rocky hump which is so prominent when you look up from the meadows. When the steep snowbank begins to level off, you will see a sharp, ice-covered peak to the west beyond the snows of Vulture Glacier. That peak is not the highest summit of Vulture, but is called South Vulture Peak. Continue up the snow, bearing to your right and diagonalling up the southwest slope of the long ridge with the rocky hump. When you can attain the top of that ridge without danger, do so. From there, at about 8,000-foot elevation, the true summit of Vulture Peak will be seen farther to the north. Its great pyramid rises beyond a quarter-mile of gently sloping snowfields comprising the western portion of Vulture Glacier. You can walk almost directly to the long ridge that descends southeast from the summit, then make your way up that long shoulder to the top. No further obstacles will be encountered, but be sure you notice your route carefully so you won't be trapped above sheer cliffs descending the wrong gully.

The small cairn on this peak was built by the U.S. Geologic Survey crew, and old bottles were found there in 1953.

The Quartz Lake Route. Distance to summit about thirteen miles, six miles of it by human trail. Elevation gained from Quartz Lake is about 5,200 vertical feet. Class 3 all the way (but an ice ax should be carried for safety on the steep snow).

This unique route was climbed by Steve Bracken, Randy Gayner, and Kim Wilson on July 21, 1981. It is perhaps the shortest and quickest route to Vulture Peak; however, it is NOT easy! The following account is based on descriptions provided by those rangers:

Hike the Quartz Lake Trail for six miles from the foot of Bowman Lake to the foot of Quartz Lake. There is a campsite there, which is a good place to spend the first night and cache excess equipment. Leave at dawn the second day, paddle the length of Quartz Lake OR bushwhack for four miles along the lakeshore, and begin the actual climb from Quartz Creek above the lake.

A short distance upstream a tributary enters from the south. Bushwhack uphill in an east-southeast direction through a maze of thick brush, heavy timber, and downfalls. Avoid the streambed, for it is choked with alders, but stay near it while gaining 1,600 vertical feet to the open areas in the northwest bowl of Vulture Peak. That grueling ordeal should require three or four frustrating hours. A large spring is in the upper basin, several hundred feet below a very long narrow snowfield that will be the next objective.

The route leads up through a large boulder field and talus slope toward the long snowfield on the west face of Vulture (the snow chute can be seen from Quartz Lake). Climb to the point where the snowfield passes through the high cliffs and reaches the talus slopes above. Stay north of the snowfield and scramble up class 3 ledges and cliffs all the way to the summit of the mountain. The 3,000 feet above timberline provides interesting climbing.

The Gyrfalcon Lake Route. See details of the approaches to Gyrfalcon Lake from Brown Pass, Valentine Creek, Nahsukin Creek, Fifty Mountain, or the McDonald Creek Trail. All are described under the "North Central Area" chapter. (Of course, mountaineers can also hike from Logging Lake to the headwall and scramble from there to Gyrfalcon Lake.) From that lake it is an easy class 3 climb up the southeast ridge to the summit of Vulture Peak.

Vulture Peak, South Summit (9,390)

The approaches to Gyrfalcon Lake were mentioned above. From that lake, climbers can cross over the southeast ridge of Vulture Peak and walk across the snow and ice to the southwest ridge. The route then leads up the ridge to the summit of this south peak of Vulture. For details, see the description under the "North Central Area" chapter.

Granite Peak Chalet, and view to snowy Vulture Peak —John Mauff

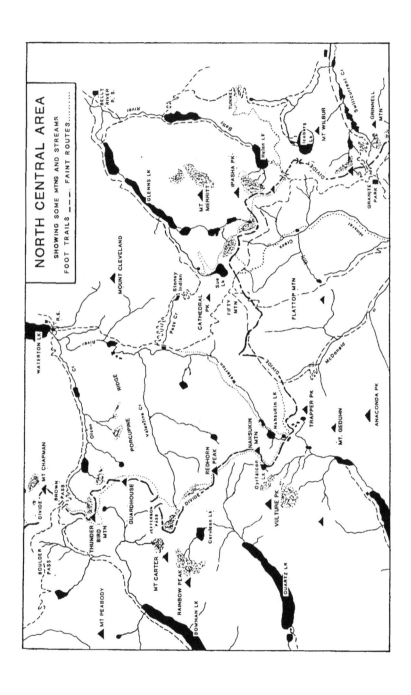

THE NORTH CENTRAL AREA

Routes Among the Peaks

This great area extends from Ahern Pass northward to Stoney Indian Pass and Brown Pass. There are many points of interest there that are too far east to be reached readily from the western edge of the park and too far west to be reached readily from the eastern trailheads. Instead of describing those routes under the sections dealing with the Livingston Range or the Lewis Range, they are therefore discussed in detail here. Obviously, visits to these destinations will require at least two days and necessitate camping in the "back country" at least one night.

The peaks that are easiest to reach from Fifty Mountain Camp are Mt. Kipp (8,800) and Cathedral Peak (9,041), while off-trail routes that are most popular there are the "short cuts" from Fifty Mountain to Stoney Indian Pass (or vice versa) that are described below. Fifty Mountain Camp can be reached by trail from Waterton Lake (ten miles), from Logan Pass (twenty miles) or from Packer's Roost (seventeen miles).

Ahern Pass is usually reached via a good trail from Granite Park Chalets or by climbing over the Iceberg Notch from Iceberg Lake. The Pass is the most reasonable approach to Ahern Peak (8,749) and Ipasha Peak (9,450), as well as the three-day mountaineering high route from Iceberg Lake to Stoney Indian Pass (described below as "The Ipasha Connection").

The other great remote area in this part of the park is the extensive meadowland between West Flattop Mountain and Jefferson Pass. Of special interest there are Gyrfalcon Lake, Two Ocean Glacier, The Carter Glaciers, and a number of small peaks seldom visited by anyone (Mt. Geduhn, Nahsukin Mountain, Trapper Peak, and Redhorn Peak). Details of the routes from Brown Pass or Frances Lake to Porcupine Ridge and Jefferson Pass are presented below under "Jefferson Pass Approaches."

Climbing routes on Thunderbird Mountain and Mt. Chapman are covered under the Livingston Range section, Mt. Merritt and Pyramid Peak are in the Lewis Range discussion, and Iceberg Peak, the Pinnacle Wall, and the great goat trail from Ptarmigan Tunnel to Ahern Pass are described in detail in the "Many Glacier" section of this guide.

Alice Edwards supervising movie sequence by Gordon Edwards
—Ira Spring

FIFTY MOUNTAIN CAMP TO STONEY INDIAN PASS
VIA HIGH SHORT CUTS

These short cuts permit mountaineers to avoid the long, dull trail between Stoney Indian Pass and the Fifty Mountain area. In addition to the basic routes (described below), the mountaineer may want to make side-trips en route, climbing Pyramid Peak from Sue Lake meadows or climbing Cathedral Peak from the north ridge short cut. During the first "ascent" of this circuit the author met other hikers on Stoney Indian Pass and watched them leave at 11 A.M. en route to Fifty Mountain via Waterton Valley. They reached Fifty Mountain at 6:30 P.M., exhausted. Meanwhile, the author had returned to camp via the Cathedral Ridge, climbed Mt. Kipp with his family, and prepared and finished dinner. It really IS an effective short cut!

By utilizing these routes, competent backpackers who are familiar with cross-country travel can backpack from the Belly River Ranger Station to Sue Lake and Chaney Glacier, then hike down to Granite Park for the night. (An even easier trip in the reverse direction, of course.) More likely these short cuts will be used just for the pleasure of campers who are at Fifty Mountain and want to spend the day reconnoitering around the Fifty Mountain and Sue Lake areas, carrying light packs.

The Chaney Glacier Route. Leave the Highline Trail at about 7,300-foot elevation, where a stream crosses the trail in the large basin southwest of Chaney Glacier. Scramble up near the stream to Chaney Notch (the lowest notch in the ridge above the glacier, at 8,100 ft.). A few yards downhill, east of the notch, walk right onto the snow from the steep scree, and descend the glacier gradually, toward the north. Approach the bedrock by the north end of the glacier, and walk uphill from there toward the east. Pass between the two large moraines there, then stroll through grassy meadows toward Sue Lake. (A short distance eastward the meadow ends in great cliffs, providing views of Margaret and Ipasha Lake in the valley far below.) WARNING: Ralph Thornton reported that in 1987 the bare ice of the glacier was exposed and there were "quite a few large crevasses over much of its surface." Obviously, then, mountaineers should take precautions there! If you have no ice ax (for probing the snow cover), rope together during the glacier crossing, or at least leave ten or fifteen feet of space between party members and travel single-file (so that only the leader is in danger). Continue north to unbelievably blue Sue Lake, nestled thousands of feet beneath tremendous walls. Views to the north from the outlet of that lake are dominated by the rugged Stoney Indian Peaks and the matterhorn of Wahcheechee Mountain, with Stoney Indian Pass pinched between them. The largest mountain near Sue Lake is Cathedral Peak, with several graceful waterfalls leaping thousands of feet into the basin south of Stoney Indian Pass. The descent into that basin begins far east of the lake, at the northern edge of the great meadows. From the base of Pyramid Peak a moderately steep grassy ramp descends for 600 vertical feet, reaching the basin floor near the bottom of the waterfall that issues from Sue Lake.

Climbers with a half-hour to spare may want to walk up Pyramid Peak before descending the ramp. From that peak there are remarkable views of the lakes in the long, narrow valley toward the east, as well as the unique lakes at the south base of the mountain (Margaret Lake is half milky and half blue!). The summit of Pyramid Peak is guarded by a very deep transverse cleft. Just as you think you are nearly to the summit, the bottom drops out before you and you must lose considerable elevation descending toward the south and skirting the end of the cleft. From there, traverse eastward along the south side of the mountain until finding an easy route to the ridgetop.

After going down the long grassy ramp to the bottom of the great waterfall, cross the stream above the alder thickets and go north along the edge of the vegetation until approaching the human trail. (Another route from the bottom of the ramp involves a game trail that descends the east side of the waterfall stream, but it leads to brush thickets and wet areas before reaching the foot trail.) It is still about 900 vertical feet up the winding trail to Stoney Indian Pass (7,800 ft.).

The Cathedral Peak Ridge Route. From Fifty Mountain Camp, hike to the north end of the great meadows. Leave the trail at 6,900 feet and scramble up easy slopes while traversing northward to the high ridge north of Cathedral Peak. The lowest part of that ridge is 8,700 feet in elevation and it should be crossed at that point. (For details of the easy climb of Cathedral Peak from there, see the description elsewhere in this guide.)

From the north ridge, walk down gentle slopes and steep meadows into the narrow basin northeast of the Pyramid Descend into the narrower lower portion of that basin and follow goat trails down easy class 3 cliffs beside the stream. Below the cliffs, head across scree slopes and vegetated soil toward Stoney Indian Pass. The only remaining obstacle is the steep, snow–filled gully beneath Wahcheechee Mountain. Approach that gully via a large grassy slope that extends horizontally toward it, and use any of several narrow ledges that lead safely to the edge of the snow. If no ice ax is available, carry a long, sharp-pointed rock with which to (hopefully) stop yourself in case of a fall on the snow (or at least to steer yourself onto the dirt and rocks beside the gully). Beyond the snow, cross the boulder field and gently sloping hillside that will bring you to Stoney Indian Pass in a few minutes.

This route is certainly the shortest and fastest from Fifty Mountain to Stoney Indian (or vice versa) and can be used by experienced mountaineers, even bearing heavy packs. If doubts arise, as you struggle over the high ridge, consider the fact that you are missing a dull, hot ten miles of insect-infested trail . . . and that the trail descends 2,900 vertical feet to Waterton Valley, then gains most of it back again on the laborious climb back up to Fifty Mountain meadows. Besides, this high route is SCENIC!

THE IPASHA CONNECTION:
HIGH ROUTE FROM ICEBERG LAKE
TO STONEY INDIAN PASS

This three-day high-level backpacking experience should only be attempted by mountaineers in good condition, equipped with ice axes and rope. Register with the rangers in advance. Distance from Iceberg Lake to Stoney Indian Pass is about eighteen miles, none of it by human trail, ascending 4,200 vertical feet and descending 1,900 feet en route. Class 3 most of the way, but class 4 on the Iceberg Wall and class 5 on the "Nervous Traverse" between Ipasha Glacier and Chaney Glacier.

Hike 4.5 miles from Swiftcurrent Camp to Iceberg, gaining 1,200 vertical feet. Climb 1,600 vertical feet to Iceberg Notch (via route described elsewhere in this guide). Descend 600 vertical feet to Ahern Pass. Good campsites are at the pass and on the flat ridge 200 feet up the southeast corner of Ahern Peak. Walk 1,750 vertical feet up the marvelous goat trail on the southeast ridge of Ahern Peak and down to the meadows beyond the summit (see description of route to Ipasha Peak via the Yo-Yo route, for further details). Walk north along the broad ridge toward Ipasha Peak until the ridge narrows abruptly, then descend the west side of the ridge to the bottom of the broad black diorite sill. Walk north on the goat trail at the bottom of that sill until reaching the lower slopes of Ipasha. (For details, see Route to Ipasha in this guide.) Continue to traverse northward until reaching the ridge overlooking the head of the Belly River Valley, then walk down that ridge until it is blocked by large cliffs. The basin below, toward the northwest, contains Ipasha Glacier (the next objective). A descent must be made via the huge steep snowfield that covers the north-facing slope below the high ridge. Ice axes are a necessity for the safe descent of this snowfield, for it can be deadly to anyone who slips and slides down it out of control. All the mountaineers should be given instructions concerning how to hold the ice ax and how to use it for effective self-arrests if they fall here. If some members do not have ice axes, one person should descend and carry back up enough ice axes so that those left at the top can also descend in safety. Walk westward below the snowfield, to the lake at the lower edge of Ipasha Glacier. The glacier basin is wild, remote, and beautiful, with spectacular views of Mt. Merritt and the upper Belly River Valley. Marvelous campsites are there, in the lush grass between the lake and the lip of the waterfall that drops a thousand feet into the nearby cirque.

Cross the stream and walk up the great snowfield north of the lake, staying near the east edge of the snow. Near the bottom of the cliffs above the snow a distinct goat trail eventually appears beside the snowfield. Follow it uphill and onto the sheer east face of the mountain (above all vegetation). The traverse of that face can only be made at one place, and the goat trail there is only a few inches wide ... with 2,000 feet of exposure below it and an overhanging precipice above it. Hikers with packs must face the wall and side-step along the narrow ledge for fifteen or twenty feet. Fortunately there are good handholds all the way; nevertheless, on the first ascent we all agreed that this part of the route should be referred to as the "Nervous Traverse!" The ledge soon widens a little, but then ends and it is necessary to "switchback" downward six to eight feet to a lower ledge that continues to the northeast corner of the mountain. Careful balance is required during the switchback maneuvering! When the corner is reached, Chaney Glacier comes into view. Walk down the ridge to a deep notch between the major cliff-face and the sharp formations on the northeast ridge. Scramble down easy scree slopes from that notch to the snow covering Chaney Glacier, and take the long walk to the far northern end of the glacier. Leave the snow there and pass through a large gap between huge moraines. The extensive meadows beyond lead to dazzling Sue Lake (7,145 ft.), and marvelous campsites. (We spent the first night at Ahern Pass and the next night at Sue Lake.) The stream flowing out of the lake immediately plunges over an immense cliff, and nearby there are even higher waterfalls leaping from the sheer face of Cathedral Peak.

From the deep basin below the cliff a human trail zig-zags up to Stoney Indian Pass. To reach that basin, follow the top of the cliff from Sue Lake toward the east. Soon the cliffs end and you walk down a broad, gentle ramp of green vegetation, with trees along the right side. That descending passageway extends all the way to the bottom of the falls that originated in Sue Lake just seconds earlier. (For more details of the route from Chaney Glacier to Stoney Indian Pass, see the description of the routes from Fifty Mountain to Stoney Indian Pass elsewhere in this guide.) From Stoney Indian Pass (7,800 ft.) the well-maintained human trail proceeds another nine miles to the head of Waterton Lake. The launch leaves two or three times daily, cruising to Waterton, where the pleasures and luxuries of civilization await the hungry, thirsty conquerors of strenuous trips through Glacier National Park.

First "ascent" of this route in early August 1976, was by Mavis Lorenz, Alice and Jane Edwards, Scott Burch, Chip Youlden, Jim Walker, Fred Reese, and J. G. Edwards.

JEFFERSON PASS APPROACHES

The Continental Divide Route, described elsewhere in this guide, goes from Forum Peak in Alberta, to Boulder Pass in Glacier National Park, and down the trail to Brown Pass. It then ascends to Thunderbird Glacier and traverses the west face and the south slopes of both summits of Thunderbird Peak, to reach a deep notch directly south of the Sentinel (8,875), which everyone should take the time to climb. From the deep notch, traverse the east and south slopes of The Guardhouse until reaching the meadows that extend to Jefferson Pass (6,660 ft.). From Jefferson Pass it is a long but pleasant cross-country hike to Fifty Mountain Camp and the trails to Granite Park and Logan Pass.

Brown Pass to Jefferson Pass. Ascend around the east slopes of the large hump between the pass and Thunderbird Glacier, staying just below the sheer cliffs formed by the dark igneous sill. Above the hump, head westward and cross the snow, when necessary, to reach the northwest ridge of Thunderbird Mountain. Every backpacker attempting this route to Jefferson Pass should have an ice ax, but persons without axes may be able to cross the snowfield if they go straight up the snow until reaching a gentler slope for the traverse (AND if they carry a strong, sharp-pointed rock in each hand with which they may be able to stop themselves if they slip toward the abyss).

Scramble a few feet down the west side of the northwest ridge to a distinct game trail that traverses the entire west face at an elevation of 8,000 feet. Follow it to the saddle below the southwest corner of the mountain. Camping there is likely to be a windy experience, but the views are fantastic! (Carry water, in case there is no snow nearby.)

From the southwest saddle, look far across the south face of Thunderbird to the narrow, deep notch in the ridge between Thunderbird and The Guardhouse. The game trail continues for nearly two miles across the ledges and scree slopes to that notch, but it becomes very faint, and is usually covered partially by steep snowbanks. When the notch is reached (8,000 ft.), it will be seen that the broad valley between there and Porcupine Ridge lies nearly a thousand vertical feet below, and that there are intervening cliffs and steep snowfields, even in August.

From the notch, traverse southward across the east face of The Guardhouse, just above the 7,600-foot level. Even in August much of that long traverse may be covered by steep snow. When directly above the saddle that connects The Guardhouse to Porcupine Ridge, climb straight up the summit ridge of The Guardhouse for the remarkable views in all directions

View northwest from The Guardhouse. The Continental Divide Route traverses the side of Thunderbird Mountain, visible in right foreground
—Dan Spencer

and a panorama toward the south that reveals the entire route from Jefferson Pass to Trapper Peak. From the hillside above the saddle, traverse around the south end of The Guardhouse ridge to the meadows near Jefferson Pass. Steep snow and troublesome cliffs make that descent hazardous below the saddle. Dan Maturen and Dan Spencer (who were investigating this route in 1983) scrambled directly down several hundred feet to a large grassy bench with small evergreens (at the 7,200-ft. contour level) and then traversed westward to Jefferson Pass. Even though that was in early August, they had difficulty negotiating a long steep gully filled with snow, just above the bench, with a dangerous little cliff above a large snowbank. They recommend traversing west above the elevation of the saddle until directly above Jefferson Pass, then it is an easy walk down to the pass.

To continue south from the pass, walk to the gap between Redhorn Peak and the unnamed peak just northwest of it. Scramble 1,500 feet up the north slope of Redhorn and walk along a marvelous game trail on the ridgetop for two miles, to the summit of Nahsukin Mountain. Descend from Nahsukin to Gyrfalcon Lake (and Two-Ocean Glacier), then walk about 1.5 miles down great slopes of flat, scoured rock surfaces to the small lakes astride the Continental Divide at 6,100 foot elevation. Traverse around the east side of Trapper to reach the McDonald Creek trail.

Follow it eastward for about three miles to Fifty Mountain Camp, or south for ten miles to Packer's Roost at Going-to-the-Sun Highway.

For mountaineers wishing to return to Waterton rather than going to Fifty Mountain or Packers Roost, a good route exists from Nahsukin Lake down to the Waterton Valley Trail. From the small lakes straddling the Divide, follow the 6,300-foot contour elevation toward the northeast. A scree area on the west side of the ridge above you extends to the top of a long steep gully that descends toward the center of Nahsukin Lake. A short distance downhill a game trail traverses eastward to a gentler gully where it descends to the foot of the lake. Bushwhack 400 vertical feet down to the small lake east of Nahsukin, then cross the inlet of that lake. In the meadow north of the small lake is the "old Waterton Valley Trail," which follows the left bank of the Waterton River for about four miles down to the junction with Kootenai Creek (4,700 ft.). In mid-season it is easy to ford the river just below that junction, where the current is moderately swift but the water is not much more than knee-deep and the bottom is solid. After about another mile, the trail east of the river joins the Waterton Valley Trail. It is then five more miles to the head of Waterton Lake.

The Valentine Creek Approach. Hike the trail from Waterton Lake to Kootenai Lakes. Shortly after passing the lakes, bushwhack ford it near the confluence with Valentine Creek. Follow up the Valentine Creek valley for about seven miles, on remnants of the old trail that once led to a fire lookout high on Porcupine Ridge. Beyond that trail there should be even fainter traces of a "manway" that was used many years ago for travel up to Jefferson Pass.

The Lake Frances Approach. In 1965, Robert Pfister and Richard Cussler hiked from the McDonald Creek trail to Jefferson Pass and up to the saddle between The Guardhouse and Porcupine Ridge, then descended (in late August) directly down steep slopes and cliffs to Lake Frances, as follows: Climb down 500 feet of class 3 and 4 cliffs from the saddle to the large lake below, toward the north. An ice ax traverse toward the west along a broad slope of snow (below the steep upper cliffs) leads to much easier slopes extending down to that lake. Walk past another small lake, and around to the outlet of the third lake in the basin. Carefully work down more cliffs from that outlet, to scree slopes below, then bushwhack to Olson Creek and up to the foot trail beyond it. Perhaps mountaineers might reverse this route and climb up that 2,100 vertical feet en route to Jefferson Pass.

Other Routes. Not highly recommended by anyone is the notorious bushwhack up the east fork of Bowman Creek (nearly five miles of impenetrable bush and downed trees, while ascending 2,600 vertical ft.). In the early days a horse trail went all the way up that valley, but it had vanished by the end of the Second World War in 1945.

Routes to the Summits

Ahern Peak (8,749)

It is difficult to imagine a more spectacular hike anywhere in the park. The views in all directions are impressive, especially those toward the south, where the great glaciers and peaks beyond Logan Pass show up very well. Along the western horizon many great snowfields shine in the sun, with massive pyramids of rock thrusting skyward between them. Mt. Merritt is also impressive from this angle, with the icy cloak of Old Sun Glacier covering the upper half of the east face and with great waterfalls plunging thousands of feet into the Belly River Valley. This easy walk to the summit should not take more than an hour from Ahern Pass and will surely be considered one of the most rewarding trips anywhere in the park.

The Southeast Ridge Route. Distance to the summit from Ahern Pass is about one mile, via an excellent goat trail, gaining about 1,750 vertical feet en route. It is a class 2 walk-up all the way . . . IF you don't slip off the trail and tumble 3,500 feet down into Helen Lake! Ahern Pass is about five miles north of Granite Park, thus about 12.5 miles from Logan Pass, 12.5 miles from Swiftcurrent Camp (via Swiftcurrent Pass), and nine miles from "the Loop" on the highway below Granite Park Chalets.

From Ahern Pass, walk uphill near the edge of the great cliff that drops down toward Helen Lake. At a large flat area between the cliff and the nearby alpine forest there is a fine campsite close to a large permanent snowbank that provides good water. Continue uphill from the campsite, following game trails through broken cliffs. Soon the trails consolidate into one well-beaten path that leads to the summit, staying very close to the cliff edge most of the way. That trail passes beside several thrilling notches in the cliff edge, each providing breath-taking views straight down to azure Helen Lake.

Cathedral Peak (9,041)

Summit views are similar to those from Mt. Kipp, but in several respects they are much better. Blue, snow-flecked Sue Lake is spectacular, nestled at the base of an awesome north face of Mt. Kipp, and the long, deep valley containing Glenn's Lake and Crosley Lake lies at your feet. Toward the west the panorama is mostly snowy, with Longfellow Peak, Vulture Peak, Rainbow Peak, and Mt. Carter dominating the scene. At the foot of Vulture Peak (with its three rugged summits surrounding Vulture Glacier) is beautiful Nahsukin Lake, which drains into some smaller ponds below it. Perhaps the most interesting view of all from this lofty peak, however, is that of Waterton Lake and the town of Waterton. Beyond the graceful saddle of Stoney Indian Pass (and between the spire of Wahcheechee Mountain and the Stoney Indian Peaks) the broad ribbon of Waterton Lake extends northward, hemmed in on either side by rugged peaks and ridges. (You may be sure that hundreds of people are returning your gaze from the Waterton area, for Cathedral Peak is the impressive snowy "sugarloaf" mountain that is so prominent from Waterton and Waterton Lake.)

The Northwest Couloir Route. Distance to summit about nine miles, eight miles of it by trail. Elevation gained from Fifty Mountain meadows is about 2,100 vertical feet. Class 3 and 4 all the way.

Hike from Waterton Lake to the north end of the extensive meadows north of Fifty Mountain Camp. (This area can also be reached via the highline trail from Granite Park, or via the Flattop Mountain trail from McDonald Valley.)

From the meadow, look toward the summit and observe the route. A broad formation of brown igneous rock extends entirely across the southwest face of the mountain, creating a formidable obstacle. A prominent vertical gully, partly filled with steep snow, extends up through the lower cliffs to that dark igneous formation, and is dangerous to ascend or cross until very late in the summer. Above the igneous rock the dome-shaped upper portion of the peak rises, composed entirely of sedimentary formations. Climbers must climb nearly a thousand vertical feet of scree and small cliffs in order to reach the igneous (lava) cliffs. The easiest route through the lower cliffs is far south of the snowy gully, where scree slopes extend nearly up to the lava formation. Above the scree, traverse north just below the lava, and cross the snow gully at that point (a short rope should be used for belaying the climbers across that steep snow).

Just north of the snow-filled gully there is a broad (fifty-foot-wide) couloir that extends upward entirely through the lava formation, affording very easy access to the summit dome of the mountain. Scramble up that class 3 couloir for about 200 vertical feet, then continue up through easy sedimentary formations while angling toward the right (south). The rocky hump astride the northwest ridge of the summit dome is easily bypassed around its south side. After reaching the notch between that hump

Altar built at Stoney Indian Pass by Father Tom Best's Exodus hike group—John Mauff

and the main summit dome, climb up easy cliffs and gullies just east of the northwest ridge and reach the top with nothing more difficult than class 4.

Alternate route. From Stoney Indian Pass, follow the "short cut" route to Fifty Mountain, which leads to the broad gully up through the lava formation near the NW ridge.

Mt. Geduhn (8,375)

The Gyrfalcon Lake Approach. From the summit there are unusual views of Longfellow Peak as well as a great panorama northward to Vulture Peak and the Rainbow-Carter massif. Particularly impressive is the deep, green valley embracing Grace Lake and Logging Lake 4,000 vertical feet below toward the west. Nearly the entire hiking route from the McDonald Creek trail to Jefferson Pass and Porcupine Ridge can be studied from this vantage point.

For details of the approaches to Gyrfalcon Lake and Two Ocean Glacier see description in this chapter under "Jefferson Pass Approaches."

From the three small lakes on the Continental Divide 1.5 miles southeast of Gyrfalcon Lake, follow game trails up the ridge west of the large basin of ponds and meadows just under the west face of Trapper Peak. The ridge leads to an unnamed peak (7,869 ft.) and from there over to Mt. Geduhn, passing a beautiful formation of fossil algae that stands out in high relief as a result of extensive weathering. Dan Spencer and Dan Maturen provided these details.

Perhaps nobody will make a trip this far just to climb Geduhn, but mountaineers who are passing through these meadows along the Continental Divide route will surely enjoy the short side-trip to visit that summit! (See Trapper Peak routes for a description of the ridge that connects these peaks.)

Of course, Mt. Geduhn can also be reached from the west, via the Logging Valley, but incredible bushwhacking and the twenty-mile approach will probably prevent that from becoming anyone's favorite climb.

The Guardhouse (9,336)

The views from the top are terrific because there are high peaks in every direction: Mt. Chapman, Kinnerly and Kintla peaks, Mt. Carter, Rainbow Peak, and Vulture Peak fill the skyline in the north and west, while Mt. Cleveland, Cathedral Peak, and Mt. Merritt are especially impressive further east and southeastward. The extensive green areas that are noteworthy are Hole-in-the-Wall Basin to the north, Jefferson Pass and Fifty Mountain Meadows to the southeast, and West Flattop and Flattop mountains further southward. Far down Porcupine Ridge, toward the east, are the impressive spires that overlook the Waterton Valley. All in all, a very worthwhile climb to make, and the time required to reach the summit from the saddle on Porcupine Ridge should not exceed two hours.

The approaches to the base of this great mountain are infinitely more difficult and exhausting than the climb itself. For details of the easiest approaches see the descriptions in this guide of Jefferson Pass Approaches. The closest route is that described by Pfister and Cussler, which leaves the trail just downstream from Frances Lake, 6.3 miles west of Goathaunt (at the head of Waterton Lake). Ford Olson Creek and scramble up the steep valley with the three small lakes, heading directly toward The Guardhouse. A less-hazardous approach is described in detail under the route from Brown Pass to Jefferson Pass. It involves a traverse of Thunderbird Glacier, followed by three miles of poor goat trail across the west face and south slopes of Thunderbird Mountain at the 8,000-foot contour level.

From the broad saddle between Porcupine Ridge and The Guardhouse climb up class 3 cliffs to the summit ridge, staying between the large snowfields to the south and the more difficult cliffs on the north. (Mark well the point where you reach the ridge, so it can be followed on the descent.) Walk several hundred yards up the ridge toward the north to reach the sky-scraping summit!

The gain in elevation from Frances Lake to the top of The Guardhouse is about 4,000 vertical feet, so a base camp in the valley might be preferable to a high camp on the saddle.

Ipasha Peak (9,450)

The Yo-Yo Route. The reason for this name will be evident to all who climb this route. The numerous ups and downs will eventually induce fatigue in persons who are not quite in shape, but for most climbers this will be merely a challenging but strenuous hike. The total elevation that must be gained during the ascent is about 6,050 vertical feet, while even on the way "up" the climbers must descend about 1,400 feet!

Summit views are remarkable. Looking toward Mt. Cleveland and Stoney Indian Pass one is impressed by the large number of sharp peaks, including Cathedral and Wahcheechee (left of the pass), Stoney Indian Peaks (to the right), and Pyramid Peak (in the foreground). Four thousand feet below the latter peak is the wild trailless valley west of Mt. Merritt, displaying an attractive assortment of blue, emerald, and milky-colored lakes. In the other direction, Helen Lake sparkles at your feet, embraced in the lush green valley and surrounded by thousands of vertical feet of brilliant red rock formations. The entire Livingston Range sprawls across the western horizon, culminating in Kintla and Kinnerly peaks beyond the top of Cathedral Peak, but they seem dwarfed by the northern neighbor of Ipasha, 10,000-foot-high Mt. Merritt. Merritt's east face appears tremendously steep from this angle and Old Sun Glacier, clinging to that face, is simply stupendous. The unclimbed spires between Ipasha and Merritt cannot be reached from either peak without a descent of a thousand feet down the west face and a hazardous climb directly up to their base from there. The largest of those spires is called the "Lithoid Cusp." Toward the south, Jackson, Blackfoot, and Sperry glaciers fairly gleam above the verdant valleys around and beyond Logan Pass. The roof of the Many Glacier Hotel can barely be seen from the summit of Ipasha, IF you can stand on someone's shoulders long enough to focus on it, and the buff-colored ridge behind the hotel parking lot may be seen without climbing on each other.

The Yo-Yo route, briefly summarized, involves the following elements: Hike to Iceberg Lake, gaining 1,200 feet in 4.5 miles; climb up to Iceberg Notch, gaining 1,600 more feet; run down the coarse scree and boulders 650 vertical feet to Ahern Pass (a descent often referred to as the "Boulder-dash" by climbers with a decent sense of humor); walk up the southeast ridge of Ahern Peak gaining 1,750 feet; descend 400 feet to the scree-covered saddle toward the north then drop another 200 to 300 feet in order to reach the traverse routes on either side of the narrow rock ridge there; and finally struggle up the last strenuous 1,500 vertical feet to the summit of Ipasha Peak. Details of the first part of the route are discussed under *Iceberg Notch* in this guide, and the route above Ahern Pass is outlined under *Ahern Peak* in this guide. From the top of Ahern Peak, walk down the broad scree slopes just to the north until reaching the scree-covered saddle at the lowest level (about 8,300 ft. in elevation). Good campsites are halfway down the scree slopes, with level areas and a permanent water supply. From the saddle, there are two alternative routes, one on scree and goat trails along the west face of the ridge and the other involving snow and ice along the east side of the ridge. The ridgetop itself can be walked along easily, with impressive cliffs all along each side. Unfortunately, at the north end of the ridge there is a sudden sheer drop off to a scree-covered lower ridgetop beyond. The twenty-foot cliff could probably be descended far enough to permit a safe jump to the bottom, but the ascent on the return trip would be very unlikely without pitons and rope. Climbers who are thus equipped may wish to save time and energy by rappelling down that cliff and leaving the rope in place for aid on the return.

The West Shelf Variant.   From the scree-covered saddle, walk down the side scree-filled couloir toward the west. When the couloir branches, descend further down the right (north) fork for another 150 feet. The scree gives way to a rocky, narrow gorge which is easily descended but exposes climbers to considerable danger from dislodged rocks. Below that gorge an excellent goat trail traverses north along the dark igneous rock formation called the "diorite sill." Follow that trail for more than 100 yards, until below a large, deep notch in the cliffy ridgetop above, then scramble straight up the scree-chute that leads to the notch. This joins the Ahern Glacier Variant on the scree-covered saddle a few feet further north, and both routes become the same from there to the summit.

The Ahern Glacier Variant.   This should never be attempted unless the climbers are equipped with ice axes and experienced in self-arrest techniques. Unequipped climbers would be unlikely to complete the northern part of the traverse without slipping, whereupon the body would probably have to be retrieved near Helen Lake. For the properly equipped climber this route is a simple walk northward across the steep snow below the summit cliffs along the east side of the ridge. Beyond the north end of the ridge, climb up to the scree-covered saddle and join the West Shelf route. The two routes become the same from there to the summit.

From the saddle, the route to the top of Ipasha is easy but time-consuming. Walk northward, past the dark igneous spires, toward the great pyramid several hundred feet high. Traverse around the east base of that pyramid, on snow or scree, until directly beneath a prominent gap in the ridge between the pyramid and the main summit mass of Ipasha Peak. Scramble up toward that gap, but not far below it watch for a narrow rift angling up toward the north. It is easy and safe to climb that rift; however it may be necessary to remove all packs in order to squeeze through it. Mark the top of that rift well, so that it can be found on the descent. Walk up the long cliffy ridge, first on one side then the other, avoiding unnecessary risks and exposure. Soon it becomes less rocky, and the final approach is up a simple scree-covered ridge. WARNING: The great snowbank along that summit ridge usually has an overhanging cornice. It can be studied while approaching the gap in the ridge, but it is always safest NOT to walk on any snowbank near a ridge unless it has been carefully investigated from below. Even massive cornices may break off under the weight of a lightweight person!

The Yo Route. (Shortcut to the Yo-Yo Route.) Obviously it is not necessary to approach Ahern Pass only via Iceberg Notch. Good trails lead to that pass from Logan Pass (12.5 miles), from Swiftcurrent Camp via Swiftcurrent Pass (also 12.5 miles), and from "the Loop" (the big switchback in the highway below Granite Park Chalets). From Ahern Pass it is only about three miles to the summit of Ipasha Peak, ascending about 3,250 feet en route. If the west shelf variant is followed around the ridge between Ahern and Ipasha, there is nothing worse than class 3 in the entire climb. If weather, time or fatigue interfere with the completion of the climb, nobody should be disappointed by turning back after having reached the top of Ahern Peak!

The Cattle Queen Route. Distance to summit about 17.5 miles, sixteen miles of it by trail from Logan Pass or Swiftcurrent Camp, or 13.5 miles, twelve of it by trail (from "the Loop" in the highway below Granite Park). Elevation gained from the trail is about 2,500 vertical feet. Class 3 all the way.

Hike up the Highline Trail for about eight miles from Granite Park, to Cattle Queen Creek. Above the creek crossing, the hillside sweeps upward and culminates in rocky ridges and crags, the largest of which is the great pyramid on the ridge southwest of Ipasha's summit. Leave the trail and scramble up 1,500 vertical feet of scree and class 3 cliffs, to the lowest part of the ridge directly above the stream crossing. From that scree-covered ridge (8,400 ft.), follow the route described under the Yo-Yo Route up the last 1,000 vertical feet to the summit of Ipasha Peak.

Mt. Kipp (8,800)

From the Highline Trail directly above Fifty Mountain Camp there is an easy scree scramble all the way to the summit of this peak. A more interesting route is closer to the sharp west ridge of the mountain, and is approached via the short spur trail that leads to the "Sue Lake Overlook." The distances to this peak from Waterton, Goathaunt, Logan Pass, Swiftcurrent Camp, or Granite Park are so variable that it would be confusing to give them all here. It seems unlikely that anyone would backpack into this region simply to climb Mt. Kipp anyway, so most climbers will simply be hikers who are overnighting at Fifty Mountain.

The West Ridge Route. From the Sue Lake Overlook, traverse a short distance toward the south and enter a steep vertical couloir (class 3). Climb easily upward for more than 100 feet, realizing that you probably could not climb out of that couloir even if you wanted to. The danger from falling rock will surely impress climbers up this route. Above the couloir is a safe ridgetop from which access to the summit is not difficult via the southeast face or via a ledge across the steep north face to the final summit ridge. Views are attractive in every direction, and the descent is a thrilling, speedy scree-run all the way to the Highline Trail.

Thunderbird Mountain (8,800)

From this summit, Bowman Lake and valley are overshadowed by bulky Mt. Carter, with the 500-foot icefall of Weasel Collar Glacier plunging down its northeast flank. In the other direction the Waterton Valley is clearly seen, with monstrous Mt. Cleveland looming above it (Waterton Lake is not quite visible). Hole-in-the-Wall Cirque is concealed by the north ridge of Thunderbird, but an easy scramble to a lower point north of the summit provides a view of it.

The West Face Traverse Route. Distance to summit about twenty-one miles, eighteen miles of it by human trail. (Taking the launch from Waterton to Goathaunt will save ten miles of that distance.) Elevation gained is about 4,600 ft. Class 2 and 3 all the way, except for the steep snow on the glacier (carry ice axes!).

Hike the trail from Waterton Lake to Brown Pass (6,400 ft.) and begin the climb from there. Make an ascending traverse around the east side of the prominent hump north of Thunderbird Glacier ("Logan Glacier" on old maps) to the broad saddle between that hogback and the main mass of Thunderbird Mountain. Cross the west lobe of Thunderbird Glacier and attain the northwest ridge of the mountain near some large rock "fingers" at the base of summit cliffs. The snow is less steep a hundred feet above the lower edge, but ice axes are useful even there. (If you have no ax, carry a slender, sharp-pointed rock that you can drag through the snow with both hands as you slide down the snow, feet first, on your stomach . . . and can stop yourself IF the slope is not too steep or ice-covered.) If the party is equipped for steep snow climbing, the glacier can be traversed all the way, instead of being skirted.

Descend twenty feet below the northwest ridge to the broad scree ledge that extends entirely across the west face of the mountain. Follow the faint game trail for several hundred yards southward along this scree ledge, to the southwest ridge. A saddle there separates the main mass of the mountain from a prominent peak further south. The saddle proves to be one of the most spectacular campsites in the entire park! (Carry water, though!) The game trail continues, traversing the entire south side of Thunderbird Mountain and passing through the prominent notch that is visible beyond it, toward Porcupine Ridge. It offers access to the meadows on the broad saddle between The Guardhouse and Porcupine Ridge, from which mountaineers can work their way to Jefferson Pass (see description of route along the Continental Divide from Canada to Marias Pass).

From the saddle southwest of the main mass of Thunderbird Mountain, study the steep ridge above. Not far east of the ridge, climb the second

Joe Steffen, on Ipasha Peak, examines Mt. Merritt and the Lithoid Cusp—Eric Schwab

couloir (counting eastward from the southwest ridge) until it becomes difficult, then traverse to the 4th couloir and climb to a high scree ledge. This ledge leads westward through the top portions of three couloirs and passes around the southwest ridge and onto the west face of Thunderbird. The interesting dark brown rock there is Purcell Lava, above which there are formations of greenish sedimentary shale. Scramble northward up the great west face, on easy ledges. At last the summit ridge is reached where a deep notch in the ridge affords access to the east side of the mountain. Follow easy ledges toward the north, beneath the east face of the uppermost cliffs, until just beneath the highest peak. A rotten class 3 chimney leads up almost 60 feet, to the summit cairn.

Trapper Peak (7,702)

This remote peak can only be reached after a long approach without very good trails. Mountaineers who are already in the area, either to climb Vulture Peak or to follow the Continental Divide through the wild Jefferson Pass region can hardly avoid scrambling up to Trapper Peak just to get a good look around. The quickest route of approach is via the McDonald Creek trail, from Fifty Mountain Camp. The trail can also be followed up from Packer's Roost in the McDonald Valley for about ten miles to the vicinity of Trapper Peak. (This trail is abandoned and extremely difficult to follow.)

Hike uphill from the McDonald Creek trail toward the peak, passing over a small knob encountered en route. Traverse the east side of Trapper to reach the north ridge, then walk to the summit (class 3 all the way from the trail).

Most climbers will also want to ascend Mt. Geduhn while in the area, and the two peaks are joined by a high ridge which can be traversed. The only difficulty is where the diorite sill (dark igneous rock) crosses the ridge. A descent of thirty or forty feet down the west side of the ridge at that point leads to cliffs that are more easily climbed, then it is easy to regain the ridgetop and continue the traverse.

For description of the views, see those from Mt. Geduhn, which are very similar.

Vulture Peak (9,638)

The Gyrfalcon Lake Route. From this high lake it takes only two or three hours of easy climbing to reach the summit of Vulture Peak, but the approach to Gyrfalcon Lake is difficult and very time-consuming. (See descriptions of the Jefferson Pass Approaches, earlier in this chapter, for details.)

From the lake, the route to the summit is described as follows by Dan Spencer and Dan Maturen: "Climb directly up to the saddle between the main peak and the smaller knob to the southeast (8,361), either across gentle snowfields or along the small ridges that ascend the knob. From the saddle it is mostly class 3 climbing to the southeast ridge, with occasional short traverses needed onto the broad south face until one can scramble back up to the ridgetop."

Other Routes. The Logging Lake Route begins at the north fork road, 4.5 miles downstream from Logging Lake, and the Quartz Lake Route begins at the head of that lake after a lengthy approach. For details of those routes, see the chapter describing climbs in the Northern Livingston Range.

Vulture Peak, South Summit (9,390)

This route was described by Ranger Dick Mattson after he and Ranger Wyatt Woodsmall reached the summit in 1980.

From the saddle southeast of Vulture Peak traverse around, on Vulture Glacier, to the saddle between that peak and the South Peak. One set of tricky cliffs is encountered on the southwest shoulder of Vulture en route. From the latter saddle, head up the north shoulder of the South Summit. At one point it is necessary to drop down onto the northwest side of the ridge (with a rope belay for protection) and traverse until reaching an easy route up to the ridgetop again. The actual summit is then reached via broken cliffs along the eastern side just below the top (class 3).

When Mattson and Woodsmall reached the summit they found a register placed there on July 27, 1958, by Dick Rieman and Don Eberlie. Nobody had been there in the intervening twenty-two years!

Chief Mountain, from the great eastern prairies—NPS Photo

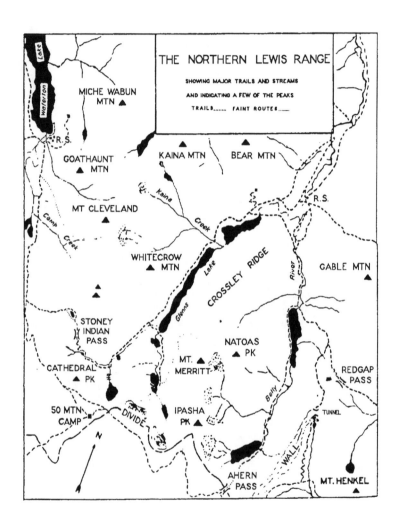

THE NORTHERN LEWIS RANGE

SHOWING MAJOR TRAILS AND STREAMS

AND INDICATING A FEW OF THE PEAKS

TRAILS_____ FAINT ROUTES........

THE NORTHERN LEWIS RANGE

Routes Among the Peaks

The climax of the Northern Lewis Range in Glacier National Park is Mt. Cleveland (10,466), the highest peak in the Northern Rockies of the United States. The Sierra Club mountaineers who placed the register on the summit in 1924 indicated the nature of the climb by writing in their 1925 Bulletin that their consensus was "that the ascent of Mt. Cleveland involves all the difficulties and hardships of the Red Kaweah, Mt. Whitney, and Mt. Shasta combined."

There are other high peaks just north of the border, in Waterton National Park, Alberta, but all are simple one-day climbs. Harder to approach than Cleveland, and only slightly lower, is Mt. Merritt (10,004). Most people who have stood on that summit agree that the view northwest from Merritt is the most beautiful and spectacular of any in the park. A few miles west of the base of Mt. Merritt is lofty Stoney Indian Pass, from which several other peaks are available. These include the Stoney Indian Peaks (9,350), Wahcheechee Mountain (8,477), and Cathedral Peak (9,041).

A lonely outlier far east of Mt. Merritt is Chief Mountain (9,080). Chief is perhaps more interesting from a historic or cultural aspect than from its challenges to mountaineers. Some of the details are included under the discussion of the climb.

Far up in the isolated valley between Waterton Lake and the Belly River Valley there are two other mountains worthy of mention as goals for climbers, namely Miche Wabun Peak (8,861) and Kaina Mountain (9,489).

Routes to the Summits

Mt. Chapman (9,406)

Summit views are impressive, especially toward the southeast and southwest. Porcupine Ridge, with its great eastern spires, extends toward

Mt. Cleveland, while Cathedral Peak and Mt. Merritt are slightly further to the south. Closer at hand the west end of Porcupine Ridge rises into the jagged peaks of The Guardhouse, The Sentinel, and Thunderbird Mountain. In the west, there is an ascending row of great peaks, from Longfellow (far south) past Vulture, Rainbow and Carter, to Kintla, Kinnerly and Long Knife peaks. The lower regions are also photogenic . . . the great basin in which Hole-in-the-Wall Camp is located lies almost at your feet, with long and slender Bowman Lake stretching away toward the southwest below it. Far beyond The Guardhouse the rolling meadows extend to Nahsukin Mountain and beyond, bearing many small glaciers and snowfields.

The West Slope Route.   Hike 8.5 miles up the trail from Goathaunt to Brown Pass (6,500 ft.). Continue for about one-half mile toward Boulder Pass, watching for likely routes above the trail. It is a simple class 3 scramble for 2,900 vertical feet to the lofty summit of Mt. Chapman.

The North Face Route.   (Garth Uibel, of Calgary, has provided the data upon which the following description is based.) Drive to Cameron Lake, twelve miles west of Waterton. Hike the trail eastward, toward Carthew Pass. Leave the trail at the highest point (6,400 ft.), and bushwhack straight south along the large ridgetop, then drop through open meadows toward Lake Wurdeman (5,265 ft.). Good campsites are near that lovely lake. (The lake can also be reached by following the Boundary Trail down to the valley floor, then bushwhacking up to the lake, but the brush and downed timber there is awesome.)

Mt. Chapman rises 4,200 vertical feet directly south of Lake Wurdeman and many routes exist on its great north face, but the most "interesting" route for well-equipped climbers (having ice axes and crampons) follows: From the south end of Lake Wurdeman, climb up the snowfields to small cliffs on the right (west) side of the waterfall. Climb those cliffs to reach the main mass of the glacier. The middle of the glacier is heavily crevassed, and those deep crevasses may be masked by weak "snowbridges" early in the summer (which will not support the weight of a hiker). Circle below the crevassed area, staying south of it, then climb up through the "neck" of the glacier. Above that narrow neck, angle upward toward the southeast while crossing the glacier. Leave the snow and scramble to the top of the ridge, from which it is an easy walk to the summit.

Chief Mountain (9,080)

Although this is not one of the high peaks in the park, views from its

Along the summit ridge of Chief Mountain —Robert Megard

summit are always pleasing. To the west, the lofty peaks which dominate the horizon are Mount Merritt (with Old Sun Glacier covering much of its east face) and its ponderous neighbor, Mount Cleveland. Beyond Cleveland and somewhat hidden by it is the pointed spire of Kinnerly Peak, with the broad pyramid of Kintla Peak slightly to the left of it. The beautiful azure lake southwest of Chief Mountain is Slide Lake. It was formed after 1914, when a tremendous rock avalanche from Yellow Mountain blocked Otatso Creek. Many peaks in the southern half of the park are visible, including thumb-like Mt. St. Nicholas, which appears between Red Eagle Mountain and Going-to-the-Sun Mountain. The endless green prairies are impressive toward the east, dappled with small bright blue lakes. All in all, it is a most delightful viewpoint, in exchange for a relatively small expenditure of energy.

The Indians of this region tell of a Flathead brave who carried a bison skull from the area around Flathead Lake, over the high passes, through the territory of the hostile and bloodthirsty Blackfeet Indians, and up the long slopes to the base of Chief Mountain. Then, even though several accounts were known of Indians who had disappeared on its cliffs, he dragged himself and the bison skull to the summit and began fasting. Legend does not specify which side he climbed but it was probably the

Specter of the Brocken . . . A rainbow formed around climber's shadow cast upon top of cloud—J. G. Edwards

west slope. For four nights he stayed on top, sleeping with the skull for his pillow, and four days he paced the summit, chanting warrior songs and attempting to make peace with the Gods who were to decide his destiny. The Spirit of the Mountain attempted to drive him off of the peak constantly during his vigil, until at last, on the fourth night, it yielded. The Spirit then smoked the peace pipe with the brave and gave him the sacred token which was to protect him so well that no peril of battle or of the hunt could overcome him. He died of old age, the greatest of Flathead warriors, but just before his death he told the young men of the tribe the source of his powerful "medicine."

No white man climbed this peak until 1892, when Henry L. Stimson (Secretary of State under President Hoover and Secretary of War under President Franklin Roosevelt) and two friends, one a full-blooded Blackfoot Indian, made the ascent. Mr. Stimson was reluctant to creep up on the majestic Chief from the rear, so he pioneered a spectacular route up the east face. On top he found the weathered remains of an old bison skull. It had rotted away until little remained but a piece of the frontal bone and stubs which had borne the horns. The party left it on the very summit where they had found it, wedged among the rocks. Apparently no other ascent of the east face was made until 1951, when Alice and Gordon Edwards decided to try it. . . and discovered that it was really quite easy, and very interesting. East face climbs became common during the following years, and Rangvold Kvelstad personally led two or three groups up that face every summer for a least six or seven years. Horace M. Albright, formerly the National Director of the National Park Service, visited with Warren L. Hanna in California and learned of Mr. Hanna's intense interest in the early history of Glacier National Park. He told of meeting Henry L. Stimson in Washington early this century and of discussing the Chief Mountain ascent with him. Stimson was so impressed by Albright's interest that he presented him a copy of his privately-printed book, *My Vacations.* That little book has provided a tremendous amount of information that was not available elsewhere, much of which was incorporated into this guide. For additional data, refer to Warren Hanna's remarkable book, *Many Splendored Glacierland.*

On July 31, 1972, thousands of tons of rock fell from Chief Mountain as the entire northeast corner collapsed. The roar was heard from as far away as Lake McDonald and the dust cloud was seen from Ptarmigan Tunnel and Granite Park. The fragile alpine meadows below were abruptly smashed and squeezed both laterally and longitudinally. The resulting devastation was tremendous, and covered an area at least a half-mile in each direction from the base of the cliff.

Dozens of ascents of the west side of Chief Mountain have been made, including one by the U. S. Geological Survey team (their buried record on the summit was uncovered by climbers in 1976). The Nature Study Club of Indiana placed a register on Chief in 1921, and it was still being signed by mountaineers in the early 1960s. When the boy scouts of Cardston, Alberta made the climb in 1932 they also left a register, and it was still there in 1969. Despite the many climbs during the past ninety-seven years, the lure of Chief Mountain has not faded, and dozens of visitors to Glacier National Park still make it one of their goals each summer. In 1989 a group of thirty-six climbers from the Glacier Mountaineering Society enjoyed a day on the famous mountain's colorful summit.

There are many routes up Chief Mountain, and they are described in the sections which immediately follow. Access to Chief Mountain changed in 1993 when the Blackfeet Tribe closed the Humble Oil Road to all non-tribal members in order to protect the sanctity of religious practices. Please respect this closure.

The Slide Lake Approach. The southeast approach to Chief Mountain should be accessed from Glacier National Park. Drive north from Babb to the "Y" and take the west fork, toward the Chief Mountain Customs Station. After 4.5 more miles, a narrow dirt lane is reached, heading across the fields toward Chief Mountain. That rough lane formerly extended to Slide Lake. You can park at the pullout across the highway to the North or inside the barbed wire gate. Please close the gate behind you. This road is very poor and impassable to low-clearance vehicles. Walk about 4.6 miles down that lane inside the park boundary, to an overlook of Otatso Creek. From the old cabin site there, bushwhack uphill to the narrow meadow below the south face of Chief Mountain. That meadow provides easy access to the southeast corner of the mountain. From the meadow it is also an easy walk to the southwest side of the mountain, with its great scree slopes.

After reaching the base of the cliffs on the south side of the mountain, climbers have the choice of three common routes to the summit: (1) *The Southwest Slope Route* (class 2 and 3); (2) *The Solid Northwest Ridge Route* (class 3 and 4); and (3) *The East Face Route* (which is much more hazardous).

The Southwest Slope Route. Distance to summit about four miles, two miles of it by lane or trail. Class 2 or 3 all the way, except for one class 4 pitch along the summit ridge. Traverse around the south end of the mountain, through small meadows with monstrous boulders (some as large as 15 to 30 feet square). Continue westward until beyond the low cliffs of the southwest corner of the mountain. The entire west slope of Chief is clearly visible from there, and the route of ascent can be studied. Angle up the great hillside of loose talus and scree, seeking to step only on larger slabs that do not easily slip. Either climb to the base of the upper cliffs and then traverse northward, or make a long, long diagonal upward toward the far north end of the mountain. Near the north end, a very deep notch appears in the summit ridge. Scramble up the scree to the bottom of that notch and walk through it to the east side of the ridge. A well-worn climbers' trail leads up to the summit ridge from there. Walk south along the ridgetop, to the summit cairn. A nine-foot-deep notch in the ridgetop is the only obstacle. The descent into that notch involves great exposure, but if care is taken in seeking good handholds, the descent into the notch can be made with safety. (Packs should always be *passed down*, rather than worn while descending, lest the climber be pushed forward by the pack and plunge head-first down the west face of the mountain.) Approach the true summit along the west side of the final cliffs, and ascend the last fifteen-foot pitch with ease.

NOTICE: To avoid the bushwhacking above the Slide Lake trail and the long traverse of the great southwest scree slopes, many climbers might prefer hiking up the trail to Gable Pass (7,200 ft. elevation) and then approaching the Chief by going around the two little peaks west of it.

Chief Mountain with prairie grasses in the foreground—John Mauff

Those peaks are called "The Papoose" and "The Squaw." From the saddle west of Chief, scramble straight up a "climbers' trail" to the great notch near the north end of the summit ridge. A fast descent can be made from the great notch down the scree to the southwest corner of the mountain, and it is then not difficult to bushwhack down to the human trail below.

The Solid Northwest Ridge Route. Distance to summit four or five miles, depending on which of the following routes are selected.

(1) Follow the route suggested above to the southwest corner of the mountain, then make a low traverse of the entire southwest side, below the great scree slopes. From the saddle between Chief and the small peak west of it (The Squaw) a definite climbers' trail leads straight up the scree to the great notch near the north end of the summit ridge. Scramble up that climbers' trail until finding a route across the loose scree to the solid rock of the northwest ridge of the mountain.

(2) A longer, but perhaps easier, route is also possible. From the Slide Lake Trail, hike up to Gable Pass, then approach the saddle west of the Chief by traversing around the two small peaks there (The Papoose and The Squaw). Scramble up the climbers' trail from there until finding a route across the loose scree to the solid rock of the northwest ridge.

Once the solid rock is reached, elevation is gained easily and rapidly all the way to the top of the north end of the summit ridge. At the top of the ridge there is a great steep hump that may deter some climbers. It is easier than it looks from below (class 4) and it is then an easy walk over the top of the hump and into the deep notch in the summit ridge (where the *Southwest Slope Route* is encountered). If some members of the party prefer, they can by-pass the steep hump by traversing southward along the base of the great cliff. In ten minutes they will reach the upper section of the *Southwest Slope Route* and can follow it through the great notch. The route from there to the summit is described under the *Southwest Slope Route*. As mentioned, a fast descent can be made from below the great notch down the scree to the southwest corner of the mountain, and it is then easy to bushwhack down to the Slide Lake trail, below.

The East Face Route. Distance to the summit about three miles, two miles of it by lane or trail. The first ascent of this face was made by Henry L. Stimson, Dr. Walter B. James, and William Kipp on September 8, 1892. They lassoed pinnacles at times, and went up the rope hand-over-hand. For more details, see page 134. Their written account of the climb was so frightening that it was not attempted again until Alice and Gordon Edwards repeated it in the early 1950s . . . and found that it was really not as difficult as anticipated.

Follow the route suggested above to reach the southeast corner of the mountain. Pause there to study the lower 500 feet of the east face. A cone-shaped scree-slope extends far up the cliffs a little further north, studded with a few extrusions of bedrock. Scramble up that cone, which is almost directly below the narrow deep notch in the summit ridge. From the top of the scree cone move to your right and up a steep gully on the south side of the prominent buttress that protrudes eastward from the main cliff face. Proceed up that class 3 gully for about 60 feet, then traverse to the right and pass around the buttress on a scree shelf, to reach a couloir north of the buttress. Ascend that couloir for about 30 feet until it steepens to a cliff, then scramble southward to a ridge that is directly above the basal scree cone. Continue up that ridge for another 20 or 30 feet and then angle northward into a big couloir. The class 4 cliff at the head of that couloir must be climbed, to reach a basin that ascends gradually toward the south. Walk up that basin, to the great transverse scree area that extends across the east face of Chief Mountain. A small cliff divides the scree area into an upper and a lower scree slope, and chimneys further south provide easy access to the upper slope.

After reaching the upper scree slope, walk to the bottom of the steep vertical couloir that extends completely up to the prominent narrow notch in the summit ridge. (Another couloir, a bit further north, is broader, but is rotten and is usually wet and slippery.) The lower section of narrow couloir is easy to climb, but it then steepens abruptly and goes almost straight up. At that place, climb up the north wall for about 10 or 15 feet (class 4) to get entirely out of the narrow couloir and onto a broad, scree-covered shelf that extends around a ridge, toward the north. (That is the last place where it is possible to get out of the narrow couloir). Walk around the easy scree shelf and enter the great diagonal couloir that leads to the summit. It is an easy scramble all the way up that diagonal couloir. Near the top it narrows to an easy chimney where the only danger will be the possibility of falling rocks. Above that chimney it is an easy scramble to the summit.

It is recommended that climbers descend via the *Southwest Slope Route*, which is faster and safer, and will provide them with different interesting experiences. (Do not go down via Gable Pass, however . . . It is much easier to make the long diagonal descent across the scree slopes or to follow the goat trail southward below the great west cliff-face.)

The steep vertical couloir above the broad scree area halfway up the mountain has attracted some experienced rock-climbers with appropriate cliff-climbing equipment. (That narrow couloir is the one described above, on the route to the great diagonal couloir). Lou Wendt climbed up it to the cleft in the ridgetop, but failed to get from there to the summit. He said the first 60 feet above where it "steepens abruptly" were easy, but then the north wall overhangs and had to be by-passed via a 35-foot chimney on the south wall (*Mountain Ear*, 1964). Jim Kanzler and Don Cook (*Mountain Ear*, Oct. 1965) described it as a "very difficult class 5 cliff with a large overhang on the right side." Kanzler wrote: "Proceed to the ceiling of the overhang, traverse left on an 8-inch-wide sloping ledge under the overhang until it may be by-passed, then climb directly up into the couloir above the pitch." From there, they climbed to the deep notch in the summit and then down about 20 feet to a scree shelf on the southwest face. They traversed northward on that shelf, passing below two bad couloirs they avoided climbing. "The shelf gets very narrow, with 900 feet of frightening exposure, and a belay would be useful." They then climbed a class 5 crack above the third couloir to reach the summit. It should be noted that Kanzler has been a professional guide in the Grand Tetons for several years, and his description should be considered with that in mind.

Citadel Spire (On Porcupine Ridge) (7,750)

This prominent Spire is visible from anywhere on Waterton Lake and from many other places in the Waterton Valley. It is more than 350 vertical feet in height, and is a challenge for technical rock climbers. Those who have reached its summit recommend taking along two ropes, rappel slings, several pitons (including angles), some chocks or nuts, and hardhats. Depending upon the route, this is a class 3 or class 4 most of the way if the easiest route is found, or class 5 and 6 for those who seek out the sheer faces. The first ascent was made by Jim and Jerry Kanzler, Ray Martin, and Clare Pogreba in the summer of 1967. The climb was described in a good article in *Summit* magazine, May 1968, with photos by Hal and Jerry Kanzler.

Hike the trail for 2.8 miles from Goathaunt to Kootenai Lake, after riding the launch from Waterton. Wade the Waterton River below the lake, and bushwhack up the side of Porcupine Ridge. The upper third of the ridge becomes easier (less brush). Finally the base of the great spire is reached. The climbers scrambled up the southeast side for about 250 feet of class 3 rock, troubled only by excessive rock-fall. They roped up there and climbed thirty feet around a vertical rib, onto the south side of the spire. With an angle piton for protection they climbed up a large crack of loose rock, placing other angle pitons at twenty-five, forty, and sixty feet up the crack. They worked out onto the face for the next pitch, then up a final roped pitch of about thirty feet of very steep rotten rock. It was only an easy short walk from there to the summit. Pogreba wrote: "The

Yellow Mountain avalanche that blocked Otatso Creek and formed Slide Lake (view from Chief Mountain)—J. G. Edwards

Mt. Cleveland, the highest in the park, rises beyond ten-mile-long Waterton Lake—J. G. Edwards

climb was my first experience with Glacier Park mountains, and I was really impressed. Although much of the rock is rotten, the exposure is tremendous and the scenery beautiful. The interesting possibilities are unlimited."

Jim Kanzler has become one the most proficient alpinists in the United States, and his accomplishments have included first ascents of the north face of Mt. Siyeh and the north face of Mt. Cleveland. Excellent photos in the Summit article showed that north face of Cleveland. Ironically, Jerry Kanzler, Ray Martin, and Clare Pogreba were among five valiant climbers who were swept to their death by a great avalanche on the upper west face of Mt. Cleveland in December 1969. Their loss has deeply affected everyone associated with Glacier National Park.

A second ascent of Citadel Spire was completed on July 21, 1968, via the southeast corner. The climbers were Helmuth Matdies and Dick Wallner (of Whitefish and Kalispell, respectively). The photo in the Summit article by Pogreba was taken looking directly at the southeast corner climbed by these two men. Matdies was formerly a professional climbing guide in Austria, and climbed most of the mountains in that great country before coming to Montana. He wrote that he didn't think the climb would be much fun if they traversed back and forth seeking easy ledges, because the rock where class 3 and 4 are is very bad. "If you take a route of class 5 or 6 the rock is excellent and makes for enjoyable climbing," he said. After reaching the summit, Matdies and Wallner rappelled down the center of the south face on their descent.

Citadel Spire climbers should be well-equipped and know the techniques of rappelling, how to place pitons correctly, how to establish trustworthy rappel slings, and so forth.

Referring back to his experience in Austria, Helmuth often stated that "Glacier Park can offer equally good climbing" and that "the reputation of the peaks in the park deserves to be better."

Mt. Cleveland (10,466)

This massive mountain, the highest in Glacier National Park, has been climbed via several routes. The customary approach is described below as the West Face Route, but there have been many ascents made by way of the Stoney Indian Peak traverse. The east face has been recently climbed at least twice from Glenns Lake, and one memorable assault on the 4,000-foot-high north face was successful. The northwest ridge is easy, up to the extensive scree slope beneath the summit cliffs, but it was necessary to traverse below the cliffs for a mile and a half before ascending further on the West Face route.

Although Mt. Cleveland is only a little higher than several other peaks in Glacier National Park, the summit views impart a feeling that you are vastly above everything else. To the north, south, and west lie all the giants of the Rockies of British Columbia, Alberta, and Montana.

Eastward as far as you can see are the prairies dotted with small lakes, interrupted only by the low Sweetgrass Mountains about 100 miles across the plains. Far to the northwest are peaks in the Purcell and Selkirk ranges, and on a clear day it is possible to see the sharp matterhorn of Mount Assinboine, west of Calgary. Practically every peak in Glacier National Park may be singled out — even such spires as those of Porcupine Ridge now far below. Waterton Lake lies more than 6,000 feet below the summit; at its far end the town of Waterton, the Prince of Wales Hotel is barely visible on a point of land just south of town.

The West Face Route. Distance to summit about eight miles from Goathaunt, two miles of it by human trail. Elevation gained is about 6,100 vertical feet. Mostly class 3, but there may be a few class 4 cliffs high on the west face.

Take the launch from Waterton Townsite to Goathaunt and ask the rangers there for recent information regarding the approach to this great mountain. Register for the climb there.

Hike the Waterton Valley trail for two miles. Camp Creek is the long stream draining the basin between Stoney Indian Peaks and Mt. Cleveland. It is too brushy and forested to follow up toward Cleveland. About a half-mile north of Camp Creek a much smaller stream crosses the trail, and it is there that the route to Mt. Cleveland begins. Walk toward the peak through an open grassy forest for several hundred feet until encountering the elk trail that parallels the foot trail. Follow that trail south and southeast for perhaps two miles, as it gradually angles uphill toward the east and parallels Camp Creek (staying far above the stream and the impenetrable brush and downed timber near the stream). At forks in the trail, always take the lower fork until approaching the head of the valley. Near the head of the valley the trail leaves the forest and traverses a steep slope that is densely covered by alders. Above that slope, toward the left, is the great basin that will provide the best access to the southwest face of Mt. Cleveland. Following that elk trail up to this point has saved four hours and a great amount of energy (as compared with bushwhacking up close to Camp Creek without any trail).

After leaving the forest, the elk trail is soon crossed by a rocky streambed with dense, overhanging alder branches. Walk up that streambed into the great basin not far above the elk trail. A great waterfall drops over the high cliffs that rim the basin, and above the lip of the waterfall there are thousands of vertical feet of scree ledges, small cliffs, chimneys, diagonals, and usually some steep snow-chutes. (Another waterfall is formed by that same stream far below the basin in the morass of brush and windfalls, but is not visible from this upper basin . . . many climbers take a downhill fork in the elk trail and eventually find that waterfall above them, after which their only solution is to fight their way uphill for another hour in order to reach timberline and the correct waterfall.) Most Cleveland climbers establish a high camp in the upper basin, below the waterfall, although conditioned climbers may leave the head of Waterton Lake at 7:00 A.M. and return in time to catch the late afternoon boat back to Waterton that same day. It is far better to make this a two-day climb and enjoy it more fully.

While facing the waterfall, notice the steep scree chute far south of it, extending up through the cliffs to a horizontal shelf that can be followed back toward the north into the great basin above the waterfall. After that, simply scramble straight upward for about 3,500 vertical feet. There are dozens of cliffs, but none with dangerous exposure need be climbed. Often there are easier pitches further to the right. The gully in the center of the face usually has a steep snow chute lingering into late summer. (The gully was the source of the tremendous avalanche that swept five capable young climbers to their death in December 1969.) Just below the top of the great face there is a jumbled mass of black blocks of rock unlike any seen elsewhere in the park, and requiring careful climbing to safely reach the broad ridgetop above. It is a gradual slope up to the summit from the ridgetop, but a most beautiful stroll. For the first time you see the vast prairies, the colorful mountains around Chief, the verdant Belly River Valley with its deep forests, open meadows, and spectacular lakes. A register was placed in a large aluminum box cemented to the summit cairn in 1924, and provided great pleasure for subsequent climbers during the next forty years. Unfortunately, some person or persons were personally offended by the presence of cairns and registers during the 1960s and most of the historically valuable and interesting summit registers disappeared from many summits throughout the park beginning at the time. The register and box on Cleveland were suddenly missing, and the cairn had been levelled. The author searched for remnants of the aluminum box at the base of the great north face for more than an hour, but without success.

An article by John J. Mazza, "The Sierra Club Ascent of Mount Cleveland," was published in the *Sierra Club Bulletin* in 1925, pages 156-157, with three plates.

The Stoney Indian Route. In 1937 Norman Clyde led a group of Sierra Club members to the summit of Cleveland via the west face, then decided to take a chance and try a different route down. (The club campsite that night was to be at Stoney Indian Lake, and the climbers disliked the idea of going all the way down to Waterton Valley, then hiking up to Stoney Indian for the night.) Clyde wrote of the descent as follows: "From the saddle south of the summit we then followed a horizontal course along shelves to the east of a line of sharp pinnacles. Although it looked somewhat difficult and hazardous from a distance, it proved to be a hike of comparative ease and safety . . . the imposing form of Mt. Merritt sweeping grandly upward from the valley and surmounted by striking cliffs and pinnacles towering over four thousand feet above the lakes. After proceeding along the narrow benches about two miles we crossed through a notch to the west side of the sharp line of sharp peaks, dropped down a chimney for several hundred feet and then continued along the ledge to Indian Pass."

In 1969, Jerry DeSanto and Fred Goodsell, rangers at Waterton, provided details of the route in the opposite direction, as follows. Climb northeast from Stoney Indian Pass to the base of the first peak. Go east about 150 yards to a break in the cliff that leads up through the dark igneous sill and the white marble strata above it. Traverse west and head north along the west slope of the peak. When directly below the saddle between the southern-most Stoney Indian Peak (just traversed) and the highest peak just ahead, climb up to that saddle and cross to the east slope of the peak. Stay above the grey limestone layer that extends all the way to the upper slope of Mt. Cleveland. Although not difficult (class 3), the ledge is only three feet wide in places. A broader scree ledge parallels it about seventy-five feet higher. It takes energy to traverse these loose-surfaced slopes, but no technical ability. Late in the summer there will be no water from Stoney Indian Pass to the snow near the top of Mt. Cleveland, so hikers should carry a canteen or two.

The Southeast Face Routes. Ranger Terry Kennedy and his brother, Dan Kennedy, reached the summit via this new route on July 19, 1983. Hike from Highway 89 at the Chief Mountain Customs Station on the Canadian border 6.2 miles to the Belly River Ranger Station. Continue for about four more miles, to the foot of Glenns Lake, then leave the trail and begin bushwhacking up Whitecrow Mountain Ridge. The brush was heavy and slowed progress so much that the Kennedys bivouaced at 6,600 feet elevation on the ridge. The next day they traversed to Whitecrow Glacier and crossed it, to reach the southeast face of Mt. Cleveland (elevation 7,600 ft.). Most of the remainder of the 2,800 vertical feet was on steep snow and ice, requiring great skill and stamina. They reached the summit at 5 P.M.

An easier route of the southeast face is that via Whitecrow Lake (6,147). Hike about 2.5 miles further up Glenns Lake, to the stream that drains Whitecrow Lake, then bushwhack uphill for 1,500 vertical feet to reach the lake. Next, scramble 2,800 vertical feet up steep scree and a few hazardous cliffs, to reach the ridgetop. The last 1,700 feet above the ridgetop is just a walk up the great south ridge of Cleveland.

The North Face. This face was ascended in 1971 by Minnesotans John Patten, Bud Nelson, Denny Morren, Jake Wenzel, and Brian Ranke. They traversed around the final pyramid to reach the summit. In 1976 Jim Kanzler, Terry Kennedy, and Steve Jackson went up the entire north face, including the summit pyramid, in 18 hours. The base of that 4,000-foot wall is approached from the old Goathaunt Lookout trail. Leave the trail at about 5,200 feet and traverse toward Mt. Cleveland on faint game trails, while gradually climbing. Beyond the steep hillside of meadows go about 100 feet up the bare ridge overlooking the fork in the stream (Cleveland

Creek), walk down the stream and cross it. Trails lead up the south fork, which very quickly becomes a dry streambed during most of the summer and is an easy walk to the great talus slopes beneath the 4,000-foot north face. The wall is not nearly as sheer as it appears from a distance, and the deep couloir that is just above the talus and steep snow is not difficult (but it is a giant funnel for rocks falling from above). Higher on the face there are dozens of gullies, spires, ridges, ledges, and steep scree slopes. It looks easier than it actually is, but remember how FAR it is to the great shelf that crosses the face not far below the summit! This is a major mountaineering project, and should not be taken lightly. A very strong game trail (elk as well as goats and sheep use it) angles upward to the right (west) to the northwest ridge of Cleveland and traverses the entire west face of the mountain. Lest anyone considers this as a shortcut to the climbing route there, be assured that it is not. The trip to the foot of the north face and back to the Ranger Station will take most of the day, and it is mostly tiresome cross-hill scrambling on very faint traces of trails. It is, however, an interesting trip, especially if you continue onto the northwest ridge for a look around from the 7,000-foot level.

Goathaunt Mountain (8,641)

Views from this peak are especially impressive looking up Olson Creek to Brown Pass and the surrounding mountains. The extensive meadowlands south of Jefferson Pass are splendid, and the view down onto Waterton Lake is unique. In the deep valley northeast of the peak Miche Wabun Lake sparkles amid acres of bright green grassland. Undoubtedly, however, the object of greatest interest to most climbers will be the north face of Mt. Cleveland, which is completely visible from this vantage point. Distance to summit about three miles, half of it by human trail. Elevation gained is about 4,400 vertical feet. Class 3 all the way.

The Ridge Route. From Goathaunt, at the head of Waterton Lake, take the old trail that goes steeply uphill to the site of the old fire lookout on a broad grassy shelf overlooking Waterton Lake. A dry streambed is encountered there that extends all the way to the top of the ridge, 1,600 feet above. It is a tiring climb to the ridgetop, but well worthwhile. Walk south along that bright red ridge, to a broad saddle of fine red scree. South of that saddle the ridge becomes precipitous and it is easier to traverse along the right (west) side of the ridge for awhile and then regain the top beyond the steep cliffs. The ridge suddenly turns eastward and approaches the base of Goathaunt Mountain. Work out onto the south slope of that mountain and scramble easily up to the ridgetop near the summit.

The peak can also be climbed from the faint game trail that traverses south from the old fire lookout trail at about 5,200 feet then climbs as it parallels Cleveland Creek along the open but steep slopes far above the creek. When directly beneath the summit of Goathaunt, walk up the great brushy and grassy slopes for more than 2,000 vertical feet, to the summit. (Obviously, this is not as pleasant or interesting as the other route!)

ADDED ATTRACTION: From the summit of Goathaunt it is easy to follow the high ridge toward the southeast for half a mile, to the sheer spire formerly called "Hawk's Bill" (elevation 9,167). The upper 100 feet requires ropes and pitons, but even without reaching the actual summit most climbers will find this a pleasant and interesting ascent. It was unclimbed until July 1987, when rangers Chuck Sigler, Dick Mattson, and Dan Wirth succeeded in reaching its summit. Because clouds carried by prevailing southwest winds are often "captured" by massive Mt. Cleveland, leaving this peak in the sunshine, the rangers have proposed the name "Rain Shadow Peak" for this impressive spire. They point out that there is already a "Hawk's Bill" on the map of Glacier National Park (west of Lake Francis). For further details of the route, see "Rain Shadow Peak" later in this chapter.

Kaina Mountain (9,489)

The South Ridge Route.   Distance to summit about twelve miles, 9.5 miles of it by trail. Elevation gained is about 4,500 vertical feet from the trail. Easy class 3 all the way, but it is a long way up! First known ascent: William Wanser and his father DeWight ("De") Wanser, in August 1931. (De and his wife, Berith, managed Crossley Lake Tent Camp from 1924 to 1938, so Bill Wanser practically grew up there.)

Hike from Chief Mountain Customs Station to the head of Cosley Lake, and bushwhack up Kaina Creek. Ascend the ridge on your right to the unnamed peak (elevation 8,374 ft.), then walk northwest along the spectacular summit ridge for another mile to the top of Kaina Mountain.

Far below the summit, Kaina Lake is nestled in a high cirque with a tremendous waterfall plunging from its outlet down into Kaina Creek. In the other direction (northwest) is beautiful Miche Wabun Lake, with the jagged spire of Miche Wabun Peak above it. Much of the north face of Mt. Cleveland is seen here in profile, although partially concealed by the 9,167-foot "Hawk's Bill" in the foreground.

The Northeast Valley Route.   Distance to summit about sixteen miles, eleven miles of it by trail. Elevation gained is about 4,300 feet. First known ascent: Charles Fisher, Hal Kanzler, and Thomas Sweeney, June

High clouds cast shadows on the face of Goathaunt Mountain on Waterton Lake. Mount Cleveland is in the background —Hileman

30, 1962. Follow the approach described to Miche Wabun Mountain in this guide. When the stream is reached that enters the North Fork of the Belly River from the valley between Bear Mountain and Kaina Mountain, follow it up the valley for three miles. It is a lush, verdant valley of open meadows blanketed with wildflowers. From near the headwall of the valley, follow a good goat trail up a steep ridge that leads to the major southeast ridge of Kaina Mountain. The easy walk along that ridge to the summit requires another hour, but there will be no complaints about the scenery!

Kaiser Point (9,996)

This is the name suggested for the peak adjoining Mt. Cleveland on the northeast. The name is that which was given to Mt. Cleveland by the U.S. Northern Boundary Survey of 1872-76.

Distance to summit about fourteen miles, ten miles of it by trail. Class 3 and 4. First known ascent: July 14, 1985, by Rangers Chuck Sigler and Dick Mattson, who provided the following details: Hike from Chief Mountain Customs Station to the Stoney Indian Pass Trail. Leave the trail at Kaina Creek, between Cosley Lake and Glenns Lake. Bushwhack (!!) up into Whitecrow Basin by traversing the north side of Kaina Creek, then Whitecrow Creek. A good campsite is in the last tall spruce trees near the head of this valley. From these trees, climb north through a band of cliffs,

149

then traverse north and west into the drainage between Kaiser Point and the unnamed rounded peak to its southeast. A challenging set of cliffs there can be climbed in the drainage and waterfall area. (This would be difficult earlier in the season, when wet.) Above the cliffs, climb easily into the saddle and angle up toward the northeast side of the ridge that leads to the summit. The broken cliffs just below the summit are not difficult. Great views all around, with tremendous exposure in the northwest and northeast!

Mt. Merritt (10,004)

The views from this great mountain are probably the most beautiful and spectacular of any in the entire national park. Immediately to the north-

Mt. Merritt, with Old Sun Glacier, viewed from goat trail to Redgap Pass—John Mauff

A sea of peaks fills the skyline northwest from Mt. Merritt —J. G. Edwards

Looking Northwest From Mt. Merritt. (1) Stoney Indian Peaks; (2) Wahcheechee Mtn.; (3) Pyramid Pk. (in foreground); (4) Kootenai Pk.; (5) Mt. Carter; (6) Kintla Pk.; (7) Mt. Peabody; (8) The Guardhouse; (9) Kinnerly Pk.; (10) Porcupine Ridge; (11) Northeast Ridge of Thunderbird Mtn.; (12) Long Knife Pk.; (13) Mt. Chapman.

west, beyond the head of Glenns Lake, is Mt. Cleveland, the highest peak in the park. Farther eastward a portion of Cosley Lake is visible, beyond which the broad grassy valley of the Belly River winds out toward the prairies. South of the Belly River, Chief Mountain rises abruptly from its pedestal at the near edge of the prairies. In the immediate foreground the long, slender finger of Natoas Peak (the eastern summit of the Merritt Massif) points toward the red mountains near Redgap Pass. A diagonal trail climbs the red slope from Elizabeth Lake and disappears into Ptarmigan Tunnel. Beyond the Ptarmigan Wall and Pinnacle Wall are (left to right) Mt. Henkel, Allen Mountain, Mt. Siyeh, Mt. Wilbur, and Mt. Gould. Due south, beyond Ipasha Peak, is Mt. Cannon, and northwest from it is the snowy Livingston Range. Almost west of the top of Merritt, on a bench high above Margaret Lake and directly beyond it, Sue Lake snuggles against the sharp shadow of Mt. Kipp. Far beyond, in the Livingston Range, is ice-clad Vulture Peak, while further north rises the massive pyramid known as Mt. Carter, flanked on the left by Rainbow Peak. All these are impressive, but even better is the vista just west of Mt. Cleveland. Kintla Peak (another broad pyramid) is closely flanked by the matterhorn of Kinnerly Peak. Long Knife Mountain cleaves the clouds a little farther north, and a jumbled series of sharp spires, pinnacles, and jagged ridges marvelously adorns the gaps between the major summits. Of all the mountaintop views in Glacier National Park, this is likely to be the most pleasing to the beholder, especially early in the season or after a summer blizzard has embossed the stratified cliffs with a beautiful tracery of white on a background of red, green, and buff-colored rock.

The Mokowanis Lake Route.   Distance to summit about eighteen miles, fourteen miles of it by human trail. Elevation gained from the trail is about 4,600 vertical feet. Class 3 all the way, if correct routes are chosen (possibly some class four pitches just north of the great saddle). First known ascent by Norman Clyde, July 28, 1924. From the Chief Mountain Customs Station, on Highway 89, hike 6.5 miles to the Belly River Ranger Station. Continue for 2.5 miles to Cosley Lake, then through dense forests for another four miles to the head of Glenns Lake. Pause to study the mountain and observe the climbing route through the large cirque (A) and up to the saddle (B). From the head of Glenns Lake take the trail toward the left, past White Quiver Falls and up a faint path for almost another mile to Mokowanis Lake.

Beyond Mokowanis Lake there are many elk trails leading toward Margaret Lake. Follow the best of those to the open meadows within sight and sound of the high unnamed waterfall just below Margaret Lake. Leave the valley there and ascend the meadows toward the north and east, following well-worn elk trails. Many trails lead in that direction but it is difficult to describe which one is best. The trail passes around the great northwest shoulder of Mt. Merritt (below the cliffs) and enters the huge cirque on the northwest side of the mountain (A). Another way to locate the best trail is suggested by Pat Caffrey, as follows: Just beyond Mokowanis Lake, look up and study the slopes below the great upper cliffs. Three large drainage gullies extend down from those cliffs to the valley floor. The northern one is vegetated near the bottom (the other two are mostly gravel). Ascend the vegetated gully, which soon becomes easier as it reaches the steep meadows that extend entirely across the mountainside there. Not far below the huge cliffs the dirt-sided gully broadens, and a game trail crosses it. Traverse on that trail, which becomes very distinct as it goes northward. It crosses the meadows on a sloping shelf about twenty feet wide and eventually approaches the northwest cirque.

Enter the great basin, or cirque, and walk through the small trees, shrubs and boulders toward the saddle (B) above the steep wall at the head of the cirque. It is a steep climb up to that saddle, but the lower half is an easy scree scramble. Above that there are three couloirs extending upward. All are passable, but the one on your right is easiest. Follow it up to the algal reef, then traverse thirty feet to the right to climb through the reef, then return to the couloir and scramble easily up to the saddle. A good alternative route with fewer cliffs is shown in the diagram: It begins with a gradual ascent from the west side of the great basin, leading to the algal reef below the saddle. (No difficulty, but it is a long hillside traverse.)

Pass over the saddle and onto the (hopefully) sunny southern slopes high above the middle portion of Old Sun Glacier. Convenient goat trails lead upward along the south side of the great east ridge. Be sure to stay off the steep snowbanks unless equipped for safe ice-climbing (or using a solid rope belay). It is easy to skirt all the snow, by climbing to the ridgetop and approaching the summit dome from there. The two peaks of the summit are similar but the one on your right (north) is slightly higher. (It only takes an extra five minutes to stand atop both of them!)

The Old Sun Glacier Route. This climb begins below Old Sun Glacier, which can be approached via several routes (most likely through Ptarmigan Tunnel from Swiftcurrent Camp or via Belly River Ranger Station, from Chief Mountain Customs Station). Nothing worse than class 4 on the rocks, but great danger on the steep snow (which has a maximum slope of fifty degrees). Essential equipment: 100 feet of good rope, ice ax for each climber, and crampons for at least half of the climbers. Essential knowledge: correct self-arrest technique, correct ice ax belay technique, and correct way to hold ice ax while ascending and descending steep snow. First ascent of route: Craig B. Sutter, John G. Replinger Jr., and Charles E. Wilson, August 27, 1971 (all from Illinois).

After the approach of twelve to thirteen miles, leave the Helen Lake trail where it crosses the stream draining Old Sun Glacier into Belly River. Follow up that drainage, using the dry overflow area north of the stream. Camp near the two parallel streams entering from Old Sun Glacier.

Walk up the open meadow south of those two streams, then up the diagonal scree passageway through the red cliffs, jump the three small streams just above a prominent waterfall, and continue northward along the broad scree-covered ledge. Pass around the long ridge and into the north basin (which usually has two large snowfields). NOTE: That long ridge looks promising, but becomes impassible at the top, so avoid it. Walk up on or near the large snowbanks, while observing the great waterfall far above, and studying the two large rock "thumbs" beside it. (The south thumb has two prominent white blotches near its base, and the climbing route traverses just below those blotches.) Scramble up the scree and class 3 cliffs, staying to the right of the right-hand rock thumb, until about seventy feet below the great gray "reef" of fossil algae. At that elevation seek an easy traverse across the base of the two thumbs, leading to the ridge just above the lip of the great waterfall. Several ledges extend part-way across, but only one goes all the way, and it bears some green vegetation.

Strap on crampons and prepare for serious use of ice axes from here on. Walk straight up the steep snow between the ice cliff on your left and the cliffs on your right. Above that steep area, traverse toward the south on relatively gentle snow slopes far above the steep ice-fall area. A large transverse crevasse (the "bergschrund") blocks the way upward. Walk around the south end of that bergschrund and climb up the steep snow between it and the large rock outcropping above it. It is an easy walk up toward the summit, bearing slightly toward the right. After leaving the snow, scramble up easy scree slopes to the summit dome.

Miche Wabun Peak (8,861)

The Southeast Face Route. Distance to summit about twelve miles, 10.5 miles of it by trail (via Chief Mountain Customs Station, Three-mile Camp, and N. Fork Belly River Trail) or a mile less if the poorly marked route is taken from the Belly River Bridge on Chief Mountain Highway 22.6 miles from Babb. Elevation gained is about 3,500 vertical feet. Class 4 (possibly class 5) pitches occur half-way up the southeast face, requiring ropes, pitons, and slings. First ascent: Charles Fisher, Hal Kanzler, and Thomas Sweeney (of Columbia Falls) June 29, 1962.

There are two possible approaches to Miche Wabun Lake: (1) Hike from the Customs Station toward Belly River Ranger Station for three miles to Three-Mile Camp, ford the Belly River and go three miles northwest to the northeast ridge of Sentinel Mountain, then descend for a mile to reach the North Fork of Belly River and carefully ford it; join the other approach route on the north shore of that river, then ford the river again and walk 3.4 miles up the south shore to Miche Wabun Lake; (2) Hike from the Belly River bridge mentioned above for 5.4 miles to the warden's cabin, follow the northwest side of the river for a little more than a mile and join the trail discussed above, ford the river and walk 3.4 miles up the south shore to Miche Wabun Lake.

Wade the outlet of the lake and plod straight up the timbered slope to open hillsides plainly visible from below. Continue up the scree slope and angle to your left around an early summer snowbank. Climb up to a good bench below sheer cliffs and traverse to your right along that bench for more than fifty feet. Climb diagonally up toward the left (south) to a smaller ledge, and traverse twenty feet to the south along that ledge. A major vertical chimney extends up from there, which should be ascended with care (and possibly with pitons for safety). At the top of the chimney are pitons and slings used by previous parties for rappelling down, but do NOT trust them without thoroughly testing them (they often loosen during the winter freezing and thawing of cliffs). Above the chimney, continue to the left for a few feet and climb onto the diorite bench near the knob on your left. Make a climbing traverse across the diorite cliffs, toward the north ridge, reaching it at a skyline notch just above a small pinnacle. Walk up to the summit along the west side of that north ridge. Be very careful of poor rock on this peak, for everything seems to be loose, and the strata slope downward toward the east. (Based on description written by Hal Kanzler in the *Mountain Ear,* May 1963, pp. 4-7, illus.)

The Northwest Face Route. Distance to summit about four miles, none of it by human trail. Elevation gained is 4,665 feet from Waterton Lake. Plan on spending at least seven hours on the ascent and four hours returning to the lakeshore. Class 3 climbing, except for class 4 in a chimney near the top.

Travel by boat to Street Point (the Street Creek alluvial fan) on the east shore of Waterton Lake. From Street Point follow the Street Creek drainage for about two miles, into the large cirque northwest of Miche Wabun Peak. This struggle involves difficult bushwhacking along the north side of steep-walled Street Creek gorge. Once in the cirque you are above timberline and have a clear view of the northwest face of Miche Wabun. Climb the ridge on the west side of the cirque (from the top, there are great views of the south end of Waterton Lake). From this ridge, follow a goat trail proceding south and east toward the peak, until reaching the middle of the northwest face of the mountain. At that point the trail becomes very narrow, with tremendous exposure. Scramble upward from there until about fifty feet below the black diorite (metagabbro) sill. There is another goat trail there, which parallels the sill and leads to the north or northeast ridge of the peak.

A *good* rope belay is recommended here, while climbing up the next 100 feet of class 4 pitches. Follow an "open book" route slightly to the right of the north ridge, up to the diorite sill. The sill at that point consists of fragmented rock, and it is an easy scramble from there to the summit.

The first ascent of this fantastic route was made on August 1, 1982, by Chip Youlden (of Billings) and Dan Downey (of Kalispell), both of whom were on the boat crew at Waterton Lake that summer. They provided the details upon which this description is based.

Natoas Peak (9,360)

The Southwest Ramp Route. A very long, but easy, class 3 scramble. Distance to summit about eighteen miles, fourteen miles of it by trail. Elevation gained is about 4,200 vertical feet from the trail below. First ascent: William P. Matthews and Bruce D. Murphy, August 16, 1964. The climbers made the following comments: "The most difficult aspect of the climb was the arduous scramble to the top of the saddle above Old Sun Glacier. At the summit we built a cairn and therein put a Band-Aid box containing a notebook. The summit of the mountain is less than a yard wide and the exposure was devastating to our morale. On two sides of the summit the faces drop off 1,000 feet or more, and the eastern aspect is the knife edge ridge! Total time for the ascent was six hours, descent four hours."

Rain Shadow Peak (9,167)

An approach to this impressive spire is mentioned under the Goathaunt Mtn. description. A more direct approach was described by the climbers who made the first ascent of the peak in July 1987. They are Rangers Dick Mattson, Dan Wirth, and Chief Ranger Chuck Sigler. The distance to the summit is about 3.5 miles, one mile of it by human trail. The final cliffs are class 5, so carry good rock-climbing equipment!

Hike the trail from Goathaunt Ranger Station to the Goathaunt Overlook. Continue by game trail to Goathaunt Ridge and traverse up to the saddle above Goathaunt Lake, then follow the ridge around to Goathaunt Mountain. After admiring the spectacular views from there, walk up the ridge toward the southeast and traverse around the south and east faces of Rain Shadow Pk., below the sheer cliffs.

Climb up through the red cliffs to the diorite sill (dark igneous rock). A crack leading upward from the sill is the most logical route up the next pitch. The first thirty feet of the crack is topped by a small overhang. The rock is unstable and good points for protection are hard to find. Forty feet of easier climbing leads to the ridgetop, and a good belay/rappel point. From there a short pitch with poor protection goes up to a ledge on the east face. Work north on narrow ledges with great exposure, then up a couple of chimneys to the summit. Great views from there, but many climbers will entertain worries about the descent.

This abbreviated account is based on the description provided by the first ascent climbing team.

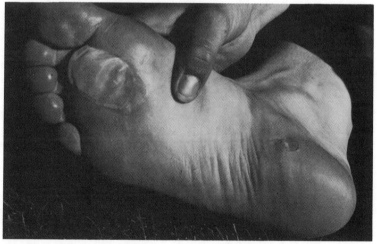

Don't hike too far on the first day—J. G. Edwards

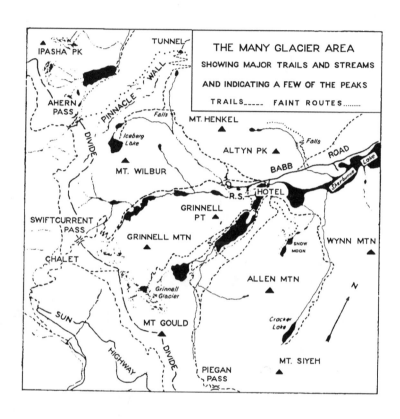

THE MANY GLACIER AREA

SHOWING MAJOR TRAILS AND STREAMS

AND INDICATING A FEW OF THE PEAKS

TRAILS_____ FAINT ROUTES........

THE MANY GLACIER AREA

Routes Among the Peaks

Although some people may believe the Many Glacier area is too barren, windy, and cold, for most mountaineers and serious hikers there is no more satisfying region in all of North America. There are several great valleys radiating from the Swiftcurrent Lake environs and at least ten other lakes nearby, many of them excellent for fishing. The greatest attraction of the region, however, is surely the encircling array of mountains. All of the peaks normally climbed in this vicinity are easily reached in a single day, and there are good facilities for eating, sleeping, buying supplies, enjoying entertainment, doing laundry, taking showers, and receiving medical attention at the conclusion of those climbs.

The most challenging peaks in the area are Mt. Wilbur (9,321) and Mt. Gould (9,553). The recommended route up Mt. Gould begins from Logan pass, but Mt. Wilbur is usually climbed by way of that wonderful east face that is so impressive from the Swiftcurrent Valley. Rising directly from the shore of Swiftcurrent Lake opposite the hotel is a beautiful red spire known as Grinnell Point (7,600). It is really the east end of a long ridge that abuts the Continental Divide between Grinnell and Swiftcurrent valleys. The highest point of Grinnell Mountain (8,851) may be reached via various interesting routes described in this chapter.

North of Swiftcurrent Lake there are two bright red mountains, named Altyn Peak (7,947) and Mt. Henkel (8,770). Either can be climbed easily in half a day, and each offers fine views of the Lewis Range and the Many Glacier area. A foot trail was constructed to the top of Altyn in 1922, but only small portions of it can be found there now. It was still being used by naturalist-guided parties in the 1940s.

Southwest of the hotel, rising far above the shore of Swiftcurrent and Josephine lakes, is Allen Mountain (9,376), a deceptively high peak requiring considerable endurance to climb. To the east, a trail from the hotel leads up the great U-shaped valley between Mt. Allen and Mt. Wynn, continuing to Cracker Lake in the shadow of the sheer 4,300-foot north face of Mt. Siyeh (10,014 ft.).

Three major valleys converge at Swiftcurrent Lake. The Josephine Lake Valley has a great trail to Piegan Pass, Preston Park, and Going-to-the-Sun Road, and a shorter trail climbing easily up to Grinnell Glacier.

Mt. Gould, in the background, is three miles beyond the Many Glacier Hotel—Brian Kennedy

The Swiftcurrent Valley trail makes a memorable ascent to Swiftcurrent Pass, then angles down to Granite Park Chalets, where it connects with the Garden Wall Trail from Logan Pass (7.6 more miles). Northward from Granite Park the trail continues for twenty-two rugged miles to Waterton Lake, where scheduled launches carry grateful hikers eight miles further to Waterton, Alberta. The Wilbur Creek Valley is the location of the very popular 4.5 mile trail to Iceberg Lake (where floating "snowbergs" are never out of season). Along that trail a north fork goes uphill just beyond Ptarmigan Falls, and passes through Ptarmigan Tunnel (a man-made short cut to the Belly River Valley, that was completed in 1931). After descending the tremendous slopes of brilliant red rock the trail reaches the Belly River Valley. From there it is not far to the highway at Chief Mountain Customs Station, while in the opposite direction the trail goes fourteen miles to Waterton Lake, via spectacular Stoney Indian Pass.

Because of the convergence of so many great valleys and ridges in the Many Glacier area there are a great many off-trail hikes and scrambles that are challenging, in addition to actual summit climbs. Several of these are mentioned briefly below, but more detailed descriptions are presented in the following pages.

(1) Hike up the trail through the valley above Apikuni Falls. When the trail ends, cross the small streambed and go straight on uphill toward the west, staying north of the cliffs. From the top, walk downhill through the forest to beautiful Natahki Lake for lunch. The return to Swiftcurrent Lake is usually made by walking up the steep meadows to the saddle west of Altyn Peak and running down nearly a thousand vertical feet of loose scree to the meadows near the road.

(2) Reach the old Josephine Mine by way of the eastern or southern routes to Grinnell Point, which are described in detail in this guide.

(3) Follow the high game trails from Many Glacier Hotel to Snow Moon and Fallen Leaf Lakes. This is also the recommended approach to the summit of Allen Mountain. (See descriptions of routes on the following pages.)

(4) The easy climb from near Red Rock Falls up to Shangri La, the great bench lake basin northeast of Mt. Wilbur. It can be reached more easily from Iceberg Lake. The routes are described in this guide.

(5) With hardy companions, follow good game trails from the top of Mt. Wynn up the long, long ridge to the summit of Mt. Siyeh. (Siyeh is described under the St. Mary Valley Area in the guide because most routes up Siyeh begin from Going-to-the-Sun Road.)

(6) Traverse northward from the trail just east of Swiftcurrent Pass via a goat trail along the bottom of the diorite sill on the east face of Swiftcurrent Peak. That trail leads down into the basin containing North Swiftcurrent Glacier. From the north end of that basin, Iceberg Peak can be climbed (see details under that peak). Other alternatives are to climb the ridge west of the north end of the basin and walk up the long north ridge to the fire lookout or descend from the ridge down to the highline trail a few hundred feet below.

(7) Leave the trail east of Swiftcurrent Pass and descend steep meadows into the basin north of Swiftcurrent Glacier. Pass around the left end of the big moraine and enjoy exploring that small glacier. (See descriptions of route to Grinnell Mountain from there, and routes to Granite Park Chalet and the Grinnell Glacier Overlook.)

(8) Hike the incredible goat trails that begin near Ptarmigan Tunnel. One trail can be followed all the way to Ahern Pass, and the other goes over the ridge between the north end of the tunnel and Redgap Pass. From that Pass, other good goat trails lead around Mt. Seward, to the summit of Yellow Mountain, and to the high ridge overlooking Poia Lake. (See details provided elsewhere in this guide.)

THE HOLE IN THE PINNACLE WALL

Persons looking at the Pinnacle Wall in late afternoon often notice a bright spot about thirty feet below the top of the ridge which, upon close examination through binoculars, proves to be a large hole extending all the way through the wall. Many climbers have climbed up the wall to examine that hole. The route is described below. The distance to the hole from Swiftcurrent Camp is 4.5 miles, four miles of it by human trail. Elevation gained is about 2,500 vertical feet.

Hike four miles up the Iceberg Lake trail, gaining a thousand feet in elevation. Beyond Ptarmigan Falls, pass through the forested area and continue across the open slopes to the permanent stream that crosses the trail. Beyond that stream the trail soon passes through an area of bright red cliffs. Leave the trail just beyond them and walk up the steep grassy meadows to the great scree slopes above. Enter the largest, longest streambed that extends down from the great scree slopes and follow it up, taking advantage of the solid footing there. When the streambed fades, scramble upward toward the left to reach the ridgetop near its lowest point.

Walk southward on or near the top of the ridge until reaching the large pyramidal spire. Descend ten or fifteen feet down the west side of the spire and then traverse to the great rock rib that extends down that side of the spire. The best route around that rib begins at a gentle, almost flat portion of the rib. Scramble up to the ridgetop again south of the pyramidal spire and walk along that ridge until it steepens abruptly and cannot be climbed. Traverse around the east side of the wall on easy scree slopes, horizontally, until reaching a position directly below the famous hole in the wall. Even though the hole cannot be seen from below, the overhang above it can, and the wind can usually be heard whistling through it.

The thirty-foot climb up to the hole is hazardous because it is steep, the rock is quite rotten, and a falling climber would likely roll hundreds of feet down the mountain over those abrading cliffs, gathering momentum all the way. Roping climbers together will not do much good, for there are no belay positions. If the leader climbs up very carefully and drops a rope for use by the other climbers, he can provide a good belay from a secure position inside the hole.

The hole in the wall is about four feet high, six to eight feet across, and perhaps five feet through. Views from there are no better than from elsewhere along the Pinnacle Wall, but it is a very interesting place to see, and with a wide angle lens it is possible to photograph other people in the hole, with the distant mountains in the background in focus too.

Joe Steffen, who has climbed to this hole dozens of times and led many parties up by various routes, describes a more precarious route for the descent. He likes to climb along the west side of the ridge, south of the hole, to reach Iceberg Notch. The route involves class 4 ledges with great exposure.

PTARMIGAN TUNNEL TO AHERN PASS
VIA PINNACLE WALL GOAT TRAIL

Distance along goat trail about four miles. Class 2 and 3 most of the way, but a slip off the trail would be fatal in many places. Carry ice axes before July 4th, *and water after July 4th!* This hike should interest persons wishing to enjoy a circle route from Swiftcurrent Valley to Ptarmigan Tunnel then to Granite Park and return to Swiftcurrent via Swiftcurrent Pass (twenty-four miles). If the shortcut over Iceberg Notch from Ahern Pass is taken it is only sixteen miles and is usually completed in nine hours.

Hike the human trail to Ptarmigan Tunnel to begin this trip. Just east of the south entrance to the tunnel, scramble to the ridgetop above it (be very careful not to knock rocks onto the trail). Follow the excellent goat trail westward on that ridge, up to the bottom of the HUGE cliff and then around onto the great scree slope on the north face. (Shun the goat trail that goes onto the north side of the ridge earlier, for it ends in awful cliffs.) The trail heads west after passing around the cliff base, providing great views of Mt. Merritt, Elizabeth Lake, and the Belly River Valley. Soon it descends sharply to pass around the head of an awesome couloir, then continues to the northwest corner of the Ptarmigan Ridge. Views become even grander at that point. Far to the south, above Helen Lake, is Ahern Pass, the southern terminus of this remarkable trail.

From the corner, the trail ascends southward, skirting the base of the great cliff. After 100 yards a bright red cliff perhaps twenty feet high is approached. Carefully climb up and over that little cliff, then traverse around the head of the large, very steep couloir beyond it (this is the only reasonable way to get across that couloir, so you cannot miss it). After crossing over the couloir the trail heads for the sheer vertical shoulder beyond and passes around it above hundreds of feet of exposure. It continues into a smaller steep couloir, then around another seemingly impossible shoulder. After traversing two or three couloirs and the intervening ledges and shoulders (all very photogenic), the trail reaches a steep scree slope and leaves the cliff faces. Shortly the scree slope ends, overlooking a very broad basin of scree and small cliffs, above which rises a spectacular spire on the ridgetop. That "Ptarmigan Spire" is actually the

Majestic Mountain Sheep rams, dwarfed by Mt. Wilbur—Hal Kanzler

abrupt north end of the Ptarmigan Wall, and the next objective is to reach the saddle below the spire. The easiest way is to climb straight up to the saddle, rather than getting into the loose rock in the great basin. The hillside is easy class 3 walking, with good ledges and fairly solid footing all the way. In fifteen or twenty minutes you will gain about 300 vertical feet and be on the ridge (saddle) overlooking Ptarmigan Lake. The usual lunch spot is there, with remarkable views of the lake, Ptarmigan Tunnel, ridge after ridge of bright red rock, and (to the northwest) Mt. Merritt and Old Sun Glacier looming above blue Elizabeth Lake.

At the base of the great spire the "Main Trail" to Ahern Pass begins. Walk along the west wall beneath Ptarmigan Spire on the very well-maintained goat trail that heads directly toward Ahern Pass. There is really no need for further clarification of the route from this point, for nobody could ever get off course. The wide, deep trail goes on and on, skirting the tops of frightening cliffs and clinging to small ledges with an overlay of loose rocks and pebbles. To avoid carelessness, consider the result of a simple slip on one of those pebbles. Soon a small snowbank is reached (until late summer) that might produce water. Just beyond that is the best picture-postcard view of Helen Lake with your climbing party on a scree shoulder overlooking it. The steep exposure ends and the trail heads around a great basin of scree, going toward an enormous cliff that apparently blocks further progress. In the hanging valley below the cliff there is green vegetation, red rock, and good water. The water drops down toward Helen Lake as a large waterfall leaping down brilliant red cliffs (unfortunately not well seen from above). Halfway across the great upper basin of scree, the trail passes through a gap in a vertical strip of scrubby alpine fir thickets. A descent into the hanging valley is easy from there, but a more important feature is the deep notch in the ridgetop above you. If a quick escape from the long goat trail is necessary, scramble up to that notch and straight down the other side (angling southward to avoid the basal cliffs there) to the Ptarmigan Lake trail. You can reach the road in an hour and a half from this point on the goat trail!

Continuing along the goat trail, south of the thicket of trees, the trail gradually descends and heads straight toward that 2,000-foot wall . . . *and then traverses completely across it for several hundred yards!* Lichen-covered cliffs overhang the tenuous trail most of the way, and a foot or two from the trail edge is the lip of the abyss. It may be disconcerting to see Helen Lake, nearly 3,000 feet below, directly beside your foot as you make each carefully placed step along that narrow trail, but it is probably a sensation that most mountaineers will enjoy. (Photo on p. 168)

West of the great cliff face the trail finally reaches a broad scree

Two views looking south along a goat trail from Ptarmigan Tunnel to Ahern Pass. The pass is visible in the lower picture —John Mauff

shoulder from which there is a clear view of Ahern Pass, about another half-mile away. It is an easy but boring scree walk, with the trail staying 100 feet below the bottom of the great upper cliffs all the way to the snowfield that guards the pass. The ancient trail that was scooped out by Colonel Ahern's men in the late 1800s, so they could take horses from Helen Lake up and over the pass, is still visible. It joins the goat trail near the bottom of the snow field and you suddenly realize you are on a much broader trail.

Before venturing onto the snow without ice ax support, take a long, sharp-pointed rock in each hand, to hopefully stop you in case of a slip on the steep snow. Walk carefully up the snow, kicking deep steps where possible and stepping on pieces of rock that may be embedded in the surface. Following the leader here makes it much safer for all who follow in his or her footsteps. Stay away from the cliffs above the snow, because huge ice caves melt out *beneath the surface* near those cliffs. Avoid getting too far from the cliffs, however, for the slope steepens a little further downhill and death would result from a slide down the snow and off the cliffs at the bottom. If a reasonably cautious route is followed, there is little danger on the walk up to Ahern Pass.

From Ahern Pass it is about five miles by trail to Granite Park Chalets and nine miles more to Swiftcurrent Cabins (or seven miles to Logan Pass, or three miles to the highway below the Chalets). From Ahern Pass, most climbers will want to scramble up 500 feet of scree to see the view from Iceberg Notch and some will then descend to the trail near Iceberg Lake. See the description of that descent elsewhere in this guide before attempting it. The correct route is not very dangerous but the rest of the great wall may be impossible without ropes and pitons.

PTARMIGAN TUNNEL TO REDGAP PASS
VIA GOAT TRAIL

This short cut route to Redgap Pass involves a beautiful, high-level approach to a remote pass that normally is reached only after a tiresome fifteen-mile hike from Swiftcurrent Camp. It is a wonderful limbering-up trip prior to making a long climb, or a relaxing day for mountaineers between climbs. The route is class 3 all the way, unless snow conditions are hazardous (in which case it may be impossible to make the northern descent safely without ice axes and rope belays).

Hike five miles by trail from Swiftcurrent Valley to Ptarmigan Tunnel. From the north end of the tunnel, study the red ridge that rises above the

Along the goat trail from Ptarmigan Tunnel to Ahern Pass. Four miles of pleasant "exposure" for mountaineers—John Mauff

trail northeast of the tunnel. Redgap Pass lies directly beyond the highest part of the ridge. South of that high point there is a broad notch in the top of the wall that is very obvious when viewed from Ptarmigan Tunnel. The climb to that notch is easy, via a series of long diagonal scree ledges.

To reach the easiest climbing route, hike down the trail north of Ptarmigan Tunnel until the great red wall suddenly is replaced by a green rock formation. The trail curves westward there and passes around a tongue of scree beneath green rock outcrops. Climb up that scree, then angle up to the left beneath steep rock walls until reaching a broad gully.

Descend a few feet and cross the gully, then go horizontally to the north until reaching the obvious diagonal route that extends to the broad notch at the top of the ridge. WARNING: Be very careful not to dislodge rocks that may fall on the trail below. Before venturing onto this wall, either from above or below, look carefully for people on the trail, then do not move in any direction while they may be below you.

From the notch, take time to admire Kennedy Creek and Poia Lake. In the opposite direction incredible Mt. Merritt, bearing Old Sun Glacier, steals the show, but the "Lithoid Cusp" between Merritt and Ipasha Peak is also spectacular (as of 1990 it is apparently still unclimbed). Looking northeast you can clearly see Redgap Pass, but sheer cliffs prevent an approach via the east side of the intervening ridge. Instead, traverse the west side of the ridge, on a marvelous goat trail that follows ledges horizontally across the entire face, then descends into a deep notch further north. A look down through that notch toward Redgap will surprise and delight even the most jaded mountaineer. A sensational goat trail drops 400 feet at a sixty-degree slope as it clings to the precipitous northeast face of a huge, bright red cliff. If snow completely covers any part of this steep trail it may be wise to turn back, unless equipped for rope belays and ice-climbing. If the snow has melted, however, a ten-minute descent leads to a broad saddle, and a good game trail traverses the gentle slopes from there to Redgap Pass. The hike from Ptarmigan Tunnel to Redgap Pass should not require more than an hour and a half, and the return trip will take about an hour.

Beyond Redgap Pass there are other destinations that can be reached via game trails from the pass. A faint trail passes around the west side of Mt. Seward, to the tremendous broad ridge between Seward and Gable Mountains. A much better trail traverses the southeast side of Mt. Seward, to "Seward Saddle," overlooking the head of Otatso Valley. Because of the bright red color of the scree all around Seward Mountain and the pleasant gradient of those game trails, history professor Dick Schwab suggests that they be referred to as "The Red Scree Strolls." Beyond Seward Saddle an excellent goat trail continues eastward to the very summit of Yellow Mountain, and a side-trail near the summit goes along a ridge to the rounded peak overlooking Poia Lake. (See the Yellow Mountain route described elsewhere in this guide for details.)

The Many Glacier Hotel, seen from Iceberg Notch. Shangri La is visible in the hanging basin far above Iceberg Lake—John Mauff

SHANGRI LA

The short trip into this charming isolated basin that hangs from the north wall of Mt. Wilbur and Bullhead Point is always interesting and the destination is always enjoyable. Most climbers will approach Shangri La from the eastern cliffs, have lunch by the lake, then climb over the ridge to descend to Iceberg Lake and hike back to the road via the Iceberg Lake trail. The following descriptions are written with that approach in mind.

Hike up the trail toward Redrock Falls from the Swiftcurrent Camp area. At the top of the long, gentle hill, the east end of the long ridge is seen just above the trail. Scramble easily to that ridgetop and walk on faint trails and through open groves of aspen and pine for about a mile, until emerging into an open hillside of meadows with the stream just below toward the south. (Another approach is up that stream drainage from where it crosses the trail near Redrock Lake, but bushwhacking cannot be avoided there.) Cross the steep meadows and walk up the hillside beside the snow chute, to the red cliffs above.

Instead of going out onto the steep snow, climb the deep little gully in the cliff just north of the edge of the snow chute (class 3). Turn right and continue up a rocky route to a large grassy shelf further north. Walk uphill, angling back and forth to find the easy routes, but when the next big cliff is encountered go to the far south end of it (almost beneath the waterfall) and climb twelve to fifteen feet up a steep but broken rock couloir just north of a thicket of alders. Now, traverse north again for sixty to seventy feet to a deep cleft that angles up between cliffs toward the right to another broad grassy slope. Above is the last cliff. It forms a continuous cliff band about twenty feet high, which is quite sheer except far to the north. Look for the safe route up, via a steep gully with good holds all the way, near the north end of the grassy shelf. A pleasant stroll through open woods and small meadows soon brings hikers to the small lake. On the way, a brief search will locate the old miner's claim marker (a large, tall, inscribed rock) and the nearby canal that he dug.

To continue to Iceberg Lake, walk straight up to the bare skyline ridgetop west of the lake. From that ridge there are breathtaking views of Iceberg Lake, full of floating cakes of snow and ice, and usually reflecting the cliff walls in its still, blue surface. Views to the east are also impressive, with Swiftcurrent Lake and the Many Glacier Hotel just "over the ridge" from Shangri La, and Lake Sherburne stretching eastward between densely wooded ridges almost out to the great prairies beyond. Walk around onto the west side of the scree-covered ridge, then angle southward until above open scree slopes. It is a fast run down the slope, frequently made faster if a final glissade down to the lake shore on the large snowfield is still possible.

Hikers who are at Iceberg Lake might wish to attempt a return to Swiftcurrent Camp via this lake basin. It is easy enough to enter Shangri La from Iceberg Lake, but more difficult to find the route down through the cliffs and to bushwhack down to the trail. If you intend to try it, be sure to notify someone who is hiking down the trail so they can report your name to the rangers, or at least wait in the camp or the cabins or hotel until you return and notify them. A simple broken leg on this route could become fatal if nobody knew you were stranded up there!

Many climbers will find themselves in this marvelous area with time available to do something else before descending into the valleys. An obvious choice is to climb to the top of the great ridge along the south side of Shangri La. Although not named on topographic maps, that ridge is well-known to mountaineers by the name "Bullhead Point." Although not very high above sea level, it provides an interesting scramble as well as spectacular views. From the summit, a quick descent can be made to the Swiftcurrent Valley trail near Redrock Falls. The details of four routes are given below, under Bullhead Point. Three of those routes begin in the Shangri La Basin. On the descent, it is more pleasant to go down into the great basin directly east of Wilbur's summit, thence down the valley to the meadows that lead to the foot trail, rather than the more direct "South Slope Route."

THE SKYLINE EXPERIENCE
FROM MT. WYNN TO MT. SIYEH

This route is a great one for climbers and mountaineers who enjoy off-trail travel and long ridge-walks. Begin by climbing Mt. Wynn, as described elsewhere in this guide. From that summit, examine the long ridge that joins the mountain with distant Mt. Siyeh. Notice how far away Mt. Siyeh appears to be! Actually, it is only about 5.5 miles via the ridgetop game trail, and can be reached easily in three or four hours. Nobody has ever been eager to return to Mt. Wynn, so it is wise to plan descending the south side of Mt. Siyeh to Preston Park and hiking down to the highway at Siyeh Bend (another 3.5 miles from the summit).

From the top of Mt. Wynn follow the faint game trail toward the east, across a great scree-covered plateau, thence southward on and near the ridgetop. Pause to admire the perfectly circular little lake east of the ridge. The trail becomes much stronger as it traverses the 8,200-foot contour around the west side of the next scree dome and descends gradually to a

The final ridge up the east side of Mt. Siyeh —John Mauff

high saddle. Beyond that saddle the trail climbs steeply up a long ridge, entering the great red Grinnell Argillite formation. When the route is blocked by huge red cliffs, a short detour to the right leads to an easily climbed cliff and the ridgetop can be regained. Soon a much higher rocky ridge rises ahead, which must be traversed along the east side. The slope is very steep, but is covered with tall, soft grass and has marvelous little streams of icewater splashing down from the permanent snowfield atop the ridge. After resting and drinking, climb straight up to the ridgetop and head south again. A very cliffy hillside must be ascended to reach the higher ridge (9,190 ft.), and it looks difficult . . . but turns out to be a walk-up, following easy scree gullies and ledges all the way without difficulty. From the top, the trail to Mt. Siyeh is fantastic! The long gentle rise through the meadows is made even more interesting because you are almost as high as the top of Going-to-the-Sun Mountain, while strolling through flat meadows of flowers! Soon the cliffy pyramid of Cracker Peak (9,833 ft.) is approached, and an old mining claim is passed at the top of the scree ridge with a great view down onto Cracker Lake. It is not possible to traverse around Cracker Peak because of sheer cliffs on its southwest face, so just plod up to the top and follow the west ridge on toward Mt. Siyeh. Fortunately, the appearance of Cracker Peak from a distance is misleading, and there is not actually much of a descent between Cracker Peak and the last steep ridge leading up to the summit of Mt. Siyeh. Stay slightly south

173

It is nearly 4,000 vertical feet down north face of Mt. Siyeh
—John Mauff

of the steep ridge and climb easy class 3 pitches all the way to the top of the mountain. (Of course, it is also possible to traverse the south side of the summit pyramid and walk easily up the gentler west slope to the top of Siyeh.) "Well worth the trip" will surely be the thoughts of the mountaineers as they sign the register and admire the sea of peaks in every direction . . . and the deep blue of Cracker Lake 4,000 feet below the cairn.

WARNING: Before attempting to descend from the summit to Preston Park, see the description of the south slope route in the "St. Mary Valley" chapter. There are dangerous cliffs if you go too far to the west. From Preston Park, hike south a mile to the trail junction, then follow the descending trail to the road just a pleasant mile further. The highway is reached at "Siyeh Bend," where the road crosses Siyeh Creek (elevation 5,850 ft.). Hopefully arrangements will have been made in advance for transportation back to Many Glacier from there.

SNOW MOON LAKE BASIN (6,700)

This beautiful basin is occupied by two idyllic mountain lakes and many acres of steep snowfields. There are no trails near it, except game trails (but those trails are nearly as distinct as many human trails in the park). The two routes to the basin are described below.

The High Traverse Route. Distance to the basin is about 1.5 miles from Many Glacier Hotel, none of it by human trail. Elevation gained is about 1,800 vertical feet. Class 2 and 3 all the way, *unless* the trail is blocked by steep snowbanks. (This route should not be attempted before July 4th unless the hikers are carrying ice axes and know how to use them.)

From the Many Glacier Hotel parking lot, hike straight up the ridge toward Allen Mountain. After leaving the shrubs and small aspens the route goes up a very solid rock formation along the top of the ridge. When the ridge approaches the forest descend a short and very steep trail down the cliff toward the east and follow it for more than ten feet to another ridge further east. The trail heads uphill again near that ridge but soon angles to the west and follows up another extensive bedrock outcrop for about 150 feet through the trees. It then enters the dense forest and climbs steeply uphill until reaching open hillsides and extensive talus slopes. Mark well the place where you emerged from the forest, so you can find it during the descent.

Plod up 500 vertical feet of loose talus, following well-worn trails that zig-zag up toward the huge cliffs far above. History professor Dick Schwab refers to this section as the "Dread Scree Stroll." Stay west of the smaller cliffs that crop out on your left. Near the top of the slope it is easiest to climb up the deep stream gully in the center of the talus slope. At last the bottom of the great cliffs is approached, and a very well-worn game trail is encountered which traverses the entire mountainside just below the cliffs. That trail goes all the way to Snow Moon Lake, but the following details may be helpful.

The trail ascends rather steeply as it heads east along an exposed rock stratum and soon enters the forest. After a steep switchback there, head east along the base of the great cliff. There are no difficulties if the snow has melted off the trail; however, before July 4th the route may be very dangerous because of steep snow in the broad couloir that must be crossed soon after entering the woods. When it is dry and bare, that couloir presents no problem. It is about thirty feet wide, with dozens of very small ledges extending across it to the continuation of the good trail on the far side, but it steepens to a sheer cliff below the crossing, with considerable exposure. Any slip on snow there would send the hiker over the cliff, with serious injury or death resulting. Consequently, if there is snow in the couloir, climbers should take the alternative route, which passes below that sheer cliff then traverses eastward for two or three hundred feet and climbs up to join the main trail again. To reach the lower trail, back-track toward the west from the couloir, until above a steep slope of soil that can be walked down. Angle from the bottom of that descent down to the level of the cliff bottom. The crossing at that lower level has no exposure (except for exposure to rocks falling from above). After the upper and lower trails join, cross an open hillside covered with grass and herbs and climb slightly while approaching a bare ridgetop from which views open up toward the south and east. A perfect place for lunch! There are great views back from there which reveal the incredible steepness of the face just crossed, as well as the grandiose setting of the hotel and the lakes in Many Glacier area. This may well be the final destination of some hikers, yet it is only an easy half-hour further to the lake basin from there.

Descend the trail toward the south (toward the big waterfall, called Schwab Falls), and walk along the excellent game trail that parallels the base of the impressive overhanging cliffs. Do not loiter there, for large masses break off frequently. When the trail reaches a small streambed (far above the waterfall) scramble up to an easier place to cross it. The red ledges beyond the streambed lead to a grassy slope up which the trail continues. Walk up it to a fine red scree-slope that overlooks the big stream that drains the entire lake basin. Where the trail forks there, take the upper fork through the fringe of trees. Suddenly Fallen Leaf Lake comes into view, with a huge snow-rimmed basin of red rock beyond it. Climb uphill for a good look at Snow Moon Lake (further west), then hike the trail along the north side of Fallen Leaf to reach the upper lake. The time required to reach the lakes from the hotel should not exceed three or four hours, and the return (with great scree-running) is easily accomplished in about half that time.

The Bushwhack Route. This route to the lakes basin is much less scenic, and involves half an hour of uphill bushwhacking. Hike the Cracker Lake trail from the hotel parking lot until nearly to the fork in the trail at Cracker Flats. Look up the vegetated slopes toward Mt. Allen and locate the place where the high sheer cliffs suddenly become much lower. A distinct broken area extends up through the cliffs there, providing a class 3 route up through them to the forested basin beyond. Bushwhack up the steep hillside to that break in the cliffs and follow the game trail through it and into the basin. From the top of the break the game trail goes along the bottom of a huge talus slope, near the upper edge of the forest. As the large waterfall is approached, the trail climbs steeply up a broad scree-covered ridge. After passing the elevation of the top of the falls watch for the trail of the High Traverse Route which approaches along the cliff-base from the north. See that description for further details of the approach to the lakes.

Routes beyond the lake basin. Several other objectives may tempt climbers after they reach the lakes. A few possibilities are:

(1) Ascend the broad green ridge southeast of the lakes, to get a glimpse of Cracker Lake. While still walking through those meadows you will be higher than the top of Mt. Altyn or Grinnell Point, and can see all the great peaks in the north and northwestern parts of the park. Reach that high ridge by either angling up from the head of Snow Moon Lake or going straight up from the stream below Fallen Leaf Lake (where the game trail begins).

(2) Scramble up the scree to the deep notch in the ridgetop west of the lakes, then to the top of the north peak. (A descent can be made to the human trail directly below that notch, but there is too much bushwhacking on the route and if you angle to the right you end above awful cliffs.)

(3) From the notch mentioned above a natural ledge can be followed into the basin far above Snow Moon Lake (but it is not an easy walk).

(4) With ice axes, climb the steep snowfield directly toward the (invisible) summit of Allen Mountain, up to the great gap in the mountain ridge above all that snow. The summit can be reached from there in another hour, and the views are superb!

(5) Follow alternative 1, then continue up the rocky east ridge of Mt. Allen to the highest point visible from the lakes . . . and along the summit ridge toward the west from there. (See the description of this route to Allen Mountain in this guide for more details.)

SWIFTCURRENT GLACIER BASIN
(AND GRINNELL MOUNTAIN)

From Swiftcurrent Valley, hike toward Swiftcurrent Pass for about six miles, while climbing nearly 2,300 vertical feet. Pass beside the great waterfall high on the headwall, then the trail climbs eastward around "The Devil's Elbow" and soon crosses the stream that drains Swiftcurrent Pass. After a long switchback it crosses the stream again, then goes uphill toward the top of the pass. About a hundred feet up the hill, leave the trail and look through a break in the fringe of trees on the left side of the trail. When the "correct" break is reached, you will find a steep gravel hillside that can be walked down to the stream in the meadow not far below. (That stream and meadow can also be reached by leaving the trail beside the great waterfall downhill from the Devil's Elbow and climbing straight up the steep cliffy slope beside the stream for about ten vertical feet. Although the climbing is only class 4, a slip there would likely result in a roll down the slope and a plunge over the cliff by the waterfall.)

Walk up the gentle meadows beside the stream as it curves toward the south and approaches a large moraine. Instead of climbing that moraine, descend beside it and find a safe route around it. The great snow-filled basin of Swiftcurrent Glacier lies directly before you as you pass beneath the lower end of that large moraine, and can be safely explored for many hours. From that dwindling glacier it is possible to scramble over the ridgetop toward the west and descend to the trail to Granite Park Chalets, but most mountaineers will seek a higher destination. The summit of Grinnell Mountain is easily accessible from the glacier, and is a very interesting climb.

Walk across the entire snowfield, climbing gradually as the east edge of it is approached. When the talus slope east of the snow is reached, scramble straight up the slope to the saddle above it (8,100-ft. elevation). Walk up the long, gradual ridge toward the east for about half a mile, while gaining over 700 vertical feet, and stand triumphantly on the very highest point of Grinnell Mountain.

The views are great in every direction, with lake-filled valleys 4,000 vertical feet below on each side of the summit and Grinnell Glacier at the head of the cirque to the south. Hundreds of square miles of pastel-colored prairies extend to the eastern horizon, while all the great snowy peaks of the Livingston and Lewis ranges glisten in the sunshine. While enjoying this lofty summit in August 1982, Rolf Larson was digging around the bottom of the cairn and uncovered a flat metal box containing an old register. It had been placed there, with an appropriate installation ceremony (it stated), on August 12, 1919 by Dr. Frank B. Wynn and two friends from The Nature Study Club of Indiana. Dr. Wynn and various friends also placed registers which this author enjoyed finding on many other mountains in the park (Jackson, Gould, Edwards, Gunsight, Chief, Reynolds, Going-to-the-Sun, etc.), but during the 1960s some person or persons routinely destroyed the cairns on most peaks in the park and either destroyed or took away all of those sacred records of the preceding forty years. After Dr. Wynn died on Mt. Siyeh, the Park Service named Mt. Wynn in his honor. The register on Grinnell Mountain was also signed by: Norman Clyde in August 1923 (with Fred Herz and Lee Stopple, of the Sierra Club); by George C. Ruhle (Park Naturalist) on September 7, 1929 (twenty years before he wrote his *Guide to Glacier*); by Leo Seethaler (*The Glacier Guide*) in 1929; by climbers from Germany, Switzerland, Oxford University, Princeton, etc.; by a large Sierra Club party in 1937, guided by Norman Clyde (his third time up); by James Dyson (author of *World of Ice*, voted best non-fiction book in the U.S. in 1962) on July 31, 1937; and by six climbers guided by G. M. Kilbourn (the trail guide at Many Glacier) on July 23, 1940. Such records were always a thrill to read during the years before they were destroyed! To protect this register from that fate, Ranger Larson and his friends (Robert Horodyski and Jane Edwards) decided that it should be taken to park headquarters for safe keeping. Good xerox copies are available at headquarters, so please leave the xerox copy that has been placed on Grinnell Mountain for others to enjoy.

The descent toward the Grinnell Glacier trail from the saddle or from the south side of the long ridge is very hazardous, but below the very top of the mountain the cliffs give way to steep scree slopes extending to the meadows far below (stay west of the big snowfield). When the cliffs are reached, just above the meadows, traverse to the west on game trails until finding easy pitches that will give access to the trail below the small meadow.

Routes to the Summits

Allen Mountain (9,376)

Because it is so broad and so close to the road it is difficult to realize just how big this mountain is. Climbers who struggle up to its summit, however, will always remember that it is HUGE . . . and will also cherish the surprisingly spectacular views they saw from the top. Grinnell Point (seen from Allen Mountain) is so far below that it nearly escapes notice, as does the Pinnacle Wall. Just beyond that wall Mt. Merritt looms up, with Old Sun Glacier completely visible from this elevation. The massive peak north of Merritt is Mt. Cleveland, highest in the park. Nearer at hand, just beyond the long east ridge of Grinnell Mountain, Mt. Wilbur rears its formidable east face. In the west, much of the snowy Livingston Range is visible, while the gaudy red and yellow ridges north of Sherburne Lake attract the eye. There are great views in every other direction also, including the north face of Mt. Siyeh, the east face of Mt. Gould, and large expanses of snow and ice beyond Logan Pass. Many climbers will be especially impressed by pictures they can take of Many Glacier Hotel from this summit, with Snow Moon and Fallen Leaf lakes in their bright red basin on the right side of the same photograph! It is indeed well worth the effort expended to reach that exalted peak.

The Northwest Slope Route. Distance to summit about 3.5 miles, one mile of it by human trail. Elevation gained is about 4,500 vertical feet. Class 3 all the way.

Hike the high trail above the south side of Lake Josephine, from Many Glacier Hotel. Slightly more than a mile from the hotel the trail leaves the dense forest and emerges into a great avalanche slope covered with alders, mountain ash, and maple. In the 1950s it was an easy walk up that hillside to the base of the cliffs above, because a recent avalanche had scoured the slope clean of vegetation. By the 1970s the slope had become so brushy that it earned a reputation as one of the worst "bushwhacks" in the area (even descending it had become a nightmare). Climbers who still wish to try the route are advised to stay in or beside the streambed below the big waterfall, for easier walking. A distinct game trail follows the base of the cliff from the bottom of the waterfall eastward and into the outlet of the great hanging valley on the north side of Mt. Allen.

An alternative approach to that hanging valley exists about a quarter of a mile east. It is more difficult to describe, but climbers who carefully inspect the hillside from a distance can see the route and hopefully can find it when they reach that area on the high trail from the hotel. The approach involves the alder-covered hillside where a small permanent stream flows down beneath overhanging alder boughs and crosses the trail a few feet east of the junction with a human trail that descends to Josephine Lake valley. Far above the alder thickets there is a large ravine of bare soil that extends up to the base of the cliffs that are above all of the trees. Late in the summer it is possible (but grim) to clamber up the wet streambed, crouching or crawling up under the overhanging alder branches. If there is still too much water flowing there, ascend a much narrower, but dry, "overflow" streambed a few feet to the east. This one extends about

Mt. Siyeh's humps rise above Mt. Allen, in view from Grinnell Mountain
—John Mauff

halfway up to the large area of bare soil, and from there on up the climbers must be ingenious and perseverent. (This is still MUCH better than the old route up to the large waterfall!) When the dirt slopes are finally reached, walk easily uphill into the broadening basin, then angle toward the west. A game trail parallels the top of that large denuded area and it is an easy hike along that trail to the outlet of the great hanging valley mentioned above.

Regardless of which approach is used in order to reach that hanging valley, walk up the east bank of the stream toward the great slopes of scree and cliffs. Upon reaching the scree slopes stay north of the steep streambed and scramble up the unstable slope for 3,000 vertical feet to the left end of the long summit ridge. It is then a pleasant 200 yards along that ridge to the highest point.

It is unfortunately more difficult to find the large open hillside if seeking to descend this route without having first ascended it. The following description should help. After walking down the great hanging valley and reaching the heavily-forested "drop-off" into the Swiftcurrent Valley, traverse eastward through scattered trees and open grassy slopes, staying not far below the bare cliffs that rise above all the vegetation. Two game trails lead in that direction, either of which may be followed. A small "open hillside" below the vegetation is soon encountered, but it does not extend very far downhill. Continue eastward to the much larger open area of exposed soil, sparse vegetation, and (frequently) a large snowbank. This open area extends very far downhill, and can be walked down easily until it narrows into a streambed that drains it. Continue downward on easy but steep slopes along the east side of the streambed until finally reaching extensive alder thickets. From that point downward it is easiest to go twenty to thirty feet east of the streambed, and descend a rather steep grassy hillside (angling down toward the left) until it ends in alders also. From there, either struggle over to the main stream and go down the rocky streambed beneath dense overhanging alders, OR enter a very narrow dry streambed directly below the grassy slope and only a short distance east of the main streambed. Alders overhang the narrow streambed and there are obstacles like slick rocks, branches and tree trunks in the gully, but it is not more than fifteen minutes down to the trail and it is easier than descending in the larger streambed.

The Snow Moon Basin Route. This is the more highly recommended route, because it is much more pleasant, interesting, and scenic than any other route on Allen Mountain. Follow the route described elsewhere in this guide to reach the Snow Moon Lake Basin from Many Glacier Hotel. Walk up to the great rounded ridge southeast of the lakes in that basin, and follow the game trail up the ridge for 1,600 vertical feet to the high steep cliffs that ultimately block the ridge. (The trail begins by the outlet of Fallen Leaf Lake, but can be reached from the head of Snow Moon Lake via a great walk across the meadows.) Finally, the rounded ridge becomes

The Many Glacier Hotel, seen from Allen Mountain. Snow Moon and Fallen Leaf lakes are visible in the great basin on the right
—J. G. Edwards

cliffy but the game trail becomes even more distinct. Follow it up the bright red gullies and slopes for a few hundred feet more, until suddenly tremendous sheer cliffs totally bar any further progress. The trail crosses a broad scree shelf toward the west and fades away. After traversing for perhaps 100 feet from the ridge, study the great cliff above the scree. A very steep "break" (not quite a shallow gully) offers a questionable way up for twenty or thirty feet, but even climbers who have gone up the route before may find it difficult to believe that the break is actually the route. Searching elsewhere across the cliff soon impresses climbers that the "break" is the only possible route, and a great cairn of rock directly below it helps to confirm that fact.

Carefully climb the first thirty-foot pitch, one person at a time, and the leader will then begin to express more optimism. The break becomes easier to climb and angles slightly to the right (but still is going almost vertically). It continues up semi-chimneys and steep, narrow, shallow gullies, always with good handholds and footholds, and even beginning climbers should feel completely secure on the route. It goes, and goes, and goes! The major danger will be from dislodged rocks, so behave accordingly. Either climb very close together, in groups of not more than two or three, OR stay a hundred feet apart so the lower climbers have time to take cover if a rock falls toward them. The climbing is either class 3 or 4, but there is very great "exposure," which should make all climbers extremely careful. The danger of falling might be equated with the danger of falling from a 300-foot-high stepladder!

The great break can be ascended all the way to the top of the ridge, although it is safer to leave the break near the last cliff and traverse to the east on a scree shelf that leads around the ridge and onto the south side of the ridge. It is then an easy scramble, without exposure, staying just below the ascending ridgetop, for hundreds of feet. As a great snowfield further south on the east face is approached, the entire mountainside becomes a steep scree-slope with small cliffy outcroppings, and in another half hour the east end of the long summit ridge is reached. Josephine Lake comes into view and the jagged western horizon, and it is a glorious stroll along that last gentle ridge for several hundred feet to the highest point of Allen Mountain. (First ascent of this route was by John Mauff, Keith Hollister, and Alice, Jane, and Gordon Edwards, in 1968.)

The Snow Moon Notch Route. This alternative approach from Snow Moon Lake is much closer and faster than the ridge route described above, but may require ice axes in early summer. Ascend 1,400 vertical feet up the great snowy slope due south of the head of Snow Moon Lake and then angle up toward the west in order to reach the great notch in the north ridge

Relaxing on the brilliant red summit of Mt. Altyn, with Swiftcurrent Lake and the Many Glacier Hotel below—J. G. Edwards

of Mt. Allen (elevation 8,100 ft.). Pass through the notch and into the great northern scree basin, then scramble upward for another 1,100 vertical feet to the east end of the summit ridge. The stroll along that ridge to the summit is uncomplicated. Climbers who have ice axes and know proper glissading techniques, AND who have just climbed up the snowfields above Snow Moon Lake may enjoy the 1,300-foot glissade down the snow to the lake on the descent. (It is always dangerous to glissade down slopes that have not been recently climbed, because of lack of knowledge of ice conditions or bergschrunds or cliffs that are hidden from above!) Of course, climbers without ice axes should never attempt to descend via this great notch unless there is a bare passageway entirely across the top of the slope to the meadow-covered slopes further east. This route is not nearly as interesting as the other Snow Moon Basin route that is described above, and it actually seems to be much more exhausting than that route.

The Cracker Lake Route. This rather unimaginative route presents no difficulties other than fatigue. Hike from Many Glacier Hotel to Cracker Lake (about 5.5 miles) while climbing about 1,000 vertical feet. Walk around the head of the lake to its west shore, then scramble upward on scree and small cliffs for 3,200 vertical feet. More than halfway up, follow the ridge along the south side of the large snowfield then angle toward the north while climbing and finally reach the east end of the gentle summit ridge. The descent via this route is infinitely easier than the ascent!

Altyn Peak (7,947)

From the top of this very convenient viewpoint, hikers will enjoy a marvelous panorama of the entire Swiftcurrent Valley. All of the peaks in the vicinity are displayed to good advantage, the most striking being Mt. Gould and Mt. Wilbur. The trail up the broad Swiftcurrent Valley may be traced past several lakes to the cliffy cirque at the head of the valley, then up to Swiftcurrent Pass. Toward the south massive Allen Mountain rises directly above blue Josephine Lake, while the long, high ridge of Grinnell Mountain stretches from Swiftcurrent Lake to the Continental Divide. Three thousand feet straight down the red slopes of Altyn Peak is beautiful Many Glacier Hotel, with its colorful parking lot, and the launch seems to cross Swiftcurrent Lake almost constantly while the climbers relax and luxuriate on this idyllic peak.

The South America Route. This route goes up the steep streambed above the road junction beside Swiftcurrent Falls. After passing the big snowbank that is shaped like South America (early in the summer) angle slightly eastward and climb to the base of the cliffs above the broad red talus slopes. A wide diagonal ledge covered with scree extends upward and eastward from the sparsely wooded slope, passing around a projecting shoulder almost directly beneath the summit. The ledge soon emerges on the top just east of the huge summit cairn. Very little rock work is necessary on this route but the amount of exposure above cliffs near the top may make some hikers feel insecure.

The Western Saddle Route. Distance to summit about 2.5 miles, none of it by human trail. Elevation gained is about 3,050 vertical feet. Class 2 all the way. From the highway around the north side of Swiftcurrent Lake, walk up the steep meadows toward the top of the mountain. After passing the half-way point, scramble up loose scree directly toward the broad saddle west of Altyn. The scree is bright red and very loose, so seek out bits of vegetation and small outcroppings of solid rock for better footing. There are also many trails made by mountain sheep on this hillside, which may aid in the ascent, and frequently climbers see ewes and lambs grazing on the upper hillsides. The red scree chutes and gullies extend to the saddle, after which it is an easy walk up gentler slopes to the summit of Altyn Peak.

A good game trail leads westward from that long saddle, traversing red scree slopes all the way into the center of the south basin of Mt. Henkel. (It is more difficult to find when traversing from Henkel to the saddle.)

Apikuni Mountain (Appekunny Mountain) (9,068)

The Southwest Ridge Route, via Mt. Henkel. Distance to summit from Mt. Henkel is about a mile, gaining about 1,000 feet in elevation (after descending to the intervening saddle). Mostly class 3, except for the short class 4 couloir descending to the Apikuni saddle. This is much more pleasant and interesting than the more obvious scramble of 1,000 vertical feet of loose scree from the valley above Appekunny Falls to the summit of this mountain.

Ascend from Swiftcurrent Camp to the upper south basin of Mt. Henkel then follow the strata up to the east ridge of the mountain. Go up that ridge, enjoying the splendid views of Natahki Lake and the spectacular panoramas to the west and south. At about 8,500 feet in elevation, just before reaching the low eastern peak of Mt. Henkel, a scree slope is reached which extends across the east slope of that eastern peak. The slope is eight to ten feet wide with tremendous cliffs below and a sheer wall above. Walk across the scree and onto the northeast ridge of Mt. Henkel. At the very nose of the ridge descend toward the saddle between Henkel and Apikuni. A twenty-foot cliff extends entirely across the northeast face of Henkel but a steep, narrow couloir angles down toward the right (east) from that northeast ridge, ending slightly east of the nose of the ridge. The couloir is only twenty feet long, and has large handholds and foot ledges all the way down. The next cliff on the descending ridge of Mt. Henkel is easily by-passed along the east side, and the rest of the descent (about 400 vertical feet) presents no problems at all.

The long walk up the flat slabs of the southwest ridge of Apikuni is scenic, interesting, and easy. Summit views are unique and spectacular, especially toward the west and northwest.

WARNING: If a descent to Apikuni Falls is attempted, follow the summit ridge very far to the east before starting down, in order to avoid the cliffs on the south slope of Apikuni Mountain. Look over the entire southeast slope *before* starting down, to determine where the treeless routes are that lead to the human trail above the waterfalls. If cliffs are encountered anywhere on the descent, they can be avoided by going further east.

The Apikuni Falls Route. This route is not really much fun. Hike the trail up to Apikuni Falls and into the broad hanging valley above the falls.

Continue westward until reaching the stream that crosses the faint foot trail, then head up the stream gully. Keep going up the loose footing until reaching the ridgetop about 4,000 vertical feet up the hillside. From the ridge it is a pleasant walk westward to the broad, rounded summit. This route is much more fun on the descent, but be careful not to start down until rather far east of the summit.

B-7 Pillar, by Iceberg Notch (8,500)

This spire is the huge, square-sided pinnacle just north of Iceberg Notch and is the highest point on the Pinnacle Wall. The ascent is a technical rock climb and should not be attempted without 120 feet of good climbing rope, rappel slings, and at least three pitons.

Distance to the summit about six miles, 4.5 miles of it by human trail. Elevation gained from Iceberg Notch is about 250 vertical feet. Class 5 pitches on the wall (one pitch is almost class 6). First ascent: Keith Hollister and Philip Shinn (Swiftcurrent employees), August 16, 1967.

Hike from Swiftcurrent Cabin Camp to Iceberg Lake and follow the normal route from there to Iceberg Notch (8,250 ft.) as described elsewhere in this guide.

The Northwest Chimney Route. Walk north on goat trail along the base of the west side of the wall until the middle of the Pillar is reached. A steep gully cuts up through the diorite sill (the black formation of hard igneous rock). The first pitch leads nearly 100 feet up good rock in a chimney, and is class 4.5 (scarce handholds). The second pitch is up a narrow class 5 chimney that is nearly blocked thirty feet up by an overhanging slab that leaves only twelve inches of clearance for climbers in the chimney. A *thin* leader can get through and belay the next climbers as they climb out of the chimney and around the slab. (On the descent, rappel 120 feet from above that slab to the scree below the cliffs.) Above the chimney, angle to the north and climb seventy feet up a class 4 gully that is capped by an overhang. The last fifty vertical feet to the summit is a steep scramble toward the northeast. Shinn and Hollister built the cairn and placed a register therein.

The South Arete Route. From Iceberg Notch climb class 3 scree to a small notch south of the Pillar, follow the ridgetop to the Pillar, then descend ten feet below the east side of the ridge (class 3). In a letter Kroger describes the climb from there as follows: "We climbed a small dihedral up through relatively solid rock for about seventy feet to a large shelf squarely on the arete, or ridge (about class 5.6, with protection adequate but tricky to place). The second pitch goes up very rotten rock just left of the arete for about 110 feet to another good ledge (4th or low 5th class). We climbed on to the summit, 3rd class. There was a register left by the first ascent party. The easiest descent route is via the northwest gully. Scramble down 3rd class ledges to a block in the chimney, then rappel about 120 feet to the talus. On the climb we used two pitons plus various nuts and runners." First ascent of route was by Chuck Kroger (Stanford Alpine Club) with Jim Anderson and Roy Harrison, August 25, 1968.

Mt. Gould (9,553)

Easier routes begin from Logan Pass and the Garden Wall Trail, and are described in that section of this guide. There are two routes that have been climbed from the Swiftcurrent Valley, however, and those are covered below.

The Northeast Face Route. This is only for expert mountaineers who are equipped with ropes and pitons and proficient in their use. Distance to summit about eight miles, none of it by trail. Elevation gained is about 4,600 vertical feet. Several class 4 and 5 pitches in the lower half of the route. First ascent: Robert E. Pfister, Ranger, August 9, 1965.

Hike up the trail to Grinnell Glacier, then traverse the rocks and gravel east of the terminus of the glacier until far south of Angel Wing (the peak that rises directly above Grinnell Lake). A prominent 500-foot-high hump is reached just below the northeast ridge of Mt. Gould. Walk around the east side of that hump, then traverse the south side of it and scramble into the narrow notch between the hump and the main wall of Mt. Gould. Go up easy scree ledges until reaching the sheer cliffs of Gould then traverse about fifty to seventy feet to the right. Pass two steep shoulders and reach a steep, narrow class 4 or 5 gully. Thirty feet up that precarious gully go to the left along a narrowing rock ledge (*crawling* past the place where the overhang makes it impossible to walk). The top of the cliff is reached at a point directly above the big notch at the base of the main wall (where the climb began).

Next there is a class 3 scramble up slopes and ledges to the pale marble formation that is just below the broad sill of dark igneous diorite (metagabbro). On the first ascent, Pfister climbed a dry waterfall channel near the northeast ridge. He easily got up through the 100 feet of diorite, then reached the most difficult cliff of the entire climb. From the northeast ridge he traversed west past two chimney bases, then around a prominent vertical rib, and reached a small waterfall. He went twenty feet up the cliff on the east side of the waterfall then traversed further east before climbing the next twenty feet . . . all with *tremendous* exposure. In a letter, he wrote:

The incredible view north from Mt. Gould—J. G. Edwards

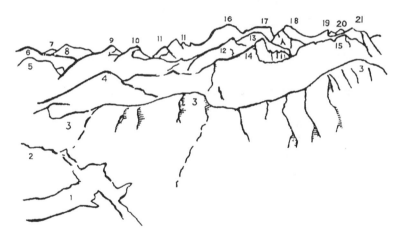

Looking North From Mount Gould. (1) Salamander Glacier; (2) The Garden Wall; (3) Grinnell Mtn.; (4) Swiftcurrent Mtn.; (5) Kootenai Pk. (6) Porcupine Ridge; (7) Mt. Custer; (8) Mt. Chapman; (9) Cathedral Pk.; (10) Mt. Kipp; (11) Stoney Indian Pks.; (12) Ahern Pk.; (13) Ipasha Pk.; (14) South end of Pinnacle Wall (Iceberg Pk.); (15) Mt. Wilbur; (16) Mt. Cleveland; (17) Northeast Ridge of Mt. Cleveland; (18) Mt. Merritt; (19) Little Rakiot Pk.; (20) Kaina Mtn.; (21) Natoas Pk.

"When I became discouraged at my inability to find a safer route, it was the dreadful thought of descending the same route which prompted me to go on." Consequently, he traversed to the west until directly above where he began the waterfall pitch. After climbing another thirty-five feet up a narrow rift with good footholds, he reached a scree chute with an over-hanging boulder at the top of it. Beyond the boulder, Pfister could see the summit for the first time! He was halfway there, and the rest of the climb was made on easy scree ledges up to and around the east end of the large snowfields to the summit.A possibly easier route, scouted from above by Edwards (but not climbed) is as follows. After surmounting the big cliffs above the notch at the base, scramble up toward the west, toward the great vertical ridge, or buttress, that juts out at least fifty feet from the main face of the northeast side of the mountain. While still east of that buttress, continue easily up through the pale marble formation and into the diorite sill. Angle up toward the west in the diorite formation (excellent rock) and climb the east side of the great buttress up to the level area that can be traversed to the west side of the buttress. A good scramble up that west side leads soon to a good game trail that parallels the top of the diorite sill all the way across the northeast face, to the northeast corner ridge of the mountain. The climb up easy ledges and scree areas to the summit is the same as that used by Pfister. (The game trail, incidentally, leads to the meadow beside Gem Glacier, from which it is not difficult to descend to the Garden Wall just north of Haystack Butte.)

The East Face Route. First ascent: Roger W. Tointon of Sacramento, July 26-27, 1966. Tointon worked in the park as a tour bus driver earlier, and had studied the face with binoculars. He mentioned other Glacier Park mountains "with class 5 and some class 6 pitches" that he climbed, including Split Mountain and Ipasha Peak. He described his climb to *Great Falls Tribune* reporter Scott Sorenson, who published the following quotes in the *Tribune* on August 21, 1966: "I hiked to Grinnell Glacier, cut across the lower part of the glacier, clambered up the south headwall of Grinnell, using the ice pick to make steps, climbed from notch to notch." "I traversed (moving sideways and gradually upward) south on narrow ledges on the east face of Gould and then began the first comparatively difficult climbing. I used rope pitches (which included driving pitons into cracks in the rock) the rest of the way. The rope I had was 150 feet long." Sorenson wrote that the equipment carried included the rope, pitons, piton hammer, ice ax and carabiners, and weighed thirty pounds. The quotes continued: "Part way up the 4,000-foot cliff I ran into the big corridor (a narrow, vertical indent into the mountain where a climber may put a foot on either side of the 'chimney' and work his way up through a series of short quick steps from side to side). Once through the corridor I was confronted by sheer vertical cliffs and began a series of vertical pitches to the top." Tointon said he stopped climbing around 8:30 P.M. and spent the night about 500 feet above the black band of granite (the diorite sill). The next day he spent eleven hours (5 A.M. to 4 P.M.) climbing the last 800 feet to the summit, and "it was class 6 all the way the second day." He told Sorenson: "As I was on the mountain I wished I was not trying to climb it alone. I thought then it would be very nice to have a couple of experienced alpinists with me." Lastly, Tointon said: "I may join the Sierra Club but I don't know if I would be able to after they find out I climbed a mountain like Gould 'solo'!" It is of course difficult to provide specific routes up great faces such as this, but climbers who are seriously interested in the climb might write to Mr. Tointon in Sacramento, where he was the City Planner in 1966 and is perhaps still listed in the telephone directory there.

Grinnell Mountain (8,851)

The distance to the summit varies according to the route followed, but will not exceed eight miles, mostly on human trails. Elevation gained is 4,000 vertical feet. Four major routes to the summit are: (1) via Grinnell Point; (2) via the south slope from high on the Grinnell Glacier trail; (3) via Swiftcurrent Glacier; and (4) via a traverse from the Grinnell Glacier Overlook (above the Garden Wall trail near Granite Park Chalets).

The Grinnell Point Route. The climbing routes to the top of Grinnell Point are described elsewhere in this chapter. From the ridgetop, walk westward along the summit trail until progress is blocked by a sheer cliff. Large scree-slopes extend down toward the southwest, and by angling farther toward the west while descending scree, snowfields, and meadows you can reach the *old* Grinnell Glacier trail and follow it westward to the junction with the present Glacier trail.

If the goal is the top of the mountain rather than a long descent, pass around the sheer cliff on the ridgetop on the right (north) side and follow faint game trails westward on and near the ridgetop until a huge scree-covered hump on the ridge is approached. Either traverse around that hump on the south side or climb directly up and over the top of it. (Unless you really want to hit every high place on the ridge, save energy by traversing around it.) Beyond the hump, descend to the low saddle a little further west. That saddle can also be reached easily from the Grinnell Glacier trail that is directly beneath it (where the trail crosses the large stream with brilliant red rocks, beneath extensive steep meadows and scrub thickets). The saddle can also be reached from the steep basin south of the head of the

Swiftcurrent Valley (below Swiftcurrent Glacier), via a very well-trav-elled game trail that angles up toward the east from that basin, staying just beneath the extensive north cliff-faces of Grinnell Mountain. That trail is observed approaching from the northwest as you stand in the deep saddle. WARNING: The descent of that trail should not be attempted without ice axes, because after the first mile it becomes steeper and is completely blocked by very dangerous snowfields.

To reach the summit of Grinnell Mountain from that great saddle, descend the scree-slope south of the saddle and follow faint trails along the south side of the mountain. Soon the sheer cliffs above disappear, and a tremendous scree-covered mountainside is seen that extends all the way up to the summit, 2,000 vertical feet higher. Angle westward while scram-bling up the scree slope, so as to stay *west* of the largest snowfield on the upper slope.

The South Slope Route. Hike up the Grinnell Glacier trail until reaching the small meadow only a few hundred yards before the trail ends at the big moraines. Walk up the meadow to the easy series of cliffs just above it. After reaching the top of that series of broken cliffs, follow the game trail eastward above the cliffs until directly beneath the highest point on the mountain (just above the forest that is east of the meadow). Scramble straight up the scree, gaining 2,000 vertical feet of elevation, and staying just west of the largest snowfield that is not far below the summit. There are numerous cliffs near the top a little further west, but only easy slopes if you stay far enough to the east.

The Swiftcurrent Glacier Route. This is a very interesting but very long route, beginning with the hike up trails to the top of Swiftcurrent Pass (it can thus be approached from Swiftcurrent Valley OR from the Granite Park region). For details, see the description near the beginning of this chapter, headed "Swiftcurrent Glacier Basin (and Grinnell Mountain)."

The Grinnell Glacier Overlook Route. Hike up the short spur trail from the Garden Wall trail to the top of the ridge directly above the north end of Grinnell Glacier. About fifty feet north of the "overlook" a marvelous game trail descends an easy gully and then descends the great scree-slopes almost to the end of the Grinnell Glacier foot trail. (To avoid that last sheer cliff it is necessary to either descend the very steep snow above the meltpond, which is NOT recommended without ice axes, or to traverse northward across a scree-shelf between the upper and lower cliffs until reaching descending scree-slopes a little farther north.) (To climb Grinnell Mountain from the trail beside Grinnell Glacier, reverse this route until reaching the Glacier Overlook.)

The following description of the route from the overlook to the summit of Grinnell Mountain is based upon a more lengthy description prepared by Rolf Larson, who has climbed extensively throughout the park and is on the pictorial and editorial staff of *Going-to-the-Sun* magazine.

From the overlook, observe the great pyramid on the long ridge that leads to the distant summit of Grinnell Mountain. That pyramid is the "false summit" of the mountain, and the route leads to the saddle between the false summit and the true summit.

From the overlook, traverse the east side of the ridge, toward the false summit, angling upward across broken cliffs and gaining about 500 vertical feet by the time the great south face of the false summit is approached. Two horizontal ledges extend eastward across the great cliff face just a bit lower than the saddle on Grinnell Mountain. One traverse is on a spectacular twenty-four-inch-wide ledge and the other is on a much broader shelf about thirty feet higher. Both ledges lead to a slope just below the lowest part of the saddle east of the false summit, with 1,200 feet of exposure below! From the saddle, it is a long, easy, unforgettable climb up the great ridge to the true summit of Grinnell Mountain.

For alternative descent routes, consider visiting Swiftcurrent Glacier. From the saddle between the true summit and the false summit of Grinnell Mountain descend the boulder and scree slopes to the east end of the glacier. Cross the vast expanses of snow and polished bedrock (including remarkable exposures of fossil algal reefs that have been exposed by the last fifty years of glacier recession) and work around the lower end of the large western lateral moraine. West of the glacier, ascend to the saddle north of the false summit of Grinnell Mountain and descend easily to the Highline trail and Granite Park Chalets.

If a descent into the Swiftcurrent Valley is preferred, go north through the great meadows beyond the moraine and then up the steep grassy slope to the trail (east of Swiftcurrent Pass).

A much less pleasant route into the valley is the direct descent from the east end of the glacier down to the trail. (Be sure to stay west of all the trees and descend the *western* side of the great basin.)

Grinnell Point (7,600)

This is an easy half-day hike from Many Glacier Hotel or Swiftcurrent Camp but it provides some intriguing and spectacular views of the hotel, the cabins, the ranger station, the streams and lakes, Grinnell Glacier, the great east face of Mt. Wilbur, and many other points of interest in this great area.

There are many routes to the point, which is actually just a few spires

Hikers on Grinnell Glacier—Bob and Ira Spring

at the far east end of the very long ridge of Grinnell Mountain. A long diagonal ledge angles up the north face without difficulty, but involves a stream crossing and an uninteresting hill-climb to the lower end of the diagonal ledge. Further westward scree slopes extend all the way to the top of the ridge, but again the stream must be forded to reach the slopes and the ascent is not really enjoyable. The most interesting route follows up the east ridge from near the lakeshore, traverses the east end of the ridge halfway to the top of the point, follows a game trail across the south slope to the old Josephine Mine, then ascends directly up to the ridgetop. A shorter route on the south slope utilizes the distinct grassy ramp to get through the great cliffs east of the waterfall, then is a "walk-up" all the way to the ridgetop (passing the Josephine Mine on the way). Lastly, the old miner's foot-trail leads from the Grinnell Glacier trail eastward across extensive steep meadows to the Josephine Mine, and the route from there to the ridgetop is the same as for the other south slope routes. None of these really demand detailed description but the following discussions may be useful to some.

The South Ramp Route. Hike to Josephine Lake and continue around the north shore of the lake. Pass the small pond by the shore (below the great snow chute), then walk through the small wooded area and stop at the broad grassy slope beyond it. The great waterfall is directly above that grassy slope, and the grassy ramp (A) is only 200 feet east of the waterfall. Walk up the steep grassy slope toward the waterfall, staying fifty to 100 feet east of the stream while climbing, and finally follow up a narrow dry streambed with good footing that extends up to the great rocky "apron" near the bottom of the waterfall. Skirt that apron on the east, until near the base of the great cliff above, then walk eastward below the cliff until reaching the broad couloir. Scramble up the couloir for a hundred feet to the bottom of the great grassy ramp, and walk up it to the top of the great cliff. Continue up easy little cliffs and steep grass slopes (B) all the way to the Josephine Mine (recognizable by the cone-shaped "tailing" below the old mine entrance).

From the Josephine Mine, traverse the trail for 100 feet to the east, then begin the climb to the top of the ridge. If care is taken to find easy routes, there is nothing worse than class 3 on the entire route. Very distinct trails will be encountered soon, and they zig-zag up the hillside, skirting around difficult cliffs and staying away from the dangerous area near the steep snow chute. When the rounded ridgetop is reached, enjoy the great views toward the north and northwest, then follow the ridge further toward the east for the classic view of the hotel from the "point." Stay just south of the rocky walls, walking on safe ledges or narrow scree shelves, and in fifteen minutes the great cairn will be reached.

The East Ridge Route. Cross the bridge over Swiftcurrent Creek on the trail from the picnic ground parking area. After passing around the great curve to the right, leave the trail and walk uphill through the forest to the broad ridgetop. A game trail follows up that ridge to the open slopes of berrybushes. Traces of trails are on that steep open hillside also, leading to the low cliffs far above. Beyond the little cliffs a distinct trail continues westward along the ridgetop (D). Two great cliffs block the route as you climb higher but each is easily climbed (class 4) by following the base of the cliff on to the south side of the ridge, climbing up the steep gully for a short distance, then traversing eastward on safe rock ledges that provide access to the ridgetop again. Finally the cliff above the great snow-chute is reached. Continue upward and cross above the head of that chute, then climb straight uphill on class 3 slopes until reaching the very distinct game trail that traverses from the west and passes around the east end of the ridge. With care in walking, the trail can be safely followed across the east face in about five minutes. Beyond that traverse, walk toward the west along a faint foot trail that leads directly to the Josephine Mine opening. See the discussion above for details of the climb from the mine to the top of the ridge and the walk to Grinnell Point.

The Miner's Trail Route. This old abandoned miner's trail (C) is a great route, and ranger-naturalists led dozens of hiking parties to the old mine during the 1950s, 1960s, and early 1970s. The lower part of the trail has unfortunately become badly overgrown by brush in recent years and was difficult to find in 1983. (Before WW II this was the only trail to Grinnell Glacier, but the newer trail continues further toward the west before switching back up into the broad basin with waterfalls plunging over great walls of red argillite.) The following comments should be sufficient to enable interested persons to find the trail. Hike up the Grinnell Glacier trail until looking down at Grinnell Lake in the distance. Before reaching the big switchback where the trail abruptly angles back toward the east for a hundred yards, notice a cliff with prominent contorted strata very high above the trail. The OLD trail to Grinnell Glacier went uphill toward that high cliff, then angled sharply back toward the east for about 100 feet (until approaching a small stream with dense alder thickets), then angled sharply westward and continued toward the glacier. Although badly overgrown, the old trail tread can still be seen where it leaves the current trail, and can easily be followed to the streambed. Leave the old trail there and force a way through the alders and across the stream to a marshy meadow east of it. Above the upper edge of that meadow the good miner's trail is encountered. It leads uphill gradually across open meadows all the way to

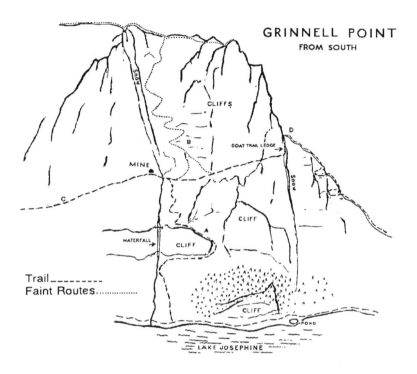

GRINNELL POINT
FROM SOUTH

the old mine entrance. From there to the ridgetop follow the route described under the other two routes above.

For hikers who do not wish to go to the top, a horizontal trail from the mine across the slopes east of the mine can be followed until it reaches the "drop-off" overlooking Swiftcurrent Lake and the hotel, truly a spectacular view! That trail was formed by the dozens of ranger parties during the 1960s, and now is being maintained by goats and sheep.

The North Face Routes. First ascent on July 11, 1990, by Randy Coffman and Tim Savee.

The approach to the base of the upper cliffs takes about an hour, via the lower east ridge. The actual time on the upper 1,100 vertical feet of rock should be seven or eight hours to the summit. The first pitch is class 5.8 difficulty and there are half a dozen other pitches of crack climbing plus one sixty-foot-high chimney in the upper half of the face. There are undoubtedly several good routes up this challenging red wall, allowing plenty of challenging opportunities for technical rock climbers to explore.

Grinnell Point, across Swiftcurrent Lake from Many Glacier Hotel
—NPS Photo

The first ascent went nearly directly up to the highest point (where a great cairn stands). That is the fourth largest hump west of the east wall of the ridge when viewed from the road.

Although no direct aid was required, pitons were sometimes placed for added protection. Randy Coffman urges climbers of this face to carry six knife blade pitons (mostly for one of the pitches) several camming device type chocks (for use in a dozen of the pitches), 165 feet of 11mm Perlon (Kernmantle rope), a good protective helmet, and several loops of nylon webbing.

Escape routes, if bad weather develops during the ascent, are mostly west of the direct climbing route, and a safe descent may be made via the long grassy ledge that angles down toward the west.

Coffman warns that pitons driven into a single crack should be at least three or four feet apart to prevent them from "zippering" out. He also observed that there are class 4 pitches between the more difficult pitches.

Before attempting routes on faces such as these, climbers are strongly urged to visit the Ranger Station and register their intentions. They may also benefit from discussing the proposed routes with the rangers like Coffman.

Mt. Henkel (8,770)

The views from this summit are marvelous, especially in the direction of Iceberg Lake, the Pinnacle Wall, and Mt. Wilbur. Snowy Vulture Peak looms up beyond the jagged Pinnacle Wall, bearing extensive glaciers and snowfields, while farther north along the horizon sharp Rainbow Peak and pyramidal Mt. Carter embrace Rainbow Glacier. Mt. Merritt completely dominates the northwest foreground, with Old Sun Glacier clinging to its steep east face. The Swiftcurrent Pass trail can be seen threading its way up the valley past a string of sparkling lakes. South of Grinnell Mountain the Garden Wall rears its serrated bastions above Grinnell Glacier. The broadly rounded dome of Mt. Jackson is nearly twenty air miles away and the snowy peak to the left is Blackfoot Mountain, with Blackfoot Glacier spread across its northern flank. On calm days a great reflection of Allen Mountain may be seen from Henkel in the lake beside the Many Glacier Hotel. Northeast of this mountain, beyond gaudy Yellow Mountain, famous old Chief Mountain rises abruptly above the seemingly endless prairies. All in all, considering the relatively small amount of energy expended by climbers of Mt. Henkel, this is the most rewarding experience one can enjoy in the Many Glacier area!

The South Couloir Route. Distance to summit about 1.5 miles, one-half mile of it by trail. Elevation gained is nearly 4,000 vertical feet. Class 2 and 3 all the way to the top. Follow the steep trail from the cabins toward Iceberg Lake. Just west of the junction where that trail joins the trail from the hotel to Iceberg Lake a stream is crossed. Instead of crossing it, climb up the bank east of the stream and follow the climbers' trail up the meadows toward Henkel. The trail is excellent until approaching the large snowbank that usually lies in the streambed below the steep cliffs. Scramble up the small cliffs and loose scree to the base of those cliffs, east of the steep stream gorge. The route up through the cliffs is obvious and climber trails can be followed all the way to the top and into the great red basin above the cliffs. Walk up that basin until the last red cliffs have been surmounted, then follow the strata upward toward the west. When the ridge is reached, climb up it all the way to the summit (class 3 only, if care is taken). WARNING: The snowbanks along the ridge are often undercut "cornices" that will collapse beneath the weight of a climber. Study them from below as you climb, and do not take risks by walking on them unless they are completely solid.

A different descent is usually favored as follows: From the summit, descend a hundred yards down the east ridge, then climb down a few easy cliffs (staying away from the steep snow) and descend toward the east in easy scree chutes. Soon the great basin of scree is reached, and the next thousand feet passes very quickly! Rejoin the route of ascent when the red formations are reached. Most climbers require about four hours for the climb up to the summit of Mt. Henkel and about half that time for the descent.

ADDED POSSIBILITIES: Apikuni (Appekunny) Mountain can be climbed from Mt. Henkel. For details, see the description under Apikuni Mountain in this guide. Crowfeet Mountain (8,914) can be reached via the long, long ridge traverse toward the northwest from the top of Mt. Henkel (and it is an easy descent from there to the trail near Ptarmigan Lake).

Iceberg Notch (7,700)

This remarkable notch is a worthwhile objective in itself, providing breathtaking views in all directions. More than that, however, it permits an interesting circuit from the Swiftcurrent area to Ahern Pass, followed by a return over Swiftcurrent Pass via Granite Park Chalet. It is only a mile, although a strenuous one, from Iceberg Lake to Ahern Pass, and (carrying small day-packs) it is not difficult to go from Ahern Pass to Swiftcurrent Camp in a little over three hours by way of this notch. (By contrast, it is a tiresome thirteen-mile hike by trail over Swiftcurrent Pass.) WARNING:

The descent from the notch to Iceberg Lake by climbers carrying full backpacks is not recommended except for very experienced mountaineers who are accustomed to climbing cliffs while carrying those packs.

The distance from Swiftcurrent Camp to the Notch is about five miles, 4.5 miles of it by human trail. Elevation gained is about 3,000 vertical feet (1,600 feet of it is up "the wall"). There is a discrepancy on the 1968 map, apparently, which should be mentioned. The previous map indicated it is about 600 vertical feet from Ahern Pass to the Notch, which seems about right when you make the climb, but the new map indicates it is about 1,300 feet up that scree-slope. Similarly, the new map indicates it is 2,100 vertical feet up from Iceberg Lake, whereas on the old maps it was only 1,600 feet, which seems correct.

Hike up the Iceberg Lake trail for a little over four miles, to the foot bridge over Iceberg Creek. Stay west of the creek, and walk through the scrub forest to the small lake that is below Iceberg Lake. There are two routes to the base of the upper cliffs from that small lake, as follows: (A) Follow a game trail from the lake shore up to the forested hump that rises from the west shore of Iceberg Lake. Scramble up the easy slopes from there, angling toward the north through small cliffs, scree chutes, and vegetated hillsides, then up the extensive scree slopes to the base of the large cliffs. Approach the cliffs by passing around the north end of the large snowbank that is there early in the summer; (B) From the small lake, scramble up the steep, hard gravel slope (or up the stream gully) to the cliffs above the scree. (A waterfall is usually near there, falling down behind a lingering snowbank.) Stay by the base of the cliff on your left and climb into the bottom of the narrow, steep gully that ascends toward the south (class 3). Climb with care, one at a time, to avoid knocking rocks on each other. From the top of that gully scramble straight uphill to the base of the great cliffs above the broad scree slope.

From either of these approaches walk south along the base of the high cliff and seek a safe route to the top of that cliff where it becomes lower. Early in summer the alternatives are: (1) use ice axes to climb up the snow on the left to get above the cliff-top, then angle north to get off of the snow and onto the class 3 slopes above the cliffs; or (2) climb up a steep, but easy open couloir for about fifteen feet to reach the top of the cliff and get to the class 3 slopes. After mid-July the snow should have melted away from the cliff enough for climbers to follow the base of the cliff southward and upward, and to reach a five-foot-high cliff between the snow and the upper slopes and easy cliffs.

Above the cliff angle up to the north on the class 3 slope and follow a faint trail to the rather flat platform on the great steep shoulder that extends down toward the small lake. The platform is about 200 feet up the cliff from the scree-slopes below. Now, look up toward the Notch and examine the route. Pay special attention to the algal reef formation, with a large gray rock bearing a prominent white blotch that resembles a capital "F" in reverse. The route leads directly to the bottom of that blotch, then passes up a steep gully a few feet south of it. From the flat platform, walk steeply upward toward the left, following a goat trail up a diagonal fracture plane that ascends in a nearly straight line for several hundred feet toward the big white blotch. When a wide scree ledge is reached (with three small trees about 100 feet north of the diagonal) the easy scramble ends. Continue straight upward in a narrow, deep gully with plenty of good hand and foot-holds. It is best to climb one at a time there to avoid injury from falling rocks. Above the gully is another one slightly further south, that leads to a broad class 3 slope from which the white blotch will be seen about 100 feet to your left.

The climb up the algal reef begins five or six feet south of the white blotch and utilizes a steep, twenty-foot diagonal gully that angles to the right above the white blotch. (On the descent, keep hands and feet far enough out on the gully walls to hold your body pressed firmly against the deep center of the gully.) Continue upward around the north side of a big knob of the same kind of rock for fifteen or twenty feet more, to the top of the reef. A fragmentary goat trail leads directly toward the Notch from there, but may be hard to follow. If in doubt, climb a little higher, after which the trail will easily be seen, and can be quickly reached. The big gap where the trail passes over the ridge is about ten feet higher than the deep notch and slightly north of it.

From the Notch it is an easy walk down the steep boulder field to Ahern Pass (the descent is jocularly referred to by some as the "Boulder Dash"). Also from the Notch, a faint goat trail leads south along the base of the cliffs and gives access to one of the routes up marvelous Iceberg Peak (a climb which will take another hour to complete).

Views from Iceberg Notch are inspiring. Helen Lake is a few thousand feet below, at the head of the Belly River Valley. The entire Livingston Range is suddenly visible, with great masses of snow shining in the sun. Ahern and Ipasha Peaks dominate the near horizon above Helen Lake and many great waterfalls plunge down their east cliffs toward the lake. Eastward the most impressive sight is certainly snow-flecked Iceberg Lake but Swiftcurrent Lake and the Many Glacier Hotel are visible beyond the north shoulder of mammoth Mt. Wilbur. The lovely hanging bench called Shangri La is directly between Iceberg Notch and the Many Glacier Hotel.

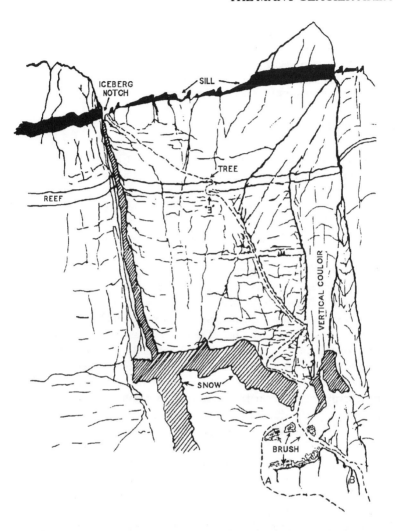

The following information is included for climbers *descending* the Iceberg Wall. From the Notch, follow the goat trail down toward the north. The algal reef must be descended at exactly the right place if excessive danger is to be avoided. Along the top of that reef there are two rounded prominences that have trees above them. The easy route through the cliff begins at the northernmost of those and was discussed in detail, above. Below the algal reef with the white blotch, traverse about 100 feet toward the north, while gradually descending, watching for a deep, steep gully below. Go down that gully, and the next one, and in five to ten minutes you will reach the top of the long diagonal rift which is an easy "walk-down" to the flat platform overlooking the small lake. Angle down from there toward the south to reach a place where the bottom-most cliff can be safely descended to reach the extensive scree slopes beneath it. It is then easy to follow either "A" or "B" on the diagram to the pond, far below.

Iceberg Peak (9,145)

The views from this sharp summit are magnificent, and for that reason alone many people will enjoy repeating this climb each summer. The main attraction is Iceberg Lake, 3,200 vertical feet straight down. The sea of peaks and snowfields and glaciers south of Swiftcurrent Pass are as attractive from here as from anywhere else in the entire park, and spectacular photographs result from pointing the camera in any direction from Iceberg Peak!

This peak is the highest point above Iceberg Lake on the southwest side of its great cirque. It can be reached easily from the Highline Trail about a mile north of Granite Park Chalets, but the route from Iceberg Lake is much more interesting and challenging, and is much quicker for persons staying in the Swiftcurrent Area. The route discussed here begins at Iceberg Notch, which can be reached from Ahern Pass or, with much more difficulty, from Iceberg Lake. Later, the other two routes will be described.

The Highline Trail Route. Walk the trail north from Granite Park until it turns sharply to the right and descends along the north wall of a great cliff and crosses an extensive snowfield that has usually accumulated there. Just north of that snowfield, walk uphill toward the top of Iceberg Peak. The only obstacle is the sill of black igneous rock, and there is an easy route visible through that sill a little farther north. From the top of the sill, it is merely a long, long scree scramble up the west side of the mountain to the summit. The elevation gained from the trail to the top is about 2,500 vertical feet. WARNING: When *descending* via this route, be sure to stay enough north to avoid the difficult cliffs. Do not angle southward until below the black sill.

The Iceberg Notch Route. Traverse south along the base of the cliffs from Iceberg Notch. Soon the trail fades and it becomes necessary to climb up one of the couloirs through the cliffs beside you in order to gain the elevation needed to get higher than the top of the large cliff that is further south. (Mark the couloir well, so it can be found on the descent.) A marvelous game trail traverses toward the south above those cliffs, between the bottom of the upper cliffs and the top of the lower cliffs, until reaching the tremendous scree area on the west side of Iceberg Peak. It is an easy scramble up the west side all the way to the top.

The South Iceberg Peak Route. Hike the trail to the east side of Swiftcurrent Pass, to the farthest north switchback there. Leave the trail at the extreme northern point of that switchback and scramble up to the ridgetop north of the trail. Walk up that gentle ridgetop toward the great cliffs. As the bottom of the great wall is approached, watch for an inconspicuous opening in the scrubby tree thickets north of the ridge, which is the beginning of the game trail that leads into the North Swiftcurrent Glacier basin. The faint trail begins below a ten-foot high rock outcrop on the ridge, which is about fifty feet from the base of the great wall. The game trail descends gradually through the trees, becoming more distinct as it goes, and leads to interesting moraines below the great snowfields in the basin. Either follow the trail across the moraines below the snow OR cross the basin on the snow.

North of the snowfields, go up the open grassy slope and follow the faint game trail that forms there. The trail skirts the bottom of the upper cliffs for a considerable distance, until reaching the huge scree slope that extends up to the low saddle on your left. From that saddle, walk up the long rocky ridge to the summit of South Iceberg Peak (not named on the map, but a very worthwhile objective in itself).

The views of the main summit of Iceberg Peak from this lower peak are both inspiring and discouraging, but the ascent is not difficult. Descend the rocky north ridge for about 100 feet, to the flat area beyond which it suddenly steepens. Continue down the cliffy hillside west of the rocky ridgetop, and it is easy to reach the saddle between South Iceberg Peak and the main mass of Iceberg Peak. Below that saddle (and west of it) begin a horizontal traverse toward the north. A game trail soon becomes very obvious there, and crosses the west face of the mountain for several hundred yards.

Eventually the cliffs above the trail end, and a great scree slope extends from the game trail almost to the very summit of Iceberg Peak. Struggle up that slope for the next half hour, watching for landmarks that will be helpful on the descent. Slightly above the long traverse there is a small wet cliff in the center of the scree (in mid-summer) where drinking water may be obtained. A hundred yards further uphill another game trail approaches the great scree slope from the north. If you intend to descend via Iceberg Notch, that is the trail you must follow after visiting the top of Iceberg Peak. If you intend to drop down to the Highline trail and go to Granite Park chalets instead, return to the damp area and run straight down the scree from there, angling slightly to the right to avoid hazardous cliffs that lie a little farther south.

As the summit is approached, angle toward the north to find more solid footing and to enjoy the tremendous views toward the north. There are no difficulties above, and one of the greatest thrills in the park is to look down the sheer red east face and see the brilliant blue waters of Iceberg Lake 3,200 vertical feet below, flecked with dazzling white icebergs! Many Glacier Hotel is seen directly beyond the hanging valley called Shangri La (just to the left of Mt. Wilbur's 3,600-foot high northwest face). A jumble of rugged peaks and sparkling snow fills the panorama toward the south, and the giant peaks of the Livingston range loom up in the west and northwest. Nearer at hand, Ahern Glacier is embraced by Ahern and Ipasha Peaks, and the water from that glacier plunges a thousand feet down spectacular cliffs to Helen Lake. The long sharp arete of the Pinnacle Wall meanders northeast, and beyond Ptarmigan Tunnel the peaks suddenly displayed are the vibrant red, orange, and white summits of Mt. Seward, Chief Mtn. and Gable Mtn. The weird pastels of Yellow Mountain and Chief Mountain are etched against the endless green background of the Alberta prairies. Other summit views in Glacier National Park are more frightening, but few are as colorful as those from Iceberg Peak.

On the descent, the alternatives are: (1) return the way you came; (2) run down to the Highline trail and hike to Granite Park chalets (thence to the highway or over Swiftcurrent Pass); or (3) go to Iceberg Notch and descend to Iceberg Lake. The first two alternatives are easier, faster, and safer, and the Iceberg Notch route should not be considered lightly. For those who DO want to reach Iceberg Notch, however, the following directions will be helpful.

Descend the small cliffs and easy scree slope from the top of Iceberg Peak until reaching the game trail that approaches from the north. If you traverse too high, cliffs will halt your progress northward (but you may then see the game trail below you). If you drop too low before traversing, you will soon end up above a tremendous north-facing cliff that cannot be descended (you must then scramble uphill to reach the game trail that leads toward the north).

Follow that good trail until it reaches a distinct gully or couloir that is easy to descend safely IF there is no snowbank at the bottom. If snow is there, avoid this gully, because the snow is very steep and hard there. Instead, stay on the trail and go further north to a safer and more interesting descent. The trail is much fainter after passing the first gully, but is still easily followed. Soon it reaches a much deeper and longer gully, which is appropriately called "the gash." That gully provides a safer descent, and the snow seldom completely blocks the bottom. In order to enter the gash, traverse above it on the game trail, then walk down the north side of it for several yards, until reaching a ramp that angles safely down into the gash.

The only danger on this descent will be from falling rocks, so do not move while other people are exposed below, and be constantly prepared to leap behind protective ledges if rockfall does occur. Below the gash, either walk across the scree slopes to Iceberg Notch OR traverse northward along the dark olive-black rock formation (the diorite or metagabbro sill) until the game trail becomes discernable. It is then an easy, fast walk all the way to Iceberg Notch.

The descent to Iceberg Lake from the Notch can be made safely by small parties, but refer to the description of the route from Iceberg Lake to Iceberg Notch, elsewhere in this guide. The trail is not easy, and it disappears frequently. The climb down the algal reef will be hazardous for some people, and a rope belay is advised for the bottom half of it. Climb down that solid, steep gully facing forward (not facing into the cliff). Use well-placed hands and arms to press your body back against the rough rock while moving your feet to lower cracks or protuberances. Descend this pitch one at a time, for if a climber were to fall there, the people below would all be sacrificed! Below the algal reef, angle sharply northward to reach to top of two steep but easy gullies, one above the other. Below them the trail is obvious going steeply down toward the left for several hundred feet, to a flat parapet above sheer cliffs. From there the route descends little cliffs and scree shelves toward the south and provides access to open scree slopes. If snow lies below the last little cliff, avoid walking on it. Instead, climb into the gap between the snow and the small cliff and walk along the cliff base until reaching unbroken scree slopes extending down into the trees. (See the guide description for the route from there to the human trail.) This descent is not recommended unless someone in the party has climbed up it recently, OR the climbers are experienced route-finders on Glacier Park terrain.

For the entire trip from Swiftcurrent Lake to South Iceberg Peak, Iceberg Peak, and return via Iceberg Notch, plan on at least twelve hours of activity.

Mt. Wilbur (9,321)

This climb is for experienced climbers only, and requires ropes, correct belaying techniques, and frequently pitons, carabiners, and slings for rappelling. Register at the ranger station the day before the climb and plan to be on the trail to the mountain by 6:00 A.M. The distance is not great but the climb usually takes a lot of time. Distance to the top via east face routes is about four miles, about half of it by human trail. Elevation gained is about 4,500 vertical feet. Class 4 and 5 pitches predominate in the upper five hundred vertical feet. First ascent: Norma. Clyde, August 20, 1923. Super-mountaineer Joe Steffen prefers to climb Wilbur above all others in the park, and has led more than forty parties to the summit!

The views from the summit are unique. Beyond the hotel and its environs Lake Sherburne extends almost to the edge of the broad expanse of prairie. The trail to Ptarmigan Tunnel meanders past Ptarmigan Lake and zig-zags sharply up to the tunnel entrance. Beyond the Pinnacle Wall is Ipasha Peak and Mt. Merritt, with the fantastic spires of the "Lithoid Cusp" occupying the gap between those great peaks. Westward, beyond the McDonald Valley, the entire Livingston Range sprawls along the horizon, replete with glaciers and snowfields. Spectacular peaks to the south include Mt. Siyeh (on the left) then Mt. Gould, snowy Mt. Jackson, and Cannon Mountain. The most stunning experience of all is to walk westward from the cairn until getting the view of Iceberg Lake 3,600 feet straight down! That deep blue lake, flecked with snow and icebergs all summer long, is surrounded on three sides by sheer walls thousands of feet high.

All east face routes begin the same way (see also "The North Face Route," later). Hike up the Swiftcurrent Valley trail to Redrock Falls, then select one of the following options: (1) Continue toward Swiftcurrent Pass until below the stream that issues from the great cirque on the east side of Mt. Wilbur, then bushwhack up to the foot of the waterfall that issues from that basin. (2) Walk up the ridge heading north from Redrock Falls, on traces of game trails. The trail later continues uphill just west of the ridge, angling back and forth to avoid thickets of brush. When the small valley downhill to the west of the ridge vanishes where it abuts against a steep transverse hillside, walk westward across the gentle slopes above the head of that valley. The large stream turned eastward below the waterfall and is now flowing directly toward you. The faint game trail leads to the north shore of that stream, but it is easier walking on the south bank, where there is a slope covered with beargrass fields. Continue uphill until almost to the bottom of the waterfall. There are two different approaches from the area below the waterfall. If the party intends to climb the *Direct Route,* the *Central Couloir Route,* or the *North Couloir Route,* follow the **"Direct Approach"** (#1 on the diagram), but if the goal is *the Chimney Route* or the *Thin Man's Pleasure Route,* follow the **"Stairstep Approach"** (#2 on the diagram). See the following discussions for further details.

The Direct Approach (#1)

Cross the stream east of the waterfall and zig-zag up the small cliffs east of the fall, then walk up the steep open slopes into the great basin, or cirque,

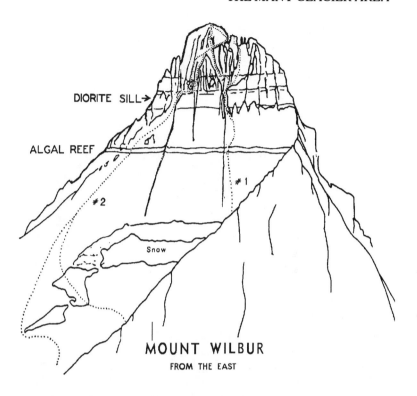

DIORITE SILL→

ALGAL REEF

#1

#2

Snow

MOUNT WILBUR

FROM THE EAST

east of Mt. Wilbur. Ascend from that basin, skirting the north end of the large horizontal (transverse) snowbank. Climb straight upward, staying north of the biggest stream gully on that great east face. Some of the cliffs are steep and are composed of crumbly rock ledges which provide no belay points, so climb very carefully. The algal reef offers little more difficulty. That hard gray formation may be recognized by the large whorls representing the fossil remains of algal colonies that lived beneath the prehistoric sea here more than a million years ago. The reef is forty to fifty feet thick here, but can be crossed rather easily via chimneys not far north of the large stream gully. (Don't risk embarrassment by falling while this far below the beginning of the real climb!) No obstacles exist above the algal reef until the diorite sill is reached. That sill is composed of dark igneous rock, which has been referred to as diorite or metagabbro, and is a very hard black rock with a greenish tint in some light conditions. Enter the big stream gully above the long snow chute that persists until mid-summer, but still about 200 feet below the dark diorite formation. The danger increases abruptly, with constant peril from falling rocks. The lower part of the diorite sill is

Mt. Wilbur, far above and beyond snowy Swiftcurrent Lake —Mel Ruder

easy to climb, but soon a sheer little wall blocks the route. A trickle (sometimes a stream) of water running down the overhanging cliff makes the rock treacherous as well as uncomfortable to hug. Climbers over the years have built up a pile of rocks below the overhang, so the first footholds can now be reached rather easily. Just above the overhang angle sharply to your left and actually climb toward the east, up the steep cliff that forms the south wall of the gully (see the photo of Robert Megard on that wall). There is great exposure below you there, but the climbing is not difficult. A great belay position is on the wide ledge just above the cliff, and the leader should always belay those following (especially in rain or snow). This belay is even more valuable on the descent, when it is easy to slip off the scree-covered ledges or the wet diorite overhang. From the belay point, traverse a narrow ledge back into the main gully and scramble up the scree to a fork in the gully at the upper edge of a broad belt of red rock. The three routes on the east face above here now diverge. See the following descriptions of (A) The Direct Route, (B) The North Couloir Route, and (C) The Central Couloir Route. (The latter is the easiest route in the center of the east face.)

(A) The Direct Route. The left fork of the gully goes straight up to the left-hand (southern) notch in the summit ridge. It is an easy chimney climb until about ten feet from the notch, but an overhang of loose rock above that long chimney is troublesome. On the first ascent, Alice Edwards had gotten into the lead and scrambled right up it, so we threw her a rope and she belayed the rest of the party up. On the descent, the author belayed the others down the overhang then looped the rope around a nub and climbed down using that support. The rope snagged and could not be retrieved, so I climbed back up and re-positioned it, then went back down ... and again failed to dislodge it. By that time I had learned much about the pitch, so climbed back up, threw the rope down, and descended without the rope for protection. A piton and a sling in the wall by the summit notch would certainly have been nice! Hopefully any parties descending that route will use protection of that sort!

(B) The North Couloir Route. The right-hand fork of the gully leads to easy slopes of ledges with a covering of scree, and in half an hour of class 3 scrambling the deepest notch in the summit ridge is reached (with a tremendous view of Iceberg Lake). Take time to admire the remarkable "fingers" of red rock just north of the notch! From the notch, climb the fifteen-foot cliff toward the summit. The small scree shelf above it leads quickly to the narrow ridgetop that is rotten and practically unclimbable. A huge detached block just east of the ridge provides the key to the pitch. "Stem" the chimney formed between the ridge and the detached block,

gaining about fifteen feet of elevation, then carefully climb onto the north edge of the narrow rotten ridge and continue up it for about twenty more feet to the top of hump between the two great notches in the summit ridge. It is easy to descend into the "next-to-deepest notch" into which the other east face routes all lead. It is an obvious class 4 climb from there up the nose of the ridge or up a steep, shallow couloir beside that ridge. After the first thirty feet, it is an easy walk up scree to the summit. First ascent: J. G. Edwards, August 1965.

(C) *The Central Couloir Route.* Leave the gully at the upper edge of the red formation, and climb about forty feet up the cliff that forms the south wall of that gully. This is a dangerous pitch to climb because of the very rotten rock, and it is much more difficult on the descent because of the lack of adequate handholds (the descent must be made using very narrow, sloping footholds, and using balance rather than handholds). Obviously a rope belay from above is desired for all climbers who can get it! Beyond the top of that south wall of the gully there is a broad, gently sloping talus slope, above which there are three easily climbed couloirs. These are readily visible from the Redrock trail, or even from the hotel porch. WARNING: These couloirs are funnels for falling rock, so stay out of the middle of any of them and climb upward as close to the ridges between them as possible. The left-hand (south) couloir is the safest, and a class 3 scramble up that slope leads to the distinct diagonal scree-covered shelf that ascends northward and ends in the next-to-deepest notch in the summit ridge. (Downward, to the south, that shelf drops off into the gully above the Chimney Route, while the next gully goes down to Thin Man's Pleasure.) From the summit notch the route to the top is obvious. Carefully climb up thirty or forty feet of rotten cliffs with good footholds, slightly west of the actual "nose" of the ridge, then walk up the scree to the summit. (Incidentally, another route from the summit down to the diagonal scree shelf is directly east of the summit via a steep, meandering couloir that leads to the top of the left-hand couloir up which you climbed.)

The Staircase Approach (#2)

From the south bank of the stream below the waterfall that issues from the great basin east of Mt. Wilbur, walk up the steep grassy hillside toward the southwest. There are many red cliffs above the vegetated slopes, however easy routes exist there that utilize safe cracks and gullies leading up through them (class 3). Choose routes carefully, for accidents have occurred there. The best routes are usually well-marked with stone "ducks" and are obvious because of heavy use by climbers. Above the red cliffs, walk up a great slope covered by beargrass (beautiful in early July,

Robert Megard climbing the overhang route on the east face of Mt. Wilbur—J. G. Edwards

213

but very slick when wet). Soon the stream draining the large snowbank is reached, and the last chance to fill canteens. Continue uphill beside the large snowbanks and onto the huge scree slope that will occupy climbers for the next hour. For easier climbing, stay near the great rounded southeast shoulder all the way to the low cliffs on that shoulder, then traverse to the right while ascending around the cliffs and enter the broad gully that parallels the upper southeast shoulder. Low in that gully the diorite (metagabbro) sill is encountered (i.e., the great horizontal formation of black or greenish-black igneous rock). That diorite is very hard solid rock, and climbing it is like climbing granite. Stay on the north wall of the gully while climbing, to avoid the hazard from falling rocks. When the gully forks, about halfway up the igneous sill, stay in the north gully. A band of hard yellow-brown rock lies above the diorite, and immediately above that is a broad sloping shelf of loose scree with steep red cliffs above it. Walk to the right (northward) along that shelf and follow one of the two available routes to the summit, described below as the Chimney Route and Thin Man's Pleasure. Both have class 4 and 5 pitches.

(A) The Chimney Route. Traverse along the scree shelf until it ends at a deep gully with a sheer wall beyond. Climb up the deep red chimney there for about sixty feet (class 4) to a small scree platform. That is a good place from which to belay other climbers and it is also a good idea to hoist the packs up from the bottom to that point. Above the platform is a deeper chimney about fifty feet high, that is usually plugged partially by huge red chockstones at the top. The climb up this chimney is more difficult than the lower one, but is quite safe for anyone familiar with chimney-stemming techniques. In mid-August 1956, a huge ten-foot-square slab covered the top of the chimney, but when the author returned four days later the big slab had broken into three pieces, and two pieces were wedged lower in the chimney. The chockstones have changed many times during the last twenty-five years!

Above the chimney the gully is easy to scramble up, but there is great danger from rocks bounding down the gully and climbers should stay on the north wall as much as possible (or be prepared to leap up the wall to avoid suddenly-appearing rocks in flight). The gully soon ends in a sheer cliff but it is easy to climb up to the right to a broad gap between the main cliff face and a great detached spire. From that gap a wide scree shelf angles up toward the north and leads into the next-to-deepest notch in the summit ridge (just north of the final summit dome). As described elsewhere, the route from that notch to the summit is an obvious class 4 climb up a steep, shallow couloir just west of the "nose" of the north ridge to the scree that leads to the top of Mt. Wilbur.

(B) Thin Man's Pleasure Route. Traverse along the scree shelf for about sixty steps to the north to a rounded red shoulder of clean rock. (This is not far south of the chimney route described above.) Look up the cliff above the rounded shoulder and observe the great overhanging ceiling about forty feet above the scree shelf ... and the hole in that ceiling, through which climbers must pass in order to reach the gully above it. The easiest route up the red shoulder to the deep crevice beneath the big hole is via the north side of that shoulder. When the cliff is dry it is not a difficult ascent (or descent) but in rain, sleet, or snow there is great need for rope support from above. After stashing all packs far back in the crevice as the climbers reach the hole in the ceiling, the last climber should pass them up through the hole before making the climb through it himself (or herself). Fortunately there is a broad solid ledge in a perfect place for climbers to place their feet while pushing their head and shoulders up through the two-foot square hole.

The gully above the hole is an easy scramble (class 3) for about150 feet, then ends in a steep cliff and a vertical crack. Climb to a narrow ledge above the head of the gully and traverse northward on it. The ledge passes across the head of the gully above the chimney route and leads to the gap (mentioned there) between the main cliff face and the great detached spire. From there, walk up the wide scree shelf that angles up toward the north and into the next-to-deepest notch in the summit ridge. The route from there to the summit is a class 4 pitch that has been described under the other routes above that notch.

Other routes may be possible, including one fromWindmaker Lake to the black jagged top of the south wall of the Iceberg Lake cirque, thence up the southwest ridge of the south summit of Mt. Wilbur.

One other route, of great difficulty, has also been climbed (and described in the *Mountain Ear* in 1961). A condensed account taken from that description is presented here.

The Northwest Face Route (from Iceberg Lake). The first ascent was made by Tom Choate, Renn Fenton, and Gil Averill on August 4, 1961. To the best of my knowledge, it was never attempted again during the following twenty-eight years.

Scramble up the scree from Iceberg Lake for 2,000 vertical feet of cliffs, ledges, staircases, and talus blocks. Rope up 300 feet below the diorite or metagabbro sill. Before the diorite is reached, climb up a damp slippery chimney with overhanging cliffs where falling rocks "screamed by occasionally."After three leads there was a ledge below the diorite where protection from falling rocks was enjoyed. After climbing through the diorite, "the whole face overhangs, including the chimney, and several chockstones hang out over you as you worm or stem your way up." One or two pitons must protect each lead "because one falls out of such a chimney, not down it." The climbers then "wiggled through small holes under several piano-size chockstones, using each for a belay point for the next lead." Another resting place is finally reached 500 feet below the top of the west ridge. Renn then led two pitches up the face in a wide chute and went up the left branch of it. After climbing two more ledges "a sheer face confronted us, not far from the top." Tom led up it, using four pitons in hard-to-find cracks for safety. In the middle, the belayer must squat under an overhang, held in only by an anchor piton, while looking straight down at Iceberg Lake 3,000 feet below. Above that is a 300-foot scramble up ledges just southwest of the ridgetop to the summit. The time required for climbing the face was just under seven hours. There ARE challenging climbs in Glacier National Park for everyone!

Mt. Wynn (8,404)

The views from this relatively low peak are unusual because they are not seen from any other vantage point. The primary attraction is certainly the Many Glacier Hotel and its surroundings, but the entire Swiftcurrent Valley is spread out toward the west, with the great cliffs of Mt. Wilbur standing over it. That alone is worth the climb, but there are other interesting sights to be seen also. The long, long ridge leading all the way to the summit of Mt. Siyeh, deserves study, and some climbers will be tempted to follow that long ridge (see the discussion of the Skyline Trail from Mt. Wynn to Mt. Siyeh elsewhere in this guide). Cracker Lake looks incredibly blue, perhaps because of the striking contrast between the color of the water and that of the bright red rock formations around it and the lush green vegetation that carpets the valley below the lake. Somewhat overpowering everything else in the canyon, of course, is the tremendous north wall of Mt. Siyeh, more than 4,000 vertical feet above Cracker Lake. There is no better view of that massive cliff than that from Mt. Wynn!

The Southwest Ridge Route. Distance to summit about five miles, 3.5 miles of it by human trail. Elevation gained is about 3,500 vertical feet. Class 2 and 3 all the way.

Hike from Many Glacier Hotel toward Cracker Lake. After leaving Cracker Flats and heading up Canyon Creek the trail climbs in earnest for the next mile, until crossing Canyon Creek on a good bridge. At the east end of the bridge a small creek enters the valley from the east. If there is not too much water in that creek it is an interesting rock climb up the canyon for several hundred yards into the wide, horizontal valley above (at

Mother goat and kid, resting on ledge—Bob Kennedy

about 6,600 ft. elevation). If there is water flowing, the steep rocks in the creekbed are too slick for safe climbing. In that case, cross the streambed and bushwhack up the wooded hillside just north of it. Either way, the object is to reach the south end of a long, high ridge that extends southwest from the top of Mt. Wynn. An excellent game trail begins there and goes gently up the ridge all the way to the summit.

Yellow Mountain (8,766)

Views from the top are unique and very impressive. Slide Lake lies directly below toward Chief Mountain. It was formed after 1914 when a massive avalanche from Yellow Mountain dammed the stream there (now called Otatso Creek). The brilliant yellow ridge southeast of the summit and the tremendous desolate basin below it fill the foreground resembling a garish moonscape. In the distance almost every large peak in the park can be seen and many look more spectacular from this vantage point than from elsewhere. The absence of vegetation along the route from Ptarmigan Tunnel and Redgap Pass to this summit may help explain the feeling of "unrealness" which grips climbers on this expedition. The experience is entirely unlike anything encountered elsewhere in Glacier National Park!

The Seward Saddle Route. Distance to summit about eleven miles, five of it by human trail. Elevation gained is about 4,000 feet. Class 2 and 3 all the way.

Travel to Redgap Pass (7,700 ft.), via Ptarmigan Tunnel (see description of route from Ptarmigan Tunnel to Redgap Pass elsewhere in this chapter). About 100 feet east of Redgap Pass and slightly above the pass a very distinct game trail forms. It ascends gradually for nearly a mile across the south slope of Mt. Seward leading to the saddle between Seward and the small sharp red peak east of it. The trail across the red scree is called "The Red Scree Stroll." About half the way across the hillside the trail crosses a small permanent stream of cold water that emerges from rock strata above. No other water should be anticipated on this route so water should be carried from Ptarmigan Lake also.

From Seward Saddle (8,000 ft.) the views are spectacular. The peaks southwest of Redgap Pass are also impressive (the high, sharp peak there is Iceberg Peak). Leaving Seward Saddle follow the game trail across the north side of the sharp red peak, cross over the ridge that extends northeast from that peak, then descend and traverse northward along the east side of that ridge. When difficult cliffs are encountered, angle back toward the south and descend to an easier traverse northward. Soon a broad rock-field is reached and the trail goes toward the sharp yellow west peak of Yellow Mountain. That peak is easily climbed but the major game trail passes eastward below the cliffs and continues to the broad saddle further east. The summit of Yellow Mountain is now only about one hour away!

Follow the ridge toward the next peak and by-pass it on the south side. Continue to the higher peak that is still further east. The true summit finally comes into view from there beyond the next peak and further to the right. It is an uneventful walk to the broad summit with its huge peculiar rocks.

Descent via Poia Lake Route. It is so far back to Ptarmigan Tunnel that few will wish to retrace their steps back to Swiftcurrent Valley. Yellow Basin offers a direct route to Kennedy Creek but the brush, debris, windfalls, and sheer stream walls provide formidable obstacles. Climbers attempting that route should stay well west of the stream gorge all the way to Kennedy Creek. The quickest and easiest route back to the road is therefore via Poia Lake and the Swiftcurrent Ridge trail as described below.

Walk westward from the summit of Yellow Mountain until reaching the broad side-ridge that extends south toward (invisible) Poia Lake. Walk southward on that side ridge admiring the small blue lake in Yellow Basin (not shown on maps prior to 1968). Eventually the ridge rises to a higher rounded hump, which must be ascended. Head southeast from the top of that hump, gradually descending diagonally along the south side of it. Flat rock outcroppings soon appear below and Poia Lake comes into view. Traverse further eastward along the top of the cliffs, until above a broad steep basin that extends all the way to the valley floor west of Poia Lake. (A rocky hump of red rock is about half-way down that scree basin but is not approached closely during the descent.)

The route down the basin is safe and easy. Scree-slopes fifty feet east of the streambed provide a rapid descent among widely scattered trees. Eventually you reach the top of a cliff over which the stream plunges as a waterfall. Traverse eastward for about 100 feet to an easy descent around the end of the cliffs. Continue straight down the slope through the forest, running down chutes and ridges of scree when possible. Angle toward the stream later and approach patches of steep meadow. Walking becomes increasingly easy as the bottom of the slope is approached and the human trail is reached several hundred feet west of Poia Lake.

Hike the trail around Poia Lake, over a large hump, and down to the lower valley of Kennedy Creek. (Notice the attractive waterfall issuing from Yellow Mountain Basin on your left.) The trail then heads uphill. It is a tiring and discouraging hike to the ridgetop where Swiftcurrent Ridge Lake is located. After passing the lake the trail descends westward and eventually reaches the road not far from Many Glacier Hotel. To save an hour take the steep side-trail about one-quarter mile from the lake and plunge straight downhill on that crude trail for about fifteen minutes to the entrance station at the road. This shortcut trail saves about three miles of hiking en route to the road.

First known ascent (and descent) via these routes was on August 14, 1973 by Lew Sabo, Dan Tyers, and Gordon Edwards.

Climbing Mt. Gould, Logan Pass in the background. —Robert Megard

St. Mary Lake in a rare reflective mood. (Left to right: Little Chief, Citadel, and Fusillade mountains)
—Brian Kennedy

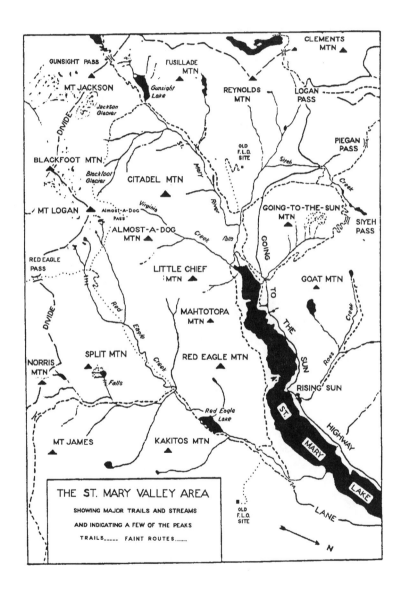

THE ST. MARY VALLEY AREA

SHOWING MAJOR TRAILS AND STREAMS

AND INDICATING A FEW OF THE PEAKS

TRAILS____ FAINT ROUTES........

THE ST. MARY VALLEY AREA

Routes Among the Peaks

This vast area includes not only the valley containing St. Mary Lake but also the long, remote Red Eagle Valley. Near the head of the St. Mary Valley there are tributary valleys extending northward to Piegan Pass and southward to Jackson Glacier and Blackfoot Glacier as well as a branch to Gunsight Pass. St. Mary Lake is generally conceded to be the most beautiful large lake in the park as well as one of the deepest and roughest. Not far below the foot of the lake is the settlement of St. Mary with stores, motels, restaurants, bars, and a garage. Along the north shore of the lake at Rising Sun there are cabins, a grocery store, a good restaurant, and a large campground.

There are dozens of impressive peaks in this valley, several of which deserve special mention. The great white pyramid south of St. Mary is Divide Mountain (8,665 ft.), an easy scramble from the old fire lookout on the northeast ridge. Mountaineers who enjoy high ridgetop walks can traverse from the end of the dirt lane east of Divide Mountain, going to the saddle south of the mountain and scrambling up to White Calf Mountain (8,825 ft.). From there, walk the spectacular ridgetop to Kupunkamint Mountain (8,893 ft.), then westward to peak 8283. The ridge goes north from there for several miles, to Curly Bear Mountain (8,099 ft.). A gap in the ridge near Curly Bear may necessitate a short detour (with elevation lost and regained) or some exposed east-side cliff-climbing. An old fire lookout was just north of the summit of Curly Bear. The trail can still be followed down toward the west to the Red Eagle Lake trail.

West of Curly Bear the Red Eagle Valley extends southwest from St. Mary Lake. The very sharp peaks rising above the valley are Split Mountain (8,792 ft.), Mt. Norris (8,900 ft.), and Triple Divide Peak (8,000 ft.). The south fork of the valley, beyond Red Eagle Lake, climbs up to Triple Divide Pass and the wild valley extending westward ends at Red Eagle Pass. The latter valley contained one of the most heavily used trails in the park, leading over Red Eagle Pass and down into the Nyack Valley, but since 1942 the trail has not been maintained. It is a mountaineering feat just trying to follow the old trail now. (See the discussion of the routes below.) From Triple Divide Pass there is a high-elevation mountaineers' route over Triple Divide Peak and Mt. Norris, thence westward on high ridgetops to Red Eagle Pass. It is described in detail as "The Norris

Traverse" under the Cutbank Valley section of this guide.

From St. Mary Lake climbers will find it easy to scramble up scree slopes and easy gullies to the summit of Red Eagle Mountain (also easy from below Red Eagle Lake). Little Chief Mountain (9,540 ft.) is a much greater challenge but the high, rounded ridgetop can be walked between Little Chief and Red Eagle passing over Mahtotopa en route. CARRY WATER! The route from Almost-a-Dog Pass and Red Eagle Pass to those mountains is described in this chapter also.

Rose Creek (Roes Creek) empties into St. Mary Lake at Rising Sun. A lovely trail goes five miles up that canyon to Otokomi Lake. Before reaching that lake, mountaineers can scramble to the 8,400-foot ridge northeast of the valley and spend the day strolling from there to Otokomi Mountain, Singleshot Mountain, and the long, long ridge of East Flattop Mountain. From the east end of that ridge a trail descends to Lower St. Mary Lake (it also goes to Napi Point) but it is not on the map inside the park boundary.

The next inlet is that of Baring Creek. The trail to Siyeh Pass (7,750 ft.), one of the highest in the park, climbs up that canyon. Beyond the pass the trail descends to Preston Park from which the easiest routes to Mt. Siyeh begin. From Preston Park, hikers can continue over Piegan Pass to Swiftcurrent Lake and the Many Glacier area, looking almost straight up the east face of Mt. Gould from several miles of spectacular trail. Most hikers feel that one pass is enough and walk down the trail to Going-to-the-Sun Highway at the Siyeh Loop instead, thus completing a half-circle around mighty Going-to-the-Sun Mountain.

On the south side of the lake a large waterfall is visible, plunging out of the high canyon between Little Chief Mountain and Dusty Star Mountain. A description of the route up that canyon, above Virginia Falls, has been included below to either entice or repel mountaineers considering it as a possible shortcut to Almost-a-Dog Pass (south of Almost-a-Dog Peak) and Red Eagle Pass.

West of Dusty Star and neighboring Citadel Mountain (9,030 ft.), a huge valley enters from the southwest. A trail from Jackson Glacier Viewpoint on the highway descends to the main trail that began at Going-to-the-Sun Point. The hike up the valley to Gunsight Lake from there is not far. The most common destination of hikers there is Gunsight Pass, from which they descend to Sperry Chalets and Lake McDonald. Climbers, however, will probably be more interested in camping at Gunsight Lake or in the Blackfoot Glacier Basin and then ascending various great mountains such as Mt. Jackson (10,052 ft.), Blackfoot Mountain (9,597 ft.), Citadel Mountain, or Mt. Logan (9,339 ft.). For those seeking real wilderness, the

Mt. St. Nicholas showing the Great Notch—Diane Ensign

Mt. Wilbur reflection and Gardner's Cabin, 30 June '54—J. G. Edwards

Joe Steffen and Joe Haugestuen approaching Thin Man's Pleasure, Mt. Wilbur—Rolf Larson

"Sam" Eischeid, North Summit Ridge of Chief Mountain—Rolf Larson

Hikers on summit of Chief Mountain—Diane Ensign

Denis Twohig on Bishop's Cap—Diane Ensign

Dan Maturen on Crowfeet Mountain above Kennedy Lake (Mt. Siyeh in background)—Dan Spencer

Dave Casteel leaping a crevasse on Grinnell Glacier—Tony Blueman

Lew Sabo looking down onto Iceberg Lake from the top of Mt. Wilbur—
J. G. Edwards

route across Blackfoot Glacier Basin to Almost-a-Dog Pass and Red Eagle Pass has been described in this chapter also. (From Red Eagle, the "Norris Traverse" extends to Triple Divide Pass and exits at the Cutbank Ranger Station, or the descent can be made to Red Eagle Lake or the Nyack Valley trail.)

In summary, the extensive St. Mary Valley area provides enough challenging destinations to keep most mountaineers occupied for several years!

ALMOST-A-DOG PASS TO RED EAGLE LAKE

From Almost-a-Dog Pass (7,900 ft.) look northward and observe an area about one-quarter mile away where the grassy slopes and scrub trees extend furthest down toward the scree slopes beneath the great cliffs. To reach that area, either hike around the west side of the rocky peak north of the pass or descend a few feet down the east side of the pass and traverse north on a good game trail that leads to the meadow. From the grassy slope look down beyond the small trees and locate a large dome of red rock about eight feet wide that is slightly separated from the main cliff face (it is called "Almost-a-Dog Dome"). Walk down to that dome and enter the gap between the dome and the cliff face. That gap leads to a marvelous steep ramp that is entirely hidden until you look down through the gap toward the north. It is six to eight feet wide and is very easy to descend (if clear of ice and snow). The steep floor of the ramp is composed of hard rock outcrops and the sides are sheer walls with many good handholds. After descending the ramp for nearly 100 feet, continue northward over a small hump and then scramble down yet another fifty or sixty feet in a similar gully that extends to the top of the talus slope beneath the great cliffs. The steep talus is easy to descend, but there is usually a steep snowbank at the very bottom of the ramp that must be crossed in order to reach the dry scree. Avoid the snow unless using ice axes OR securely anchored by rope to a piton near the bottom of the ramp. NOTICE: A safe alternate route above the cliffs also exists. Follow the horizontal game trail northward from the steep meadow above the red dome. It traverses on a broad, scree-covered shelf, all the way to the great talus slopes beneath Almost-a-Dog Mountain. It is then an easy walk down to the meadows below.

From the gentle slopes below the great cliffs it is easy to reach the old foot trail across Red Eagle Pass. Nobody should attempt the route from there to Red Eagle Lake without a good topographic map, but a brief description of the terrain is included here also. At the head of the Red Eagle

Valley, where the extensive meadows suddenly end in a steep drop-off toward the east, there is a peculiar wedge-shaped ridge that is grass-covered on top and heavily wooded on its north slope. The point of the wedge extends eastward and the old trail from Red Eagle Valley comes up onto the meadows from the south via that wedge. Descend the very steep trail to the head of the valley. There is no trace of a trail left in the thickets of maple and alder there, so a hillside traverse to the edge of the forest is recommended. In the forest the trail disappears beneath dozens of fallen trees but appears again in the meadow along the south side of the valley. The stream must soon be forded after leaving the meadow. The trail is stronger in the forest beyond that crossing. After two more stream crossings, the maintained human foot trail is reached. It is an easy hike from there out to St. Mary (seven or eight miles more). This is a fantastic trip but there are many hazards, so be SURE that somebody knows where you are going before attempting it! (For more details see "Red Eagle Lake to Nyack Creek via Red Eagle Pass.")

In addition to the possibility of going from Red Eagle Pass to Red Eagle Lake, there are other goals that may be realized by persons who reach Red Eagle Pass. The trail into Nyack Valley is not any better than the one to Red Eagle Lake and is much more remote (it can lead to Two Medicine Lake in one more day, or to West Glacier, or to Highway No. 2 after fording the Flathead River). The route called the "Norris Traverse" follows high ridges from Red Eagle Pass to Triple Divide Pass. (See description elsewhere in the guide.) It is also possible to make easy ascents of Almost-a-Dog Mountain, Little Chief Mountain, Mahtotopa Mountain, and Red Eagle Mountain from Red Eagle Pass by walking along the mile-high connecting ridges. A great many mountaineers will feel that Red Eagle Pass itself is goal enough and will enjoy hiking to the far south end of the pass to see massive Mt. Stimson rising 7,000 vertical feet above the wild Nyack Valley. For masochists, the experience of forcing a passage from Almost-a-Dog Pass to Virginia Falls (or vice versa) might be considered. (See description in this chapter of "Virginia Falls to Almost-a-Dog Pass.")

BLACKFOOT BASIN TRAVERSE
FROM GUNSIGHT LAKE TO ALMOST-A-DOG PASS

From Gunsight Lake hike approximately 1.5 miles up the trail toward Jackson Glacier. Above the first long, steep hill the trail becomes faint but with the aid of "ducks" of rock it can be followed until it nears the lateral moraine of Jackson Glacier. That moraine forms a great ridge of gravel and dirt abruptly ending the meadows through which the trail has been passing.

As the moraine is approached, drop a bit lower and parallel the small groves of trees along the lower edge of the meadow. Just before reaching the moraine descend a small, nearly dry creekbed that extends down through the trees. Follow it down for about 100 feet until below the trees, then angle to the right on a faint game trail that passes around the end of that great moraine. Continue toward the right through boulder fields and scattered shrubs heading toward the snout of Jackson Glacier. (The huge glacier shown on older maps as "Blackfoot Glacier" has melted so much since the 1930s that it fragmented into two separate glaciers named

A climber on Mt. Jackson surveys the expanse of snow and ice in Jackson and Blackfoot glaciers—Brian Kennedy

The great Blackfoot Glacier Basin, with routes indicated for
mountaineers—William Blunk and Ralph Thornton

Jackson Glacier and Blackfoot Glacier.) About 200 feet upstream there is
a huge rock in midstream with deep water rushing along both sides of it.
Leap to the near side of that massive boulder then climb up over the top of
it and down the other side, from which you can leap to the far shore. There
are flat sandy areas nearby that are good campsites and trees not far away
in which to hang packs and food.

More than a hundred yards east of the stream another moraine must be
crossed. The approach is easiest to your right near the upper edge of the
thicket of small willow trees (where the boulder field extends furthest into
the trees). After passing through most of the trees head slightly toward the
left (north) and scramble up the moraine toward several slender trees atop
it. Cross over the moraine there and descend fifteen feet down to the stream

beyond. The torrent is barely too wide to jump but a larger boulder in the middle of it provides an easy way across. Enter the beautiful undulating meadows then look uphill to scout the route. Observe the large cliffs extending across the north side of the great hump (that bears a benchmark labelled "B.M. 6879" on old topo maps). The objective to reach next is the east end of those cliffs. Walk uphill by the east edge of the first big snowfield then traverse eastward past some big trees and across the bottom of another snowfield. Along the east edge of this latter snowfield a faint game trail climbs steeply all the way up to the end of the cliffs mentioned earlier.

Next, traverse eastward across two small moraines and approach a swift stream that may be crossed only with a herculean leap. (It might be crossed upstream on the snow but there is the hazard of breaking through it and falling into the stream.) East of the stream angle to the left while climbing the next moraine, then cross the boulder-strewn area where, through fairly dense brush, you will see two small lakes below you. Descend easily to the first lake and walk along the shore to its south end. The large mountain east of this great "Blackfoot Basin" is Mt. Logan. The route heads directly toward it for the next hour. While keeping Mt. Logan

James Dyson, author of The World of Ice, *leaping a giant crevasse*

always before you, enjoy crossing the bare, polished, colorful rock formations that were so recently being abraded by the movement of old Blackfoot Glacier. There are waterfalls plunging into lakes and ponds, all kinds of rapids and rills, numerous "water-wheels," and pools and seeps everywhere. It reminds many people of some areas in Bryce or Zion national parks. Eventually the last obstacle, the eastern lateral moraine, will be reached and climbed. Beyond it there are steep horizontal strips of meadow studded with low rock outcrops and patches of small trees extending toward Mt. Logan. Two prominent streams race down through the area. The larger stream flows down just west of a big moraine and then leaps over a cliff to form a lovely waterfall. That stream must be crossed far above the waterfall. The easiest approach is to hike uphill across the steep meadows to the smaller stream (west of the waterfall). Scramble up over the ridge just beyond it. Beyond the larger stream, cross over the moraine and into the meadow (a good campsite with great views, tasty water, and plenty of firewood). Extensive strips of horizontal meadow lie ahead separated by long horizontal thickets of alpine fir. Go uphill, pass through the second steep thicket of trees, then walk northeast into the great broad open basin. Stroll up the gentle slopes to the saddle above which climbers call "Almost-a-Dog Pass." Views from the pass (7,900 ft.) are spectacular. The cliffs below toward the east are terrifying. (For a description of the route down the cliffs and into the valley, see the route from "Almost-a-Dog Pass to Red Eagle Lake" in this guide.)

A very different route across Blackfoot Glacier Basin is the "high traverse" favored by Bill Blunk and Ralph Thornton. A ice ax is essential for a safe, rapid crossing of snow slopes there. Ascend the polished rock outcroppings above the "swift stream that may be crossed only with a herculean leap" (mentioned above). Make a high traverse far above the two small lakes. Stay on snowfields and solid rock surfaces, but below glacial ice-fronts while traversing horizontally toward Almost-a-Dog Pass. The route passes just above the large lateral moraine that is east of the broad glaciated basin used on the customary route. (Ascents to the ridgetop between Mt. Logan and Blackfoot Mountain are possible on the mixed snow and rock slopes above that moraine for climbers intent upon reaching the summit of Blackfoot.)

East of that long moraine continue over another moraine about 100 yards further east and reach still more expanses of sloping bedrock and snow that must be traversed. Approach the cliffs along the west side of the low ridge extending north from Mount Logan. When above the moraine-dammed pond (shown on the 1968 map) angle slightly uphill to about the 7,300-foot elevation. Traverse above the steep lower cliffs following a good goat trail. Beyond the cliff descend the crest of a moraine for twenty or thirty feet below where it abuts against the cliff. Continue from there on a game trail along the base of the cliff. It passes around a corner where a way must be forced through about ten feet of low, scrubby trees in order to reach the meadows of the great basin west of Almost-a-Dog Pass.

This higher route takes longer because it is farther, but it may be more interesting to alpinists than the straight-line route described above. An advantage may also be the decreased likelihood of having sudden close encounters with grizzly bears, since there is visibility in all directions at all times. For hikers taking the lower route across the great glacier basin it is possible to join the high route after reaching the long moraine between the barren basin and the meadows east of it. Simply walk uphill east of that moraine until near its upper extremity, then angle eastward. Pass above the small trees, cross over the next moraine, and traverse the snow and rock until above the moraine-dammed pond. From there follow the route described above to the Almost-a-Dog Pass meadows.

THE NORRIS TRAVERSE

This remarkable cross-country route from Triple Divide Pass to Red Eagle Pass is described in detail under the Cut Bank Area section of this guide. The route involves the climb of Triple Divide Peak and Norris Mountain, then a long ridge walk on excellent game trails to Red Eagle Pass. Energetic mountaineers can then cross Almost-a-Dog Pass (described above) and continue across the Blackfoot Glacier Basin to Gunsight Lake (also described above). This is all part of the "Continental Divide Route."

RED EAGLE LAKE TO NYACK VALLEY
VIA RED EAGLE PASS

Before the Second World War this trail was one of the most heavily traveled in the park. Accounts reported that hundreds of horse-borne visitors went over Red Eagle Pass every week during the summer months. Park literature abounded with references to the beauty of that popular area. After the war the trail was never re-opened, but during the 1950s it was still in good condition. There were even good logs for crossing the streams. In 1963 the trail was still in fair condition except for two short stretches. Hikers could go from St. Mary to Nyack Creek in one easy day (as the author did with Dr. Herbert Alberding on July 22 that year). Since then many people have hiked from Red Eagle Lake to the Pass. Ranger Fred Reese led small groups of employees over from Gunsight Lake to St. Mary via Almost-a-Dog Pass and Red Eagle Valley. The trail has been deleted from the new topographic maps since it is not patrolled or maintained, so only mountaineers, bears, and hoofed creatures are likely to use it now. Because this is such an important access route to Red Eagle Pass for mountaineers, a section of the older map is duplicated here to show the location of the famous old trail.

From the trail junction west of Red Eagle Lake, in the sharp bend of Red Eagle Creek just above the inlet of the stream that drains Medicine Owl Lake, the old trail crosses Red Eagle Creek. It is possible to wade it or cross it on logs, OR to bushwhack from the east end of the present bridge, around the north side of that steep bend and reach the old trail west of the two stream crossings. For the next mile the trail passes through an open forest of small pines with moss-covered rock outcroppings and fragile herbaceous growth. There is no difficulty until reaching the next stream crossing. When the trail emerges from the forest into an open meadow, turn left and go directly to the stream. Fifty feet downstream it is wider and very shallow but the old trail crossed the stream at the south end of the meadow. After the crossing, the trail goes through extensive meadows along the south side of the forest for nearly another mile. The first troublesome area is encountered soon after the trail angles to the north and enters the forest. A massive blowdown of lodgepole pines occurred there between 1952 and

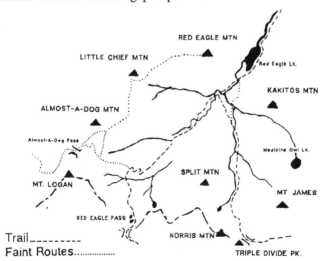

RED EAGLE PASS: CHALLENGES AND OPPORTUNITIES

1962 after which hikers had to detour around the mess or walk over the criss-crossed logs several feet off the ground for forty or fifty feet. The trail beyond the blowdown soon reaches the stream near the fork and is easily crossed there. The broad basin at the head of the valley is reached then (about 5,500 ft.) and the second obstacle is encountered. The trail has been obliterated and completely grown over by a dense growth of small willows and other shrubs. When convenient climb up the hillside north of that willow thicket and traverse that hillside toward the headwall. The old horse trail will be found there where it climbs steeply up to the tremendous meadows above the headwall. Those meadows extend for almost two miles toward the south and nearly that far toward the north. There are a number of desirable destinations accessible from this idyllic area. Some of them are discussed elsewhere in this chapter, under "Red Eagle Pass: Challenges and Opportunities."

Mountaineers who wish to spend a day or two around Red Eagle Pass while making easy exploratory trips will have a marvelous time. Those who are only intent on crossing the pass and descending into the mighty Nyack Valley must follow the old trail southward through the meadows to the small lakes, then walk toward the corridor that was cleared through the scrubby forest southeast from the lakes in the 1920s. However, any faint remnants of this long-abandoned trail in the wooded areas to the west were obliterated by the huge blowdown in that area in the winter of 88-89.

Red Eagle Lake mirrors Split Mountain with Triple Divide Peak in the background—Hileman Photo, NPS

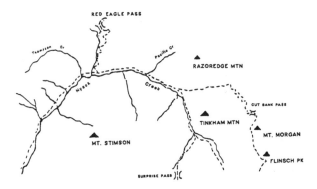

UPPER NYACK VALLEY AND SURROUNDINGS

The great alpine meadows near Red Eagle Pass extend for nearly four miles, from north to south. The pass is not easy to reach, but descriptions of various approach routes are included elsewhere in this chapter under the following headings: "Red Eagle Lake to Nyack Valley, Via Red Eagle Pass" and "Almost-A-Dog Pass to Red Eagle Pass" (preceeded by "Blackfoot Basin Traverse" or "Virginia Falls to Almost-a-Dog Pass"). From the Cut Bank Valley, Red Eagle Pass can be reached via "The Norris Traverse," which passes over two mountain summits and a long high ridge en route.

There are a large number of desirable destinations near the pass. Some are discussed elsewhere in this chapter, under "Red Eagle Lake to Nyack Valley, via Red Eagle Pass." Others include the following: (1) Scramble to the notch in the ridge south of Mt. Logan (between Logan Glacier and Red Eagle Glacier) and climb either Clyde Peak or Mt. Logan easily from there; (2) Go northwest past Mt. Logan, to Almost-a-Dog Pass, which provides access to the Blackfoot Glacier Basin and Gunsight Lake (for details, see descriptions mentioned above); (3) Go further north, below and beyond Almost-a-Dog Pass, to the great scree slopes that extend up to Almost-a-Dog Mountain. A continuous shelf 150 feet up the cliffs above the scree-slopes west of the basin, below Almost-a-Dog Mountain, is broad and flat enough to use for horse travel, and has a very good game trail extending all the way to the steep meadow just north of Almost-A-Dog Pass; (4) Scramble up 1,400 vertical feet of scree and easy cliffs directly beneath Almost-A-Dog to reach the rounded ridgetop east of that peak, thence on up the south face to the summit (8,922); (5) Continue northward along the ridge to the summit of Little Chief Mountain; (6) Walk the spectacular ridgetop east of Little Chief for miles, to Red Eagle Mountain; (7) From the south end of Red Eagle Pass, follow the game trail for four miles eastward, to Triple Divide Pass. (See details of "The Norris Traverse" under the Cut Bank Valley chapter); and (8) The very well-worn game trail that goes west from the south end of Red Eagle Pass can be followed up to a steep couloir on the southeast end of the long, long ridge of Mt. Logan. Above the couloir, follow game trails along the top or the west side of the ridge for several miles, to the summit of Mt. Logan (and on down to Almost-a-Dog Pass). There are two great notches in that long ridgetop, each with a small meadow. One is above the two small lakes in the Red Eagle Pass meadows and the other is between Clyde Peak and Mt. Logan's summit. Both can be reached rather easily from the meadows of Red Eagle Pass. (For details of the long ridge route to Mt. Logan, write to the Glacier Mountaineering Society, P.O. Box 291, Whitefish, Montana, 59937, and request a description of "The Scenic Death March.")

THE SCENIC DEATH MARCH

This scenic traverse around Mt. Logan and the long south ridge of that mountain (which includes Clyde Peak) is very interesting and extremely scenic. The distance around the mountain and ridge is about five miles, and unless the two peaks are also climbed the hike will require about six hours. Although the traverse usually will begin at Almost-a-Dog Pass, it can also be started from Red Eagle Pass. (See details elsewhere in this guide for the approaches to Almost-a-Dog and Red Eagle Pass. Obviously the trip should never be attempted solo, OR without registering with the rangers who might later be on the search and rescue mission!)

After descending from Almost-a-Dog Pass to Red Eagle Meadows, follow the faint trail southward, past Red Eagle Glacier and Logan Glacier, to the small lakes near the south end of the meadows. From the larger lake a corridor leads southeast through extensive thickets of ten-foot tall trees, and the trail continues to the actual Red Eagle Pass (6,640 ft.), where there is a great view of Mt. Stimson rising 7,000 vertical feet above the dense forests of the Nyack Valley. From that viewpoint the faint trail leading downhill is the ancient human trail into Nyack Valley, but the more distinct trail that continues westward is a well-worn game trail. Follow the game trail a short distance, to a trail fork. Take the right-hand fork and zig-zag up and around a patch of trees, then uphill and westward to a steep couloir that extends straight up for about 800 vertical feet (class 2 or 3). Above that couloir, cross over a large rock-field and locate the good game trail that traverses north along the west side of the high ridge. After about half a mile of easy walking the trail fades away. Before that time, leave the trail and climb up any safe gully for about 100 vertical feet to a large scree slope above the cliffs. Another good game trail traverses the scree above the cliffs, and enters a flat meadow on a deep notch in the ridgetop further north. (The flat area is directly above the lakes in Red Eagle meadows, which can be reached from here.) North of the flat meadow the trail leads onward along the west face of the high ridge, passing the base of Clyde Peak en route. (See description of that climb in this guide.) North of Clyde Peak there is another flat meadow, which is directly above Red Eagle and Logan Glaciers and can be reached easily from the east side. Beyond that flat meadow a trail follows a ledge northward along the east side of the great ridge, ending at a sheer wall with a good view of Almost-a-Dog Pass. Instead of going that way, climb a six-foot cliff and cross a tiny meadow to reach the *west* side of the great ridge, where another good game trail traverses northward. After a few minutes, scramble up the scree to the base of the high cliffs and follow the trail there toward the north. The great basin of scree, ledges, and small cliffs extends all the way to the southwest ridge of Mt. Logan, and can be crossed almost anywhere with safety.

From the high southwest ridge of Logan it is a short, easy scramble up to the summit. Return to that ridge before heading across the west face of Mt. Logan. It is essential that the great game trail be found there. That trail is a little lower than the southwest ridge, and follows a natural stratum across the face, descending gently all the way. Eventually it crosses a steeper portion of the face and leads to a great notch in the northwest ridge of the mountain. (Any other traverse would be very difficult, so climbers will surely locate the trail while traversing northward across the west face of the mountain.) Beyond the large notch it is an easy walk down scree or snow, to Almost-a-Dog Pass.

NOTE: This west face traverse is a good approach to Clyde Peak for climbers who have crossed the Blackfoot Glacier Basin from Gunsight Lake. If climbers are already in Red Eagle Meadows, they may climb up to either of the flat meadows along the south ridge of the Logan massif and climb Clyde Peak and/or Mt. Logan with ease.

This "Scenic Death March" was first negotiated in August 1975, by Mavis Lorenz, Paul Jensen, Al Smith, Alice Edwards, Jane Edwards, and Gordon Edwards from a base camp at the Jackson Glacier outlet. It was a foggy day, so the ridge top was invisible from the west face goat trail. The return to camp was made about midnight.

VIRGINIA FALLS TO ALMOST-A-DOG PASS

This is a DIFFERENT kind of mountaineering experience! Distance to the pass from Virginia Falls is about three miles, none of it by trail. Elevation gained is about 3,200 vertical feet. If the Park Service ever clears a trail for 1.5 miles up the valley from the human trail beside Virginia Falls, the hike to Almost-a-Dog Pass will become very popular and the round-trip hike will then be possible in a single reasonable day. At present, however, the trip is a real test of perseverence and ingenuity!

Dr. James Dyson, a remarkably tough mountaineer in the Park before the Second World War, said he was only really exhausted once, and that was in the Virginia Creek Valley. He was near Citadel Peak in mid-afternoon and was preparing to head across Blackfoot Glacier to Gunsight Lake and walk out to the road. He looked down the head of the Virginia Creek Valley and it was all grassy meadows and rather gentle. Immediately beyond the gentle meadows he saw the deep blue of St. Mary Lake, and he decided it MUST be a faster, easier route than the long trip via Gunsight Lake. He was wrong. By midnight he was wading chest-deep in beaver ponds and slogging down the center of Virginia Creek in pitch darkness . . . and then he reached the top of the large waterfall that is not visible from elsewhere and was not on the map. He finally staggered out to the road just before dawn, and vowed to prevent other climbers from suffering a similar fate. His warning was passed on by everyone he told of the experience, including this author, but eventually a group of seasoned mountaineers tried it again in the 1960s, with equally memorable consequences (even though they had lights).

My wife and daughter and I once spent a full day flagging game trails up the east side of the valley, to the end of the forest below the third waterfall. Three years later some friends joined us in the search for a route up the west side of the valley. We searched the slopes from the stream up to the cliffs of Citadel Mountain, but found only fragments of trails. The final climb up steep, brushy meadows and scree, to reach the elevation of the top of the waterfall that is above the great forested valley, was exhausting. A narrow ledge was found crossing the cliff west of that waterfall and it provided access to the meadows along the valley above that waterfall. It was a beautiful hike from there to Almost-a-Dog Pass, and in mid-afternoon we started back down. Below the upper waterfall, Lew Sabo found faint, steep game trails that got us down to Virginia Creek. We crossed it and entered the forest, but found that most of the old yellow ribbons had disappeared. Somehow we ended up on a dead-end trail that was too low in the forest, and the sun was setting as we reached the top of a cliff overlooking the great hidden waterfall. Connie Bachman and John Mauff commented that the sunset was "beautiful." In the dark, with no lights, we crossed great alder-covered hillsides and crashed through Menzesia thickets among downed tree trunks for hours. After feeling our way through the big timber blowdown, we finally started down the last steep hillside, beside Virginia Falls. It was too dark to see, but we groped our way from tree trunk to tree trunk, guided by the sound of roaring Virginia Falls. The next day we agreed that, in retrospect, it was a great hike, and Connie was still telling everyone how lovely that sunset was. Other mountaineers who enjoy such memorable experiences are urged to spend some time getting familiar with the Virginia Creek Valley. Hopefully this brief account will help them discover the best route, and will encourage them to carry plenty of flashlight batteries!

Routes to the Summits

Blackfoot Mountain (9,597)

Views from the summit are majestic, and from there one may see more distant scenes than from most other peaks in the Park. Toward the west, Hungry Horse Reservoir and the Swan Range are clearly visible, while the Sweetgrass Hills may be distinguished far out in the prairies near the eastern horizon. South of the Park are the lonely peaks of the remote Bob Marshall Wilderness Area, while toward the north one gazes upon a sea of peaks extending well beyond the Canadian border. Deeply crevassed Pumpelly Glacier clings to the south flank of Blackfoot Mountain and beyond it, across the immensely deep Nyack Valley, Mt. Stimson's mighty bulk commands attention. F. E. Matthes (1904) wrote: "Here is a scene which dwarfs the Yosemite Valley and makes the Grand Canyon seem commonplace." He especially admired Harrison Glacier, saying: "Descending 3,000 feet in tumultuous ice-cascades this magnificent glacier eclipses all others we have seen." Despite glacier recessions, this is still a magnificent reward for the perseverent climbers who attain this remote summit!

The Blackfoot Glacier Route. Distance to summit about ten miles, eight of it by trail. Elevation gained is about 4,900 feet Class 2 and 3 until almost to Blackfoot Glacier, then some class 4 to 5 en route to the summit ridge. Ice ax required for each climber, and a reliable climbing rope. The first known ascent was by Henry L. Stimson in 1894.

Leave Going-to-the-Sun Highway at the Jackson Glacier Viewpoint and hike six miles to Gunsight Lake and its primitive campground. Next day, follow the faint, steep trail toward Jackson Glacier. The trail fades away in the extensive meadows, but eventually approaches the great lateral moraine of Jackson Glacier. The meadows end abruptly, and you descend a small streambed to the lower end of the moraine. Pass around the moraine and walk upstream toward Jackson Glacier through scattered willow bushes. About 200 feet upstream there is a huge rock in midstream that will permit a dry crossing. Leap to that high midstream boulder, walk to the far side of it, and then leap to the other shore. There are flat sandy areas nearby that are ideal campsites, and trees not far away in which to hang packs and food.

Continue toward Blackfoot Mountain, climbing about 600 feet in elevation to the prominent little waterfall that drains the western lobe of Blackfoot Glacier (it flows down the hill and forms Siksika Falls far below). In the 1930s Blackfoot Glacier was huge, but it has melted so much that the remnants are now widely separated and are called Jackson Glacier and Blackfoot Glacier, respectively.

The lower cliff just north of the waterfall may be easily climbed (class 3 or 4). Above the waterfall is a large snowfield separated from the true glacier by a low rocky ridge. Walk up that ridge about one-quarter mile to the highest point of rock projecting into the edge of the glacier. Rope up and carefully walk up the glacier, testing with ice axes for hidden crevasses. Go toward the ice cliff (about sixty feet high) that hangs over a rock cliff about the same height. A big bergschrund develops on each side of this ice cliff late in summer and it is probably dangerous to attempt the ascent of the steep ice slopes beside it at any time. A safe route lies up the rocky wall farther west from the ice cliff. Climb carefully up the steepening ice to a place where the leader, safely roped and belayed from below, may cross the bergschrund from the snow onto the cliff wall (class 4 to 5). Fairly high on that wall there is a good ledge traversing to your right. Climb a bit higher and angle back toward the ice cliff to the top of this rocky outcropping. The ascent of the upper portion of the glacier above this rock becomes progressively more difficult as it steepens near the ridge. At least two large crevasses extend across this portion but are likely to be concealed by snow of varying strength and thickness. Be sure to stay roped while climbing this slope, and probe the snow with ice axes to be sure of locating concealed crevasses. Angle up toward the east and reach the ridgetop where easiest. A good goat trail follows the ridge eastward to the summit pyramid. Two small cliffs must be descended near the lowest part of the ridge, but they may be by-passed on adjacent snow slopes. From this ridge it is an easy walk up the talus slopes west of the upper snowfields and no further obstacles block the route to the summit.

Mt. Logan Ridge Route. Distance to summit about fourteen miles, eight of it by human trail. Following the description given elsewhere in this guide, cross the polished, colorful rock formations in the Blackfoot Glacier Basin. Climb over the large eastern lateral moraine of ancient Blackfoot Glacier and walk across grass-covered shelves between small fir trees (there are many good campsites there). Follow the route described elsewhere in this guide to Almost-a-Dog Pass, and the route described to Mt. Logan from that pass, until reaching the elevation of the great ridgetop extending from Mt. Logan to Blackfoot Mountain. Ice axes and rope are usually essential for safely making the long traverse between the two

Blackfoot Glacier—James Dyson

mountains along that ridgetop. There are no difficulties in getting from there to the summit. A variant of this route was climbed in August 1969 by Rangers Fred Reese and Stewart Cassidy. It leaves the meadows below the lowest part of that ridgetop and goes up the very steep snowfields to the ridge. Ice axes are absolutely necessary, and crampons are strongly recommended. For climbers accustomed to snow and ice work the descent will also be pleasant, with great glissading possibilities (remember the warning, however, against glissading down slopes that you have not recently climbed up—there are hazards of iced snow and hidden crevasses, as well as suddenly encountered cliffs).

The Southwest Cirque Route. Distance to summit about twelve miles, six of it by human trail (after fording the Flathead River). Elevation gained is about 6,300 feet. Several class 4 and 5 pitches, with great exposure, on the cirque wall. First known ascent by Rangers John E. Wilcox and Wyatt Woodsmall, August 7 and 8, 1969. This is an extremely grueling climb, requiring ice axes, pitons, carabiners, ropes, and previous experience climbing rocks and ice. The account is based on a description written by the first ascent climbers.

Leave U.S. Highway 2 about 6.9 miles east of the West Glacier highway junction (perhaps less, due to road re-routing since 1969). Descend the embankment and cross the railroad tracks to reach the Flathead River. Cross the river by wading, swimming, or by boat. WARNING: This is a large river and very treacherous, especially early in summer. North of the river head northeast for 200 feet and find the boundary trail. Follow that trail west to the junction of the Harrison Lake trail, then hike 5.5 miles to the head of that lake. Beyond the lake the trail has not been maintained for years, so plan on three miles of horrible bushwhacking before reaching the head of the valley (follow up the streambed to avoid much of the brush). Directly ahead, notice the large waterfall high on Blackfoot Mountain. That fall is interrupted by a long, wide ledge that extends across the cirque wall in both directions. Now notice a much smaller waterfall to the west of the large one. The climbing route leads up the west side of that smaller waterfall and generally up the cascading creek until reaching the meadows far above the falls. A difficult class 5 pitch must be climbed on the twelve-foot cliff just west of the smaller waterfall, then many broken cliffs to scramble up before reaching the great ledge that extends across the cirque face.

The cliffs above that transverse ledge are sheer and frightening, so avoid them by traversing westward on the ledge until reaching a clump of spruce and fir trees. Ascend a steep gully toward the right (east) over grassy slopes. The wall steepens, and soon a class 5 cliff must be climbed to reach a critical 200-foot long shelf that angles upward at a sixty-degree angle. Climb that steep pitch toward the right, via a semi-chimney technique in the lower fifty feet (the last 100 feet is mostly class 3 and 4). At last the top of the great cliff is reached and climbers can relax without so much "exposure" beneath them.

Above the great cliff, traverse to the east to the stream that later forms the large waterfall in the cirque wall. Follow up the stream, to great alpine meadows, above which it plunges down over another headwall. That headwall can be avoided by ascending due north up steep meadows for nearly an hour. Finally it is possible to angle northeastward across ridges and scree-slopes toward the high waterfall just below the summit pyramid of Blackfoot Mountain. Ascend easy cliffs beside the fall, to reach the meadows above it. THE SUMMIT OF BLACKFOOT MOUNTAIN IS STILL THREE HOURS AWAY! The meadow is a good place to spend the night.

To complete the climb, walk up to the moraine above the meadow (the stream issues from that moraine). Scramble up it and walk along its crest toward the summit. Two routes to the top are possible from here: (1) Leave the moraine and climb straight up two steep snowbanks (probably contiguous in early summer) to where the snow extends furthest uphill, then climb onto the cliffs above; or (2) Follow the moraine crest steeply uphill toward the south, then traverse upward on a lateral moraine that extends across the snowfield. When the cliffs are reached, traverse back northeast to the summit ridge. Both routes lead to the final 500 vertical feet of class 3 ledges that extend to the very top of this great mountain.

Citadel Mountain (9,030)

Perhaps the views from this mountain are not as inspiring as those from Mt. Jackson, Mt. Logan, or Blackfoot Mountain, but they are nevertheless quite satisfying. Blackfoot and Jackson Glaciers are spread across the great basin in the southern foreground, and Gunsight Lake shimmers in the afternoon sun looking hopelessly far away. Far below on the other side of the mountain azure St. Mary Lake gleams like a jewel in the bright red setting of its surrounding cliffs. Higher in the valley tiny autos creep up Going-to-the-Sun Highway, and Logan Pass is clearly visible. Beyond the narrow north ridge of Citadel Mountain, Going-to-the-Sun Mountain casts its massive shadow on Goat Mountain and Mt. Siyeh dominates the skyline beyond. Even though you can see the road and the pass, there is a great feeling of isolation, perhaps because of the long approach through uninhabited, trailless regions en route to this splendid peak.

The South Ridge Route. Distance to the summit about twelve miles, eight miles of it by human trail. Elevation gained is more than 4,000 vertical feet. Class 2 and 3 most of the way, but with class 4 pitches near the summit. First ascent: James L. Dyson, R. H. Iverson, and Alton Lindsey, July 16, 1939.

Leave the Jackson Glacier Viewpoint on Going-to-the-Sun Road and hike six miles to Gunsight Lake. Turn left beyond the bridge at the lake's outlet and follow the faint trail for nearly two miles, to the moraine below Jackson Glacier. See the description of the Traverse of Blackfoot Glacier Basin elsewhere in this guide, for the details of the complicated route from Jackson Glacier to the far east end of the great basin. After crossing the final moraine on that route (east of the big waterfall) and walking up to the narrow strip of meadow between the second and third horizontal thickets of trees, leave the route to Almost-a-Dog Pass. Head northward in that meadow as it descends gradually toward the south end of Citadel Mountain (notice the excellent campsites and numerous cold streams along the route).

After reaching the broad saddle between the St. Mary and Virginia Creek valleys, the actual climb begins. Angle up the scree toward the west and a distinct goat trail is soon reached. Follow it around the west side of the mountain, about 100 yards below the lowest sheer cliffs. A unique balanced mass of rock atop a slender pedestal is not far above the trail. Shortly after passing below that balanced rock, ascend to the top of the ridge above it and walk along that ridge toward the summit. Soon the ridge abuts against sheer cliffs but the goat trail passes onto the west face of the higher ridge and continues for a long, long distance at that same elevation. After several hundred yards of traversing on that marvelous trail, scramble up the scree toward the base of the steep cliffs that rise to the summit of the great south ridge that is still so far above you. Less than ten feet below that cliff there is another good goat trail. Follow it northward, again for a long, long time! It crosses two very steep gullies that would be extremely difficult to negotiate at any elevation below the goat trail (if snow lingers in them, the crossing should be *carefully* belayed). At each gully the trail bends sharply around a corner of the cliff, toward the right, and traverses for eight to ten feet along a class 4 ledge not more than six inches wide. North of those two hazardous gullies watch for a great couloir that extends nearly to the ridgetop south of the summit dome. Within that couloir there are two distinct gullies of scree which unite into a single constricted passage about eight feet wide near the bottom. After entering the great couloir, ascend either the right or left fork for perhaps a hundred vertical feet, above which they converge again. Beyond the convergence a single narrow gully continues upward, providing safe, easy access to the top of the ridge.

From the ridgetop one gets a very discouraging view of the summit, for it is protected by incredibly nasty-looking cliffs. Fortunately, a route exists that is relatively safe and will afford access to the summit in less than half an hour. The first obstacle is a sheer cliff about twenty feet high that completely blocks the narrow ridge and extends downward into greater cliffs on both sides of the ridge. An extremely narrow, deep chimney is located directly in the center of that south-facing cliff, providing an uncomfortable but most interesting class 4 route up the pitch. Next, traverse along the west side of the ridge, then pass through a broad notch and onto the east side. Scree slopes there provide easy access to the summit.

When the second ascent of this peak was made in 1967 (Alice, Jane, and Gordon Edwards), Dr. James Dyson's first ascent register was found in a small can rusting in the summit cairn. It was a moving experience to realize that nobody had stood there since he and his friends were there twenty-eight years earlier. Dr. Dyson, our very good friend, had recently passed away after a vigorously active life. In 1962 his book, *The World of Ice,* was judged the best non-fiction book published in the United States that year. It included many photographs of peaks and glaciers in this national park. (Unfortunately, a member of the third ascent team a few years later removed that summit register! Perhaps he was the person who removed so many other summit registers and deprived future climbers of the pleasure of sharing them!)

The North Cirque Route. Ford the cold St. Mary River, then bushwhack up the stream basin into the north cirque. Scramble up the slope to the northeast ridge, between Dusty Star Mountain and Citadel, then walk up that ridge to the summit. Dr. Robert Horodyski, who made this first ascent on September 18, 1978, referred to it as "a fairly easy hike, except for the vegetation along the St. Mary River and on the lower slopes of the mountain." He spent only 4.5 hours on the climb to the summit. In view of his abilities and stamina, this probably translates into eight hours of hell for the more average climber.

Clyde Peak (8,610)

In 1982 Bill Blunk and Ralph Thornton, two very dedicated mountaineers from Illinois, felt that the exploits of Norman Clyde in Glacier National Park in the 1920s and 1930s deserved some solid form of permanent recognition. Every other climber who heard their proposals enthusiastically agreed. While crossing the "Norris Traverse" the previous summer they had been impressed by a spectacular unnamed spire over-looking Red Eagle Pass, and thought THAT would be an appropriate mountain to name "Clyde Peak" in honor of that great man.

In 1983 the two climbers backpacked in to that remote area again, ascended the peak, and left a register on the summit. *Hungry Horse News* editor Brian Kennedy (an accomplished mountain climber himself) pub-lished an excellent account of the incident on September 1, 1983, with some great photographs. Norman Clyde made the first ascent of the spectacular peak on July 23, 1923, and the small rock cairn he made there was still in place when Thornton and Blunk reached the summit sixty years later, with no indication that anyone had been there in the interim!

Clyde Peak is not a difficult climb, but the approaches to it are very demanding. Climbers on Mt. Logan can approach it from the high southwest ridge of Logan via a scree slope descent to the saddle. The Red Eagle Pass approaches are all time-consuming. The route up Red Eagle Valley is difficult because the trail from Red Eagle Lake has not been maintained since the Second World War, and is not even on the new topographic maps. The St. Mary area map in this guide shows that trail, and it is discussed in more detail under the description of "Red Eagle Lake to Nyack Creek." Other approaches are also described in this guide: "The Norris Traverse From Triple Divide Pass to Red Eagle Pass"; "The Blackfoot Basin Traverse From Gunsight Lake to Almost-a-Dog Pass"; "Virginia Falls to Almost-a-Dog Pass"; and "Almost-a-Dog Pass to Red Eagle Lake."

The ascent route of Clyde Peak was indicated on the photograph in the *Hungry Horse News* article, but Blunk has provided the following addi-tional details in a personal letter. Walk up the moraine between Red Eagle Glacier and Logan Glacier toward the narrow saddle above. The moraine extends up to a wide scree shelf with an upward-angling goat path that eventually reaches the broken gully further south (above Red Eagle Glacier). "The climbing here is pleasant, although only one person at a time should climb in the upper gully because of loose rock." Near the top it is safer to climb the broken south wall of the gully, although it is also possible to continue up the deepest part of the gully. Above the gully is a small flat meadow in the saddle. Blunk and Thornton traversed around the west side of Clyde Peak from there, then made an ascending traverse to an open gully "between the northern-most gully and the deepest gully on that face," but they stated "It looks like the route could be chosen almost at random here." Half an hour of pleasant class 3 climbing led to the summit. Mt. Stimson, Mt. Logan, and Blackfoot Mountain (with spectacular

Clyde Peak is this graceful spire above Red Eagle Pass— William Blunk and Ralph Thornton

Pumpelly Glacier) were impressive from that vantage point. In the other direction lies beautiful Red Eagle Lake in its heavily forested valley, with miles of alpine meadows spread out at your feet above the headwall.

Hopefully, the Board of Geographic Place Names will favorably consider the formal request that this attractive peak be officially known as "Clyde Peak." Norman Clyde would have been delighted!

East Flattop Mountain (8,356)

The description of routes to this mountain from the west are discussed in this guide under the sections on Otokomi Mountain and Singleshot Mountain. The highest point of East Flattop is a rounded scree-covered knoll that is actually west and south of the top of Singleshot Mountain. The obvious procedure for most mountaineers would be to approach the mountain via Otokomi Mountain, detour to the top of Singleshot Mountain, then stroll along the three miles of the summit ridge of East Flattop, heading northeast. Descend from the east end of the mountain on the trail that joins the Napi Point trail in the lush meadows at about the 7,100-foot elevation. Downhill, to the right, that trail leads easily to Lower St. Mary Lake.

Fusillade Mountain (8,750)

The views from this long, narrow ridge are unique because of its very favorable location. The most attractive scene is surely the St. Mary Valley, with soaring cliffs of red rock rising along both sides of that long, deep-blue lake. Looking north, Mt. Reynolds is the closest peak, but to the right of Reynolds there are the impressive peaks of Going-to-the-Sun Mountain and Mt. Siyeh. Much more interesting will be the views to the south and southeast, with Mt. Jackson looming up nearly 5,000 vertical feet above Gunsight Lake in the foreground, while the broad Blackfoot Glacier basin extends eastward to Blackfoot Mountain and Mt. Logan.

The Gunsight Lake Route. The great obstacle here is the almost unbroken blanket of alder thickets on the hillside above the lake. Such hillsides change almost from year to year — it may be that the best route of ascent is up a small stream gully that extends up through the alders. To avoid the alder thickets, follow the foot trail eastward and descend until more open slopes are visible above. Bushwhack up to the meadows east of the great rock ridge of Fusillade. Traverse westward along the bottom of the south-facing cliffs until reaching the climbable couloir that provides access to the ridgetop. There are several false summits before you reach the highest point, but the climbing is easy. For safety, descend to the meadows via your route of ascent. Descending through the alder thickets toward Gunsight Lake is not bad, using the long branches as handholds.

The Twin Lakes Route (NOT the recommended route, but this is a long, interesting experience). The author and his wife bushwhacked up by the north side of Florence Falls to the flat basin above, in 1956. It was brutal. In 1991 a party reached that basin via the saddle west of Mt. Reynolds. (Game trails pass around the south sides of both lakes.) From the top of Florence Falls a game trail angles up to the bottom of a climbable couloir in the cliff-face. In late July 1991 a waterfall was drenching the couloir. A game trail goes east below the great cliff and around the east end of the ridge. Soon a wall must be crossed, and a short rope might be useful. South of that wall walk up to the bottom of the east end of Fusillade's rocky prow, then follow the details given under the *Gunsight Lake* route.

Going-To-The-Sun Mountain (9,642)

Views from the top are great, particularly toward Logan Pass and the southern part of the park. Mt. Siyeh obliterates the view toward the north, although the Garden Wall and Mt. Gould are quite spectacular. Azure St. Mary Lake lies nestled in a rugged basin of brilliant red rock. The settlement of St. Mary is hidden from view by Goat Mountain, but the wooded ridge above it is seen. The broad prairies begin just beyond that ridge and extend to the Sweetgrass Hills, nearly 100 miles east of the park. Mt. Jackson with its snow and ice is showy, while Mt. Reynolds, Bearhat Mountain and Clements Mountain encompass emerald-green Logan Pass, with autos of less-fortunate sightseers than yourself creeping their lowly way up the valley.

The West Face Route. Distance to summit about four miles, two miles of it by trail. Elevation gained from road to summit is about 3,700 vertical feet. Class 3 all the way, except for two class 4 pitches in the cliffs (B) just above the scree traverse.

Leave Going-to-the-Sun Highway at the Siyeh Creek Bridge (5,850 ft. elevation), which is also called "Siyeh Bend." Follow the trail up the east side of the creek for a few hundred feet, then it turns abruptly uphill and ascends toward the southeast for more than a mile to a trail junction. Turn sharply to the left on the trail toward Piegan Pass. Cross two medium-sized permanent streams, then leave the trail in the great devastated (avalan-ched) area. There are many good routes (in 1983) through that area or through the forest just north of it, but as the brush grows denser in future years the approach will become more difficult. If possible, walk up the rocky streambed, heading directly toward the saddle between Going-to-the-Sun Mountain and Matahpi Peak (9,365 ft.). The slope soon steepens and the streambed becomes a stairway to the basal cliffs above. Several routes through those cliffs are used by the goats, so try to locate the best ones. They are much easier to find while ascending than when approaching from above, so mark the top of your route with distinctive rock "ducks" that will help on the descent. (The easier cliffs appear to be toward the left, or north.) Once above the basal cliffs scramble uphill beside the scrub forest, then onward and upward to the 8,300-foot saddle.

Walk up the ridge from the saddle to the cliffs at the south end of it, then follow the base of the high cliffs (B) southward on a descending game trail. Soon you will reach the bottom of the great talus chute (C) that ascends diagonally upward toward the north. The chute retains snow until late in

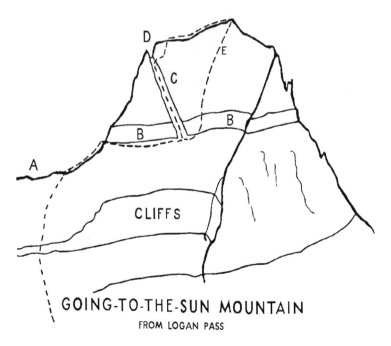

GOING-TO-THE-SUN MOUNTAIN
FROM LOGAN PASS

Going-to-the-Sun Mountain, from Mt. Oberlin—Denis Twohig

the season and is consequently very prominent in views from the west. Do NOT attempt to go up the steep snow unless equipped with ice axes and proficient in using them! If the snow in the chute has melted, it is safe to scramble up it to the top and look down the tremendous east face below the summit notch. It drops abruptly for 4,500 vertical feet to Baring Creek! After viewing the east face, descend a few yards back down the chute, to a short, easily climbed break in the south wall of the chute. Above it there is a glorious stroll up the ridgetop to the summit of the famous mountain.

Most climbers will not want to climb the diagonal chute, but will prefer instead to climb the scree slope south of it (E). By-pass the bottom of the chute and go on around the base of the cliffs. In a few minutes a deep gully is reached, extending down through the cliffs above the trail. There are difficult and dangerous pitches in the gully as well as south of it, but it is easier just north of the gully. After walking only a few yards up the bottom of the gully, climb up toward the left through a short but awkward pitch (but with no exposure). Angle more to the left then, and soon another class 4 pitch must be climbed. Above that, the route leads easily to the great scree slopes that cover the entire upper west face of the mountain. Mark the top of the short "difficult" section with a characteristic "duck" of rock that can be recognized during the descent, then plod up the scree and ledges for almost 1,000 vertical feet to the summit.

The Nature Study Club of Indiana register on this summit was moved from its lightning-mangled lead box into an aluminum tube in 1952 by the Seattle Mountaineers. The old box was ample evidence that lightning does strike twice in the same place . . . in fact, there are usually several strikes on this summit as a storm is passing down the valley. It is a very bad peak to be on during a lightning storm!

While perched on this exalted summit climbers may recall the Blackfeet Indian legend concerning their great Sun God, Napi. After he had come to them in person to help them through a period of great misfortune and was at last ready to return to his home in the sun, Napi bade them farewell and disappeared in the direction of Going-to-the-Sun Mountain. Their last view of him was as he walked up the high cliffs, from which it was only a few more steps to his heavenly home. The great snowfield on the upper east face resembles an Indian head in profile, with a great headdress . . . obviously the profile of Napi!

On the descent it is much easier and faster to scramble uphill on the game trail along the base of the cliffs, to the saddle, then go straight down to the scrub forest and the route through the lower cliffs. Otherwise it is a very long, slow traverse across that great scree slope.

The Matahpi Peak Route. From Siyeh Pass, climb over the top of Matahpi, then descend to the saddle between that peak and Going-to-the-Sun, where the route joins the west face route described above.

The Sexton Glacier Route. Leave the trail at about the 7,500-foot elevation south of Siyeh Pass. Cross the glacier and traverse southward to the great snowfield directly below the summit of the mountain. Climb up that steep snow to the top. Obviously, ice axes and rope are to be used on that route!

The Southwest Ridge Route. From the trail junction below, bushwhack up to the lower end of the cliffy southwest ridge of the mountain. Traverse northward and pass around the corner, to a ten-foot-wide gully that leads to the top of the southwest shoulder. It is an easy walk from there to the summit. This route was climbed by Dave Cummiskey (Mankato, Minnesota) and George Cook (Albuquerque) in the 1970s and they reported the route to the author. It had previously been climbed by a Sierra Club party in the 1960s but without subsequent notification of the exact route followed.

The Southeast Ridge Route. Distance to the summit about two miles, none of it by trail. Elevation gained is about 4,700 vertical feet. Class 3 except for two possible class 4 pitches in the diorite sill and another in the algal reef. ALSO, the steep snow just below the summit is potentially deadly and ice axes must be used for protection there (crampons are recommended . . . especially if the snow is hard and icy, as it will be before 10 A.M., or on chilly days.) First ascent: Dave Bush and Dan Mitchell, August 1975. The following description is based on information provided by Dave Bush.

Leave Going-to-the-Sun Road at the first big parking area east of the Jackson Glacier viewpoint (directly below the west edge of the 1969 forest fire burn, where the unwooded hillside extends down almost to the road). Walk up in or near the streambed, to the base of the great cliffs 2,500 vertical feet above the road. At each fork in the stream, follow the eastern branch. If dry, the streambed is like a solid staircase. At the foot of the great upper cliffs, leave the streambed and traverse toward the east, passing beneath another steep gully in the cliffs and entering a third gully. This one has spectacular pinnacles of black diorite forming the crest of its east wall. Climb up this black gully, continuing for several hundred feet to the ridge above. Stay west of the center of the gully as the top is approached, and reach the ridge very high on the southeast corner of the mountain.

Continue up the ridge to the gray algal reef, then angle to the south to find the easiest breaks through that reef and up the rotten cliffs just above it. The ridge provides easy access to the great snowfield on the upper east face (which resembles an Indian's head in profile when viewed from near St. Mary).

Put crampons on and grip the ice ax in the correct self-arrest manner (see the introductory portion of this guide for details), then climb carefully up the south end of that large snowbank. Near the top of it, find the safest place to get off the snow and onto the rock near the ridgetop. It is an easy scramble to the summit from there.

Bush and Mitchell spent a leisurely eleven hours on this ascent, and found the ropes were not needed except on the steep snow. They reported that they had an enjoyable time because the rock was much more solid than on the west face. Dave wrote that they were amazed by how well the route developed, because it looks so precarious from below.

Mt. Jackson, viewed from the Going-to-the-Sun Road —Brian Kennedy

Mt. Jackson (10,052)

From this summit one gets the impression of a really extensive "sea of peaks" to the north. The McDonald Valley is obscured by the sharp summits of Gunsight Mountain, Mt. Cannon, Clements Mountain, and Edwards Mountain, so not a level or low place can be seen from here except for the great glaciated basin of Blackfoot Glacier with its acres of snow and ice. Directly below, to the north, is Gunsight Pass, and in either direction from that high saddle there are beautiful lakes. Gunsight Lake lies a vertical mile below, and the incredible cliffs of Fusillade Mountain rising above it are made up of tremendously-convoluted layers of red argillite and white quartzite which are not equalled anywhere else in the park. Also of interest is the view of seldom-seen Harrison Glacier immediately below the summit of Mt. Jackson toward the south. Further south, beyond snowy Blackfoot Mountain, there are dozens of great peaks and ridges, most impressive of which are massive flat-topped Mt. Stimson and the sheer-

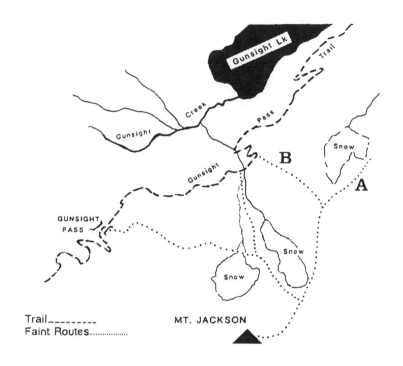

Trail_____
Faint Routes...............

MT. JACKSON

sided 1,000-foot "thumb" of Mt. St. Nicholas.

This climb usually takes two days, with the first night being spent at the foot of Gunsight Lake. Leave Going-to-the-Sun Road at the Jackson Glacier Viewpoint. Descend for a mile to the junction with the valley trail from Sun Point, then follow the main trail for nearly five more miles to Gunsight Lake. Good campsites are at the foot of the lake, but it may be difficult to get a good sleep there because of the large numbers of porcupines chewing on equipment and whimpering around the area all night.

There are four established routes from Gunsight Lake to the top of this tremendous mountain, all of which reach the summit ridge far east of the highest point. The first two of the routes involve a 3,000-foot grind up the northeast ridge after approaching it from either the east or the west.

The Northeast Ridge Routes. (A) Take the trail toward Jackson Glacier until reaching the open meadows above timberline, then scramble westward up the scree slopes to the ridgetop, OR (B) Follow the trail toward Gunsight Pass for about two miles, to the east end of the third switchback (at 6,400 ft.), then scramble eastward up the scree to the ridgetop.

After reaching that ridge, walk up it for an unbelievable distance. The rather gentle ascent eventually steepens, and the cliffy ridgetop may be by-passed a few feet toward the west. A belay rope will be very useful there if steep snow is still on and near the ridge. The summit cairn is located far to the west, along the rocky crest. A register was placed there by the Nature Study Club of Indiana in 1921 and it was a great experience to read it even in the late 1950s. Unfortunately, it was destroyed or removed by someone during the 1960s (as were most other summit registers in the park). Distance to the summit about ten miles, 7.5 miles of it by trail. Elevation gained is about 4,800 vertical feet. Class 3 all the way, unless steep snow blocks the upper section of the ridge.

The North Basin Route. Class 3 and 4, if steep snow and ice are avoided. This alternative was described in 1986 by Becky Cousins, of Lethbridge (and the Chinook Outdoor Club). She left the Gunsight Pass trail at about the 6,640-foot elevation (where the stream draining the large eastern snowfield crosses that trail), and headed uphill and slightly westward. After a few minutes the large western snowfield becomes visible (it is not visible from the trail by the stream). Climb the fairly solid ridge between the two snowfields, then continue up to the summit ridgetop. It is then a pleasant walk up that ridge to the highest point. Becky reached the summit just 2.5 hours after leaving the trail, however it should be noted that she is a truly remarkable mountaineer.

This is surely the fastest route to the summit. Climbers in good condition and traveling light can make the round trip in ten or twelve hours from the road. Of course, flashlights should be carried, in case darkness falls on the way out to the road.

The Gunsight Pass Route. Distance to summit about twelve miles, 9.5 miles of it by trail. Elevation gained is about 4,800 vertical feet. Class 3 and 4, if steep snow is avoided. The first known ascent of this route was made by Rolf Larson and Brian Kennedy, who described it in *Going-to-the-Sun* magazine (Winter 1982). The pass can also be reached by hiking 4.5 miles from Sperry Chalets.

A very old abandoned trail goes upward toward the east from Gunsight Pass. It is soon blocked by a large, steep snowbank where it cuts around the cliff near the pass. Climbers with ice axes can safely cross the thirty-degree slope of hard snow, but it should be avoided by others. If you do not have ice axes, leave the current foot-trail near the switchback just east of the pass and climb uphill east of that big snowfield to reach the ancient trail where it emerges from beneath the snow. Follow that old trail across the great basin until it approaches the largest snowfield in the middle of the basin. Angle up and across the lower section of that snowfield where the slope is gentle. Scramble 1,600 vertical feet up the scree and easy cliffs between that snowfield and the large snowfield just east of it. This portion of the route coincides with the upper part of the North Basin Route. Reach the ridgetop about a hundred feet above the snowfields, and enjoy the easy stroll along the "tightrope in the sky" leading to the highest point on the summit ridge.

Another Route? Raoul Schocher, a Swiss alpinist, hiked to Gunsight Pass alone in 1986 and climbed the northwest ridge, solo. He descended via the conventional route because "it was impossible to climb down that ridge route without a rope." Many similar faces *can* be climbed in Glacier National Park, but should only be attempted by parties equipped with ropes, pitons, carabiners, AND experience.

Little Chief Mountain (9,541)

Views from this summit are extremely satisfying. St. Mary Lake may be seen for most of its length, extending almost to the prairies. In the west the familiar landmarks around Logan Pass are at your feet. In the northwestern sector of the horizon the snowy peaks are (left to right) Heavens Peak, Longfellow Peak, Vulture Peak, Rainbow Peak, pyramidal Mt. Carter, broad Kintla Peak, and the matterhorn of Kinnerly Peak. Closer at hand the impressive masses of Going-to-the-Sun Mountain, Mt. Siyeh and Mt. Gould fill the foreground while Mt. Merritt and Mt. Cleveland loom up beyond them. To the south there are three peaks which deserve special attention: thumb-like Mt. St. Nicholas, flat-topped Mt. Stimson, and the broad dome of Mt. Jackson. Far to the southwest, beyond the park boundary, is the graceful peak of Great Northern Mountain, covered by Stanton Glacier. The panorama is truly a fitting reward for the perseverent few who succeed in reaching this lofty summit!

The West Talus Slope Route. Distance to the summit about nine miles, two miles of it by human trail. Elevation gained is about 5,050 vertical feet. Class 3 all the way, if the correct route is followed. First ascent by Henry L. Stimson in 1894. This direct route up the great mountain should begin early in the morning if climbers expect to reach the road again before dark.

Leave Going-to-the-Sun Road at the parking area 0.8 miles west of Baring Creek. A trail from there connects with the main trail from Sun Point to Gunsight Lake a few hundred yards down the hillside. Soon after reaching that trail a side trail to the left leads downhill to St. Mary Falls and (beyond that) to Virginia Falls. More than 100 yards beyond the bridge at Virginia Falls a faint elk trail leads up the hillside through the forest (just west of extensive alder thickets). Eventually the trail goes to your right,

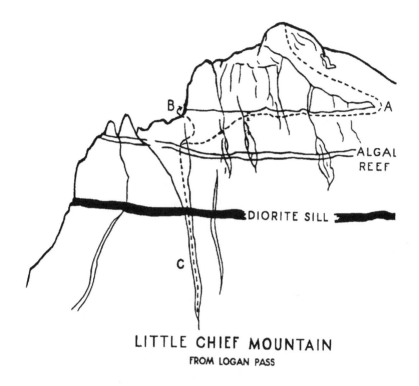

LITTLE CHIEF MOUNTAIN
FROM LOGAN PASS

horizontally, then fades away. Thirty years ago the steep elk trail continued uphill, rather than going horizontally. It was then an easy walk to the small streambed that drains the gully (C), and an easy scramble up the dry streambed to timberline. In the 1960s that trail was obliterated by a big blowdown of forest trees. Getting through the mass of downed timber was impossible for elk, and the trail therefore ended. Perhaps one of the faint trails leading uphill from the horizontal trail now leads through the old blowdown, but we could not find it in 1994. In 1980, we managed to bushwack to the downed tree trunks and climb through them, then followed the old trail through the forest all the way to the bottom of the third waterfall. (See details of the route to that waterfall, and around it, in the discussion of the route from Virginia Falls to Almost-A-Dog Pass and the Blackfoot Basin.)

Above the horizontal trail, narrow steep open strips extend through the trees toward the summit for hundreds of feet to the great rock hillside. (Mark the top of that route well, so it can be found on your descent!)

Ascend open scree slopes until finding a route to the steep stream gully (C), then climb up it until above the gray algae reef. A game trail leads south below the summit cliffs, to easy scree slopes below the summit. Traversing lower than that involves many tiring pitches and will take much longer.

The East Face Route. For experienced rock climbers only. Great exposure below several class 4 and 5 pitches on the upper east face. First ascent: Gordon Edwards, August 15, 1947.

Use the same approach as for the West Talus Slope Route, until passing through the algal reef on that face. Continue straight upward to the north end of the sheer cliffs above (B) and follow a game trail around onto the east face at about the same elevation as the top of the great gendarme. Traverse horizontally along the narrow talus-covered ledge, passing around two prominent ribs or ridges and into the next broad gully. Here there are three streambeds in the same gully. The farthest one south has the most water in it; the middle one dries up in mid-summer; and the northernmost streambed is the easiest one to climb.

Ascend the northern streambed for about 500 vertical feet. The lower 100 feet are the worst, with class 5 pitches on rotten cliffs above drops of several thousand feet. Rope belays are recommended here, if a suitable piton anchor can be placed. Above the lower five or six pitches, the climbing becomes progressively easier and it is just a scramble up to the ridgetop north of the summit dome. Pile a distinctive duck of rocks at the top of the correct gully to mark it well in case you wish to descend the same way (but the west slope route is much faster and easier). The other gullies do not appear to be feasible for climbing! Walk up the easy ridge to the summit. There are many easy breaks in the cliffs on the east side of the last bulwark guarding the highest point of this tremendous mountain.

It was while building a small cairn on this summit during a heavy snowfall in August 1947 that the author was "knocked out" by a lightning strike. A peculiar whining noise had been heard for some time but ignored. Suddenly a brilliant orange flash blinded me, followed by a total blackout. I regained consciousness while still high in the air and landed on my feet, ready to run. My descent down the north ridge (and the east face) was much more rapid than on subsequent climbs! Evidently the electrical impulse caused violent contractions of all muscles at the same time, and the extensor muscles in my legs and feet were much stronger than the flexors, so I must have leaped like a frog! (The same sensation had been experienced years earlier in a tin boathouse in Michigan, when my whole scout troop went up in the air at the same time.) The lesson learned was to pay attention to the weather and expect electrical discharges even during snowstorms.

The Red Eagle Ridge Route. It is a long, spectacular walk up the ridge from Red Eagle Mountain to Little Chief's summit via the top of Mahtotopa (8,672 ft.), but there are no obstacles en route. CARRY PLENTY OF WATER! See details of the routes up Red Eagle elsewhere in this guide.

The Almost-a-Dog Route. It is also possible to *walk* up ridges from Almost-a-Dog Pass, via Almost-a-Dog Mountain, to the summit of Little Chief. From the far north end of Red Eagle Pass meadows it is a scree-scramble to the ridge east of Almost-a-Dog Mountain, and an easy walk to the summit of Little Chief Mountain. These routes require a lengthy approach from Blackfoot Glacier Basin or Triple Divide Pass or Red Eagle Valley, thus involve at least two nights of camping en route to the mountain and back.

Human figures are dwarfed by the majesty of the Blackfoot Glacier Basin
—J. G. Edwards

Mt. Logan (9,239)

Views from the top are fantastic! Few peaks in the park can surpass this one for spectacular vistas of glaciers and vast snowfields sparkling amid sheer cliffs, far above the broad green valleys. Blackfoot Glacier still covers most of the great basin below, and the huge ice cliff in the center of it is perhaps the most outstanding single point of interest. Near the summit ridge of Blackfoot Mountain that glacier is only narrowly separated from the head of Pumpelly Glacier. (The latter clings to the steep southeastern face of the mountain, and great blocks of ice frequently break loose and thunder down the slopes toward the Nyack Valley, five thousand vertical feet below. Harrison Glacier, high on the south side of Mt. Jackson, similarly bombards the Harrison Creek Valley with occasional avalanches.) Beyond Blackfoot Glacier, Jackson Glacier and its adjacent snowfields sprawl across the eastern and southern slopes of massive Mt. Jackson. Mt. Logan provides many worthwhile views in addition to the snow and ice. Mt. Stimson looms up in the south with 7,000 vertical feet of forest and cliffs sweeping upward from the deep gash of the Nyack Creek valley. In the opposite direction the familiar peaks around St. Mary Lake and the Logan Pass area are seen, but they appear strange and exotic from this viewpoint. Split Mountain is the peculiar peak with the deep summit cleft, rising above the Red Eagle Valley, and Mt. James is the bulky red peak just beyond it. Although it is a long way to the top of Mt. Logan, the summit views make the climb a very memorable one.

The West Face Route. Distance to summit about eleven miles, eight miles of it by human trail. Elevation gained is about 3,800 vertical feet. Class 3 all the way if correct routes are followed. Allow eight hours for the round trip from Gunsight Lake.

Leave Going-to-the-Sun Road at the Jackson Glacier Viewpoint and follow the trail for about six miles to Gunsight Lake. Good campsites are located at the foot of that lovely lake, and it is recommended that climbers spend the first night there rather than attempting to complete the climb in one day. After crossing the outlet of the lake follow the faint trail toward the left for almost 1.5 miles to Jackson Glacier. See the description of the Blackfoot Basin traverse elsewhere in this guide for the best route across the complex basin and up to Almost-a-Dog Pass. From that 7,900-foot pass the actual ascent of Mt. Logan begins.

From the pass, walk up the broad scree slope toward the south. A small pyramid of rock is separated from the main upper mass of the mountain above the scree by a deep notch. A distinct goat trail leads around the west side of that pyramid, passes beside the notch, then continues around the west side of Mt. Logan. Stay on that marvelous trail, following a prominent rock stratum as it slants upward toward the south. When directly west of the summit, leave the goat trail and scramble upward and slightly to the left (north) for a few hundred feet, to the base of the steep cliffs that guard the summit. (Before leaving the main goat trail, mark it well so it can be found again for the descent.) Another goat trail parallels the base of the upper cliffs and should be followed to the north end of the mountain. The upper northern corner of the summit pyramid is an easy class 3 ascent from that goat trail.

Other Routes. (1) It is possible to ascend the snowfields east of Blackfoot Glacier to the saddle between Mt. Logan and Blackfoot Mountain, thence up the southwest ridge of Logan to the summit. Do NOT attempt this route unless equipped with ice axes and very familiar with steep snow and ice-climbing techniques; (2) From Red Eagle Pass, walk up the snow between Logan Glacier and Red Eagle Glacier, then scramble up to the great saddle between Mt. Logan and Clyde Peak (not named on 1968 maps). A game trail traverses the upper south face of Mt. Logan from that saddle up to the high southwest ridge of the mountain. From there it is an easy walk up to the summit.

Mahtotopa Mountain (8,672)

The approach via the pleasant ridgetop trail from Red Eagle Mountain is so vastly superior to any other route to this peak that no others need be mentioned. Because the peak is lower than Red Eagle (and Little Chief, its other neighbor along that great ridge) it would appear that the only reasons for climbers to visit its summit would be (1) "because it is there," or (2) because they cannot traverse from Red Eagle to Little Chief, or vice versa, without climbing Mahtotopa en route.

Otokomi Mountain (7,935)

This broad, rounded mountain is only a "walk-up," but it provides an opportunity for mountaineers to spend an enjoyable day roaming over open expanses of high meadows and scree fields while admiring the views of higher, more rugged peaks not far away. After reaching the summit of Otokomi Mountain hikers can walk for miles along the ridges of the other peaks along the same great rounded massif, Singleshot Mountain, and East Flattop Mountain.

Hike up the trail from Rising Sun Cabin Area for four miles toward Otokomi Lake, gaining about 1,800 vertical feet en route. Leave the trail at about 6,300 feet and climb 400 feet up to the flat open area east of the trail. Cross over the flat-topped ridge and descend to the stream basin east of it. Follow up the lowest tributary, toward the east, until beyond the fork that has two small ponds upstream. Walk uphill about fifty feet to a huge slope covered with scree and rocks. A good game trail leads eastward from that scree slope and continues upstream until just below the high pass that is north of the summit of Otokomi Mountain. Scramble up to that pass, and follow an excellent game trail toward the south, to the very highest point of Otokomi.

Another route, with more bushwhacking and with numerous cliffs, goes up the south end of the mountain. Walk up the trail from Rising Sun for about a mile. When the trail emerges from the south-facing hillside of dense forest and begins a traverse northward along an open hillside (at about the "K" of Creek, on the map) leave the trail and bushwhack straight up the nearby forested ridge. Soon a steep open meadow is seen east of the ridgetop. Walk up the meadow, angling further to the east, to a very extensive scree slope with good trails crossing it. Either climb directly toward the summit, up numerous class 3 and 4 cliffs, OR follow the trails eastward into the next broad grassy stream basin and walk up that basin to the easy cliffs that provide access to the high ridgetop far above and to the west of the stream. From that ridgetop it is simply a long gentle climb up scree, through scrub forest, over three false summits. Eventually the rounded dome of the true summit is reached.

Singleshot Mountain (7,926)

Climb to the summit of Otokomi Mountain, following the description elsewhere in this guide. From the saddle north of Otokomi Mountain, follow the game trail up to the west end of the great rocky crest that forms the ridge east of peak 8316. By angling back and forth along the top of that impressive rocky ridge it is possible to reach the east end of the ridge without any cliff-climbing worse than class 3. Either walk up to the summit of East Flattop Mountain (8,356) and then descend to the high saddle between that peak and Singleshot Mountain OR traverse the south side of East Flattop on faint game trails that lead to the saddle, staying about 300 vertical feet below the top of East Flattop Mountain. The walk onward to the highest point of Singleshot is easy, but may be further than it appears from the saddle. From the summit there are many interesting views. The very sheer cliffs that drop into the head of Wild Creek are impressive, as are the spires and ridges leading to Napi Rock. The great rounded ridge of East Flattop beckons true mountaineers who have the time to walk its entire length and descend from the far east end to Lower St. Mary Lake on the human trail that goes up from that lake to spectacular Napi Point. (For some reason the upper section of that trail, as well as the fork that leads up to the northeast end of East Flattop Mountain, have been left omitted from 1968 topographic map of the park, but those are good trails and lead very quickly down to the road near Lower St. Mary Lake.)

Mt. Siyeh (10,014)

This tremendous peak presents a remarkable vantage point from which may be seen almost every mountain in the entire park, as well as those in southern British Columbia and Alberta. Directly below the summit, to the north, the cliffs drop off abruptly to the basin of Cracker Lake, 4,200 vertical feet below. That lake was a beautiful blue-green body of water harboring great trout during the 1920s, but the inlet stream altered its course and by 1952 the glacial sediment caused the water to become "glacial milk" and the finely pulverized "rock flour" held in the lake in suspension caused the trout there to become eel-like in appearance and "mostly head," according to fishermen. In the 1960s the color of the lake changed from dishwater gray to vivid blue, as it remains today. Mt. Allen conceals the Swiftcurrent Valley and its chains of lakes, but west of Allen the jagged Garden Wall is clearly seen with the grand Livingston Range rising above and beyond it. Of special interest to geologists is the tremendous 110-foot-thick black band of igneous rock (diorite) that extends across the entire east face of the Garden Wall and also across the southeast face of the sheer wall on the south ridge of Allen Mountain. The Cataract Creek valley was gouged out 3,500 feet deep by glaciation *after* the igneous sill intruded between the horizontal layers of limestone beneath the prehistoric sea bottom sediments. The widely separated ridges now visible from Mt. Siyeh, each bearing the same exposures of rock formations, provide evidence of the earlier continuity of those rock formations and of the magnitude of the subsequent uplifting and erosion. The pale formation of rock above and below the diorite sill is limestone that was metamorphosed to marble by the intense heat of that volcanic intrusion. Also visible from the summit, to the southwest, are the snowy basins of Sperry, Jackson, and Blackfoot glaciers. Northeast of the mountain the brilliant red Grinnell Argillite formations of rock and scree are impressive, as are the yellow and ochre-colored ridges that extend eastward into the pastel-colored prairies.

The South Slope Route. Distance to the summit about five miles, 2.7 miles of it by trail. Elevation gained from the highway is about 4,200

The long, long ridgetop from Mt. Wynn to Mt. Siyeh—John Mauff

vertical feet. Class 2 and 3 after leaving Preston Park, but class 4 pitches may be encountered if the correct route is missed.

Leave Going-to-the-Sun Road at the Siyeh Creek crossing, three miles east of Logan Pass. Follow the trail up the east side of the stream for a few hundred feet, then it turns to the south and climbs 1.2 miles to a trail junction. Take the left fork, toward Piegan Pass, and reach Preston Park in about 1.5 miles. Take the right-hand fork in that grassy fir-studded region and head toward Siyeh Pass. While walking through the open parkland on that trail, study the areas where vegetation extends up the talus slopes of Mt. Siyeh for a considerable distance above timberline. The easternmost of those green encroachments into the talus above Preston Park is the one which leads climbers directly up to the easiest route through the cliffs.

Walk to the top of that large green strip, then go diagonally upward toward your right and enter the large streambed. If the streambed is dry, its solid rock affords excellent climbing (class 2 and 3). When difficult cliffs are encountered (class 4 to 6) traverse a little farther to the east until an easier streambed is reached, then climb up that one. (Mark the places you traversed with distinctive "ducks" of rock so that you can retrace the route during the descent.) When there are no more cliffs above, scramble straight uphill to the summit ridge, angling around the west side of the great snowbank not far below that ridge. Once on the ridge, walk easily up to the summit.

The Piegan Pass Route. Distance to summit about 7 miles, 4.5 miles of it by trail. Class 3 or 4, except for one 8-foot pitch in the gully. Angle up from the Piegan Pass trail to the ridge east of Cataract Peak. Traverse east, descending to pass below the great cliff that extends farthest down into the scree. Ascend hundreds of feet up the great gully east of that great cliff. This route may appeal to climbers approaching the mountain via the trail

The 4,100-foot north face of Mt. Siyeh—John Mauff

Edwards enjoying a sandwich on Mt.Siyeh—John Mauff

from the Swiftcurrent or Many Glacier area. (Distance to summit from there is eleven miles, 8.5 by trail.)

A short distance down the trail east of Piegan Pass, leave the trail and ascend a distinct goat trail angling up toward the notch or saddle east of Cataract Mountain. Walk up the ridgetop from there until confronted by a sheer cliff. Traverse to the southeast below that cliff for several hundred feet, until reaching an easily-climbed couloir (class 3) through the great cliffs. Mark the top of the couloir very well, so it can be located during the descent (there are no other such routes anywhere along that side of the mountain). Regain the ridgetop, then plod up that long, long ridge for about

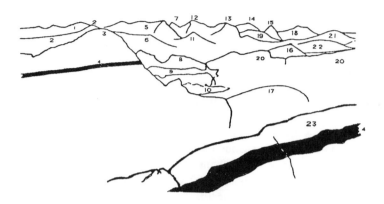

Looking Northwest From Mt. Siyeh. (1) Logging Mtn.; (2) Mt. Geduhn; (3) Mt. Gould; (4) Diorite Sill; (5) Vulture Pk.; (6) Trapper Pk.; (7) Square Pk.; (8) Garden Wall; (9) Salamander Glacier; (10) Grinnnell Glacier; (11) Nahsukin Mtn.; (12) Rainbow Pk.; (13) Mt. Carter; (14) Kintla Pk.; (15) Kinnerly Pk.; (16) Swiftcurrent Mtn. Fire Lookout; (17) Angel Wing; (18) Long Knife Mtn.; (19) Mt. Peabody; (20) Grinnell Mtn.; (21) The Guardhouse; (22) Kootenai Pk.; (23) Northwest Ridge of Mt. Siyeh.

a mile, gaining 2,000 vertical feet rather rapidly. The summit pyramid of bright red rock is easily ascended through breaks in the west face of the small cliffs.

WARNING: If you climb via this route and consider descending via the south slope, study the details of that route before starting down. (If dangerous cliffs are encountered, traverse eastward until reaching easier pitches.)

The West Couloir Route. (This is no fun to ascend, but is a speedy route down.) Climbers who wish to return to the Swiftcurrent Valley by trail and would enjoy a different route than used on the ascent may walk or run down the west ridge until reaching the large cliffs and then descend toward the north into the great scree-filled couloir there. There are no dangerous cliffs in that couloir, and small parties of climbers will find 1,500 vertical feet of scree-running there. As usual, there is considerable hazard from dislodged rocks, so each climber should avoid moving when any other climber is below him or her. The extensive flat meadows below the couloir are a pleasure to see and walk through, and the foot trail is soon reached not far above Morning Eagle Falls.

The Mt. Wynn Route. This tremendous ridge-walk follows good game trails from the summit of Mt. Wynn for five miles to the summit of Mt.

Siyeh. It is described in the Many Glacier area section, under the heading of "The Skyline Trail From Mt. Wynn to Mt. Siyeh."

The North Face Route. This route is NOT for the casual climber. In fact, it is not for most expert wall-climbers! Serious climbers who really are considering this challenge should contact Terry Kennedy or Jim Kanzler for more specific information (the National Park office can provide their addresses). A few details and comments here, however, should be of interest to all mountaineers, even if they do not feel inclined to assault the great rock walls in Glacier.

Distance to summit about 6.5 miles, 5.5 miles of it by trail (0.1 mile is up the scree slope and 0.9 mile is vertical). Elevation gained from Swiftcurrent Lake is about 5,200 vertical feet; elevation gained from Cracker Lake is 4,100 vertical feet. Class 5 and 6 much of the way up the face.

The first ascent of this sheer 3,500-foot face was made by Jim Kanzler and Terry Kennedy, on September 13, 14, and 15, 1979. They spent twenty-five hours actually climbing, and two freezing nights roped to the face. As they told reporters later, their previous attempts (in 1977 and 1978) were halted by bad weather and by "the sheer technical difficulty of the mountain." They continued to make plans. Kanzler had been climbing for nearly twenty years, and he worked as a mountaineering guide in the Tetons during the summer of 1979. Kennedy, working as a ranger in Glacier National Park, climbed almost every week during those three summers, and has been a talented rock climber for years. He has also made class 6 winter ascents in the Canadian Rockies.

The two challengers hiked to Cracker Lake in the afternoon and climbed about 1,000 vertical feet before bivouacking on the north face for the night. The next morning they had difficulty with the snow and ice, cleaning off handholds before they could use them. "It got continuously harder as we got higher," they said. One of their two ropes was badly cut by a falling rock on the third day, but they had to keep using it anyway. Because of its orientation, the north face never received any sunshine, and Kennedy referred to it as "a dark, foreboding place that got to you after awhile." They reached the top at 6:15 P.M. on the third day. Kanzler later said "It's a death route. I've never climbed the Eiger in Switzerland but I know close friends who have. From the things I've heard about it, the climb up Siyeh was just as hard." The author (JGE) has been on the *base* of the Eigerwand, and agrees. Siyeh has similar rock, but is more severe.

Ranger Robert Frauson, who was in charge of mountain rescue operations in the park, pointed out that the climbers realized that in the event of bad weather or injury it would have been extremely difficult (or impossible) to reach them on the face. He observed that "They were on their own up there, and they knew it."

Split Mountain (8,792)

The prettiest picture from the top of this peak was that of the unusual blue-colored lake 2,400 vertical feet directly below, (toward Triple Divide Pass). The lake certainly deserves the proposed name of "Blueing Lake." The unnamed lake in the cirque at the north base of the peak is also attractive. Red Eagle Lake and a small bit of St. Mary Lake are visible, as is the entire length of Lower St. Mary Lake. Looking westward beyond the extensive green meadows of Red Eagle Pass climbers will be impressed by Mt. Logan, Blackfoot Mountain, and Mt. Jackson, with extensive glaciers on their flanks and ridges. Mt. Stimson dominates the southern landscape, but there are many other great peaks visible toward the southeast. Near at hand in the north the massive ridge topped by Red Eagle Mountain, Mahtotopa Mountain, and Little Chief Mountain blocks the views, although a few peaks may be seen above that great ridgetop. The wild valley extending up to remote, seldom-seen Red Eagle Pass can be studied in its entirety from this unique viewpoint, as can the incredible ridge route described in this Guide as the "Norris Traverse" which is a mountaineer's trail from Triple Divide Pass to Red Eagle Pass.

The Red Eagle Lake Route. Distance to summit about fifteen miles, 13.5 miles of it by human trail. Elevation gained is about 4,400 vertical feet. Class 3 except for the last 120 feet, which involves class 4 and 5 cliffs above fantastic exposures. First ascent: John Mauff and Gordon Edwards, August 11, 1956.

Hike to Red Eagle Lake, then up the trail toward Triple Divide Pass. Leave the trail near the big basin between Split Mountain and Norris Mountain and scramble up the extensive scree slopes just south of the southeast ridge of Split Mountain. When the band of hard gray rock composed of fossil algae is approached, traverse to the south to find easy breaks through the reef. Continue to the summit ridge south of the impressive craggy summit.

Walk around to the west side of the sheer-walled double pinnacle and look right up the great summit cleft which is responsible for the name of the mountain. It is worth the time to go a few steps to the north and look straight down the vertical 1,800-foot face of excellent unclimbed rock! The summit pinnacle's deep cleft extends from east to west, splitting the peak into a north and a south summit. The cleft was ascended from the west and descended toward the east by the first party. About sixty feet up the

John Mauff looks down on Blueing Lake during the first ascent of Split Mountain. From Mt. Norris (on right) the long ridge descends to Triple Divide Peak—J. G. Edwards

western cleft is a wide class 4 chimney below a large chockstone. Climb out of the cleft onto the narrow scree slope north of the great chimney (which in effect forms the "floor" of the summit cleft). The steep, narrow class 4 gully enters the summit cleft from the east at that same scree slope.

The highest summit is north of the great cleft. To reach it, traverse northeast around the sheer cliff face at the bottom of the north pinnacle. Side-step across the cliff on a narrow ledge for about fifteen feet, to a narrow, shallow, very vertical gully (above 1,900 feet of sheer exposure). Delicately climb up this wall for about twelve feet (class 5) then move to the left (south) on a narrow ledge that is not visible until you actually step out of the vertical gully. This traverse leads to an easy slope just beneath the summit. WARNING: The first foothold used when leaving the gully was not solid, so step only on the inner side of it.

This peak has also been climbed from the Cut Bank area via two different routes. (See that section of the guide for further details.)

Walton Mountain (8,926)

Summit views are mostly of the unfamiliar peaks south and west of Mt. Stimson, but of course Blackfoot Mountain and Mt. Stimson are spectacular. Beyond Highway 2 is graceful Great Northern Mountain with Stanton Glacier spreading across its northeastern slopes. The lower portions of Harrison Glacier are hanging over the edges of the great cliffs above the abyss, and the numerous streams and waterfalls dashing down the 2,400-foot-high headwall toward Harrison Lake are very impressive.

The Jackson Glacier Route. Distance to the summit is about twelve miles, eight miles of it by human trail. Elevation gained is about 3,600 vertical feet from Gunsight Lake and 2,900 vertical feet from the foot of Jackson Glacier. Class 3 most of the way, but do not belittle the potential deadliness of Harrison Glacier. Study the section near the front of this guide that provides brief instructions on proper methods of using ice axes. First ascent: Tom Shreve, Mavis Lorenz, Paul Jensen, and Allen Smith, July 1974.

Leave Going-to-the-Sun Road at the Jackson Glacier Viewpoint. Descend the steep trail for 1.3 miles, to the junction with the valley trail, then hike another five miles to Gunsight Lake. Cross the outlet then turn to the left and follow a faint old trail for 1.8 miles toward Jackson Glacier. Eventually the faint trail approaches the large lateral moraine and the meadows abruptly end. As the moraine is approached, drop a bit lower and parallel the small groves of trees along the lower edge of the meadow. Just north of the moraine descend a small, nearly dry creekbed that extends down through the trees. Below the trees, angle to the right on a faint game trail that passes around the end of that great moraine. Continue toward the south and southwest, through boulder fields and scattered shrubs, to the snout of Jackson Glacier.

Climb up beside the glacier until above the terminal crevasses, then walk up the glacier (staying north of the middle of it) for about half a mile, while gaining 800 vertical feet. Head for the lowest part of the ridge between Mt. Jackson and Blackfoot Mountain, which is the easiest route to pass from Jackson Glacier to Harrison Glacier. *Additional Note*: Jaime and Lisa Johnson reached this ridge by going uphill beside the moraine and

Florence Falls, a highlight of the trail hike to Gunsight Lake
—J. G. Edwards

traversing the south side of Mt. Jackson until about a quarter of the way up Jackson Glacier, then descending to the glacier and walking up to the ridge between Mt. Jackson and Blackfoot Mtn.

Carefully climb down from that 7,853-foot notch, on class 3 or easy class 4 cliffs, to the snows of Harrison Glacier. Now, prepare for the long walk across the great glacier, for there is considerable danger of falling into hidden crevasses if the ice is covered with a concealing layer of snow. Be sure to rope up correctly, with prussik slings already attached to your climbing rope and ready for use. If there are only three in your party, all should be tied into a single rope. It is strongly recommended that travel across glaciers be undertaken only by parties on two ropes, so if a member of one roped group falls into a crevasse the other group is available to help extract the victim from the crevasse. Be sure to study the section in the early chapter of this guide which outlines a few of the essential techniques that are so important in crossing crevassed glaciers with a snow-cover obscuring the dangers!

Walk westward up the glacier, climbing a long, gentle slope and gaining about 800 vertical feet en route. Determine the safest level at which to traverse the rest of that glacier. When the snow melts, there are great numbers of large, deep crevasses exposed, but that is the safest time to make the crossing. Crevasses that are snow-covered may collapse beneath your weight, and you cannot live long wedged in the slot between ice walls, even if only fifteen or twenty feet below the surface. Watch for the slight depression in the snow which will indicate natural slumping of the snow above a hidden crevasse. Although it is time-consuming, the safest way of crossing the glacier would be for the leader to probe with the ice ax every step or two, especially in areas likely to have crevasses hidden. Of course, everyone should follow the leader across that glacier, and retrace the same steps on the way back. (The Johnsons marked their route across the crevassed section by sticking bamboo skewers, with orange tape glued to the top, into the snow, and were thus able to easily retrace their route on the descent.) Walk across the snow and ice to Walton Mountain, which should require about an hour.

Leave the snow at the 8,250-foot saddle in the ridge southwest of Harrison Glacier and scramble up the ridge toward Walton's summit. Pass over the top of the prominent hump (8,420 ft.) on the ridge and descend to the beautiful grassy shelf beyond it (a beautiful campsite with incredible views!). The final ridge extending toward the summit from there is class 3 for about 150 feet, then it steepens abruptly. Work out onto the east face and climb class 4 or 5 cliffs for about 200 feet to by-pass the cliff on the ridge, then return to the ridge and continue upward until only about 150 feet from the summit. Traverse onto the northwest face, and climb up the second gully encountered there (class 3 or 4 all the way to the top). The Johnsons suggest that future parties might seek that gully at the base of main mountain (after passing over the 8,420 hump), and follow it all the way to the summit. They descended that way in about forty minutes, to the hump. They commented that: "Both of us enjoyed this climb as much as any in the park. It has your attention the whole time, with mixed rock climbing and glacier travel. It is a remote summit, but is well worth climbing."

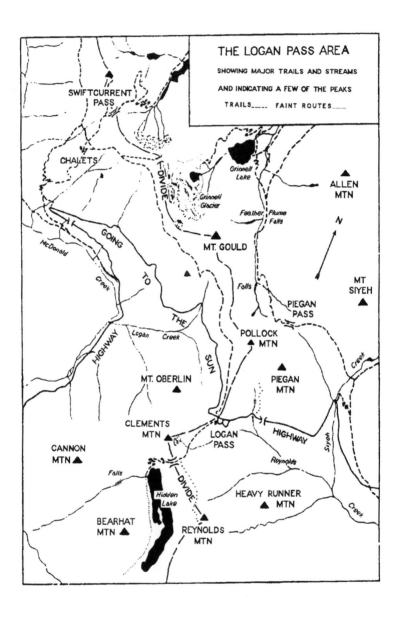

THE LOGAN PASS AREA

SHOWING MAJOR TRAILS AND STREAMS

AND INDICATING A FEW OF THE PEAKS

TRAILS_____ FAINT ROUTES........

THE LOGAN PASS AREA

Routes Among the Peaks

Most visitors to the park are so moved by the views from this spectacular pass that they do not consider going any higher. Mountaineers, however, will recognize the fact that by leaving the road at 6,646 feet above sea level they can easily attain heights that would otherwise require several additional hours of strenuous hiking and bushwhacking.

Just east of Logan Pass the highway crosses Lunch Creek. A faint trail ascends into the basin above the big waterfall there, leading easily to Piegan Mountain and Pollock Mountain. Both peaks offer marvelous views of the Logan Pass area and of the Blackfoot Glacier Basin.

At the pass you are surrounded by four primary peaks. Pollock Mountain Spur is north of the highway there, and exposes class 5 cliffs very close to the parking lot. Mt. Reynolds (9,125) is the beautiful matterhorn due south of the pass. Clements Mountain (8,760) is west of the extensive meadows, and obviously the east face of that peak offers many challenges for mountain climbers. The smaller peak north of Clements is Mt. Oberlin (8,180), and most people without previous climbing experience should be satisfied with an ascent of that lovely vantage-point as an introduction to the alpinists' world.

From Logan Pass a marvelous foot trail leads 7.5 miles north along the Garden Wall to Granite Park Chalets (and ultimately to Waterton Lake). Where that trail passes between Haystack Butte and Mt. Gould (9,553) the best route up that massive peak begins. Gould looks very different from Logan Pass than it does from the Many Glacier Hotel. It is very much less precipitous on the west face and the elevation 2,000 feet less than the east side. Even so, it is still a very long way up and provides dozens of interesting experiences during the ascent and descent! Climbers who prefer a short, steep climb rather than a long, gentle approach may prefer to drive down to the Weeping Wall parking area and scramble up the faint, steep climber's trail to reach the main Garden Wall trail just south of Haystack Butte (see the description of that route below, under "Haystack Butte and Garden Wall Trail, from Highway"). Notice that two other routes to the summit of Mt. Gould are described under the Many Glacier area chapter, because they originate from that area.

From Logan Pass a classic seventeen-mile hike leads to the Many

Glacier area via Granite Park Chalets and Swiftcurrent Pass. Strong hikers will want to detour up a steep trail to the Continental Divide one-half mile from the chalets, to the Grinnell Glacier Overlook. Some hikers may also enjoy the lung-wracking trail up to Swiftcurrent Fire Lookout to contemplate some of the greatest views in the central area of the park.

The walk from Logan Pass to Hidden Pass is the most impressive short hike in the entire park, crossing acres of beautiful meadows with vast panoramic views of the Lewis and Livingston ranges. From Hidden Pass you can study Mt. Cannon (8,952), which is not visible from Logan Pass. The lowest place in the long ridge between Cannon and Clements Mountain is called Bird Woman Pass, and both peaks can be climbed from there. From Hidden Pass it is possible to hike southward along the west side of the great rocky hump there, on a game trail that reaches the saddle between that hump and Reynolds Mountain. A better game trail reaches that saddle from the meadows east of the hump, then continues around to the southwest corner of Reynolds. In addition to leading climbers to the southern route up Mt. Reynolds, that game trail is an important link in the "Continental Divide Route" from Forum Peak in Canada to Marias Summit on Highway 2. (From Mt. Reynolds that route goes down past Twin Lakes and around the east end of Fusillade Mountain, then angles down to Gunsight Lake and across the Blackfoot Glacier Basin to Red Eagle Pass.)

A challenge to every mountaineer who spends much time in Glacier National Park is the cross-country route from Logan Pass to Sperry Chalets. The customary route follows the trail down to Hidden Lake and then climbs up to the ridge above the headwall of that lake, from which the route to the glacier is obvious. It is about seven miles from Logan Pass to the glacier, and another 4.5 miles to the chalets. Another route goes over the top of The Dragon's Tail and then descends to the glacier. Both routes are discussed in the following pages.

GEM GLACIER, FROM THE GARDEN WALL TRAIL

This is a delightful place to visit, with great views in both directions and a good chance to see bighorn sheep in the meadow. It is also the approach to the great northwest ridge of Mt. Gould which many climbers prefer to the less exciting route up the west slope to that summit.

Hike to Haystack Butte, either via the long trail from Logan Pass or the short cut route up from the road below (described elsewhere in this guide, under the heading "Haystack Butte and Garden Wall Trail, from Highway"). Proceed up the trail north of Haystack for about one-quarter mile, to a stream crossing at the very highest point along that trail (6,900 ft.). A wide "U"-shaped notch in the top of the Garden Wall is directly above this high point in the trail and a broad rocky couloir extends up to it. Walk up the steep hillside to the base of the first cliff, then follow that cliff-base toward the south until reaching an easy class 4 route up through it. Above the cliff, traverse back toward the north and into the broad couloir. Climb up the couloir until it becomes steep and dangerous near the top, then scramble up a convenient scree-chute toward your left to the top of the north wall of the couloir. A good game trail parallels the base of the huge cliff above, leading across the top of the couloir and into the meadow beyond. Curb the desire to go north along that trail, for it ends in a steep snow slope that is dangerous without ice axes. (Beyond that snow, however, is a deep notch in the Garden Wall which is reached by human trail from the Garden Wall Trail near Granite Park Chalets.) Descents to the trail between Gem Glacier and that deep notch in the wall are also discouraged, because of hazardous cliffs just above the foot trail.

On the descent, be sure to enter the head of the couloir from the north, and remember to traverse south to get down around the bottom-most cliffs.

HAYSTACK BUTTE AND THE GARDEN WALL TRAIL
FROM THE HIGHWAY

Climbers who wish to visit Gem Glacier or climb Mt. Gould may wish to avoid the long walk along the Garden Wall Trail from Logan Pass. A much shorter and quicker alternative is described here.

Park just above the Weeping Wall, along Going-to-the-Sun Road. Walk up a well-worn trail through the steep meadow south of the large stream that drains Mt. Gould and Haystack Butte. Follow the south fork, either in the rocky streambed or along its south shore. It becomes fast and easy after getting above the small cliff at the top of the meadow, and in fifteen or twenty minutes the great meadows above are reached. It is possible to traverse toward the north across the meadows, but it is faster to stay in the streambed until reaching the main trail above the meadows. WARNING: When descending this route be sure to follow the correct streambed. The larger one in that broad meadow ends in scrub forest and awful cliffs below, so traverse much further south to the smaller streambed. The correct streambed reaches the Garden Wall Trail at a point where there are several trees, and the upper several yards below the trail are surrounded by shrubs and bushes. The streambed then goes down through the meadows and stays south of extensive brush-cover until almost to the small cliff above the basal meadow.

The time required to reach the trail, from the road, should be thirty or forty minutes, and the descent only takes about half that long.

SPERRY GLACIER FROM LOGAN PASS

Mountaineers frequently study their maps, seeking interesting new ways to get places. Most will quickly notice how close Sperry Glacier is to Logan Pass, and many will be eager to try cross-country approaches to Sperry. Hopefully the following discussions will be helpful.

The Hidden Lake Route. Hike two miles to Hidden Pass and another mile downhill to Hidden Lake. After wading the outlet, walk about two miles through the meadows west of the lake, staying within 100 feet of the shore. After that shore curves sharply to the west watch for the good game trail that angles uphill for a mile toward the scree basin far above the head of the lake. (Many hikers miss this trail by starting up too soon.) Scramble up the scree to the lowest part of the ridge above that basin (7,500 ft.), and look over the other side. SURPRISE! Don't despair, though; just keep right on heading south along the ridgetop for about a half mile, until sighting a small lake below you in Floral Park (a marvelous grassy bench 900 feet below the ridgetop). Descend to the park, then walk through the meadows and boulder-fields to the constricted entryway to the great glacier basin. From there it is about two miles across the glacier basin, gaining 800 vertical feet en route.

Stay below the glacier front, walking on glacial debris, scoured rock surfaces, and snowfields. The terrain changes annually, but there is no problem finding a route up to the broad gap (Comeau Pass) south of Mt. Edwards. Beyond the small meltpond there, climb down the man-made stairway in the cliffs to reach the trail that descends for 2.5 miles to Sperry Chalets. Another six miles of trail leads easily to Lake McDonald Hotel.

The Dragon's Tail Route. Gung-ho climbers, with rope, may want to try this much more strenuous route. It is described later in this chapter. If your major objective is a visit to Sperry Glacier (or to Lake McDonald), this is not the recommended route. If you seek a great summit view, plus a challenging descent to the glacier or a circuitous return to Logan Pass via Hidden Lake, it offers interesting possibilities.

Hikers on the high, narrow goat trail along the north face of Mt. Clements—Jane Edwards

Going-to-the-Sun Mountain and the matterhorn of Mt. Reynolds, viewed from Bearhat Mountain—James Dyson

Routes to the Summits

Bearhat Mountain (8,684)

Views from this peak are among the most interesting in the park. In every direction there are jagged walls and pinnacles, splendid cliffs, and densely wooded valleys. Hidden Lake is especially handsome from this angle, and Mt. Reynolds appears above it as a fantastic matterhorn. Sperry, Jackson, and Blackfoot glaciers are all spread out in plain view. Almost every major peak in the park is visible, except for those concealed by massive Mt. Jackson.

The East Face Route. Distance to summit about four miles, three miles of it by human trail. Elevation gained is about 2,600 vertical feet (including the 500 ft. that must be lost on the approach via Hidden Lake). Class 2 and 3 all the way to the summit, if the correct route is followed. First known ascent: Norman Clyde, August 17, 1923.

Hike from Logan Pass to Hidden Lake. Cross the outlet of the lake and walk southward through the meadows until below the great rift that extends up the middle of the east face. Scramble upward, staying south of the rift and traversing further south as difficulties arise. The farther south you go, the easier and faster the climb. The register has usually been found on the north summit, rather than the central summit dome.

The highest part of Bearhat is actually at the southwest end of the mountain, where the author found part of Norman Clyde's 1923 note in a rusted tin can. The southwest peak can be reached via the summit ridge, but a sheer ten-foot cliff with inadequate "holds" must be descended to get into the gap that separates that peak from the rest of the mountain. (That gap is easily reached from below, however, after an easy traverse around the south end of Bearhat just a bit lower than the notch.)

Cannon Mountain (8,952)

From Cannon Mountain one can see almost every peak in the Lewis and Livingston ranges . . . a tremendous sea of spires and ridges extending northward into Alberta and British Columbia. In the other direction Sperry Glacier fills the great basin between Bearhat Mountain and Edwards Mountain, with high waterfalls plunging down from there into the Avalanche Lake valley (the lake itself is concealed by a shoulder of Cannon). Mt. Brown rises just south of the very deep, narrow gorge of Avalanche Creek, and a portion of Lake McDonald may be seen beyond it. South of

Sperry Glacier and Gunsight Mountain the huge dome of 10,052-foot Mt. Jackson is high enough to cut off most views of the southern part of the park. An almost surrealistic spectacle is the magnificent rock horn that is Mt. Reynolds, reflected in the deep blue mirror of Hidden Lake.

The East Ridge Route. Distance to summit about 5.5 miles, 2.5 miles of it by human trail. Elevation gained is only 2,200 vertical feet from Logan Pass, but it is more than 5,000 vertical feet down to the valley floor southwest of the summit. Mostly class 3, but perhaps one class 4 pitch along the summit ridge. First known ascent: Norman Clyde, August 15, 1923.

Hike the trail from Logan Pass to Hidden Pass and continue down the trail toward Hidden Lake for about one-quarter mile, to a place from which an easy traverse may be made across grassy slopes just below the reddish-colored cliffs of the lower south side of Clements Mountain. Traverse at that elevation until almost directly above the outlet of Hidden Lake. Scramble or walk up to the gap between Cannon Mountain and the long west ridge of Mt. Clements. From that gap, ascend gullies up the southeast shoulder of Cannon Mountain.

The best route lies just north of the southeast shoulder, ascending badly-eroded gullies that are never worse than class 3. Soon the shoulder becomes an easy scree slope to the top of the ridge. Follow the ridge westward, to a steep-walled gap that separates it from the the main summit mass. The gap is negotiated by climbing down a cliff for a few yards, traversing above a frightening cliff, then working back up toward your left, via a class 4 crack that is just south of the actual ridge. It is an easy walk from there to the summit, along scree ledges southwest of the top of the summit ridge.

The largest summit cairn ever seen in the park was constructed on the summit by the Sierra Club ... about five feet square and six feet high. The register should be easier to find in the smaller cairn that is usually there now. WARNING: On the return from Bird Woman Pass to the Hidden Lake trail make the descent directly toward the lake's outlet until reaching the elevation of the traverse used earlier. If a higher traverse is attempted it always results in complications because of the many cliffs which extend down the great hillside to that elevation.

Cannon Mountain Southwest Peak (8,800)

In 1985 James Best and Ted Steiner climbed to this summit, where they found a note placed there in a bottle on July 19, 1901 by Dr. Walter Bradford Cannon, his new bride Cornelia, and famous mountain guide Denis Comeau. The ascent was difficult, involving many class 4 pitches and one cold all-night bivouac en route, but they descended the easier northwest slope to report their discovery. After finding great interest displayed by park officials, the climbers went back up to retrieve the bottle with the historic note. It is now in the archives at park headquarters, but a handwritten copy was left at the summit in a new container. Dr. Cannon was a Nobel Prize winner in physiology at Harvard, and his wife wrote for *Harper's Magazine*. The sons and daughters of that illustrious man and wife were delighted to receive a photocopy of the note, and confirmed that it really is in his handwriting. Dr. Cannon was in every issue of *Who's Who* from 1901 to 1947. Obviously there is MUCH of historic interest still to be found in these majestic mountains!

Clements Mountain (8,760)

Rewarding views from the summit include the McDonald Valley, the Lewis Range, and most of the Livingston Range. Going-to-the-Sun Highway can be traced for more than fifteen miles as it slants down into the McDonald Valley (and for another seven miles into the St. Mary Valley). The Logan Pass area is highly photogenic, and beautiful blue St. Mary Lake is spectacular below its surrounding bastions of bright red cliffs and peaks. South of the summit there is the classic matterhorn of Mt. Reynolds rising directly above Hidden Lake, and the vast expanse of snow and ice in Sperry Glacier just beyond it on the slopes of snowy Gunsight Mountain.

The West Ridge Route. Distance to the summit about 4.5 miles, 2.5 miles of it by human trail. Elevation gained is about 2,300 vertical feet. Class 2 and 3 all the way if the correct route is followed, although there is tremendous exposure below the narrow goat trail ledge across the upper north face. First known ascent: Norman Clyde on August 13, 1923.

Hike to Hidden Pass from Logan Pass and then head down the trail toward Hidden Lake. After passing through green meadows and crossing tiny creeks, the trail descends more steeply through scree-slopes bearing sparse vegetation. Soon a series of horizontal ledges are seen above the trail, with steep green slopes between them. Just east of those ledges a large snowbank lingers late into the summer, and is drained by a small streambed surrounded by rocks and scree. Angle uphill across that scree, and traverse westward above the most prominent cliffy ledge. A faint game trail goes westward across the grassy slope there, about 100 vertical feet above the Hidden Lake trail. After a few hundred feet the trail fades away, but it is then easy to ascend to another horizontal grassy slope, about forty feet higher, and continue toward the west on that one. When almost directly

Groves Kilbourn pausing on the east face of Mt. Clements—John Mauff

above the outlet of Hidden Lake, or above the great (invisible) waterfall where the outlet stream plunges into the Avalanche basin, look for an easy route going almost straight uphill. NOTICE: It is very important to descend to this same elevation during the descent of the mountain, before traversing back toward the east, because the party may encounter unexpected cliffs and dense brush if a traverse is made higher on the mountainside, and will loose much time seeking routes down to the easy traverse with the game trail.

From the open area high above the hidden waterfall, scramble up easy gullies and steep game trails toward the ridgetop high above. Just below the uppermost cliffs an excellent game trail is encountered heading toward the large pass, or côl, between Mt. Clements and Cannon Mountain. That is the route for climbers seeking to climb the latter peak. There are two routes to the top of Clements from here, one along the south side of the ridge and the other along the north face of the ridge. Both routes lead to the Great Notch that is between the two huge rocky humps on the long west ridge of Mt. Clements. The south side route is hotter, and crosses scree most of the way, while the north side route is cool and follows a firm game trail all the way to the Notch.

To follow the south side route, simply traverse toward the east below the upper cliffs of the ridge, staying between the vegetated areas and the sheer cliffs. It is class 2 or 3 all the way to the Great Notch. (This route is

Mt. Clements, from Cannon Mountain, with St. Mary Lake in the valley beyond—Hal Kanzler

recommended on the descent because it is closer and faster than the north face route.)

To reach the north side of the ridge you must first climb to the ridgetop directly above, or slightly eastward (the route is obvious). Walk east on the ridgetop until confronted by steep unclimbable cliffs (with the huge spire that is visible from afar), then look on the north face below those cliffs, and follow the well-worn game trail there. It gains elevation steadily, staying about the same distance from the ridgetop for several hundred yards. It is cool and shady, and there should be snow lingering by the base of the cliffs. From below, it often looks as though dangerous areas lie ahead, but looks are deceiving. There is really no dangerous exposure, and the photographic opportunities are great. The trail leads directly to the

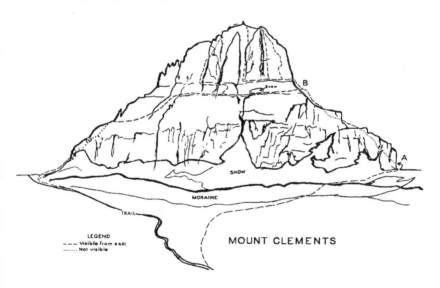

MOUNT CLEMENTS

LEGEND
--- Visible from east
.... Not visible

Great Notch, where it joins the south side route.

From that Notch a trail extends onto the north slope of the ridge, but it should be shunned because it eventually disappears on the steep north face. Instead, go further up the ridge, climbing about six small humps, until reaching a broad flat section about forty feet long. At the east end of that flat ridgetop a great cliff rises and blocks further progress up the ridge. From that location a marvelous game trail leads onto the steep north face of the ridge and extends for several hundred feet, passing entirely around the last great hump and leading to the gap between that hump and the summit. The trail bothers some climbers, for it clings to narrow ledges all the way, with sheer or overhanging cliffs above and tremendous exposure below. Any slip off that ledge would surely be fatal, so climbers should move very carefully, placing feet with precision and selecting reliable handholds. Beyond the long north face traverse it is an easy scree-walk to the summit, and a heavily-traveled trail leads all the way, traversing the west side below the uppermost cliffs, then ascending easy gullies to the top.

The East Face Couloir Route. Distance to the summit about two miles, one mile of it by human trail. Class 4 or 5 pitches must be climbed up rotten rock low in the upper couloir. First ascent: Alice and Gordon Edwards, August 26, 1950.

Hike up the Hidden Lake trail from Logan Pass until it angles sharply toward the south (left). Leave it there and climb to the top of the moraine above it. Walk the top of the moraine toward the saddle between Clements and Oberlin mountains. Pass around the cliff above the south end of that broad saddle (A) and continue around onto the north side of the mountain. WARNING: Until mid-July there may be dangerous steep snow across the last part of the traverse into the saddle. In that case, go back down the moraine until it can be safely descended into the great green basin toward the north, then walk up to the saddle from there. (See the saddle route up Oberlin for details.)

After reaching the north side of the lower northeast ridge of Clements Mountain, climb up easy gullies to the ridgetop. Walk up the ridge until stopped by a steep cliff. Traverse along the west side of that cliff on a goat trail, then scramble back to the ridgetop above the cliff. Walk up the ridge again until close to the tremendous cliffs that rise to the summit of the mountain. Traverse toward the south across the east face of the mountain at that elevation. A cairn marks the best ledge (B) on which to traverse, and the route goes just above the lingering snowpatch there and passes a few feet above the small clump of scrubby trees before reaching the bottom of the great couloir. This high traverse eliminates a few difficult cliffs that are lower on the east face below the couloir. If you find that you are below those trees it is easiest to go back to the ridge, climb to the higher ledge, then traverse south again on the higher ledge.

The great couloir in the center of the east face leads all the way to the summit. There are class 4 cliffs near the bottom but above them it is a good climb up a remarkably easy staircase of rock ledges to the summit. A detour to the right or left of the center in some places makes it easier and also reduces the danger of being struck by rocks dislodged by other climbers. (Of course, any fall in the upper couloir would almost certainly be fatal, and a climber struck by falling rock there might be knocked from

287

the ledges.) It is best to climb side by side in the great couloir, if possible, and otherwise climb one at a time. The couloir emerges at the top a few yards north of the summit cairn.

The South Ridge Route. Distance to the summit about two miles, one mile of it by human trail. Class 3 or 4 all the way if correct route is followed (mostly class 3). First ascent: J. G. Edwards, 1967.

Hike from Logan Pass to Hidden Pass. From Hidden Lake Overlook examine the great stone ridge that extends down toward the south from the summit dome of the mountain. Below the great stone "teeth" high on that ridge there is a single small "finger" of rock. (The route passes eastward below the small finger, then traverses the east face until beneath the great teeth.)

From Hidden Pass overlook, scramble up the scree to the bottom of a narrow gully west of the base of the south ridge. Clamber up that gully (almost "chimney") until it reaches the crest of the ridge. (That crest can also be reached via the steep snow on the east side of the great south ridge.) After a brief detour around the east side of a rocky hump on the ridge, ascend the west slope to reach the single rock finger mentioned above. Follow a well-worn goat trail below that finger and across the east face of the mountain. (Another traverse twenty or thirty feet higher is also possible, but involves a treacherous ledge below the great teeth.)

After walking across the east face until directly beneath the southern-most huge stone tooth on the ridgetop, a steep narrow gully with solid rock walls is reached. It angles up toward the north for twenty or thirty feet toward a black couloir. Climb up that class 4 gully to the broad scree-covered ledge just below the black couloir, then walk northward on that ledge. After passing to the north of the steep black couloir, go around the next rocky rib and climb up a broad class 3 couloir just beyond. Stay north of the center of the class 3 couloir while climbing, until reaching a higher transverse scree ledge with a faint goat trail that goes southward and passes just below a large, freestanding spire. (This is above the black couloir.) Walk south along the faint trail until reaching a couloir just south of the spire (a huge "keyhole" is in a vertical rock rib at the south side of that couloir, but appears about ready to collapse). You are now directly above the black couloir that confronted you after ascending the "steep narrow gully," and are actually in the upper portion of the same black couloir. Climb up that couloir all the way to the summit ridge of the mountain (class 4 for a short distance, then class 3 to the top). It is an easy walk to the summit from there via the west side of the ridge.

An alternative approach to the upper couloir was described by Richard E. Johnson (in a 1966 letter). He continued up the south ridge above the small single finger (staying west of the ridgetop) until reaching the base of the first huge "tooth" there. He then traversed northward across "a broad horizontal ledge above which there are impassable cliffs, then around the corner and across the east face." He then "continued across the face, past the first gully (probably class 5 and hardly a gully at all) to the second gully, then ascended straight up class 3 and 4 cliffs which lead to the ridgetop, north of the great teeth." Johnson's diagram clearly indicates the traverse from the base of the first great tooth leads to the gully with the "keyhole" (above the "black couloir"), in which case it might be a better route than that described in detail above. The traverse would be considerably above the "treacherous ledge traverse" below the great teeth mentioned briefly in an earlier description of the route.

The North Face Routes. Class 3 and 4, with considerable exposure. This face can be climbed almost anywhere, but should be attempted only by experienced climbing teams.

Hike from Logan Pass to the saddle between Oberlin and Clements mountains, following the route described for the Saddle route to Oberlin or the East Face Couloir route up Clements.

Follow the very distinct goat trail from the saddle across the north face of Clements. After a marvelous ten minutes the trail ends abruptly at the "awesome chasm," where the shelf which the trail was following disappears and a frightening cliff of unusually smooth vertical rock lies below. Goats evidently scramble and jump across it, for the trail continues on the far side; but it is not suitable for human jumping. Fortunately, a safer route exists which goes up the couloir just east of the chasm for about 100 vertical feet (class 3 only, if a zig-zag route is carefully chosen) then goes through a narrow notch on the west wall of the couloir and descends a narrow passageway down class 3 and 4 pitches to the trail west of the chasm.

Although it can be climbed anywhere, the first route up the north face was the following one. Walk the trail west of the chasm until near a prominent ridge extending down the red cliffs above, with four small alpine fir trees outlined against the sky atop it. Scramble up the cliffy gully east of that ridge (class 3) OR up the very narrow gully (almost a chimney) that starts directly below that ridge and broadens as it passes upward around the east side of the ridge. Easy class 3 ledges provide access to the ridgetop from there, at the notch in the ridgetop a little further west. There you will join the West Ridge route to the summit, described earlier. Since this route was first used (Edwards, 1967) there has been little interest in it.

The Helmuth Matdies Routes. Not long before his untimely death (not on mountains) this expert rock climber made many difficult ascents in

Glacier National Park. Two of these were on the great northeast shoulder of Clements Mountain. (See also Citadel Spire, on Porcupine Ridge.) As a professional rock-climbing guide in Austria for many years, Helmuth climbed most of the mountains in that country. He always pointed out that Glacier Park offers equally good rock climbing, and that the rock on class 5 and 6 routes in the park is excellent. Helmuth trained Kris and Dick Wallner and Cal Jorgensen (of Kalispell) in climbing techniques, and together they made many technical rock climbs in the park in the 1960s. Two of those routes were on Mt. Clements, and they are summarized below as examples of real cliff-climbing!

The approach is the same as that to the East Face Couloir route. After

The magnificent east face of Mt. Clements, showing some of the climbing routes—Helmuth Matdies

reaching the traverse ledge (B), however, rope up and climb directly up the "tremendous cliff" mentioned there (instead of going south along the ledge to the big couloir). The route that begins almost directly above the lower northeast ridgetop is here called the Northeast Shoulder Route. It is class 4 and 5 all the way, on very good rock. First ascent: Helmuth Matdies and Cal Jorgensen, September 7, 1968. The more difficult route up the shoulder begins about twenty feet further east and is here called the East-Northeast Shoulder Route. It is class 6 for 200 feet of excellent rock and class 5 the rest of the way. First ascent: H. Matdies, Kris Wallner, and Dick Wallner, September 8, 1968. The equipment used on these climbs included about forty pitons, at least twenty carabiners and a drilling outfit, wrote Helmuth, and "we also needed about 10 wooden wedges and 3 rope leaders." There is little that can be offered in the way of a "description" of these routes. They simply go more or less straight up the cliffs. A large photograph of Mt. Clements with the routes indicated by Matdies will be kept at the Glacier Mountaineering Society office in Whitefish for inspection by interested mountaineers.

The Dragon's Tail, Southwest of Mt. Reynolds (8,580)

Follow the route described elsewhere as the approach to the Southwestern Route on Mt. Reynolds. Cross the west face of the mountain on the goat trail, then relax at the southwest ridge (7,900 ft.) and study the route ahead. The Dragon's Tail offers interesting climbing opportunities as well as easy scrambling to the summit on certain routes. It provides splendid views of Hidden Lake and Sperry Glacier, and it is also possible to reach Sperry Glacier by following the Continental Divide in that direction from the top of the Dragon's Tail.

In the view from the southwest ridge, notice that the east side of the Dragon's Tail is composed of a series of horizontal ledges. A game trail follows one of those ledges, below the great upper cliffs and just above a sheer twenty-foot-high grey stratum. To reach that trail, descend westward from the saddle to the grassy area above some small clumps of trees. A faint trail crosses the scree slope west of the grassy area and leads to the beginning of the rocky ledges. Locate the correct ledge there by following the game trail onto it. Follow the trail as it gradually ascends for several hundred yards, then levels off at about 8,000 feet elevation. That trail eventually ends abruptly at a sheer-walled couloir which cannot be crossed. (It continues, on the far side of the couloir, but even the goats reach that continuation by climbing up over the head of the couloir and descending on the far side.)

From the highest part of the trail, follow up easy ledges and three or four long ascending ramps leading to the top of the ridge (class 3, if care is taken in route-finding). Mark your route carefully with distinctive "ducks" of rock slabs, so you can find it on the descent! Enjoy the easy stroll up the grassy ridgetop to the very highest grassy dome on the summit. It is possible to climb along the east side of the cliffy ridge that extends southwest from the dome, but eventually a difficult twenty-foot pitch blocks the route. A rope belay is essential for the safe descent of that cliff, but beyond that obstacle there are no more cliffs. It is also possible to descend from the grassy dome down the southeast slope, toward the right (south), until locating a passable narrow defile that can be safely descended to reach easy traverses leading toward Sperry Glacier. Both of these routes lead to the scree slopes that will provide easy access to the glacier basin. Those slopes can be followed northward, also, to the ridgetop overlooking Avalanche Lake AND the south end of Hidden Lake. A good game trail descends directly down the north side of the broad basin and into the meadows beside Hidden Lake. The walk back up to Hidden Pass from there is uncomplicated, but will usually cause fatigue.

Mt. Reynolds, in June, showing diagonal ledge across north face.
—J. G. Edwards

Looking South From Mt. Gould. (1) Heavy Runner Mtn.; (2) Jackson Glacier; (3) Mt. Thompson; (4) Fusillade Mtn.; (5) Mt. Jackson; (6) Reynolds Mtn.; (7) Gunsight Mtn.; (8) Sperry Glacier; (9) Clements Mtn.; 10) Edwards Mtn.; (11) Bearhat Mtn.; (12) Oberlin Mtn.; (13) Logan Pass. (See diagram of view north, on page 189.)

Mt. Gould (9,553)

The panorama from the summit is indeed rewarding. Although the peak is not as high as many others, it is centrally located so that no significant portion of the park is blocked from view by larger peaks. Immediately below the summit lies a broad valley in which Morning Eagle Falls is visible more than 4,000 vertical feet down to the east, and Grinnell Glacier is 3,000 vertical feet below to the north. The Garden Wall is a great arete extending south to Logan Pass, and just north of Gould it rises in great sheer-walled spires above Grinnell Glacier. Granite Park Chalets are clearly visible beyond those spires. It is a colorful scene in the east and northeast because of the peaks being predominantly bright red or yellow in those directions, but northward the general coloration of the mountains is dark gray or pale brown, and they are flecked with dozens of gleaming white snowfields. All major peaks in the northern part of the park stand out, with Ipasha, Merritt, and Cleveland rising above most of the others. West of Cleveland the matterhorn of Kinnerly Peak and the broad pyramids of Kintla Peak and Mt. Carter are most impressive. Along the western horizon the majestic summits of the Livingston Range loom up in snowy grandeur. Deep in the valley north of Lake McDonald part of Going-to-the-Sun Highway is visible between Heavens Peak and Cannon Mountain, and higher up it can be traced all the way to Logan Pass. Southeast of that pass are even more spectacular views, including Blackfoot and Jackson glaciers and the rugged peaks around them. There is almost no end to the panorama, but a favorite view photographed by most climbers from this summit will be the bright blue lakes near the Many Glacier Hotel, with the great hotel itself clearly visible along the far shore of Swiftcurrent Lake. East of the hotel, Sherburne Lake stretches almost to the pastel-green expanses of the seemingly endless prairies. More than a hundred miles across those rolling plains the Sweetgrass Hills can usually be faintly discerned. Just east of Babb is huge Duck Lake, with several smaller lakes dotting the prairie nearby. Truly a tremendous viewpoint!

The West Face Route. Distance to the summit from Logan Pass about six miles, four miles of it by trail. For a shorter approach, see the description of the route: "Haystack Butte and Garden Wall Trail from Highway." Elevation gained from Logan Pass is about 3,000 vertical feet (from the road near Weeping Wall the gain is about 3,600 vertical feet). Nothing worse than class 3 will be encountered if the route is followed carefully.

Hike north along the Garden Wall trail from Logan Pass, to the highest point of the trail between Haystack Butte and Mt. Gould. Scramble up from the trail toward the broad black cliffs low on the mountainside, angling toward the south to approach the black cliffs at the place where a stream flows down a broken couloir through them. Climb up just south of that streambed, to the base of the cliffs. Not far south of the stream there are very safe, easy routes up through the dark igneous cliffs (the diorite or metagabbro sill that is so prominent in most parts of the park in the great mountain faces and is traversed by the Garden Wall trail just after heading north from Logan Pass meadows). Be sure to mark the top of the route you climbed, so it can be located again during the descent. There are no easy routes through that cliff further to the north below Mt. Gould!

Above the diorite sill, angle upward to the north and enter the broad upper basin of the mountain. Climb up scree slopes, cliffs of any desired degree of difficulty, interesting gullies and chimneys, and usually a few snowfields or snow patches.

Those features continue all the way to the summit of the mountain, which should be reached in about three hours. With even a minimal effort expended, every climber can find safe, easy climbing routes, but remember the constant hazard from falling rocks and avoid getting directly beneath other climbers. Also, at all times keep watching for safe ledges that you can dive under when you hear or see rocks bounding down toward you. Needless to say, good climbers seek to avoid loosening any rocks while on great steep slopes such as this, and NEVER deliberately knock anything off "just to watch it go!"

The Northwest Ridge Route. This is not much further than the West Face Route, but is slightly more difficult. If care is taken to find the safest pitches, nothing worse than class 3 will be encountered.

After reaching the trail between Haystack Butte and Mt. Gould, continue north along the trail for about one-quarter mile, to a stream-crossing at the very highest point along that trail. The great couloir from which the stream comes extends up to a broad "U"-shaped gap in the top of the Garden Wall, and Gem Glacier is just out of sight beyond that gap. The bottom cliffs are difficult, but an easy route through them is about 100 feet south of the streambed. Walk up the steep soil slope toward the south and follow the base of the cliff until reaching that easy route up. Above the cliff, traverse back into the couloir above the small stream and scramble up it to the great gap in the top of the wall. (For more details, see the separate account of Gem Glacier approach in this guide.)

From the meadow beside Gem Glacier (east of the great notch in the ridge) study the route up the bottom of the northwest ridge. The easiest route goes up a steep gully of loose rock just east of the point of the ridge (other possible routes are a little further east). Within 200 feet the steep gully leads to gentler, safer terrain, and it is an easy walk up the west side of the ridge all the way to the summit.

WARNING: Climbers who have ascended via other routes but wish to take this different route down the mountain should have no difficulty until descending the couloir below the Gem Glacier notch. The entry into the head of that couloir is from the north, via a steep diagonal scree-chute. It is easy from there down to the bottom cliffs in the couloir, at which place a traverse toward the south should be made across scree and steep grassy slopes for about 100 feet. The easy route down the bottom cliff will be very obvious when you reach it, and it leads to the soil slopes just above the foot trail.

Other Routes. There are two other routes known, both of which begin on the northeast side of the mountain. Since they are approached from the Many Glacier Hotel or the Swiftcurrent Camp area, they have been included under the Many Glacier section of this guide. One route goes up close to the northeast ridge from Grinnell Glacier, and involves some dangerous class 5 or 6 pitches with fearful exposure. The other route is up the 4,000-foot-high east face, with hundreds of feet of class 6 climbing.

Mt. Oberlin (8,180)

This is probably the shortest and easiest climb in Glacier National Park, but it affords excellent scenic opportunities. There are fine views down the St. Mary Valley and up the broad McDonald Valley. To the south is the sheer east face of Clements Mountain and the great "horn" of Mt. Reynolds, with snowy Mt. Jackson beyond it. The peaks of the Livingston Range are extremely impressive when seen from this vantage point, as are the sharp ridges and spires of the Lewis Range beyond the great Garden Wall. Views of Logan Pass, with all the colorful automobiles and people, add a certain interesting element that is missing from most other climbs in Glacier National Park.

The Southeast Slope Route. Distance to the summit about 1.5 miles, almost none of it by human trail. Elevation gained is about 1,500 vertical feet from Logan Pass. Class 2 all the way.

After registering for the climb with the rangers at Logan Pass, follow their instructions for approaching the basin southeast of Mt. Oberlin, where the climb begins. In that basin there are clear pools, lush meadows, huge boulders of bright red rock, and snowfields during July and early August. There is no longer any need to describe the route to the summit, because hundreds of climbers have worn a deep trail that nobody can miss. Above the meadows, start up the scree-slope toward the summit and in a few minutes you will see the climbers' trail. It ascends toward the north and after 1,200 vertical feet of climbing it approaches the rocky ridgetop just a few yards from the summit.

The Clements Saddle Route. (Class 3, with possibly one class 4 pitch.) This more challenging route begins in the saddle between Clements and Oberlin. From the saddle, walk up the ridge toward Oberlin, pass to left of the gray cliffs, and go to the highest section of the "trail." A 2-foot-wide cleft goes 12 feet up the wall on your right, then walk about 100 feet uphill, passing over a grassy saddle and into a red depression. Climb 20 feet up red cliffs on your right, then circle around onto the west side of the ridge. Walk up a 3-foot-wide cleft for about 50 feet toward the north, then climb to the top of the red ridge. A steep gully drops down the east face from there. Descend the gully for 20 feet then climb to the flat platform on the north side of it. It is an easy scramble from there to the summit, via interesting ledges and diagonals, requiring about thirty minutes of pleasant activity.

Piegan Mountain (9,220)

Follow the route described for the approach to Mt. Pollock. After reaching the high saddle between Peigan and Pollock, scramble up the northwest ridge of Mt. Piegan (class 2) to the summit. The views are similar to those from Mt. Pollock, except for the restricted view toward the northwest (because Pollock is in the way). There are great views of Logan

Pass and Sperry Glacier, and the Blackfoot Basin displays broad expanses of snow and ice. Directly below the summit lies Piegan Glacier, which is much larger than it appears from below. Views of St. Mary Lake are spectacular beyond the lofty shoulder of Going-to-the-Sun Mountain. Climbers who may hesitate to attempt the face of Mt. Pollock should be delighted with this alternative climb. (Most climbers who ascend Piegan end up climbing Pollock before descending into the valley so far below, anyway.)

As from Pollock, climbers of Piegan can descend via Piegan Pass without difficulty if they are interested in seeing different country. From that pass they may either hike the long trail to Many Glacier and Swiftcurrent Camp OR drop down the shorter trail to Preston Park and the big switchback in the highway known as "Siyeh Bend."

Pollock Mountain (9,190)

Distance to summit about one mile, none of it by human trail. Elevation gained is about 3,000 feet. A class 3 scramble, if snow is avoided and the correct route is followed.

The views from this easily accessible peak are among the most photogenic in the park. Great expanses of snow and ice are provided by Sperry, Jackson, and Blackfoot glaciers. In the northeast, beyond the beetling 4,000-foot face of Mt. Gould, Josephine and Swiftcurrent lakes sparkle blue and silver in the Grinnell Valley and Many Glacier Hotel is clearly visible on Swiftcurrent's east shore. Beyond it are the brilliant red formations of Altyn and Henkel, the ochre-colored mass of Yellow Mountain and the varied green hues of forests and prairies. The snowy monsters of the Lewis Range are lined up along the western horizon, while Mt. Merritt and Old Sun Glacier dominate the panorama toward the north.

Drive to the first stream east of Logan Pass (Lunch Creek) and leave the road there. A faint trail goes up the east shore of that stream, to the big cliff with the waterfall. Stay far east of the waterfall and scramble up the steep slopes and easy cliffs there for about sixty feet to reach the broad basin above the cliffs. Walk straight toward the saddle between Pollock and Piegan mountains, passing through alpine meadows along the stream and then plodding up the great snowfield toward Piegan. Leave the snow and scramble up the scree and small cliffs to the great saddle above. Walk up the southeast ridge of Mt. Pollock to the base of the cliffs. From that rocky point there are two recommended routes to the summit: (1) The East Couloir Route; and (2) The Great Cleft Route.

The Southeast Couloir Route. In late August, this is the easiest way to the top, but it should be avoided in June and July because the couloir is choked with very steep, hard snow and ice. After climbing the first small cliff on the ridge, traverse along the east face of the mountain on a possible goat trail. About thirty feet from the ridge, climb up and through a narrow notch, from which the southeast couloir can be inspected. Do NOT cross the steep snow in that couloir unless equipped with ice axes and protected by rope belays. NOTICE: Climbers approaching from Piegan Pass have complained in the past that they could not find this route. The difficulty was that they were looking on the direct east face for a gully instead of on the southeast area very near the actual ridge that rises from the great saddle.

Mt. Reynolds, telephoto of the east face, from the highway
—Brian Kennedy

The Dragon's Tail, viewed from Mt. Reynolds —J. G. Edwards

Late in summer, after the snow has melted, walk into the couloir from that ridge and scramble up the scree-filled gully (class 3). The gully soon curves to the north and provides quick access to the summit. For a much more interesting climb, however, attempt the Great Cleft Route.

The Great Cleft Route. From the southeast ridge, walk across the south face at the base of the summit cliffs. The game trail there passes beneath the base of a huge "finger" of rock. Go about 110 normal steps west from the base of that finger, then look upward toward the northeast. A series of easy ledges provide access to a broad basin eaten out of the south face. Climb up and eastward into that basin. While climbing, look to your right and locate the deep, very narrow, very straight cleft there that extends to the ridgetop above the great finger. Approach that cleft from the north via a large ledge, and lower yourself into it. The cleft is less than three feet wide and has sheer walls eight to ten feet high on each side. It is very safe for the first climber, but there is a great danger of dislodged rocks striking those who follow. After ten or fifteen feet of calisthentics low in the cleft (no ropes needed) it is an easy scramble for another twenty or thirty feet to the top of the cleft. From there, a good trail ascends the steep red scree to the summit.

Reynolds Mountain (9,125)

There are fine views of the Lewis and Livingston ranges from this convenient vantage point. To the south are Mt. Jackson and Mt. Logan, with great snowfields and glaciers between them. Lofty, flat-topped Mt. Stimson rises beyond the summit ridge of Blackfoot Mountain. At your feet lies Logan Pass, bustling with tourist activity, and a careful look straight down the north face reveals a frightening 1,500-foot drop to the meadows below. Hidden Lake is seen in its entirety, nestled in its large hanging basin of emerald-green vegetation. Beyond the head of that lake hundreds of acres of ice and snow are spread across the north flank of Gunsight Mountain, and the mountaineers' route from Logan Pass to that glacier can be traced over the pass between Bearhat and the Dragon's Tail. Of course, the huge lake in the distance is Lake McDonald. Often climbers on Mt. Reynolds watch storms approaching from the west until they reach that lake, at which time it becomes evident that a hasty descent must be made via the scree-run down the southwest talus slope and a fast traverse around the goat trail to Logan Pass meadows.

The Southwestern Talus Slope Route. Distance to the summit about five miles, none of it by human trail. Elevation gained from Logan Pass is about 2,500 vertical feet. Mostly class 2, but some class 3 pitches in the uppermost cliffs south of the summit.

Leave the Logan Pass parking area, after registering with the rangers there, and descend toward the stream to the south. Follow up that stream until reaching the place where it is easy to jump across the stream on solid bedrock, then head directly toward the mountain. From the upper meadows an excellent game trail angles up a steep scree slope to the south end of the broad saddle between Mt. Reynolds and the nameless rock dome north of it. From that saddle, follow the trail around the west face of Reynolds to the southwest corner of the mountain. (Do NOT cross steep snowslopes along that trail unless equipped with ice axes . . . climb above them instead to avoid risking an uncontrolled slide onto the rocks below.)

Just beyond the southwest corner, along the base of the south cliffs, there are two broad breaks through those cliffs (class 2 or 3). Climb up through the first of these and onto the tremendous talus slopes above. A very deeply-worn climbers' trail begins there and angles upward toward the right, eventually reaching the cliffs above the center of the south face. (This is NOT a game trail, because there was no trace of it there in 1950.) When the trail reaches the cliffy south face climb up toward the west for about 100 feet to the base of very high cliffs, then walk to the left along a narrow scree-covered ledge. A steep narrow gully (class 3) goes up toward your left from there, and becomes an easy scramble after the first eight feet. The route is definite, continuing to the west until reaching a "drop off" then angling back to the right for a few feet before going west again and passing around a narrow ledge that leads onto the west face of the mountain. Continue northward on a class 2 trail that extends to the northwest ridgetop, then follows easily up that ridge and along the summit wall to the highest part of Mt. Reynolds. The old 1920 Nature Study Club register was destroyed in 1951 and replaced by an aluminum tube with a Seattle Mountaineer register in 1952. That one disappeared also, and after a series of inferior registers the present one was placed there in a plastic tube by the Glacier Mountaineering Society. Please replace it with care after reading it and (if you wish) signing it.

The North Face and East Couloir Route. This is not quite as long a route as the other one, but the upper 300 vertical feet requires some class 4 climbing with potentially deadly exposure below rotten cliffs.

Follow the same approach as for the southwest route until reaching the broad saddle northwest of the peak. Continue on the goat trail around the west side of the mountain, watching for a broad, steep gully filled with scree that extends upward for several hundred feet. (A huge cone of scree has accumulated beneath that gully and the trail bends around the cone.) The walk up that great gully is easiest if you stay on the left side, climbing up solid rock rather than fighting the loose footing in the center. Even parties of a dozen or more people can safely make the ascent IF everyone is very careful not to dislodge rocks and IF the climbers below stay up on the wall where rocks cannot reach them. For further safety, the entire party should stay very close together so that dislodged rocks will not have time to pick up momentum and begin bounding from side to side before reaching climbers below. It is safe only if everyone is careful and very considerate of the safety of the others.

At the top of the great scree gully the level "step" in the lower northwest ridge of Reynolds is reached. After gathering the party together there, climb up the ridge directly toward the summit, either on the "nose" of the ridge or in the couloir further to the left. There is again a hazard from dislodged boulders there. Above the low cliffs, plod up the slope of scree to the base of the huge upper cliffs that soar upward to the very summit ridgetop of the mountain. Near the base of those cliffs you encounter a marvelous, very distinct and well-traveled goat trail that leads around onto the north face and goes entirely across that "sheer" face as it angles gently upward. The trail is on the great "diagonal" that is very prominent when the peak is viewed from the parking lot at Logan Pass. The crossing should not be made if snow and ice completely block the trail at any point. (In that event, walk across the top of the scree slope on the west face of the mountain and join the easier route up the scree slopes on the south side.)

The great diagonal ledge leads to a small level platform on the northeast corner, from which tremendous views open up in all directions. The difficult pitches are now near at hand.

Traverse the east side of the mountain on steep scree-slopes above considerable exposure. Avoid the deep, narrow, steep cracks extending up above the scree within fifty feet of the level platform. Continue southward until only sixty to eighty feet from the southeast corner of the rocky pyramid, and then the route upward will be obvious. Carefully climb the class 4 pitches above the scree traverse until the wall steepens above you, then traverse to your right across the steep basin. A belay is sometimes desired by members of the party during that traverse. (The slightly lower level seems easier than one ten feet higher at that point.) North of the steep basin there is a very easy gully that leads directly to the summit. As usual, the danger is primarily from falling rocks, so climb one at a time in the gully and while not climbing remain in a protected place beneath an overhang or off to the north side of the gully. In ten or fifteen minutes the summit is reached. (On the descent of this route it is easy to find the top of the gully, since it is the only gully below the summit on the east face.)

The Grand Tour Route. For large parties who enjoy a more challenging route than the southern scree slope, and who really are curious to experience the diagonal ledge across the north face, this route is the answer. There is nothing worse than class 3 on the entire route!

Follow the North Face Route to the level platform on the upper northeast ridge just beneath the summit cliffs. Continue along the east face on the steep, hard scree at the base of the cliffs (descending nearly 100 vertical feet, unfortunately, before reaching the southeast ridge). Scramble onward across the great south talus slope until reaching the well-worn trail that extends up into the basin high above you. Usually the climbers angle upward all the way across that tiresome talus slope, and are nearly at the cliffs by the time the climbers' trail is reached. Follow the route up the cliffs and around the southwest ridge (as described under the southwestern talus slope route), then across the upper west face (as described there) and up the northwest ridge to the summit.

On the descent, do not hesitate to go down via the southwest talus slope trail. You cannot get lost! After it reaches the bottom of the great talus slope, carefully scramble down through the rocky gully and then follow the base of the cliffs around to the west side of the mountain. The goat trail that traverses the west side is marvelous and leads to the saddle overlooking

Logan Pass.

The Southwest Ridge Route. Approach the mountain via the South-western Talus Slope Route. After scrambling up the couloir near the southwest corner (above the saddle between Reynolds and the Dragon's Tail) start up the deeply-worn climbers' trail toward the summit. Almost immediately leave that trail and angle up toward the west, to the bottom of the green and buff-colored buttress which is the lower end of the southwest ridge. Climb up the right (east) side of that ridge toward the upper cliffs. Low on the ridge there is a large "keyhole" that makes a nice frame for photos of Mt. Clements and the expansive range beyond. When the upper cliffs are reached, work out onto the actual ridgetop and climb upward until reaching the first class 4 cliffs. The route goes up a shallow steep couloir twenty or thirty feet high, leading to a wide ledge beneath the soaring summit cliffs. Follow this ledge for a short distance eastward and around a sharp corner to the left. Just beyond that corner look up and to the left to locate a break in the cliff that contains a concave formation of black rock. The climb up through that break (class 3) provides access to the crest of the southwest ridge again. Soon a narrow platform is reached that separates two sections of the upper ridge. Cross over the platform to a sheer little cliff with a crack angling up it toward the left. This is the crux of the climb and is class 4 or perhaps 5. The crack is almost a narrow chimney, and is overhung, tending to push you out over the top of the cliff. This awkward pitch is only eight or ten feet, but requires delicate negotiation. Above this difficult crack it is class 3 the rest of the way up to the summit ridge and a class 2 walk to the highest point, which is about 100 yards further east.

This route is very enjoyable, as it almost completely avoids the great scree slopes, and it provides a stimulating alpine challenge. It was discovered by Denis and Shirley in 1980, and repeated in 1988 by Denis with Vic Davis. It is probably the shortest and fastest route up Mt. Reynolds, and because of its southern exposure it is usually devoid of snow and ice. Of course, the descent can be made quickly via the great south slope of scree, running down a thousand feet of marvelous pulverized material on the well-worn "trail" to the southwest saddle.

Rolf Larson has just traversed the goat trail across the face of Triple Divide Peak. The walk up the ridge to the peak will be safer
—J. G. Edwards

Hikers on the Norris Traverse route.—J. G. Edwards

THE CUT BANK AREA

Routes Among the Peaks

Very few park visitors get into this peaceful, attractive area. The dirt road that leads four miles in from Highway 89 to the campground and ranger station is no super highway, but it is usually maintained very well.

The trail from the end of the road heads west along the north shore of Cut Bank Creek for four miles to the important trail junction near Atlantic Falls. From there the south fork goes to Two Medicine and the north fork ends at St. Mary.

Hikers taking the south fork will enjoy Morning Star Lake and Pitamakan Lake during the ten-mile ascent to Pitamakan Pass (7,600 ft.) or Cut Bank Pass (7,900 ft.). For fifty years there has been confusion as to which pass is Pitamakan, so it seems appropriate to discuss it here. Dr. George C. Ruhle, who hiked and climbed extensively throughout the park during his twelve years as Chief Park Naturalist, wrote the marvelous book, *Guide to Glacier National Park.* In 1972 a revised edition of that book appeared. Its title is *Roads and Trails of Waterton-Glacier National Parks.* On page 95 of that revision Dr. Ruhle discussed the confusion regarding Pitamakan Pass. Historically, Cut Bank Pass was on the Continental Divide between the Cut Bank Valley and the Nyack Valley, but most maps placed it erroneously between the Cut Bank Valley and the Dry Fork Valley. Ruhle tried to get the error corrected during the 1930s but failed. He did manage to get the name "Pitamakan Pass" attached to the pass on the Continental Divide, however, hoping that would prevent the pass being given an "inappropriate" name. Finally Dr. Ruhle received help from Francis Elmore (the more recent Chief Park Naturalist), who persuaded the National Board on Geographic Names to resolve the error. Thus, as Dr. Ruhle writes, "Today, Cut Bank Pass is on the Continental Divide, where it *should* be," and Pitamakan Pass is now applied to the low point in the long ridge that extends east from Mt. Morgan. From Pitamakan Pass it is now seven miles to the foot of Two Medicine Lake, and from Cut Bank Pass it is 9.5 miles to that spot via Dawson Pass.

From the trail junction near Atlantic Falls, the other major trail heads uphill for nearly 3.5 miles to Triple Divide Pass (7,397 ft.). The last 2.5 miles presents an unforgettable grind as it gains 1,800 vertical feet in the open sun ... and usually is devoid of water! From the pass it is eight miles downhill to Red Eagle Lake and another 7.5 miles to the highway at the St. Mary Ranger Station. Triple Divide Pass is the destination of most climbers and (with permission) mountaineers should enjoy spending the night in the meadows south of that pass. The best viewpoint in the entire area is the summit of Mt. James (9,375), reached after a 2,000-foot vertical struggle up the long, long ridge from the pass.

The "Continental Divide Route" for mountaineers avoids the valleys of the Cut Bank area. It goes from the meadows east of Triple Divide Peak, around the northeast flank of Razoredge Mtn., then ascends easily to the saddle southeast of the top of Razoredge. Dr. Robert Horodyski, who pioneered that section of the route, followed goat trails along the great Continental Divide ridge toward the south and reported that the trails were good and the views were spectacular. McClintock Peak was eventually reached, from which it is a rapid descent to the human trail near Cutbank Pass.

From Triple Divide Pass a tempting challenge is the east face of Triple Divide Peak (8,020 ft.). The route is described below, and a safer route for backpackers is also pointed out under the description of the "Norris Traverse." Triple Divide is remarkable because it actually drains into three different bodies of salt water. Toward the west the water reaches Nyack Creek and the Flathead River, and ultimately enters the Pacific Ocean. The runoff toward the Cut Bank Valley begins a long trip which eventually ends in the Gulf of Mexico. The northern drainage passes through Red Eagle Lake and St. Mary Lake and finally will flow into Hudson Bay via the Saskatchewan-Nelson river system. No other mountain in North America can share this distinction!

The ascent of Norris Mountain (8,882) is also described below. That summit may well be the final objective of climbers in this area, but hardy backpackers may be interested in continuing westward along high ridges and goat trail traverses all the way to Red Eagle Pass. That route, referred to here as The Norris Traverse, is a very important link in the Continental Divide Route from Canada to Highway 2. At Red Eagle Pass it meshes with the Almost-a-Dog Pass route and the Blackfoot Glacier Basin crossing to Gunsight Lake. It is thus possible to go from Logan Pass to Dawson Pass (and beyond) without straying more than a mile from the Continental Divide. The remainder of the route is discussed elsewhere in this guide. Be SURE to register with the rangers before embarking on any such hazardous cross-country expeditions!

The interesting approach to Split Mountain from the saddle west of Mt. Norris will probably be attempted only by backpackers who are spending a night along the Norris Traverse. The customary approach to Split is from the valley north of Triple Divide Pass, and is therefore included under the St. Mary chapter of the guide, but this south ridge approach seemed to belong under the Cut Bank section of the book.

THE NORRIS TRAVERSE
FROM TRIPLE DIVIDE PASS TO RED EAGLE PASS

It is about four miles from Triple Divide Pass to Red Eagle Pass, while ascending 1,500 vertical feet and descending 2,200 vertical feet en route. Class 2 or 3 all the way, but it is a very strenuous trip. Be sure to carry plenty of water, especially late in the season when most of the snow has disappeared along the ridges.

This route provides relatively easy access to famed Red Eagle Pass. It also provides a grand experience for backpacking mountaineers who wish to savor a lengthy wilderness expedition, for they can travel from the Cut Bank Ranger Station to Gunsight Lake by continuing beyond Red Eagle Pass, following the directions given elsewhere in this chapter to Almost-a-Dog Pass and to the Blackfoot Glacier Basin traverse. There are several interesting mountain summits that can be reached from Red Eagle Pass and from Almost-a-Dog Pass, including Mt. Logan, Clyde Peak, Blackfoot Mountain, Almost-a-Dog Mountain, Little Chief Mountain, and Citadel Mountain. The Continental Divide Route from Canada to Marias Pass follows this route from Gunsight Lake to Red Eagle Pass. More details of that route are given elsewhere in the guide.

Persons contemplating this rugged off-trail experience should always register with park rangers before starting, and explain their schedule in detail. Solo efforts are strongly discouraged, because even a minor injury in this great wild area might prove fatal if the victim were to be immobilized and could not be located by rescue parties within a few days!

The tremendously deep valleys, hanging glaciers, and spectacular lakes that are visible from this high traverse are remarkable. Almost nowhere on the entire route can one see any trace of human activity in any direction, and indeed one can even see a whole valley in which there is seldom likely to be another human being!

Hike up the trail from Cut Bank Ranger Station and campground for about 7.5 miles, to Triple Divide Pass (7,397 ft. elevation), ascending 2,300 vertical feet en route. Camping is possible, with ranger permission, south of the pass in meadows with small rivulets nearby. Hikers who have only small, light packs can climb the 600-foot-high east face of Triple Divide Peak (class 4 if the correct route is followed) but it is not recommended for backpackers with full packs. Persons with large packs should hike through the meadows south of the pass and scramble up the scree-slope below the lowest part of the saddle south of Triple Divide Peak. For details of the route up the east face of Triple Divide Peak, refer to the description under that heading later in this chapter.

From the saddle between Triple Divide Peak and Mt. Norris, follow a goat trail for 600 vertical feet up the southeast ridge of Norris, to the summit cliffs. The 200-foot climb to the summit from there is easy and worthwhile.

Traverse westward below the south-facing cliffs, and then northward below the west-facing cliffs, to reach the long northwest ridge. Unfortunately, there is no distinct trail around the south and west sides of Mt. Norris, but the distance is not great at that elevation, so plod on around in the loose scree. An excellent goat trail leads down the northwest ridge for 1,200 vertical feet to the saddle, then traverses the south side of the large hump beyond the saddle. The latter traverse is made on distinct game trails skirting the upper edge of the scrub forest, then descends steep scree to a lower saddle toward the west. (This saddle is the lowest point between Red Eagle Pass and Triple Divide Pass, with decent campsites with melting snow nearby.) A side-trip to Split Mountain may be made from the saddle, following the route described by Bill Blunk and Ralph Thornton elsewhere in this guide.

A very well-worn goat trail climbs steeply for 300 vertical feet directly west of the low saddle to the ridgetop, then goes southwest along the top of the horizontal ridge for several hundred feet. Along the ridge the trail ascends two or three steep but easy pitches, only fifteen to twenty-five feet high. Hikers may want to hoist packs up on a rope so they can climb the pitches unhindered by the weight. After passing over the last red hump on the long ridge, observe the scree slope ahead on the north side of "Goat Peak." A very deep goat trail traverses that slope, beginning west of the red hump and leading directly to a deep notch in the ridge northwest of Goat Peak. (A fainter goat trail traverses the slope about 100 feet higher and goes down the ridge to that notch.) After reaching the deep notch in the ridge, follow the trail down around the west side of a small rocky hump on the ridge and continue to the very lowest point on the ridge. From there the goat trail continues westward along the south side of the next knoll (which has a bell-shaped summit) to a slightly lower saddle that overlooks a lovely little lake. Hike the ridgetop westward from the saddle above the lake, ascending about forty feet up the cliffy east end of the ridge and then following the broadly rounded summit to the final descent to Red Eagle Pass five minutes later.

The first traverse of this route was made (in both directions) on August 14, 1976 by Alice, Jane, and Gordon Edwards, after seeking the route on several trips during the previous three summers.

For details of the other routes involving Red Eagle Pass, see the descriptions in this guide of "Blackfoot Basin Traverse, From Gunsight Lake to Almost-a-Dog Pass"; "Red Eagle Lake to Nyack Creek, via Red Eagle Pass"; "Almost-a-Dog Pass to Red Eagle Lake"; and "Virginia Falls to Almost-a-Dog Pass."

Routes to the Summits

Mt. James (9,375)

This huge mountain is a simple ridge-walk up from the human trail at Triple Divide Pass. Distance to the summit from Cut Bank Ranger Station is about nine miles, seven miles of it by human trail. Elevation gained is about 4,500 vertical feet from the Ranger Station. Class 2 and 3 all the way. Although an easy climb, it will prove quite tiring for most climbers. The views are superb, and it is well worth the effort involved.

Norris Mountain (8,882)

This pleasant peak will seldom be the final objective of climbers, but it must be ascended by mountaineers en route from Two Medicine Pass to Red Eagle Pass (via the "Norris Traverse Route"). The views from nearby Mt. James are more spectacular and include the added bonus of seeing Triple Divide Peak and Norris Mountain in the foreground. From the summit of Norris the most impressive panorama is that toward the southwest, with Mt. Stimson dominating. A bit further north is the great green expanse of Red Eagle meadows, overshadowed by the attractive pyramid of Mt. Logan. The ridge between Norris and Red Eagle Pass is the route taken by the game trail that leads to the pass and beyond to Gunsight Lake. North of Red Eagle Pass there is the long rounded ridge above Red Eagle Valley, with high points along the ridge being Almost-a-Dog Mountain, Little Chief Mountain, Mahtotopa, and Red Eagle Mountain (all look very different from this unusual angle). Directly below the north face of Mt. Norris is a beautiful basin, 2,500 vertical feet below, with small lakes or tarns of great beauty. Further to the northeast there are impressive views of Red Eagle Lake and St. Mary Lake.

The Southeast Ridge Route. Distance to the summit from Cut Bank Ranger Station about ten miles, seven miles of it via human trail. Elevation gained is 4,000 vertical feet from the Cut Bank Ranger Station. Class 3 all the way after leaving the trail.

Hike seven miles up the trail from the ranger station to Triple Divide Pass (7,397 ft.). The trail gains 1,800 vertical feet in that last long hill climb, and there is usually NO water. To reach Norris Mountain it is necessary to go over the top of Triple Divide Peak.

From the pass there are two routes to Triple Divide Peak. The direct climb up the east face is not technically difficult, but the rock is very rotten. (See description of the "Norris Traverse" for more details of the route.) The other route is far south of the east face, and is a simple scramble up a scree slope to the low saddle there, followed by a pleasant ridge-walk back north to the summit.

From Triple Divide Peak descend about fifty feet to the saddle between that mountain and Mt. Norris (good campsites are there). Walk up a faint game trail from that saddle all the way to the upper cliffs of Mt. Norris, staying on the southeast ridge or slightly west of that ridge for easier walking. When the steep cliffs of the final summit pyramid are reached, traverse to the west below them for about 100 feet, studying the numerous gullies and ledges above. There are many class 3 routes to the summit.

For mountaineers who wish to continue westward along the ridge toward Red Eagle Pass, it is easy to descend the center of the west end of the summit pyramid of Mt. Norris.

Split Mountain (8,792)

The customary route up this beautiful spire begins in the valley above Red Eagle Lake, and is described under the St. Mary Valley Area chapter in this guide. The following routes are included here because they are approached from the Cut Bank Valley.

The South Ridge Route. (Thanks to Bill Blunk for providing these details.) Hike to Triple Divide Pass (7,397 ft. elevation) either from St. Mary or from Cut Bank Ranger Station, then proceed over the top of Triple Divide Peak (8,000 ft.). From that summit, follow the faint goat trail for 1000 vertical feet up the southeast ridge of Mt. Norris. Traverse the south side and west side of the upper summit cliffs of Norris, then descend another goat trail for 1,200 vertical feet down the northwest ridge. Traverse at 7,600 foot elevation across the south side of the large hump (7,912 ft.) beyond the bottom of the northwest ridge of Norris, following the good game trail just above the scrub forest. Another good trail heads northward across the west side of that large hump and leads to the ridgetop north of the hump. (Notice that from Triple Divide Pass to this large hump the route is simply the beginning section of the "Norris Traverse," which is described elsewhere in this guide as the high-level route to Red Eagle Pass and Gunsight Lake.)

Walk north on the ridgetop, toward Split Mountain. When it "cliffs out," descend to a lower trail on the west side of the ridge. When that, too, cliffs out, descend still further and follow another goat trail northward to a large rectangular notch in the ridgetop. Cross over to the gentler slope east of that notch, then traverse easily to the summit pinnacle where the regular route is joined. First ascent of this route: William Blunk and Ralph Thornton, July 30,1982 (while en route from Cut Bank Ranger Station to Gunsight Lake via the Norris Traverse, Red Eagle Pass, Almost-a-Dog Pass and Blackfoot Glacier).

The Triple Divide Pass Route. Distance to the summit is about nine miles, seven miles of it by human trail. Elevation gained is 3,700 feet (but 800 ft. must be lost and regained). This route was pioneered by Jaime Johnson and Mark Pearson in July 1989. Hike the trail from Cut Bank Campground to Triple Divide Pass (7,397 ft.). From the Pass, descend beneath the northeast face of Norris Mountain. Glissade or walk the easy snowfields and scree slopes, toward the south face of Split Mountain. Traverse high along the west end of Blueing Lake until the southern scree slopes are reached. From that point follow the standard Red Eagle Lake Route to the summit. This approach is obviously closer and faster than the Red Eagle Route, however it does involve a long hot climb up to Triple Divide Pass.

Triple Divide Peak (8,020)

Distance to summit about eight miles, almost all of it by human trail. Elevation gained from Cut Bank Ranger Station is about 2,900 vertical feet, but only 600 vertical feet from Triple Divide Pass. Class 3, but with unusually rotten cliffs.

Hike up the trail from Cut Bank Ranger Station to Triple Divide Pass, then examine the routes to the summit of the peak. About four miles south of the peak, at the lowest part of the saddle between Triple Divide and Razoredge Mountain, a steep little scree slope extends from the gentle meadows up to the saddle. It is a pleasant walk from there to the summit, up the gentle ridge. The more precipitous route up the east face of the mountain will be more interesting to mountaineers, but is not recommended to those who are carrying heavy or clumsy backpacks. The following details of the route will be helpful to climbers wishing to minimize their risks on the face.

Walk up the ridge from the trail toward the summit of Triple Divide Peak. The ridge is class 2 through the formation of black igneous rock, then the pitch steepens abruptly. Traverse left (south) for a few yards and into the broad basin. Climb directly upward on class 3 gullies and ledges. A little higher it is best to angle toward the right, because the rock is more solid there, but either way will lead to a distinctly orange ledge that extends entirely across the upper east face. That ledge traverses just beneath the sheer upper cliffs and provides easy access to the south ridge of the mountain. Mark the ridge carefully at that point, so the correct ledge can be found for the descent. It is only 100 vertical feet to the summit from there. A bucket of water poured carefully on the summit cairn will drain off into three different directions; part toward the Pacific Ocean, part toward the North Atlantic and part toward the Gulf of Mexico!

Rising Wolf Mountain towers 4, 500 vertical feet above the Two Medicine Valley—Marion Lacy

THE TWO MEDICINE AREA

Routes Among the Peaks

Although most of the mountains around Two Medicine Lake are relatively low, it is by far the most brightly colored portion of the park. A large campground is located below the foot of Two Medicine Lake, with a gasoline station nearby. A small store and good boating facilities are at the lakeshore, but there are no motels, lodges, or formal restaurants there.

Many of the peaks in the area are brilliant red, contrasting pleasantly with the deep blue of the lakes and the greens of the heavily-forested surroundings. It is a friendly, quiet place, very little commercialized, with easy trails leading to nearby high passes, marvelous meadows, and fish-filled lakes. There are few difficult climbs; many of the peaks are scrambles up grassy hillsides and scree-slopes and can be completed without much need for careful route-finding. As usual, however, there is danger from steep snowbanks and from rock-fall on the steeper hillsides. Popular climbs nearby include: Scenic Point (7,522); Appistoki Peak (8,164); Mt. Henry (8,847); Mt. Ellsworth (8,581); Never Laughs Mountain (7,641); Grizzly Mountain (9,067); and Painted Tepee (7,650).

A good trail leads north from the campground and into the large valley of Dry Creek, affording access to Oldman Lake, then climbs steeply to Pitamakan Pass (7,600). Mt. Morgan (8,781) rises above the trail between Pitamakan Pass and Cut Bank Pass (7,900), which overlooks the Nyack Valley toward the west. Morgan is surrounded by difficult cliffs, but a break in the wall occurs near the northeast corner of the mountain.

A great circular route may be completed by continuing southward from Cut Bank Pass to Dawson Pass and down to the head of Two Medicine Lake. This great circle is easier if traveled in the opposite direction, since it can then be begun with a launch ride to the head of the lake and a fresh start up to Dawson Pass. From Dawson Pass a faint trail leads up the ridge to Helen Mountain (8,538), and Flinsch Peak (9,225) can be climbed without difficulty up its south face. Both of these summits provide impressive views of the entire southern part of the park, with Mt. Stimson (10,142) and Mt. St. Nicholas (9,376) dominating the scene.

Rising Wolf Mountain (9,513) is best climbed via its long west ridge from Dawson Pass, but can also be ascended from the lower Bighorn Basin or even from the shore of Two Medicine Lake. (Be sure to

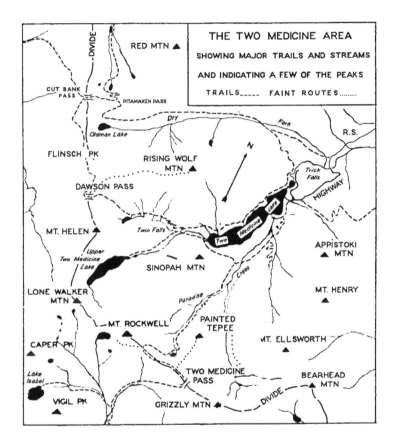

THE TWO MEDICINE AREA

SHOWING MAJOR TRAILS AND STREAMS

AND INDICATING A FEW OF THE PEAKS

TRAILS_____ FAINT ROUTES........

descend via exactly the same route climbed, or you may end up above some impassable cliffs.)

A good goat trail leads from Two Medicine Pass around the backside of Mt. Rockwell (9,272), then climbers can scramble down to the head of Upper Two Medicine Lake or down to Aurice Lake. In addition to Mt. Rockwell, climbs can be made there of Lone Walker Mountain or Caper Peak.

From the south shore of Two Medicine Lake a good trail heads up toward the southwest, to the high ridge of Two Medicine Pass, south of Mt. Rockwell. It then goes south along the ridgetop for about a mile. When the clouds are boiling up from the valleys below, this trail really deserves to be compared with "a tightrope in the sky!" The following pages discuss the climbs that may be made easily from this great pass.

En route to Two Medicine Pass, a mile beyond Aster Creek, a faint trail can be followed up the east side of Paradise Creek for two miles to Buttercup Park or Paradise Park. From the ridge above Buttercup meadows (east of Grizzly Mountain) game trails follow the Continental Divide south to Firebrand Pass and eventually to Summit Mountain. The descent to the Autumn trail from there is easy, and the trail leads out to Marias Pass, thus completing the southern extension of the Continental Divide Route that begins at Forum Peak on the Canadian border and stays within a mile of the Divide for more than 110 miles.

THE SCENIC POINT RIDGE WALK

This remarkable route has been described in greater detail by Rolf Larson in *Going-to-the-Sun* magazine, Volume 3, Number 2 (Summer 1983) which is available from P.O. Box 291, Whitefish, MT 59937. The route covers thirteen miles of exhilarating open country, most of it far above timberline along great rounded ridges. Allow ten hours for the entire circuit.

From the foot of Two Medicine Lake, take the trail to Scenic Point, 2,240 vertical feet above the lake. Walk two miles southward through ridgetop meadows, to the summit of Medicine Peak. The lower domes to the east are Bison Mountain and The Head. From Medicine Peak, follow the rounded ridge southwest to the summit of Mt. Henry (8,847 ft.). For the final fifty yards, the ridge narrows to a sharp arete. Either carefully climb along the top of the arete OR descend 100 feet to the southeast and enter a gully that angles up to the summit of the mountain.

The great ridge heads due west from Mt. Henry, to an unnamed peak with a steep north face. Either go over the top of that peak OR follow the game trail around the north face of it about 100 feet below the summit. Next there is a great descent down the ridge toward the north, losing 1,000 vertical feet before reaching the saddle south of Appistoki Peak. A walking ascent of 500 feet is necessary to reach the summit of Appistoki from there. There are great views of the Two Medicine area from the top of that peak.

North of Appistoki, follow one of the following two alternative routes: (1) Descend to the eastern cliffs which were seen from the Scenic Point trail during the hike up, in the morning. There are several class 3 gullies extending down almost to the scree, but most of them steepen to class 4 near the bottom. Continue down the scree to the streambed then climb up the far bank to hit the trail below the big switchback; (2) For a safer alternative, go only 500 feet down the north ridge of Appistoki and locate a "ramp" that leads around to the east side of the mountain. Follow it around, then descend easily to the stream basin below. Work down the streambed until at the 6,000-foot contour level, then leave the stream and traverse to the trail just below the big switchback in the Scenic Point trail.

As Rolf Larson observes, "Along the Scenic Point trail there are several beautiful points from which to enjoy the Two Medicine drainage. The trail also takes you through a couple of beautiful, age-gnarled stands of several-hundred-year-old limber pines. From Scenic Point, on a clear day, the Sweetgrass Hills stand out on the eastern horizon. On the walk through alpine meadows up to Medicine Peak, past Mt. Henry, you enjoy nice views into the southeastern and central sections of the Park. From the unnamed peak west of Mt. Henry there is a good possible alternative route following a spur ridge from there to Mt. Ellsworth. From there it is possible to follow a number of other routes, all of which make for longer days but provide great experiences."

THE MAD WOLF GRAND CIRCUIT
MAD WOLF , EAGLE PLUME, and BAD MARRIAGE

The classic circuit between these attractive peaks covers about eleven miles, none of it by trail. The vertical gain in elevation is roughly 3,200 feet. Nothing more difficult than class 3 need be climbed. This circuit route can be started from either of two locations, as described below.

(1) Drive to the base of Mad Wolf Mountain (after leaving U.S. Highway 89 approximately two miles north of the Kiowa Campground). The unimproved dirt road then winds for several miles across pastures and coulees on the Blackfoot Indian Reservation. Gates must be opened on occasion, and it is advisable to stop and ask permission at the house near the trailhead. It will require thirty to forty-five minutes of slow driving to reach the starting point on the northeast flank of Mad Wolf Mountain (in section 32 on the topo map). This road is not good, at present, having high centers and some mud-holes, and in wet weather a 4-wheel drive vehicle may be essential.

(2) The other starting point is near Cut Bank Campground, or Cut Bank Ranger Station. Cross Cut Bank Creek then bushwhack up through open forest for roughly one mile, occasionally encountering open grassy areas. Gain about 1,000 feet of elevation, until near the top of Cut Bank Ridge, on the north side of Mad Wolf Mountain. Proceed up the drainage on the northeast corner of that peak until attaining the summit. Nothing worse than class 3 in encountered in the roughly 2000 feet of elevation gained after leaving the ridge.

After resting on the summit, one can enjoy a fantastic ridge walk for about three miles, to the base of Eagle Plume Mountain. Unique views along this ridge include the entire Lake Creek drainage, with seldom-visited Lonely Lakes and Running Crane Lake. This entire drainage district has no trails, and is truly one of the most pristine areas in the eastern portion of the Park. Beyond the drainage, thousands of feet of brilliant red argillite comprise the elongate bulk of Red Mountain (9,377 ft.). This is surely one of the most inspiring ridge walks in Glacier National Park!

After reaching the base of Eagle Plume Mountain it is an easy class 2 or 3 climb of 700 vertical feet to the summit of the peak. The view toward the west, to Medicine Grizzly Peak, is spellbinding, with abundant high cirques and ice fields. Virtually all the peaks in the Cut Bank Valley are visible. From the summit of Eagle Plume, descend westward to about the 8,000-foot level, then work north toward the saddle between Eagle Plume and Bad Marriage. Some class 3 cliffs may be encountered during this traverse. From the saddle it is an easy stroll to the summit of Bad Marriage Mountain. Views are similar those from Eagle Plume, but more of the Cut Bank Valley is visible.

Descend toward the northeast from the summit, into the cirque on the southeast face of Bad Marriage. Enter this cirque near the area marked "falls" on the topo map. Nothing worse than class 3 should be encountered. Two beautiful waterfalls are near the base of the cirque. After crossing the creek, follow along the base of the north side of Mad Wolf Mountain. Slide areas will slow progress considerably, but eventually the western end of Cut Bank Ridge will be reached, and the descent to the campground area is easy from there. We are grateful to Bill Hedglin for the details of this marvelous circuit, as well as the routes up several other peaks in the colorful Two Medicine Area!

Routes to the Summits

Calf Robe Mountain (7,920)

Distance to summit about eight miles, four miles of it by trail. Elevation gained is approximately 2,800 feet. Class 2 or 3 all the way. Leave Highway 2 about 6.2 miles southwest of East Glacier Park, near False Summit and Lubec Lake. Cross the fence and walk along the dirt road through the meadow for about one-half mile. The trail starts at the edge of the meadow, near Coonsa Creek. Follow the trail for about a mile, to the junction with the Autumn Creek Trail. Leave the trail at this junction, and bushwhack roughly one-quarter mile through open forest. After breaking through the trees, continue northwest, toward the north end of this elongate flat-topped mountain. The ascent up the northeast flank is straightforward and virtually all class 2. Exceptional views into the Ole Creek drainage reward you at the summit. Mt. Despair, Barrier Buttes, and other impressive remote peaks rise beyond the valley toward the west. To the east there is a sea of peaks in the Lewis and Clark Forest and the Flathead Forest.

This summit may also be reached from Firebrand Pass, by climbing roughly 1,000 feet of class 2 and 3 terrain on the northwest flank of Calf Robe after leaving the trail at that pass.

Mt. Ellsworth (8,58l)

This beautiful peak is accessible via several routes. It can be approached from Aster Park, Scenic Point Trail, Mt. Henry, and from the south along the traverse from Firebrand Pass to Two Medicine. The most commonly used route is described here.

The Scenic Point Route. This trek affords great views, and numerous options for alternate peaks, should weather become a factor. Distance is twelve miles, three or four miles of it by human trail. Elevation gained is 3,500 to 4,000 feet. Difficulty is mostly class 2, with occasional class 3 stretches.

Start the hike at the Scenic Point trailhead in the Two Medicine Valley. Follow the trail for roughly one and one-half miles, to the point at which the trail starts ascending briskly up toward Scenic Point. Leave the trail, and follow Appistoki Creek, climbing grassy slopes up into the basin. This lower basin is separated from an upper basin by an easily climbed class 2 slope. In early season, a beautiful waterfall is present, plunging from the upper cirque into the lower basin. Continue through the high cirque toward the saddle between Appistoki Mountain and Mt. Henry. The massive wall of the north face of Mt. Henry towers above you for 2,000 feet, giving this cirque a splendidly isolated aura. The saddle between Appistoki and Mt. Henry, at an elevation of roughly 7,700 feet, affords fine views of the Two Medicine Valley. From this saddle, one can easily ascend Appistoki (8,164) in fifteen minutes. A rapid descent on scree to the south shore trail on Two Medicine Lake is possible. If continuing Mt. Ellsworth from the saddle, climb the ridge (class 2 or 3) to the summit of the unnamed peak (8,650 ft.) directly west of Mt. Henry. From there it is an easy ridge-walk for a half-mile to the summit of Mt. Henry (8,847), or a descent southwest to the long ridge extending about a mile and a half to Mt. Ellsworth. From that lofty summit there are unique views of Mt. Henry, Aster Park, and

Buttercup Park, as well as the Continental Divide toward Firebrand Pass. The impressive east face of Grizzly Mountain occupies much of the view to the southwest, and the cliffs of Mt. Rockwell and Sinopah Mountain dominate views to the west and northwest. A quick descent via Aster Park is possible, once the snow has melted in this drainage.

For additional pleasure, descend northwest from the summit of Ellsworth to the saddle below Never Laughs Mountain. From there, Never Laughs (7,641) can be climbed in a matter of minutes, before descending from the saddle into Aster Park. CAUTION: do not drop too low into the Aster Creek drainage, but stay roughly at timberline while traversing north along the base of Never Laughs, then descend into the trees along the north nose of the ridge. Down in the trees, the old Aster Park trail should be located, and it can be followed down to the south shore trail by Two Medicine Lake. Although the Aster Creek drainage appears open in its upper reaches, it rapidly degenerates into a horribly tangled bushwhack, so stay higher, and away from the creek. The wildflowers in Aster Park are truly memorable.

Grizzly Mountain (9,067)

For hikers who are already at Two Medicine Pass, this great peak provides an easily accessible vantage point almost on par with Mt. Rockwell but much easier to reach. From the point where the human trail begins its descent into the Park Creek valley, continue straight ahead toward Grizzly Mountain. It is nearly 1,500 vertical feet up to the summit, but there are no obstacles and the views are phenomenal all the way. The entire southern part of the park is visible, including all of those peaks with romantic Indian names that most visitors to Glacier National Park hear about but never actually see: Eagle Ribs, Red Crow, Bearhead, Brave Dog, Calf Robe, Lone Walker, and Little Dog. Also there are numerous seldom-seen peaks with descriptive English names, including Vigil Peak, Battlement Mountain, Mt. Despair, Skeleton Mountain, and Peril Peak. This is quite an experience even for long-time hikers and climbers in Glacier National Park. The distance to the summit from Two Medicine, via Two Medicine Pass, is about eleven miles.

Another route to this summit is closer but not as scenic, yet may be attractive to climbers. Follow the old abandoned trail up Paradise Creek and into Paradise Park (the route of the original human trail to Two Medicine Pass), then climb directly up the north side of Grizzly Mountain. This is class 3, if care is taken, all the way.

ROUTES TO THE SUMMITS

Painted Tepee (7,650)

This class 2 route leads hikers to a marvelous point from which to view the entire Two Medicine area. Distance to summit about 10.5 miles, nine miles of it by human trail. Elevation gained is about 2,500 vertical feet.

Hike from the foot of Two Medicine Lake around the south shore and onward to Two Medicine Pass. About a mile south along the ridge from the place where the trail first tops that ridge south of Mt. Rockwell is Chief Lodgepole Peak (7,682). From there, walk along the fantastic red ridge toward the northeast, to the top of Painted Tepee. (That summit may also be reached by scrambling straight up from almost any place around its base, and of course the descent can also be made much faster via those other routes to the trails below, either northward toward Rockwell Falls or eastward to the trail below Buttercup Park and Paradise Park.)

Not everyone who reaches the summit will actually get to the highest point, for that is a "balanced rock" about ten feet high. With a boost from below it is possible to reach the top of that little pinnacle.

Pumpelly Pillar (7,600)

This tremendously impressive narrow ridge attracts the attention of every mountaineer who sees it. It appears to be guarded by impregnable walls on both sides, but two of the park's best climbers recently scouted a possible route and their attempt on the south face was wonderfully successful. That first ascent was made by Ranger Dick Mattson and Chief Ranger Chuck Sigler in September of 1982. Details of the route are given below.

Head up from just below Upper Two Medicine Lake toward the great wall and locate a class 4 gully through the first set of cliffs (Sigler and Mattson rappelled there, on their descent). Scramble up broken cliffs from there toward the east, reaching the bottom of the final set of cliffs somewhere on the eastern half of the face. The top of the eastern end of the ridge is then easily attained by angling up toward the right. From there, traverse west on a ledge just below the top, by-passing the highest part of the ridge along the south side. Gain the ridgetop west of the highest point and climb from there to the top. A short section just before the summit has considerable exposure on the north, and a rope belay is advised there for safety. No cairn was found on the top by the rangers. No Name Lake seems only a stone's throw (and 1,695 vertical feet) away!

Flinsch Peak, above the long west ridge of Rising Wolf Mountain
—John Mauff

Rising Wolf Mountain (9,513)

There are great views of the entire Two Medicine area and the vast prairies east of the park. Most of the peaks in the south-central area of the park are also visible, including Mt. St. Nicholas and Mt. Stimpson. The most spectacular views are those nearer at hand, however, for no other place in the entire park can match the brilliant coloration of the mountains and spires above Two Medicine Lake and the surrounding valleys.

The West Ridge Route. Distance to summit about nine miles, 6.5 miles of it by human trail (two miles less, if the boat is taken to the head of Two Medicine Lake). Elevation gained is about 4,400 vertical feet. Class 2 and 3 all the way.

Hike from Two Medicine Lake to Dawson Pass, gaining 3,000 vertical feet en route. Leave the trail at the switchback half a mile above Dawson Pass, where it cuts back toward the west. Angle up the scree slope to reach the ridgetop between Flinsch Peak and Rising Wolf Mountain. Walk eastward on or near the top of that tremendous ridge all the way to the summit, following a well-defined game trail that has been improved upon by a generation of humans intent on sharing the unique experience of lingering for a while on a great mountaintop.

The prominent hump halfway along the ridge may be traversed on either side, but the steep step east of it should be climbed only after you have traversed at least sixty feet along the south side of the cliffs.

The time required to hike from Dawson Pass to the top of the mountain should not exceed two hours. Do NOT attempt unscouted routes down the mountain from there, for there are a great many hidden cliffs on the way down that are not visible from above. Instead, why not walk back along the same ridge and make a climb of Flinsch Peak before descending to the trail? It is a very impressive matterhorn, and extremely photogenic.

The South Face Route. Beginning from the streambed halfway along the north shore of the lake, it is an easy obvious scramble to the ridgetop far to the east of the summit, and a gentle walk up that ridge to the top.

WARNING: DO NOT attempt unscouted routes down this mountain, for there are many hidden cliffs that are not visible from above!

Mt. Rockwell (9,272)

The West Face Route. Distance to the top about eleven miles, eight miles of it by human trail. Elevation gained is about 4,100 vertical feet. Mostly class 3, but class 4 pitches may be encountered near the top. First known ascent: Norman Clyde, July 15, 1923.

A tremendous array of peaks is visible to the north, and the western horizon is dominated by Mt. Stimson and Pinchot Peak. The sharp spire further south is Vigil Peak, beyond which is Mt. St. Nicholas (the most difficult climb in the park). Rising Wolf looms up nearby toward the northeast, with a long ridge connecting it to the impressive matterhorn of Flinsch Peak. Upper Two Medicine Lake is hidden by a small summit in the foreground and Two Medicine Lake is concealed by the beautiful red flanks of Sinopah Mountain. Brilliant red and yellow rock formations predominate in the peaks visible toward the southeast, and many rugged concentrations of mountains far south of the park boundary are visible on clear days.

From Two Medicine Lake, follow the trail to Two Medicine Pass (gaining 2,200 vertical feet en route). When the ridge is topped, follow a steep game trail that climbs sharply toward the west just south of Mt. Rockwell. The game trail crosses over the southwest ridge also, and then traverses the west side of Rockwell through a scrub forest of dwarfed alpine fir. About halfway around the west side of the mountain, leave the trail and scramble up easy scree slopes and small cliffs for about 1,500 feet of elevation to the summit. From the lower scree slopes it is difficult to determine which peak is actually the highest, but veer to the north while gaining altitude and you will reach the true summit (which is near the extreme northern end of the mountain) .

The Upper Two Medicine Lake Route. Distance to summit about seven or eight miles, 5.5 miles of it by trail via the south shore trail along Two Medicine Lake, or 4.7 miles via the north lakeshore trail. Hikers can save two miles of trail travel by taking the boat to the head of the lake, but the timing is bad. The boats don't leave early enough, and it is unlikely that climbers can catch a boat for the return trip. Mostly class 3, but there are possible class 4 pitches near the summit.

Hike to the foot of Upper Two Medicine Lake, then cross the outlet stream (usually possible on log jams). Follow a game trail along the south shore (mostly fifteen to twenty feet above the shore) until near the inlet stream that is near the head of the lake. Just east of that stream the cliffs are broken into a series of ascending ledges that are easily climbed. Angle toward the east (left) near the lip of the hanging valley above, then (after in that upper valley) traverse through dense thickets toward the stream far above the waterfall. Follow the stream up the hanging valley until almost to its head, then scramble up scree slopes and ledges toward the deep notch just north of Mt. Rockwell. Stay north of the great cleft that extends downward from that notch, and attain the top just north of the notch. It is an easy, although rather exposed, route from there along the crest of the ridge, veering onto the east side if the crest becomes too dangerous. After reaching the main mass of Mt. Rockwell continue a short distance southward along its east face until beneath easy class 3 and 4 ledges and cliffs. A careful scramble up these leads directly to the summit.

Sinopah Mountain (8,271)

This impressive peak, although far from being the highest in the Two Medicine Valley, is unquestionably the most photographed peak there. It is also a favorite subject for numerous artists and photographers. Distance to the summit is about five miles, 3.3 miles of it by trail. Elevation gained is roughly 2,700 vertical feet after leaving the trail. Difficulty is no worse than steep class 3 if the proper route is taken.

Hike along the south shore trail of Two Medicine Lake, and take the fork which goes to Two Medicine Pass. Leave the trail near Rockwell Falls. Do not cross the creek, but bushwhack directly up through the sparse alder thickets and grassy avalanche chutes for about one-quarter mile.

Upon breaking through the bush, climb scree slopes to the base of the cliffs. A wide couloir at the eastern end of the cliffs, directly above the vegetated scree slope, affords the least difficult route. (Other narrow couloirs further west can only be described as "narrow and nasty," and should only be attempted by experienced climbers.) The wider couloir, however is an enjoyable class 3 climb through roughly 1,000 vertical feet of cliffs. Care should be taken in the couloir, for there is much loose debris present on ledges. The summit cairn is located several hundred feet west of the precipitous east face of Sinopah. Views from the summit include beautiful blue Two Medicine Lake, the magnificent east face of Mount Rockwell, massive red Rising Wolf Mountain, and the tremendous expanse of green plains filling the eastern horizon. The sharp matterhorn of Flinsch Peak is especially inspiring from this angle. By dropping down a few feet, and traversing to the eastern end of the summit ridge, one can enjoy an exceptional view of Middle Two Medicine Lake. This climb is a relatively easy seven to eight-hour trip, and is always well worth the effort.

Squaw Mountain (7,280)

This somewhat isolated peak yields excellent views of the southeastern front of Glacier National Park. To the east lie the vast plains, interrupted by the far-away Sweetgrass Hills. Closer at hand, a multitude of peaks in the Lewis and Clark National Forest and Flathead National Forest are visible.

From East Glacier, follow the Autumn Creek Trail for about three miles, to the point at which the trail most closely approaches the east face of Squaw Mountain. Leave the trail there and bushwhack for roughly one-quarter mile. After breaking out of the trees, work up toward the southeast corner of the peak and climb the southeast ridge. About 800 vertical feet must be gained along the ridge, but it is all class 2 or 3 in difficulty.

After a rest to enjoy the summit views, a two to three mile walk along the long ridge to the southwest is worthwhile. The highest point on the ridge is a small unnamed peak which is labelled on the topo map with an elevation of 7,695 feet. Nothing worse than class 3 is encountered in a short climb to that summit. From this vantage point one is rewarded with grand views of the headwall area of the Midvale Creek drainage and the vertical east face of Bearhead Mountain, and Mt. Henry (8,847) is very impressive when viewed from this area. Total distance (if ridge walk is included) is fourteen miles round trip, about half of which is on human trail. Total elevation gained is approximately 2,500 feet.

THE SOUTH CENTRAL AREA

Routes Among the Peaks

The great southern quarter of the park is poorly known and seldom visited. It is barely mentioned in Dr. George Ruhle's otherwise remarkable complete guides to the trails in Glacier National Park. One reason for the apparent lack of interest in the area is that there is no dry way of getting across the broad middle fork of the Flathead River anywhere between West Glacier and the Walton Ranger Station (a distance of more than thirty miles). When the bridge at Nyack was removed it effectively isolated more than 300 square miles of park and as of 1990 the Park Service has not yet installed any cable carts (which were discussed many years ago). Hikers and climbers must treat every crossing of the river as potentially lethal. Some hiker will drown there soon . . . don't let it be *you!*

From the north shore of the Flathead River, the trails lead through groves of giant cottonwood trees in the broad flat valleys below the 4,000-foot elevation. Many of those trees have trunks more than three feet in diameter and a few even exceed four feet at chest height. As elevation is gained the forest changes to white pine, Engelmann spruce, and lodgepole pine. Near the alpine meadows, of course, lodgepole pine predominates, and there are also large numbers of white-bark pines.

The most impressive peaks in the southern region are Mt. Stimson (10,142) and Mt. St. Nicholas (9,376). "St. Nick" rises more than 5,000 vertical feet above the surrounding stream valleys, and Stimson soars more than 6,200 vertical feet above Nyack Creek! There are many other high peaks in this great wilderness area. They are so far from the highway and they rise so far above their bases and are protected by such densely forested slopes that most mountaineers hesitate to even attempt assaults on them! Because the valleys below those mountains are less than 4,000 feet above sea level, all of the peaks are very demanding ascents.

Mt. Pinchot (9,310) and Eaglehead Mountain (9,140) are close neighbors south of Mt. Stimson, while Peril Peak (8,645), Mt. Doody (8,800), and Cloudcroft Peaks (8,710) are nearby. St. Nicholas stands nearly alone but there are other respectable peaks just north and east of it. Not far away along the Continental Divide there is Little Dog Mountain (8,610), Summit Mountain (8,770), Bearhead Mountain (8,406), Grizzly Mountain (9,067), and Mt. Rockwell (9,272). (The latter two are climbed most often from the Two Medicine Area.)

The great circle route (thirty-seven miles) up Nyack Creek, over

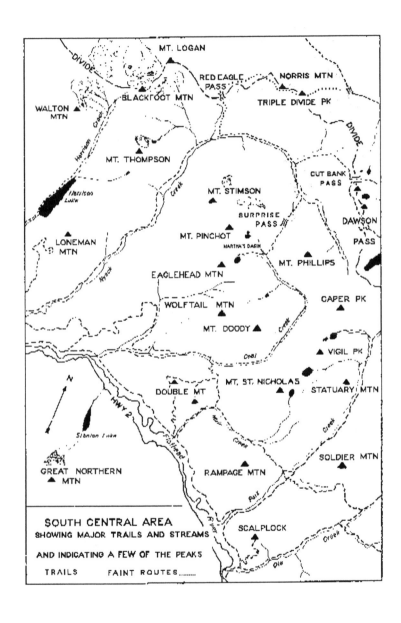

SOUTH CENTRAL AREA
SHOWING MAJOR TRAILS AND STREAMS
AND INDICATING A FEW OF THE PEAKS
TRAILS   FAINT ROUTES.........

Surprise Pass, and back down Coal Creek to the Flathead passes dozens of lesser peaks as it encircles the southern behemoth among Glacier's mountains, Mt. Stimson. A famous side trail branches from the Nyack Valley trail 12.7 miles upstream and climbs 2,600 vertical feet to the legendary Red Eagle Pass. That trail has not been maintained since 1942 and was severely damaged during the 1964 flood, so the ascent to Red Eagle Pass is now a mountaineering expedition instead of a simple hike. For more details, see the St. Mary Valley chapter, where the route from Red Eagle Lake to Nyack Creek via Red Eagle Pass is described. Four miles further upstream another side trail gains 3,300 vertical feet in five miles en route to Cut Bank Pass. It provides access to Cut Bank Ranger Station (ten miles to the northeast) or to the Two Medicine Area (eight miles southeast). The Nyack Creek trail curves to the east, then to the south, where it climbs quickly to densely forested Surprise Pass (5,760 ft. elevation). Mt. Pinchot rises 3,500 feet higher, west of the pass, and Mt. Phillips (9,494) is 3,700 vertical feet uphill toward the east.

Descending from Surprise Pass the "loop trail" soon reaches Coal Creek, and a short side trail to the west leads to Martha's Basin with its glorious meadows and picture-book lakes. From there it is sixteen miles down the Coal Creek trail to the Flathead River (and another hazardous crossing). Rising nearly 5,000 vertical feet west of Coal Creek are the Cloudcroft Peaks and Mt. Doody, while the eastern wall of the valley is capped by Caper Peak (8,310), Battlement Mountain (8,830), and spectacular Mt. St. Nicholas.

East of Coal Creek, the eleven-mile trail up Park Creek to Two Medicine Pass is seldom hiked (except part-way by Mt. St. Nicholas devotees). At Essex the highway finally crosses to the north shore of the Flathead River, and the Walton Ranger Station is located near the mouth of Ole Creek. The Ole Creek trail seems to go on forever, but it is only 19.5 miles before it finally zig-zags up to Firebrand Pass (6,951).

West of the great Nyack Valley a trail leads up to Harrison Lake and beyond it to the foot of the Harrison Glacier Basin. Blackfoot Mountain has been climbed from there, but the more customary approach is from the north via the Blackfoot Glacier basin.

Joe Biby writes glowingly of backpacking trips taken in the "Nyack Wilderness." He and Greg Nelson and Doug Nelson (all of Kalispell) climbed Mt. Doody and camped in Dunwoody Basin. The next day they climbed Cloudcroft Peaks, then descended and walked the ridges over to Peril Peak. They camped just below the summit, with spectacular views in all directions. The following day they descended miles of alpine meadows to reach Martha's Basin, hiked sixteen miles down to the Flathead River, and waded across to Highway 2. They expressed it well when they said: "Any journey through the Nyack at high elevations is a trip through paradise where wilderness is still wilderness."

Routes to the Summits

Mt. Doody (8,800)

This is one of the peaks between Mt. Stimson and Mt. St. Nicholas, and summit views in both directions are therefore fantastic. The Coal Creek Valley lies nearly 5,000 feet below the summit, while a beautiful hanging valley (Dunwoody Basin) with two small lakes is just northeast of the peak. Cloudcroft Peaks (8,710 ft.) are northeast of Doody, along the same ridge, and can easily be approached from the upper lake in Dunwoody Basin. Remote, spectacular Peril Peak (8,645 ft.) rises above the ridge northwest of Dunwoody Basin, and two miles of sloping meadows extend down toward Buffalo Woman Lake from that peak. The trail up Coal Creek to Surprise Pass has a branch that climbs into Martha's Basin and game trails cross the meadows there to Buffalo Woman Lake and Beaver Woman Lake. Both Eaglehead Mountain (9,140 ft.) and Mt. Pinchot (9,310 ft.) can be climbed easily from Martha's Basin.

To reach Mt. Doody, wade the Flathead River near the Coal Creek inlet and hike six miles up the Coal Creek trail to Elk Creek (3,900 ft. elevation). Scramble up the barren talus slope just upstream from Elk Creek for 2,500 vertical feet to the ridge overlooking Dunwoody Basin, then climb up the class 3 ridge to the summit.

Mt. Phillips (9,494)

Bushwhack south from Surprise Pass toward the west ridge of Mt. Phillips. An avalanche chute just to the right of this ridge offers fairly easy climbing up to the treeline. From there, it is an easy walk up to the summit. There are very good views of Martha's Basin, Mt. Stimson, Mt. Doody, and the Cloudcroft Peaks, and numerous other photogenic peaks and valleys.

The first known ascent was by Rangers Chuck Sigler and Dick Mattson, August 4, 1986. Distance to summit about seventeen miles, fifteen miles of it by human trail.

Mt. Stimson (10,142)

This is truly a monster of a mountain! It is 6,000 vertical feet from Nyack Creek up to the summit, and nearly that far up from any other approach. The most notable views are those toward the north, but in the southeast Mt. Pinchot is in the foreground and the lithoid thumb of Mt. St. Nicholas rises spectacularly just beyond. The southern side of Mt. Jackson bears Walton Glacier, while Blackfoot Mountain's southeast face displays massive Pumpelly Glacier with its tremendous icefall dropping debris and ice into the remote valley at its foot. Mt. Logan is connected to Blackfoot by a long ridge, and the broad green expanse of Red Eagle Pass lies just east of Logan. Beyond those meadows you see Going-to-the-Sun Mountain and Little Chief Mountain (which arise from opposite sides of St. Mary Lake). Going-to-the-Sun is somewhat dwarfed by the broad summit of Mt. Siyeh, just beyond it. The sea of jagged peaks in the north and northwestern regions of the park are inspiring, as usual, and when seen from this great an elevation the impression is much like views from an airplane would be. Mountaineers who have an interest in the Norris Traverse from Triple Divide Peak to Red Eagle Pass will enjoy seeing the entire route as it works its way over Mt. Norris and along the great ridge from there to the pass.

The view toward the southeast from atop Mt. Stimson —J. G. Edwards

The West Face Route. For hikers with considerable fortitude and perseverance, in addition to some ability as rock climbers. The time required for the trip from the highway to the summit should be at least fifteen to twenty hours of actual hiking and climbing. It is suggested that the first night be spent at the base of the mountain, so a very early start can be enjoyed the next day. Carry lights, so the descent to camp can be made after dark! The distance to the summit is about eighteen miles, twelve miles of it by trail. Elevation gained is about 6,750 vertical feet. Mostly class 2 and 3, but with a few class 4 pitches in the upper vertical feet.

Cross the Flathead River along Highway 2 (register for the climb at the Nyack Ranger Station). Make local inquiry concerning the best places to wade that mighty river at the time of your climb. There are several places possible, but they vary depending upon the water level at the time and the current configuration of the mud flats and sandbars. Also, even though there are no cable carts across the river as of this writing, there may be some such facilities constructed in the future.

Hike twelve miles up the Nyack Creek trail until two miles beyond a snowshoe cabin, where a bench mark on the OLD topographic maps marked the 4,082-foot elevation beside the stream. That marker has not been seen in recent years, so check your position by watching for the mouth of the stream that drains the entire west face of Mount Stimson. It is very dangerous to cross Nyack Creek at that point (it is very deep and *very* swift, so the crossing should be made upstream where it is wider and shallower). Beyond the location of the old benchmark, the trail was rerouted in 1979. The old trail was near the creek, but the new one is higher in the forest. About 500 yards along that new trail, descend a wide, rocky dry streambed to Nyack Creek, crossing the old trail near the stream. The widest part of the stream is slightly downstream from that dry streambed. Even there it is potentially dangerous, but logs usually span the stream in that vicinity. After reaching the east bank, walk south on good elk trails for about 250 yards to the mouth of the drainage stream that was observed from the opposite shore earlier. The actual climb begins there, and the summit is still more than 6,000 vertical feet above you!

Tiresome uphill bushwhacking is required for possibly three hours before timberline is approached. The easiest route through the brush is on or near the ascending ridgetop just south of the small stream, but the streambed itself is open and clean later in the season. About 2,000 feet uphill a relatively flat bench area is reached, and it is crowded with dense stands of maple and alders. Cross to the north side of the stream there and bushwhack to the low cliffs far upstream. Easy routes up those cliffs are abundant in the streambed, so follow it until the stream curves northward.

A much more difficult cliff is encountered there (class 4), but there are open slopes of beargrass above it. Walk up the steep beargrass slopes to a much larger cliff, over which at least two streams drop as waterfalls. The larger of the streams is near the center of the cliff, and the easiest route up is just east of that large waterfall (class 4). In spite of slight overhanging ledges the ascent is not very hazardous.

Above this waterfall is the upper cirque of the west side of Mt. Stimson. Although it may not look it, the summit is still 2,000 feet above you and the hardest part of the climb is yet to come. The safest and quickest route from this point to the summit is as follows: Climb directly toward the peak, trying to follow a straight line from the lip of the waterfall toward the summit (be sure to remember this guideline on the descent, too). Relatively easy couloirs and cliffs (class 3) extend up to and through the 100-foot-thick sill of dark igneous rock (diorite or metagabbro) that extends across this face of Mt. Stimson. Immediately below and also above the black band are difficult pitches of light-colored partially metamorphosed rock which is more troublesome (perhaps class 4). Above that black diorite sill you must endure at least another hour of class 3 climbing up easy cliffs interspersed with scree slopes. The rock is too rotten for good cliff climbing, so search out the easiest possible breaks through the cliffs. (Remember how far you are from potential rescuers at this point — and exercise great caution).

Continue climbing almost directly toward the summit until reaching a

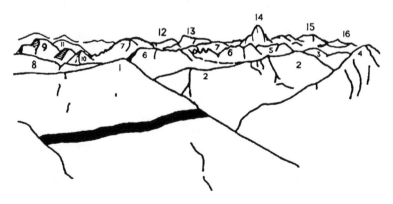

Looking Southeast From Mt. Stimson. (1) Mt. Pinchot; (2) Peril Pk.;(3) Wolftail Mtn.; (4) Eaglehead Mtn.; (5) Mt. Doody; (6) Cloudcroft Pks.; (7) Battlement Mtn.; (8) Caper Pk.; (9) Mt. Despair; (10) Vigil Pk.; (11) Barrier Butte; (12) Statuary Mtn.; (13) Church Butte; (14) Mt. St. Nicholas; (15) Scalplock Mtn.; (16) Riverview Mtn.

prominent yellowish-brown layer of rock about three feet thick above which the cliffs suddenly become much more difficult. It is an easy, safe traverse along this yellow-brown rock layer to the south ridge of Stimson. The elevation of that layer is 9,740 feet (according to the altimeter reading by Bill Blunk and Ralph Thornton), and it is about 100 feet higher than the top of the prominent west or southwest peak of Mt. Stimson.

The ridge above the yellow-brown layer is an easy climb until it suddenly becomes sheer. It is no problem to traverse slightly to your right onto the southeast face until reaching easy breaks in the wall, then scramble back up to the ridgetop. After three or four such interruptions you will be within thirty feet of the summit. Another sheer cliff is astride the ridge there, and also extends onto the southeast face. For the first time since starting up the ridge, the west face is not a sheer wall, so it is easy to traverse onto that face and within a few feet a couloir and a short chimney are reached. The top of that chimney is almost at the highest part of the summit, and nearby is a low cairn of rocks in which is a register that has been signed by very, very few people! When Alice and Gordon Edwards reached the summit in 1951 there was no register, but a few rocks were already there in the form of a small "duck" so obviously someone had already been there. The identity of the first climbers there has never been discovered. Dick Mattson and Wyatt Woodsmall (park rangers) were there on July 25, 1978, and noted that the earlier register was "completely destroyed by critters." Amazingly, Greg Nelson, Joe Biby, and Doug Mason (from Kalispell) followed on July 30, 1978, but climbed via Martha's Basin and Mt. Pinchot, thence up the south face of Mt. Stimson. On August 7, 1979, Brian Cooper and Mark Wisner (from Maryland) reached the summit. Blunk and Thornton were there on August 15, 1979, and copied the data in the register at that time. This is an amazing number of climbers in a short period of time, when compared with the previous twenty years during which not over half a dozen people got there. The mountain has certainly not gotten easier, but the mountaineers have become more numerous . . . and probably "tougher."

The Southeast Spur Route. Distance to the summit about twenty-one miles, sixteen miles of it by human trail. Elevation gained from Martha's Basin is about 4,000 vertical feet. Class 3 or easy 4 all the way, unless grizzly bears chase you out onto the sheer east face. First ascent was by Joseph Biby, Doug Mason and Greg Nelson, dedicated trail crew employees and naturalists, on July 30, 1978.

When the water level is low, ford the Flathead River at Coal Creek. Hike the Coal Creek trail for sixteen miles, taking the side trail at Martha's Basin to reach Buffalo Woman Lake. Very beautiful campsites are there.

From that basin, hike about a mile northwest through a boulder-strewn cirque to the pass (7,400 ft.) between Eaglehead Mountain and Mt. Pinchot. Traverse the southwest face of Pinchot, then cross the western scree slope for another mile to the saddle between Pinchot and Mt. Stimson. Traverse the southwest face of Pinchot, then cross the western scree slope for another mile to the saddle between Pinchot and Mt. Stimson. (There are no game trails across that loose scree slope, unfortunately). From that saddle (7,500 ft.) the enjoyable part of the climb begins. The first ascent team climbed directly up the spine separating the south face of Stimson from the very steep east face, and found that the ridgeline was good consolidated rock that affords excellent climbing but requires no roping up.

Partway up that 2,500-foot-long ridge the climbers experienced a close encounter of the worst kind. They saw a large grizzly bear working its way down a steep chute above them. Thinking to alert the bear to their presence, Greg Nelson began to holler at it . . . but it kept coming directly toward them. Since they were thousands of feet above the nearest trees and could certainly not outrun the bear, the men began to consider climbing out onto the cliffs of the east face in order to avoid being attacked. Fortunately the bear halted when about seventy-five yards above them and suddenly sprinted out across the steep south face of Mt. Stimson "and proceeded to cross that entire face, snow chutes and all, in a matter of minutes." As Joe Biby recalls, "All three of us agreed that it probably would have taken us the remainder of the day to cross that same face." Without further difficulties the summit was reached and the summit views were exceptional. As they point out, "the attraction of Mt. Stimson relative to the other mountains in Glacier is the feeling of being on top of the largest thing around, as Stimson so dominates that entire area and Nyack Creek seems so very far below."

The Pinchot Creek Route. Drive along Highway 2 until about 4.5 miles southeast of Nyack (to Section 26 on the 1968 map of Glacier National Park). Near the Garry Lookout Tower, watch for a small dirt lane that descends to the railroad tracks and continues toward the Flathead River (which is visible from the highway). The elevation there is 3,500 feet above sea level, while the mountain (seen in the distance) is more than 10,000 feet in elevation!

Eric Schwab, who pioneered this route in 1988 with Dave Leppert and Russ Watts, was able to wade across the river, but cannot recommend it under normal conditions because of the water depth there. Even later in the season, during very dry years, the water will still be waist deep at that point. Instead of wading, it is recommended that the crossing be made by boat, if possible.

North of the river, walk down the Boundary Trail toward Coal Creek. Forest fires and subsequent underbrush growth in the area have nearly obliterated parts of the trail near Coal Creek, but it is not difficult to travel cross-country toward the junction of Pinchot Creek with Coal Creek. Cross the creek there and ascend the low but steep point between the two creeks. At the top of that point, look for the old (but distinct) human trail that parallels above the east bank of Pinchot Creek. Ascend on that trail gradually for about a half-mile, then descend from the burned area to where the trail crosses Pinchot Creek. Continue along the trail for another mile, until it turns westward and leaves the creek. Leave the trail there and head up the broad creekbed toward Mt. Stimson. After about a mile and a half of easy travel the creekbed angles to the right (northeast) and there are great views of Mt. Stimson. When the bed becomes cliffy, leave it and find a marvelous elk trail about 100 feet west of the creek and parallel with it. That trail leads through the scattered forests and flat meadows east of Three Suns Mountain and eventually re-enters the creekbed near the upper limits of tree growth. Great camping areas will be found in the open terrain above tree line, which is about as far as most backpackers want to go on the first day, anyway. Grizzly bears abound in that valley, but have not yet caused any difficulties for climbers. The trees nearby provide supports for hoisting food and other belongings high enough above the ground to prevent vandalism by animals, and climbers will want to leave their backpacks there while continuing to the summit carrying only light daypacks.

From the camping area, continue up the creekbed toward the saddle between Mt. Stimson and Mt. Pinchot. From there the route to the summit of Stimson is obvious (for details of the route from that 7,500-ft. saddle to the summit, see the *Southeast Spur Route* description, above).

This is obviously the most direct route from the highway to the summit of Mt. Stimson, and the elevation is gained gradually from the river to the open area above tree line. Unfortunately the river crossing must be considered extremely hazardous, so when the water level is high climbers should seek other routes to the Boundary Trail. Joe Biby fords the river almost directly across from Coal Creek to gain access to the lengthy trail that leads up that stream to Surprise Pass. Perhaps his crossing is less hazardous? A light-weight boat would obviously be great for ferrying two or three people with their packs, unless it overturns or sinks, and it would certainly be nice to have one there on the return trip (*if* the current permits landing at a convenient place). An inflatable boat could be deflated and hidden in the trees on the north side of the river for use on the return trip.

Hikers and climbers in the southern region of the park continue to yearn for a safe and convenient way to cross that potentially deadly river, and perhaps in the future the NPS might stretch a cable from bank to bank that could be crossed by climbers (or fire fighters) suspended by a carabiners and pulling themselves along by hand. (A cart on the cable would probably be too expensive, although one could be added later, if funds became available.)

Mt. St. Nicholas (9,376)

Summit views are not especially rewarding, but this is still a marvelous mountain to climb! From the top, Mt. Stimson and Mt. Pinchot dominate the view to the northwest, while far beyond them, around Logan Pass, many familiar peaks can be identified. Nearby, in the northeast, there are low but extremely sharp, jagged mountains such as Vigil Peak, Flinsch Peak and Grizzly Mountain. The many lesser peaks in the southern area of Glacier National Park are also worthy of examination, yet none are more impressive than Great Northern Mountain with Stanton Glacier, which rises southwest of the park boundary.

Most climbers will not fully enjoy the time spent on top, because they will be preoccupied with thoughts of the poor rock, the sheer cliffs and the tremendous exposure awaiting them during the descent. This peak is considered the most dangerous and difficult mountain for climbers in Glacier National Park, although of course there are many more difficult technical climbs (such as the north face of Mt. Siyeh and the east face of Mt. Gould).

Equipment recommended for the climb includes two 100-foot service-able climbing ropes, at least twenty feet of sling rope for rappel anchors, and at least four pitons (including at least two large angle pitons).

There are several known routes up this spectacular spire, and several ways to approach it. Most ascents have been made via the Northeast Ridge Route, which involves first reaching the Great Notch. The fastest approach to that Notch, and the one which avoids fording the Flathead River, will be described below. We (Britton and Edwards) packed into high camp in the afternoon via that approach, made the climb the following morning, and returned to the the highway that afternoon. Most other climbers have taken three or four days for the climb and return.

The Northeast Ridge Route, via the Great Notch. Distance to the top is about eighteen miles, twelve miles of it by human trail. Elevation gained is about 5,500 vertical feet. Class 4 to 6 much of the way up

MOUNT ST. NICHOLAS
FROM THE EAST

the last thousand vertical feet.

Hike west from the Walton Ranger Station on Highway 2, for nearly four miles, to Park Creek. Follow the Park Creek trail upstream five miles to the Muir Creek trail junction and onward for three more miles, until opposite a large valley that extends up toward the northwest (east of Park Creek). The 7,724-foot peak above the south side of that valley was labelled "Salvage Mountain" on older maps, but the 1968 map applied that name to the 8,328-foot summit a mile north of the 7,724-foot peak. That 8,328-foot summit was labelled "Church Butte" on previous maps, but the 1968 map places the name "Church Butte" further northeast, on the 8,808-foot peak bearing a triangulation point labelled "Salvage." To avoid misunderstandings, the *elevations* of the peaks will be used here, instead of the *names* of the peaks.

The valley west of Park Creek heads toward peak 8,328, bypassing peak 7,724. Leave the Park Creek trail and cross Park Creek on logs (hopefully) to enter that valley. Bushwhacking up the valley is easy, especially along the north bank of the stream. Follow the main stream, as it eventually curves northward along the base of the cliffs that bear several huge pinnacles. Good campsites, with water and wood, are about 150 feet below the head of the valley, just above the "l" of "Salvage Mountain" on the 1968 map. (For tremendous views of Mt. St. Nicholas, scramble up to the notch at the south end of peak 8328, above the sharp bend in the streambed.)

Break camp early next morning and travel light. Walk to the pass just above the campsite and then proceed to the slightly higher saddle toward the west. Suddenly you get the first view of Mt. St. Nicholas! It looks unclimbable!! From the saddle, walk northward up the gentle ridge toward a low peak. A game trail soon cuts across the southwest slope of that peak and descends the southwest ridge to the small lake east of St. Nick. (That lake was not even shown, on earlier maps.) From the lake it an easy scramble up to the small sharp peak (B) beside the northeast shoulder of St. Nicholas. Between that peak and the main mountain is the prominent notch that climbers refer to as "The Great Notch." The climb of the last thousand vertical feet begins in that notch.

To get up the overhanging cliff that is the first obstacle above the notch, the lead climber must stand on something high, such as the shoulders of another climber, in order to reach the first good handholds above the overhang. The following climbers can then wriggle up a rope that is held firm by the leader. Above that pitch, angle east and scramble up class 3 pitches for about 100 feet. Squarely astride the ridge there is a convenient "cannon-hole" formed by a huge slab resting across a notch in the ridgetop.

Beautiful Mt. St. Nicholas remains aloof. This telephoto picture was taken from the highway—Scott Crandell

Crawl westward through that hole (about three feet wide) and follow a narrow mossy ledge around toward the north face. At that point it is wise to rope up for the rockwork ahead.

The cliffs above are mostly a mosaic of huge blocks of red argillite (shale), but on at least one cliff face the strata are thin, with layers of quartzite alternating with thin layers of red shale. The route upward is flexible, but perhaps the following comments will be helpful. Above the cannon-hole climb a steep fifteen-foot cliff, then angle upward and a bit further onto the north face. Soon you will see a large block of red rock resting on the edge of a shelf about thirty feet above you. It is almost on the ridgeline, above a rather smooth vertical cliff face. (Rappel down it on the descent.) A ten-inch ledge leads eastward from a gap below this large block, and out onto a great cliff face above a 1,500-foot drop. A strong belay is desirable here, with a good anchor piton. Move cautiously, noting that a fall from that ledge, even with a good belay, will "pendulum" a climber quickly against the cliff wall below the belayer. Place a good piton above your head before starting to climb up that fragile cliff face from the narrow ledge. The handholds above the narrow ledge are thin slabs of quartzite and and red argillite an inch or two thick, and will not stand the strain of any outward pull. Keep elbows and body close against the cliff, and make certain that the pull exerted on the tiny slabs is straight downward, so that they are wedged between neighboring layers. The fragile cliff is not really very high, but it may take several minutes to reach the top. Belay the other climbers up, protected by another solid belay, *assuming* that at least one might slip off the cliff face. An alternative to this fragile cliff climb is to go directly up the sheer little wall to the "large block of red rock on the edge of a shelf" that was mentioned earlier. That climb does not have the fearsome exposure of the fragile cliff, but it will probably require pitons and some direct aid to reach the big rock. (Most climbers will rappel down that pitch on the descent, perhaps even using the big red rock for a rappel sling placement.)

Above this awesome cliff there is a broad shelf with a deep crack appropriate for the placement of a rappel piton. (Remember, do NOT trust old pitons unless they have been carefully tested . . . they loosen during the freezing and thawing of rocks.) One more class 5 cliff is ahead and then there are progressively easier fissures and cliffs all the way to the summit. It may be easiest west of the ridgetop, and the final 200 feet is so simple that there is no need for ropes.

On the descent, all climbers except the last person should be belayed down the cliffs (even if rappelling). The last climber should be belayed from below. Obviously, carabiners or slings must be left on the mountain, but should never be trusted by subsequent climbing teams. Most climbers will rappel at least five times on the descent to the Great Notch, and will be relieved when they finally reach it.

Other approaches. Young and Young (1933) went to Rotunda Cirque and approached from the northeast, spending five days on the round trip. Snell and Walker (1934) reported climbing the east face all the way to the summit, but no further details are known concerning their route. Parker and Vielbig (1952) attempted the south ridge but ran out of pitons, descended, and detoured to complete the climb via the Great Notch two days later. Black and Ward (1966) went up Coal Creek and climbed to the summit via the northwest ridge and the great northwestern couloir (see the *Northwest Couloir Route* for details). In late December 1985, Tom Cladouhos and his son, Trenton, succeeded in making the first winter ascent of Mt. Nick . . . They forded the river, skied up Park Creek, climbed to the Great Notch, and reached the summit after seven rope pitches. On top they observed the rare phenomenon known as the Specter of Brocken! (See *Going-to-the-Sun* magazine, Fall 1985, for details and photographs.) Ted Steiner and Kenny Kasselder climbed the direct southwest face in 1985 and again in 1986. (See *The Hungry Horse News,* June 11, 1986, for details and photos.)

The Northwest Couloir Route. This is a difficult and hazardous route. Take plenty of rope and pitons, and wear hard hats. First ascent: Reverend Hugh M. Black and Reverend John Ward, August 18, 1966.

Ford the Flathead River just upstream from the mouth of Coal Creek, then follow the trail up Coal Creek to the base of the northwest ridge of Mt. St. Nicholas. Cross the creek and bushwhack 1,500 vertical feet up toward the great rock thumb on the northwest corner of the mountain. The northwest ridge provides access to the large couloir that ascends southeast-ward toward the summit. (The great notch of the standard route is visible beyond the north face, on the northeast ridge, above a long narrow snow chute in the couloir.) Traverse almost to that snow, then climb up and to your right (class 3 and 4) to the bottom of the upper couloir. Traverse to the right beyond the first chimney, and climb the next one (200 feet further). It becomes class 5, with great exposure near the top and with much loose rock. Above that chimney, traverse east (class 4) to a large overhanging chimney with a chockstone. Ten feet above that chockstone traverse eastward for about fifteen feet (class 5) and climb up over a class 5 shoulder. Above that there is another overhanging chimney in the couloir, but then the route eases as it alternates between the couloir and the cliffs just east of it. About 100 feet from the top of the couloir, traverse westward along a large scree ledge for about 120 feet, to feasible class 5 cliffs that lead to the south face just below the summit. On the descent, two rappels down the last 300 feet of the upper couloir are suggested by Black and Ward.

The author is grateful to Father Black for providing the details of this unusual route up spectacular St. Nicholas. Incidentally, Hugh's brother Roscoe, who is also an outstanding mountaineer, owns and operates numerous excellent tourist facilities at St. Mary, on the eastern edge of Glacier National Park.

Summit register data through the years has been reported by various climbers. Although known to be incomplete, the following list enumerates most of the climbers who have reached the elusive summit of this spectacular spire. Persons who know of additional records are urged to write to the Glacier Natural History Association and provide the details.

Conrad Wellen is believed to have made the first ascent, in 1926. Robert T. Young and R. T. Young, Jr., made the second ascent (1933). Hampton Snell and Cliff Walker of Missoula (1934). L. A. Muldown, James Caughren, and R. F. Haines of Whitefish (1937). Ole Dalen and Chuck Creon of Whitefish (1941). J. Murphy and K. Brueckner (1948). Klindt Vielbig and Dick Parker of Portland (1952). J. G. Edwards and Dale Britton (1952). Martin Faulkner and John Merriam (1954). Dick Rieman and Eddie Gilliland of Whitefish (1958). Dick Rieman, Marion Lacy, and Eddie Gilliland (1959). Gil Averill, Tom Choate, and Renn Fenton (1961). Hal Kanzler, Jim Kanzler, and twelve-year-old Jerry Kanzler (1963). Hugh Black and John Ward (1966). Bob Pfister (Mich.) and Don Witt (Ariz.) (1966). Larry Burton, Jim Kanzler, Mike Cheek and Roy Barker (1966). Jim Anderson and Charles Kroger (1968). Terry Kennedy and Carl Sanders (1972). Terry Kennedy and friends (1974). Chuck Sigler, Dick Mattson, and Wyatt Woodsmall (1979). Terry Kennedy and friends, again (1979). Tom and Trenton Cladouhos, in winter (1985). Ted Steiner and Kenny Kasselder (1985 AND 1986). Jaime Johnson and Mark Pearson (1988). Dale Lee and Martin Sosa (1988). Terry Kennedy, solo (1989). Question: WHO was there, between 1974 and 1979??

Robert T. Young, Jr., wrote to Hal Kanzler in 1968, describing the climb of St. Nick that he shared with his father in 1933. He also discussed his father's conversation with Conrad Wellen at a meeting of the Missoula Mountaineers in 1933, where Wellen said he approached from Coal Creek and "climbed more or less directly up the north side of the mountain, coming up quite close to the northeast col, or perhaps a bit to the southwest of it."

An interesting event occurred during the 1966 climb by Larry Burton and friends. They found two registers on top and sorted out the bits of paper to put them all under one cairn. They then descended to the Great Notch, where Mike Cheek fell from the overhang and landed on a huge slab of shale, breaking it. Larry then saw an old register book beneath the broken slab of shale. It was the original Conrad Wellen register! The climbers gave the old register to Bob Sellers, the West Side District Ranger, to place in the Park Museum for permanent preservation, but it apparently never got there. The greatest mystery, of course, is why Wellen's old register was in the Great Notch instead of on the summit of mighty Mt. St. Nicholas.

Walton Mountain (8,926)

This remote mountain is discussed in detail in the St. Mary Valley Area chapter. Although it is located south of the St. Mary Valley drainage, it is best approached via the trail to Gunsight Lake. From that lake, hike the trail to Jackson Glacier and proceed to the head of that glacier. It is then a one-mile traverse over badly crevassed Harrison Glacier to the base of the summit pyramid of Walton Mountain, and the top is only 500 vertical feet above the glacial snowfields.

INDEX

346

Selected Literature

Ahlenslager, K. E., *Glacier: The Story Behind the Scenery*, KC Publications (1988), 48 pp., with great color photographs.

Alt, D. D., C. W. Buchholtz, B. Gildart, and R. Frauson, "Glacier Country . . . Montana's Glacier National Park," *Montana Magazine* (1983), 104 pp. of great color photographs.

Alt, D. D. and D. W. Hyndman, *Rocks, Ice and Water, The Geology of Waterton-Glacier Park*, Mountain Press, Missoula (1973), 112 pp., illustrated.

Bailey, V. and F. M. Bailey, *Wild Animals of Glacier National Park*, U.S. Govenment Printing Office (1918), 210 pp., illustrated. (Mammals on pp. 1-102, birds on pp. 103-210).

Blunk, W. and R. Thornton, "Clyde Peak," *Hungry Horse News* (September 1, 1983).

Buchholtz, C. W., *Man In Glacier,* Glacier Natural History Association (1976), 88 pp.

Bueler, W. M., "Chief Mountain; Early History," *Off Belay* (1977), 3 pp.

Caffrey, P., *Climber's Guide to Montana*, Mountain Press, Missoula (1986), 1150 peaks, 237 pp., illustrated.

Christopherson, E., *Adventures Among the Glaciers,* Earthquake Press, Missoula (1966), 88 pp., illustrated.

Clyde, N., "First Ascent of Mount Wilbur," *Sierra Club Bulletin* (1924), 11:1, pp. 4-6, 3 pls.

Clyde, N., "First Ascent of Mount Merritt," *Sierra Club Bulletin* (1925), 12:2, pp. 165-167.

Clyde, N., "The Mountains of Glacier National Park," *Appalachia* (1934), 20:4, pp. 22-36, illustrated.

Davis, W. E., "Climbing in Glacier National Park," *Trail and Timberline* (1958), No. 479, pp. 147-152.

D'Evelyn, M. N., "Over Red Eagle Pass," *Glacial Drift* (1934).

Dyson, J. L., *The Geologic Story of Glacier National Park*, Glacier Natural History Association (1949), 24 pp. (Out of print).

Dyson, J. L., *The World of Ice,* Alfred A. Knopf, N.Y. (1962), 292 pp.

Edwards, J. G., "General Observations on the Ecology of Glacier National Park," *Wasmann Journal of Biology* (1957), 15:1, pp. 123-151, 5 figs.

Edwards, J. G., "Entomology Above Timberline," *Mazama Annual* (1956), 38:1, pp. 13-17.

Edwards, J. G., "Continental Divide Route, Part 1, Gunsight Lake to Red Eagle Pass," "Part 2, Triple Divide Pass to Red Eagle Pass," *Going-to-the-Sun* (1981), 2:1, pp. 31-34; 2:2, pp. 36-38, illustrated.

Elrod, M. J., *Elrod's Guide and Book of Information,* (1924). (Out of print).

Gildart, B., "Montana's Glacier National Park," *Montana Magazine* (1983).

Grinnell, G. B., "The Crown of the Continent," *Century Magazine* (1901), pp. 660-672. (Out of print).

Hanna, W. L., *Montana's Many-Splendored Glacierland*, Superior Publishing Co., Seattle (1975), 215 pp., illustrated with many color plates. Reprinted (1987) by University of North Dakota Foundation, Grand Forks, N.D.

Hanna, W. L., *The Grizzlies of Glacier*, Mountain Press, Missoula (1978), 154 pp., illustrated.

Hanna, W. L., *The Life and Times of James Willard Schultz (Apikuny)*, University of Oklahoma Press, Norman (1986), 382 pages.

Hanna, W. L., *Stars Over Montana: Men Who Made Glacier National Park History,* Glacier Natural History Association (1988), 204 pp.

Harvey, G. H., "Our First Sierra Club Outing," *Sierra Club Bulletin* (1925), 12:2, pp. 158-162, illustrated.

Holterman, J., *Place Names of Glacier/Waterton National Parks,* Glacier Natural History Association (1985), 169 pp.

Horodyski, R. J., "Stromatolites of Glacier National Park, Montana," *Precambrian Research 2*: (1975), pp. 215-254, illustrated (fossils). Inside Trail. (Periodical published by The Glacier Park Foundation, P. O. Box 824, Helena, Montana 59624.)

Kennedy, T. and J. Kanzler, "On the Path of Mad Wolf," (Ascent of Siyeh's North Face), *Going-to-the-Sun* (1980), 1:1, pp. 20-24, 46-47, illustrated.

Larson, R., "Scenic Point to Appistoki Peak; The High Traverse," *Going to-the-Sun* (1982), 3:2,pp. 20-21, illustrated.

Larson, R., "Mt. Jackson, From Gunsight Pass," *Going-to-the-Sun* (1982), 2:3, pp. 14-15, illustrated.

Larson, R., *Mountain Hazards*, Glacier Natural History Association (1984), 30 pp., illustrated.

Lechleitner, R. R., *Mammals of Glacier National Park*, Glacier Natural History Association (1955), 92 pp. (Out of print).

Long, G. W., "Many-Splendored Glacierland," *National Geographic Magazine* (May 1956), pp. 589-636, with many color pictures.

SELECTED LITERATURE

Matthes, F., "The Alps of Montana," *Appalachia 10*: (1904), pp. 255-76.

Mazza, J. J., "The Sierra Club Ascent of Mount Cleveland," *Sierra Club Bulletin* (1925), 12:2, pp. 156-157, 3 plates.

Mountain Ear Journal, published by Rocky Mountaineers of Western Montana in 1970s, 2100 S. Ave. W, Missoula, MT 59801.

Montana Magazine, 1983. A Special Photographic Issue on Glacier National Park.

Nelson, A. G., *Wildflowers of Glacier National Park*, privately printed (1970), 47 pp., 80 color plates. (Out of print).

Parratt, L. P., *Birds of Glacier National Park*, Glacier Natural History Association (1964), 64 pp., illustrated. (Out of print).

Parsons, M. R., "The Glacier National Park Outing," *The Mountaineer* (Seattle Mountaineers) 7: (1914), pp. 17-42, illustrated.

Pogreba, C. E., "Glacier Park's Citadel Spire," *Summit Magazine* (1968), pp. 20-23, illustrated in color.

Raup, O., et al., *Geology Along Going-to-the-Sun Road*, Glacier Natural History Association (1983), 62 pp., illustrated with maps, charts, and color photographs.

Reiner, R. E., *Flowering Beauty of Glacier National Park*, privately printed (1974).

Rinehart, M. R., *Through Glacier Park with Howard Eaton*, Houghton-Mifflin Co. (1916), 92 pp., illustrated (Mary Roberts Rinehart).

Robbins, M., *High Country Trail: Along the Continental Divide*, National Geographic Society (1981), 199 pp., with dozens of color photos by Paul Chesley.

Robinson, D. H., *Trees and Forests of Glacier National Park,* Glacier Natural History Association (1950), 48 pp. (revised, 1961). (Out of print).

Robinson, D. H., *Through the Years in Glacier National Park*, Glacier Natural History Association (1960), 127 pp., illustrated. (Out of print).

Ross, C. P. and R. Rezak, "The Rocks and Fossils of Glacier National Park," U.S. Geological Survey, Professional Paper 294-K (1959), pp. 401-438, illustrated.

Ruhle, G. C., *Guide to Glacier National Park*, Campbell-Mithuen, Inc., Minneapolis (1954). (Out of print).

Ruhle, G. C., *Roads and Trails of Waterton-Glacier National Parks*, John W. Forney, Minneapolis (1972), 164 pp. (Out of print). Revised in 1986 by Becky Williams, Glacier Natural History Association, 146 pp., illustrated. (Excellent).

Seattle Mountaineers, *Mountaineering, The Freedom of the Hills*, The Vail-Ballou Press, Binghamton, N.Y. (1960), 430 pp., well illustrated.

Shaw, R. J. and D. On, *Plants of Waterton-Glacier National Parks and The Northern Rockies,* Mountain Press, Missoula (1979), 160 pp., illustrated in color.

Sperry, L. B., "In the Montana Rockies," *Appalachia* (1896), Vol. 8.

Standley, P. C., *Plants of Glacier National Park*, U.S. Government Printing Office, 1926, 110 pp., illustrated. (Out of print).

Stimson, H. L., "The Ascent of Chief Mountain," *Hunting in Many Lands* (1895), Forest & Stream Publishing Co., New York. (Out of print).

Stimson, H. L., *My Vacations* (privately printed by Stimson) (1949). pp. 43-74 are about climbing and hunting in what is now Glacier National Park.

Ulrich, T. J., *Birds of The Northern Rockies*, Mountain Press, Missoula (1984), 160 pp., illustrated in color.

Ulrich, T. J., *Mammals of the Northern Rockies*, Glacier Natural History Association (1986), 160 pp., illustrated in color.

Vielbig, K. N., "An Ascent of Mt. St. Nicholas," *Mazama Annual* (1952), 34:13, pp. 29-34, illustrated.

Yenne, W. J., *Switchback (50 years in the mountains of Montana and the west),* WY Books, San Francisco (1983), 170 pp.

Glacier Natural History Association

The Glacier Natural History Association (GNHA) is a cooperating association of the National Park Service incorporated in the State of Montana in 1946 and recognized by the Internal Revenue Service as a nonprofit 501(c)3 organization.

A primary purpose is to operate bookstores in the visitor centers of Glacier National Park and other Montana land management agencies of the Department of the Interior and Department of Agriculture; such as Big Hole National Battlefield, Grant-Kohrs Ranch National Historic Site, National Bison Range, and Flathead National Forest. Guidebooks, maps, videos, and publications about the natural and cultural resources and histories of these areas are the primary educational and informational items provided at reasonable cost to visitors.

Proceeds from bookstore sales are returned to the Interpretive Division of Glacier National Park, as well as the other agencies served by GNHA to further the support of research, educational, and interpretive activities, cultural preservation, and specialized equipment and project needs related to visitor services.

Anyone wishing to support the goals and activities of the Association may become a member. Members receive a 15 percent discount on purchases from the Association and similar discounts from many cooperating associations in other national park areas. For information on membership and dues, please contact: Glacier Natural History Association, Box 428, West Glacier, MT 59936 or call (406) 888-5756.